Charles Williams – Lord Williams of Elvel – has enjoyed a distinguished political career, becoming a Labour Life Peer in 1985 before being elected Deputy Leader of the Opposition in 1989. As C.C.P. Williams he played cricket for both Oxford University and Essex, captaining Oxford in 1955 (between M.C. Cowdrey in 1954 and M.J.K. Smith in 1956) and making a total of 4,090 runs in first-class cricket at an average of 28.20. He twice hit 1,000 runs in a season, with a top score of 139 not out.

Charles Williams now lives in Wales and London, and is the author of one previous book, *The Last Great Frenchman*, a brilliantly received biography of Charles de Gaulle.

Bradman

AN AUSTRALIAN HERO

Charles Williams

An *Abacus* Book

First published in Great Britain in 1996
by Little, Brown and Company
This edition published by Abacus in 1997

A CIP catalogue record for this book
is available from the British Library.

ISBN: 0 349 10940 0

Typeset in Bembo by
Palimpsest Book Production Limited,
Polmont, Stirlingshire
Printed and bound in Great Britain by
Clays Ltd, St Ives plc

Abacus
A Division of
Little, Brown and Company (UK)
Brettenham House
Lancaster Place
London WC2E 7EN

For Jessie Bradman,
an Australian heroine
in her own right

Contents

LIST OF ILLUSTRATIONS

Many of the uncredited illustrations are reproductions of photographs which comprise the fifty-one volumes of Sir Donald Bradman's personal scrapbooks, compiled by the State Library of South Australia. Every effort has been made to contact copyright holders, but in many cases copyright proved difficult to trace because the illustrations carried no accreditation. Should any person feel that photographs or illustrations have been used without proper authority, he or she is invited to contact the publisher.

ἀντεβόλησεν τῶν ἀνὴρ θνατὸς οὔπω τις πρότερον

He achieved things that no mortal man had achieved before[†]

[†] Pindar, on Xenophon of Corinth, who, in the Olympic Games of 484 BC, won the short sprint and pentathlon on the same day. Oxford Text (1947) of *Olympia* XIII, lines 41–2; tr. author.

PREFACE

THIS IS A STORY ABOUT AUSTRALIA as well as a great
Australian. I put it this way because – although much has
been written about Don Bradman as a cricketer – nobody, as far
as I know, has written the story of his life as an Australian.

What this book attempts to do is to put Bradman's cricketing
achievements into the context of an Australia feeling her way,
gradually, towards something that the world would recognise as
'nationhood'. The truth is that the years spanned by Bradman's
career, from the late 1920s to the late 1940s, represented a decisive
period in the history of modern Australia. During that period
Bradman was an icon for many Australians. Nothing, of course,
can detract from his cricketing genius, and that can never, nor
should it ever, be diminished. What I have tried to do is show
how that genius became a focus for Australian aspirations during
a crucial period in the country's history.

Pant-y-Rhiw
August 1996

PROLOGUE

'Sport was part of the cultural baggage brought out to
Australia by the convicts.'[1]

IT MUST HAVE BEEN IN EARLY December 1992, when I was in
labour with my first literary child, that Ted Willis, a much
missed friend and colleague, walked up to where I was sitting
in one of the bars in the House of Lords and said bluntly: 'I
have got the subject for your next book.' Since Ted had been
of the greatest help to me, and was himself a writer of the most
fertile imagination (much, much more than the mere author of
Dixon of Dock Green), I listened to him with my mind smartly to
attention. 'Bradman,' he said. When I had recovered my poise,
I replied that either he had gone mad or he had been in the bar
longer than I had, with consequential effects. Not a bit of it,
he said, and went on to explain his reasoning: Bradman was as
much in the heroic mould, although in a different country and
in a different context, as was de Gaulle; and since I was in the
business of heroes – and a former cricketer – this was a natural
book for me to write. I went away to think about it.

Two weeks later Ted died. The book had to be written.

Sporting heroes are not new to Australia. They go back a
hundred and fifty years or more. The first of the genre, so it
seems, was a flamboyant character who went by the name of
The Flying Pieman. The Pieman was by profession a circus
stuntman; but he was also a runner of remarkable endurance
– hence his nickname. In 1848, the year in which the cities of
old Europe were convulsed by popular revolution, the Pieman
decided to launch a revolution of his own. He would race, he

said, the coach that ran from Brisbane to Ipswich – a distance of some fifty miles. Furthermore, he would carry a handicap for the whole race, a long carriage-pole. Bets were laid. The odds have not been recorded, but it takes little imagination to assume that the heavy money must have been against the Pieman and in favour of the horse-drawn coach. If so, the punters were sadly mistaken, since the Pieman beat the coach by a full hour.

Encouraged by this success, and realising that his new career held promise, the Pieman then took on the Sydney-to-Windsor coach – again a distance of about fifty miles. But this was no ordinary coach from distant Queensland: it was the fine and fast coach that carried the Royal Mail from the most important city of New South Wales to its satellite town to the north-west. This time the Pieman wore a top hat as a handicap – and again he won easily. From this triumph he went on to others, competing against any rival who presented himself, always carrying a handicap – once in the form of a live goat slung around his shoulders. There was no beating him, and his exploits were relayed from town to town throughout the continent. Australia had found her first sporting hero.

The Pieman had chosen his moment for fame well. The gold rush of the 1850s not only increased the amount of spare cash in people's pockets, particularly in the colony of Victoria, where the finds were most spectacular, it also showed the benefit of gambling. If those who had sold all they had to search for gold had struck it lucky, there was every reason to believe that anybody and everybody could achieve the same result – but without the unpleasant nuisance of long and arduous journeys into the bush. Gambling thus became a prominent – and largely uncontrolled – feature of life in all the Australian colonies.

The urge to place a bet found its most spectacular outlet in horse-racing. For Australians racing was a natural day-to-day activity. The horse was the main means of conveyance over long distances before the arrival of the motor car, and it made obvious sense to the possessor of a horse, in a society which was already becoming aggressively competitive, to race it against his neighbour's. These informal events quickly became institutionalised; indeed, as early as 1810 races were held in

Sydney's Hyde Park. But it was not until 1861 that the most prestigious of all, the Melbourne Cup, was first run. Although late in arrival, it quickly gained a popularity superior to all rivals in other colonies. By 1865 offices in Melbourne were closed for the afternoon of the Cup, and by 1883 it was said to have been watched by no fewer than 100,000 people – one-third of the population of Melbourne at the time.

The sums laid on the contending horses were prodigious. In mainly Catholic Melbourne, Protestant congregations resorted to holding seaside picnics on the day, in order to obstruct their flock from engaging in such sinful activity, although it does not seem to have deflected them to any serious extent. Nevertheless, disapproval in prudish Melbourne was to the gain of the richer and more flamboyant Sydney, since the scene for the big money soon moved to the Sydney Tattersall's Sweep. Melbourne provided the race and Sydney provided the money: the Sweep paid out huge prizes for the lucky holder of the ticket with the name of the Melbourne Cup winner.

As horse-racing became ever more popular in the late nineteenth century, so did the reputation both of the horses and of their jockeys. To be sure, none of the horses approached the fame of the great Phar Lap, winner of 31 out of 33 races – including the Melbourne Cup – in the late 1920s and early 1930s, whose statue stands proudly in the Melbourne Museum and whose name is even now only mentioned in Australia in reverentially hushed tones. But great horses there were, and they provided much sport for the public throughout Australia. Almost every small settlement, let alone town or major city, had its own racecourse.

Admiration for the horse spread to admiration for the jockey. Tommy Corrigan, for instance, an Irishman whose most distinctive feature was a moustache of exaggerated proportions, and who won the Grand National in Victoria seven times in the 1880s and 1890s, was regarded as almost a deity. 'What's Tommy riding today?' was a familiar question on arrival at a racecourse, and the reply would be the signal for pockets to open and money to be laid on the nose of the animal so privileged.[2] Such was the near worship of Tommy Corrigan that when he was killed in an accident at Caulfield racecourse in 1894, Melbourne went into deep mourning. At his funeral all traffic was stopped for two hours, and by the time his coffin – with his green and white colours and riding boots on top – reached the cemetery, the end of the procession was still wending its way along St Kilda Road some two miles back.

Tommy Corrigan was by no means the only Australian sporting hero of his time. If horse-racing was the preferred spectator sport of Melbourne, Sydney looked to the water for its entertainment. The banks of the Parramatta River, at the western end of Sydney Harbour, were the favoured point from which Sydneyites could watch races, both rowing and sailing. Individual scullers were particularly favoured, and it is said that no fewer than 25,000 enthusiasts turned out to cheer the return of Edmund Trickett, after he had won the world sculling championship on the Thames in London in 1879. No less exalted was Henry Leach, who followed Trickett in winning the championship in 1889; and, in terms of funerals, Leach's rivalled Tommy Corrigan's. Leach died of typhoid almost immediately after his return to Australia. Sydney was distraught, and his funeral was attended, so it is reported, by no fewer than 170,000 people.

Cricket started to attract crowds in the latter half of the nineteenth century, particularly in the major cities. The English team of 1861 were astonished to see how many spectators turned out to watch their matches. By the end of the century the names of Spofforth and Bannerman were widely known, to be followed in the early 1900s by Noble and Trumper. The 'Ashes' – the symbol of the 'death of English cricket' through defeat by an Australian XI at the Oval in 1882 – had become the outward expression of the rivalry between the mother country and her presumptuous colonies. Test matches between England and Australia to compete for the Ashes quickly became regular events.

As a popular daily press developed in the major cities of the Australian colonies, particularly after the agreement between them in 1901 to form a Commonwealth; as public transport became more widespread and more efficient; and as the standard of living edged upwards, so the attraction of spectator sports became more evident as a way of occupying leisure time. Nevertheless, however competitive they might be, they were always perceived as sport. In the political and social atmosphere of relative Edwardian calm, they did not generate any specifically nationalist passions. Indeed, when the Olympic Games were held, for the first time in the modern era, in 1896, Australia did not even send a team. As it happened this did not prevent an Australian, Edwin Flack, from winning the 800 and 1500 metres – presaging future Australian Olympic triumphs. But he was only in Greece because he was living in London at the time, and he entered the Games as a private citizen.

THE FIRST WORLD WAR changed the whole nature of spectator sport, just as it changed the world in which sport was played. For four years in Europe and the British Empire, and for two in the United States, nationalist emotions had been roused to prolonged and violent heights. The strategy on both sides had been, understandably enough, to gain maximum popular support for the war effort, which was costing so many lives and bringing such unimaginable horrors. In the aftermath of the War the Central European and Russian belligerents, all in their own way defeated and exhausted, used up their remaining energies in internal disputes and rumbling civil wars. But no such option was available for the victors, particularly the United States and the British Empire – neither of which, unlike France, had suffered invasion of their national territories. Yet once great emotions have been stirred they are not easily calmed, and need outlets through which they can be worked out.

There was no easy way in which the trauma could be laid to rest. Further war was obviously out of the question – witness the outright rejection by the Allies to fight for Poland against Soviet Russia in 1920–21. For many the only way was to bury the experience of the War in neurotic oblivion; for others, particularly those who had participated, the way was to relive the War in solemn and ritualised ceremonies of remembrance. But for the majority it was a question of trying to forget the tragedy which they had witnessed from the safety of home. This is turn took two forms: escapism into hectic and frivolous jollity, and – to work out the darker side of the nationalist passion – by re-enacting heroic events in a medium that did not require anything other than enthusiastic audience applause: literature, for instance; painting; music; the theatre or cinema. The exploits of heroes of the past featured yet again. Even the battle of the shepherd boy David (perhaps entitled, in the use of his sling, to be called the western world's first sporting hero) against the giant Goliath was put on film. Other heroes were dug out to satisfy the public need for intense and dramatic – but uninvolved – action.

In almost every country it was not difficult to find the heroes that symbolised the spirit of warlike nationalism, even if their exploits were largely the product of myth rather than history. For example, France had her Joan of Arc, England her Shakespearian kings, Scotland her Robert the Bruce, Italy her Caesar, Spain her El Cid, and Germany – *absit omen* – her Wagnerian pantheon. But the case of Australia was different. There was, quite simply, nobody who fitted the bill. Ned Kelly was something of a hero, but he was a rogue, and certainly would not do as a symbol for the new nationalism. Australia had never fought a war of independence; thus there was no Washington or Bolívar. Australia had never fought a civil war; thus there was no Cromwell or Abraham Lincoln. Australia had never been at war with her neighbours; thus there was no Foch or Wellington. Australia had never had a revolution; thus there was no Robespierre, Garibaldi or Lenin. It was all very difficult. Australia needed an icon, but there was none to hand.

Furthermore, it had never been entirely easy to define an 'Australian' identity which an icon was meant to represent. Australia itself is a vast continent, stretching some 3000 miles from east to west and some 1500 miles from north to south. Its climate is hopelessly unbalanced: rain only falls in any reasonable quantity in the coastal belt; inland there is waterless desert. The population is for the most part confined to a relatively small area in the south-eastern corner of the continent and a tiny pocket in the south-west. Furthermore, it is far from homogenous, deriving from a variety of widely different countries and cultures. It is little wonder that visitors, and sometimes residents, feel that

Australia is only, as Prince Metternich said of Italy, 'a geographical expression'.[3]

The task of Australians after the First World War, as the British Empire struggled to recover from wounds which were eventually to prove fatal, was to discover some unifying force which could propel them into what was clearly going to be a post-colonial era, and was therefore one of great difficulty. Some returned for comfort to suck at the drying teats of the mother country, adopting even more 'British' attitudes than they had before the War. But most felt instinctively that it was time to move on, and to find some way of expressing their rising nationality without offending the majority who were still loosely, but umbilically, attached to the 'old country'.

In the end, it was as much a matter of elimination as anything else. Everybody was tired of war; party politics varied from State to State, were frequently sectarian and in many instances corrupt; and revolution could only be against the British, and was, therefore, unthinkable. It was thus that Australia turned to spectator sport as the prime vehicle for the aspirations to national identity which the War had produced. In retrospect, it was an obvious – if unconscious – move. It suited the temperament of the people, the climate of the country and the social disposition: the climate in the inhabited areas was ideal for outdoor sports both in summer and in winter; and it was on the playing field that class and religious antagonisms could be most successfully resolved.

Sport in Australia thus became an integral part of politics. (Of course, it was politics in the wider sense – the binding together of the polity rather than another manifestation of the parochial squabbles of the political parties. But it was politics nonetheless.) Sport allowed Australia to stand up in her own right. It both encouraged and disciplined the egalitarian individualism that was emerging as an identifiable Australian characteristic. It was to be Australia's way of showing the rest of the world that the continent was not just an appendage of the British Empire but a real and living nation.

There was a clear consequence. It followed naturally that the sporting hero achieved in Australia a status several ranks above sporting champions of other countries. He was treated, and to some extent still is treated, with a reverence, or hysterical enthusiasm, depending on the age and character of the hero, reserved in other countries for royalty or successful military commanders. But whereas after the Second World War there was a variety of sports in which Australians excelled, after the First World War there was only one sport of any consequence – cricket. Cricket was the means whereby the adolescent Australia could prove its worth. Cricketing heroes were its Davids and the British Empire its Goliath.

Of these, there is no doubt that Don Bradman was the greatest. He was so much superior in ability to his contemporaries that at times it seemed that the fate of all Australia depended on him alone. The adulation that he aroused, unwelcome as it was to Bradman himself, is witness to his almost royal status. The fact that he played his finest cricket at a time when economic and political circumstances were at their most difficult only served to highlight his role as the most visible binding force of the Australian polity. Furthermore, his standing was so much higher than his contemporaries that the respect in which he was held, both as a player and as a person, stretched well beyond the shores of the Australian continent. He was, in his day, a world figure. As Jack Ingham, sports editor of the *Star*, wrote in 1938: 'It is strange, but I think true, that all the time, day and night, somewhere in the world someone is talking about Bradman'; and it comes as little surprise to hear that Nelson Mandela, when released from his long period in prison, wanted to know whether Bradman was still alive. Bradman was, and still remains, one of the great Australian heroes; but in the end it can without exaggeration be said that he was the greatest of them all.

1

FROM SUFFOLK TO SYDNEY

'To beat the English team was a special goal, far more satisfying in Australia than beating the New Zealanders or South Africans or whoever came here. The special quality came from class antipathy and post-colonial irritations. It was great fun to beat "Mum", as it were, and the gentlemen with whom she associated. The favoured icon was the little Aussie battler – the man who breasts up to the whole world and wins. Bradman was that. I don't think he was loved as a national figure, but you don't have to love your heroes. If he had come from one of the upper-class schools I doubt if he would have been quite the hero that he was.'[1] Thus a correspondent from Australia.

Nevertheless, it was interesting, as it always is, to know more about 'Mum', and it was Bradman himself, during the 1930 Australian tour of England, who set out to discover his ancestral origins. His search was by no means unique; indeed, the pattern is familiar. The young Australian, like many other young Australians – or Americans or Canadians or South Africans, for that matter – wished to know where he had come from. He had been told by his father, handing on to his son the stories told by his own father, that the family had originated in England, and that the precise area of England which had nurtured their family for many generations was East Anglia; in particular, that western section of East Anglia at the meeting point of the boundaries of Suffolk, Essex and Cambridgeshire. The pilgrim – since that was what the young Don was – now wished to know for himself. He therefore set off from Cambridge, where the Australians were playing against the University, south-eastwards on a journey to try to trace his inheritance.

The result was not altogether satisfactory. Certainly there were those who told him that his family came from this or that village, or indeed from this or that county. But it was difficult to tell the difference between those who wished to tell the true story and those who wished to embroider the truth in order to claim parentage of this new object of international curiosity. Rivalry between the three counties, each one forming part of the area which everybody admitted was the soil from which the new warrior had sprung, made it difficult to determine which of the three had the prior claim. The judgement came down, as indeed – on the evidence, but only on a delicate balance – it must, in favour of Suffolk; and, in particular, on the village of Withersfield.

Withersfield, as a village, is pleasant enough for a visitor who happens to be passing through, but in truth cannot aspire to be considered a major tourist attraction. It is set in a hollow, protected from the arid summers and the winter winds of the East Anglian plain. In this hollow there grew a settlement, probably of Saxon origin, which developed into a place of shelter for travellers on the Norwich–London turnpike. As the years passed, it accumulated an elegant, middle-sized stately home, Hantchet Hall; two public houses, a village green, a small school and a population of some two or three hundred. It is what it is, an oasis in the middle of a harsh, flat and unyielding landscape. Unlike the towns and villages of east Suffolk or the fishing ports of Essex, there is little sign of past wealth, either from the Flemish wool trade, which brought the great churches to Lavenham and Kersey, or from the North Sea fishing catch – and, it must be admitted, the smuggling – which enriched north Essex. The county of Suffolk was, in any event, sliding into long-term decline before it was rescued by the arrival of the London commuter. There had been no growth at all – indeed, possibly a slight decline – in the population between the fourteenth century and the early twentieth; and, worst of all, the town of Eye had missed the chance to dominate central East Anglia by voting not to let the railway stop there, ceding the position to the Norfolk town of Diss, which eagerly seized its chance.

The village of Withersfield is perched uneasily in the furthest south-western corner of the county. It seems to be nearer Cambridge and the Fens than to Bury St Edmunds or

Colchester; and Cambridge, of course, is Cromwell country. Indeed, the influence of protest against the arbitrary exercise of authority has pervaded the history of the whole of East Anglia, apart from the Royalist towns. Electorally, the vote turned against the landowners – first to the Liberals and then to Labour – right up to the conversion of the countryside in the 1970s and 1980s to an extended belt of commuter land. Even now, a scratch below the surface will reveal a distrust of authority, particularly central authority, which is quite unlike the docile attitudes of more southern English counties.

It was protest, and an accompanying lack of hope, that led Charles Bradman to emigrate to Australia in the early 1850s. The times, after all, were dismal. The depression of the 1840s had led to famine in Ireland and severe malnutrition in the rural areas of England. The accounts of the period make melancholy reading: rural poverty led to disease, which in turn led to unemployment, which in turn led again to poverty. Whatever might have been the external grandeur of Britain at the time, the everyday life of the agricultural labourer was little short of perpetual misery.

The despair of that era is reflected in the gravestones in Withersfield churchyard. Most are now covered in lichen or have disintegrated to the point where the inscriptions are no longer legible. Unlike the burial place of Sir John Jacob within the shelter of the church, the graves of the lower orders lie covered only by coarse grass. The stones marking a later period are more visible, but still tell their story of hopelessness. The path leading to the door of the church itself – simple enough, with a vacant mounting above the door from which Cromwell's soldiers had hacked away the statuette of the Virgin Mary, who had given her name to the church – is lined on the right-hand side with a series of headstones carrying the name of Bradnam, clearly spelt as such. There lie John and Ada, Elizabeth and Jacob, William, Ernest, Herbert William and Martha Annie, all of them bearing mute and posthumous witness to the presence of the Bradnam family in the precarious and uncompromising life of Withersfield in the nineteenth century.

Charles, son of John, was christened Charles Bradman in Withersfield church on 26 May 1833. The variant in the spelling

11

of the baby's surname should not be a matter for surprise – most of the villagers were illiterate and even the church authorities made muddles from time to time. The spelling of names among the rural working class of the day was anyway a matter of wide choice. Charles's brother was recorded as a Bradnam, so the whole thing was probably a mistake. But mistake or not, Bradman it was.

The Bradnams or Bradmans – according to choice and circumstance – were, by any measure, rural working class. As such, they were not only illiterate or, at best, semi-literate, but could not in reality hope for anything much better than their present lot – at least in the England of the mid-nineteenth century. Agricultural labourers, since that is what they were, could entertain only the most limited of aspirations.

In 1852, at the age of 18, Charles Bradman decided that he had had enough of rural England. He dared to join a group of Suffolk farmworkers who had heard of the discovery of gold in a country which until then had been little more than a penal colony at the other end of the earth. Together they left their families (in Charles Bradman's case, his parents and seven brothers and sisters), scraped together what means they could and set off on the long and dangerous journey to the British colonies on the east coast of the Australian continent. The precise point of landfall, whatever the original destination, was far from certain. The journey took months and conditions were appalling. It was not just the natural hazards of crossing rough seas in cramped quarters, or even the filth or the foul food. Among those they expected to meet on arrival were convicted criminals who, under the harsh system of the day, had been sentenced to forced deportation. It was not, to say the least, the recipe for a happy cruise to the Southern Hemisphere.

But in spite of the dangers and hardships the small group was only one among many. In all, some 95,000 English, Scots, Welshmen and Irishmen made the same dreadful journey in 1852, nearly seven times as many as in the previous year. They were all intent on the same aim: escape from the poverty of the British Isles and – with perhaps a half-suppressed whisper – the pursuit of gold.

The pursuit of gold, as is often the case, proved to be a dream which faded quickly. Although the first discoveries had been made in the colony of New South Wales in early 1851, the richest fields – and those most easy to mine – were in the neighbouring colony of Victoria. But the young Bradman had chosen New South Wales. In the circumstances, there was only one thing to do: to use the skills he had learned in his native Suffolk, the hard skills of agricultural survival, and to make the best of them.

It was far from easy. Sydney, apart from the core of British expatriates who surrounded the colonial government, was a rough town. New immigrants, not least those accustomed to the neighbourliness of Suffolk villages, found the place uncomfortable and unwelcoming. But the hinterland of New South Wales was much more attractive, and Charles Bradman soon settled down at a settlement in Mittagong, a small but self-sufficient farming community some eighty miles or so to the south of Sydney in the pleasingly fertile Southern Highlands of New South Wales. There he set about earning enough money as a labourer to buy his own land. It took him eleven years – in the course of which he married a fifteen-year-old Mittagong girl, Elizabeth, of Australian birth. By now with two sons, the couple in 1874 moved 150 miles westwards and inland to the village of Jindalee, where land was cheaper, but dusty and harder to work. Jindalee, now vanished, was their home until Charles's death in 1907, and rough farming – mixed arable and livestock – was their living.

It was at Cootamundra – or Cootamundry as it was then known – that the third son, Don Bradman's father, was born two years after the parents' move to Jindalee. There appears to have been no particular reason for the choice of birthplace; after all, Cootamundra was only a few miles from Jindalee. But the larger village at least had the advantage of a practised midwife and some of the medical attention which Jindalee lacked. George Bradman, as he was named, grew up in Jindalee and helped, as was the family tradition, on his father's farm. His adolescence, however, was far from easy. There were family rows, to the point where one of George's elder brothers walked out of the house never, as far as is recorded, to be heard of again. George himself asserted his independence by marrying at the age of seventeen. His bride, Emily Whatman, was, like his mother, from a farming family on the Mittagong range.

As it turned out, although Emily was five years older than her husband, the two were admirably suited. The marriage lasted for 51 years, surviving all trials on its way. One of the most daunting of these was the production by Emily, as a last effort in 1908, when she was nearly 37, of the fifth in a series of children, a small son – duly baptised Donald George Bradman. Cootamundra was the birthplace once again.

The life into which the baby was born was one of unease and uncertainty. To be sure, the depression of the 1890s, during which a number of banks had crashed, leaving their clients impoverished, had passed. Moreover, the price of wool – the barometer of prosperity in the rural interior of New South Wales – had doubled in the previous forty years. Furthermore, the arrival of the railway, passing as it did through the Cootamundra district, had opened communications both to the east and to the west, which, together with the accompanying postal service, brought isolated communities in touch with the strange and seemingly hurried life of the big cities.

But the end of the nineteenth century had seen the end of exploration, the final chapter of expansion which had been fuelled by the unshakable optimism that there was always better land 'further out'. The north and west of the continent held little promise. The centre was largely uninhabitable semi-desert, scrub or dry beds of sand; and the south-east corner fully colonised. Professional managers had replaced the stockmen and 'jackeroos' on company-owned properties in the fertile areas, while the suburbs of the large cities expanded to house the bank managers who were taking over from the old colonists. Australia had become more stable institutionally – less buccaneering – more integrated economically, because of the development that followed the railways and the telegraph, and stronger politically, because of the binding-together of the colonies into a federal Commonwealth in 1901.

Life in Cootamundra, or in nearby Yeo Yeo, where the family lived at the time of Donald's birth, had felt the effect of these changes. The Sydney–Melbourne railroad passed that way – Yeo Yeo itself was a small railway halt – and the prosperity from the growing wool trade was leaving its mark. The Bradman family were able to afford a home of some substance, admittedly wooden, as were most houses in the little village, but at least with enough room, in its two interconnected sections, to allow the children a measure of space. Most important, George Bradman owned the land which he farmed. However poor the land, the life of Cootamundra was certainly preferable to the landless poverty of his cousins in far-away Suffolk.

The climate, however, was harsh – too harsh in fact for George's wife Emily. Nor did the life of a smallholder's wife suit her. Her own family, the Whatmans, were a cut above the Bradmans in the size and worth of their holdings of land and had been able to afford a greater degree of comfort. Besides, the Bowral/Mittagong area of New South Wales, where the Whatmans farmed, was largely concentrated in the gentle and grassy uplands, whereas the Cootamundra district lay in the inhospitable valley of the river Murrumbidgee. It was because of his wife's health that George Bradman finally sold his farm at Yeo Yeo in 1910, when his youngest son was some eighteen months to two years old. The family then moved – or, in the case of Emily, moved back – to Whatman country. George gave up farming and took up carpentry in the town of Bowral. Life for the Bradmans had once again taken a new direction.

Bowral life was, of course, quite different from that in the railway halt of Yeo Yeo, but it was far from resembling life in the towns of today. Bowral at the time was only at the beginning of what was to become rapid development. Only eighty miles or so south-west of Sydney, it was starting to attract the rich from the city – building summer homes or making weekend excursions to avoid the steamy heat of the coast. At an altitude of 2,210 feet, Bowral offered a pleasant enough climate when Sydney was sticky. On the other hand, the winters were cold, particularly when the west wind blew. Nobody would come from the city during those months and the little town had to live with itself. With a winter population of just under 2,000, the town was on the margin of self-sufficiency. Admittedly, there were two local newspapers and a butter factory, as well as a few quarries; and there were two banks, a hospital and four small hotels. But most of the population did the best they could working for themselves. It was not by any means easy. The mostly wooden houses frequently had rough corrugated iron roofs (only public buildings were built with brick); the streets were basic and without pavements; people either walked, rode on horseback or in a horse-drawn buggy; there was no town water supply, and if there was no rain, there was no water; consequently there was no indoor sanitation – people had to make do with earth closets, cleared weekly by the 'sanitary man' (known colloquially as the 'shit-carter'); and there were no radios, indeed no entertainment at all unless it was home-grown.

But George Bradman was lucky in one respect at least. Through his Whatman brothers-in-law, George and Richard, he was taken up by a builder from the town – indeed he owned the only joinery works in Bowral – by the name of Alf Stephens. It was fortunate not only because Stephens was able to find him work but also because he was much respected in the town and, above all, president of Bowral Town Cricket Club. He even had a practice wicket at the back of his house which he let the local boys use.

Don Bradman's first home in Bowral was like many others in small Australian towns of the time: a timber-framed weatherboard bungalow. His first school was like many others also: a gaunt brick building with an unpaved yard in which to play, the whole divided into two – one half for the five- to ten-year-olds and one for the ten- to fourteen-year-olds. As for his academic record, it was equally unremarkable: 'I nearly always finished third,' he himself said in later life.[2] In appearance, he was small, already with a slightly square face and with the right eyebrow arching quizzically higher than the left; a shy, tough little lad unable to suppress a look of amused irony when photographed as a choirboy at the age of nine.

He was not a lonely child, in the strict sense of the term, since there were many friends at school and he lived, after all, in a large family. He was also popular. Even while still in the primary school – for the five- to ten-year-olds – he was invited on occasion to play in the makeshift games of cricket organised by the high school boys in the yard which the two schools shared. Yet none of his school friends lived near him, nor was there any organised sport outside school that could keep him entertained. Inevitably, there were times when life was solitary – after school, for instance, when he went home 'at, say, four o'clock in the afternoon . . . to amuse myself by playing or doing some gardening, chopping some wood or doing the vegetables, or something like that'.[3]

Left to his own devices, young Don invented games for himself, as small boys will. Tennis he played against a garage door; football by kicking whatever kind of ball was available around whatever open space was available. Best of all, however, were his solitary cricket games. Behind his home was a rainwater tank set on a round brick base on a concrete floor. Near the tank was a laundry, which was joined to the back of the house. The game, in essence, was simple. The boy threw a golf ball at the base of the water tank with his right hand while holding a cricket stump in his left. The ball flew back off the brickwork at an unpredictable angle. While it was fizzing back at him he gripped the stump with both hands; the point was to hit the ball before it could get past him and strike the laundry wall or door. The feat is difficult enough at the best of times, but such was the speed of eye and co-ordination of eye with arm that the boy, even at the age of nine or ten, managed to hit the golf ball with his stump, as he said himself in later life, 'more often than not'.[4]

Such was life for the schoolboy in the Bowral of the First World War: games, lessons, jobs in the house and garden, piano lessons from his sister Lilian, family 'singalongs' in the evening. It was a very far cry from the grisly battlefields of the European War. Indeed, the whole business of the War seemed to pass Bowral by. Certainly there had been great excitement in August 1914, when the parades were held and volunteers crowded the recruiting tables, but as the War dragged on it started to have its effect even in far distant Australia. The closure of European markets and the shortage of available shipping forced the coal mines of New South Wales to lay off workers. Coincidentally, drought struck the agricultural districts, so that the wheat harvest of 1914–15 was only a quarter of that of the previous year. Unemployment rose quickly from 5.9% of the workforce to 11%.

As a consequence, the unemployed made up a large part of the Australian Imperial Force (AIF). It did not make for good discipline. 'I think we have to admit that our force contains more bad hats than the others,' wrote one commentator.[5] There was a high incidence of venereal disease and a good deal of drunken rioting when the Australians, now joined by New Zealanders to make up the Australian and New Zealand Army Corps (ANZAC), went on leave in Cairo on the way to war. In the 'Battle of the Wozzer', for example, an altercation in a brothel led to a street fight of such violence – accompanied by random arson – that the military police gave up trying to keep order. It was only on the following day that the Anzacs could be shepherded aboard their troopships in Alexandria, leaving, not unnaturally, some of their number behind in military prisons.

The Australia that emerged from the smoke in 1918 was, like all belligerents, changed in many ways – some subtle, some not so subtle. Not so subtle were the returning Anzacs. They were rough, coarse, and full of bombast about their own achievements. But they had faced the enemy in battle; and had, moreover, shifted from the romantic view of 1915. 'We have been told that we will probably land under fire . . . we are full of joyous expectancy,' a soldier wrote home in that year. 'I am at present about to enter into the joy of my life.'[6] Instead the mood was one of horrified realism. 'Mother,' wrote one survivor of the 1916 offensive, 'it's quite indescribable; it was just awful.'[7] And they had lost comrades. In the end, of the 330,000 Australians who had put on a uniform during the War – two-fifths of the eligible male population – 59,000 had died and 167,000 had been wounded. Last, but by no means least, they had established the warrior image of the Anzac soldier, part of the corpus of national identification that had found its expression at Anzac Cove on the Turkish peninsula of Gallipoli.

'There ain't no religion out here, sir,' said one Anzac to his chaplain. 'We're all brothers.'[8] And brothers they had been. The hoops of fraternal steel that had been forged in the heat of Gallipoli, the mud of Flanders and the waste of the Somme were unbreakable, and created bonds that long afterwards – even in peace – distinguished those who 'went out' from those who did not. 'Diggers', they were called, from the digging their forbears had done in the gold-fields and that they too had done in the trenches; 'diggers' they remained. Above all else, they had discovered an abiding contempt for the British officer class.

The noise of this thunder was only distantly heard in the 'backblocks' of New South Wales. Bowral had certainly sent some of her young men to war, had read the reports of Gallipoli and the Western Front in the newspapers, and had voted in the conscription referenda. But both the Bradman and the Whatman families had been lucky enough to avoid direct involvement (apart from Ernest Bradnam, who was buried in Withersfield churchyard after his death on the Western Front in 1917). George Bradman was in his forties when the War started, as were his Whatman brothers-in-law, and the young men of the next generation were too young.

Life in Bowral might have been unaffected by the War, but those years brought people together in a surprising way, and it was because of this that Don Bradman met his future wife, Jessie Menzies. Old relationships had been renewed – Bradman's mother Emily and his future wife's father had started school together in the 1870s, and their parents were friends before that. Jessie lived with her family on a farm about six miles out of Bowral. Since she was too young to travel to school by herself, when the time came her family asked the Bradmans whether she could board with them during the school week for a year, until her sisters were of an age to form an impressive enough group to go to school with her in safety. So it was that at an early age there began, in the troubled aftermath of war, the relationship which, in Bradman's own words, 'has been a tremendous stabilising influence in the whole of my life'.[9]

As for cricket, Bradman was twelve years old when he made his first hundred. He had graduated to the Bowral Intermediate High School in 1918. Two years later he was asked to play for his school in a rough-and-tumble match on a football field. Not only did he manage to prevent a hat-trick but he made 55 not out. This ensured selection for the next match, this time on a 'proper' wicket of concrete covered with matting – for Bowral High School against their great rivals Mittagong High School. It was, in its own way, a famous day. Bowral made a total of 156 – of which the twelve-year-old Don made 115 not out. Quite simply, none of the Mittagong bowlers could get him out; nor, indeed, could they contain his ability to score apparently at will. The great career had well and truly begun.

The next step in the career was an invitation to act as scorer for the Bowral Town team for the 1920–21 season. This was competitive cricket at close quarters. There was sharp rivalry between the towns in Berrima District, one of which was Bowral, for the Tom Mack Cup, the object of the District Cricket Competition. Saturday afternoons were spent travelling around Berrima District (mostly in a truck with solid tyres on pot-holed roads) and watching Uncle George captaining the Bowral team, with George Bradman himself acting on occasion as umpire.

The story-book then took over. On one Saturday the Bowral team found itself one man short at Moss Vale, with no possibility of summoning a reserve from Bowral, which was a good six miles away. The young Don, still in knickerbockers, was promoted on the spot from scorer to player, went in at number ten and made 37 not out. One of the Bowral team, Sidney Cupitt, rewarded Don with a present of one of his old bats. It was dented, cracked and far too big for the boy; but it was the first proper bat he had ever owned, and, once cut down by three inches off the bottom by his father, a treasure of unimaginable glory.

The third event in the story-book summer of 1920–21 was a first visit to Sydney itself. As a treat, George Bradman took two days off work in February to take his young son to the Sydney Cricket Ground (known then and now simply as the SCG) and the England–Australia Test being played there. For the small country boy it was thrilling beyond measure. The crowds were such as young Don had never seen before (30,000 on the Saturday when Charlie Macartney made 170, full of delicate leg glances); the turf was nothing like the rough Bowral grass; the pavilion was of unheard-of splendour; the crowd, many of them old Diggers, rough and raucous; the stands and the Hill overwhelming. The excitement of it all was almost too much. 'I shall never be happy,' Don told his father, 'until I play on this ground.' His father smiled 'with affectionate tolerance'.[10]

At the end of 1922, Bradman left school, aged fourteen. He had passed his Intermediate Certificate examination, in which he had performed 'very creditably', and finished with a shining report from his headmaster which described him as 'truthful, honest and industrious, and an unusually bright lad'.[11] It was now time to earn his living. He put on a wing collar, black tie, waistcoat with a watch-chain and fob and a frock coat, and set off to work as clerk in the estate agency of Deer & Westbrook in Bong Bong Street. It was far from being the most exciting of jobs, but his employer, Percy Westbrook, was a kindly man and sympathetic to Bradman's requests for time off on Saturdays to play cricket.

There was also time to play lawn tennis – Westbrook's main interest was bowls, but tennis was next in his sporting affection. Indeed, for the next two years Bradman played more tennis than cricket. In the summer of 1923–24 he played no cricket at all, and in 1924–25 very little, and then only towards the end of the summer.

But life for the young Bradman seemed to be settling down comfortably enough. His job was secure. His future lay in working his way up to a partnership in the estate agency. Bowral was growing, and free from the political disturbances that led to the post-War riots in Sydney – 'Diggers' against what was thought to be communist infiltration of the New South Wales government. And the economic depression, with the accompanying slump in wheat and wool prices, had not yet taken its toll of employment and good temper. The future for the young man seemed clear enough: a lifetime of simple and comfortable obscurity.

That option, if it ever was one, vanished with Bradman's return to cricket in the following year. At the start of the 1925–26 season, now aged seventeen, he became a regular member of the Bowral Town Cricket Club. At first, his efforts were unremarkable, but everything changed on the Saturday before Christmas in 1925. Bowral were due to play Wingello, holders of the Tom Mack Cup from the previous year, won thanks largely to the bowling of one of her famous sons, W.J. O'Reilly. O'Reilly was in many respects Bradman's opposite: he was of Irish Catholic origin, where Bradman was English Protestant; he was tall and lanky, where Bradman was short and dapper; he was a great bowler, where Bradman was a great batsman; and, although each respected the other's ability, the contrast between their two personalities was such that there was never to be much friendship between them, and in the end the distance was to develop into outright hostility.

On that day in December 1925, Wingello had brought O'Reilly into their team, although he was at the time living in Sydney. Bowral won the toss and batted, O'Reilly taking the new ball despite being a bowler mainly of medium-pace leg breaks. One wicket went down quickly and Bradman came in. 'What struck me most about him,' O'Reilly recalled later, 'was the difficulty he seemed to be having in taking normal steps to the wicket. His pads seemed to reach right up to his navel. His bat was small and had reached the sere and yellow stage, where the yellow was turning to dark tobacco.'[12] By the end of the day the little lad was 234 not out.

O'Reilly might have had Bradman caught out twice before he reached 50, but in each case the catch went to the Wingello captain, Selby Jeffery, an old Anzac who had been at the landing at Gallipoli. Jeffery's cricket outfit, however, made life difficult for him in the slips. In O'Reilly's account — disputed, needless to say, by Bradman — apart from the big brass 'A' of a Gallipoli veteran, he wore a black waistcoat in which he kept a pipe, a tobacco pouch and a box of matches. These were frequently in use during play, and it was just at the point when Jeffery was employing his two hands in lighting his pipe that the first chance from the young Bradman hit him in the midriff. The second one was no less complicated, travelling through a cloud of smoke of such density that the fielder could not possibly have seen the ball. 'Sorry, Bill,' said the veteran on both occasions, and that was the end of that. Nobody spoke in anger or in disrespect to the veterans of Gallipoli. But, whatever the truth of the story, O'Reilly had his revenge. The game continued on the following Saturday, on the Wingello ground, and this time O'Reilly bowled Bradman first ball.

In the following match, the final game of the 1925–26 season, Bradman made 300 against Moss Vale, and informed his mother that she now owed him three bats as a reward. One was all that his mother was prepared to offer; the offer was accepted and, at the age of seventeen, Don Bradman took possession of the first new bat he had ever owned. Bowral went on to win the match, and with it the Tom Mack Cup, by an innings and 338 runs. The match lasted five Saturday afternoons.

All this soon came to the attention of the New South Wales Cricket Association (NSWCA) in Sydney. On 5 October 1926 a somewhat stilted letter arrived, addressed to D. Bradman, Esq., c/o A. Stephens, Esq., Boolwey Street, Bowral – for some reason the NSWCA could not be bothered to find out Bradman's own address – inviting him to a practice session at Sydney Cricket Ground on the 11th. They had not given the young man much notice, but he was urged to 'give this matter the consideration its importance warrants' and to 'realise that this is an opportunity which should not be missed'[13]; in addition, they offered to pay his expenses.

For the eighteen-year-old it certainly was an opportunity not to be missed. He sought and obtained leave to go to Sydney, and duly went, accompanied by his father, George. It was the first time Bradman had performed for selectors and, indeed, the press, but he was, in the words of one reporting journalist, 'undismayed by the size of the gallery'.[14] The visit was not wholly satisfactory, however, not least because the Sydney club which wanted to sign him up, Central Cumberland, were unable to pay his expenses for a weekly trip from Bowral to Sydney. There was therefore no immediate entry into Sydney club cricket. Furthermore, although he was selected to play for the 'Possibles' in a trial match on 10 November, his 37 not out was not considered good enough to achieve selection for the State side.

By way of compensation, Bradman was offered, and accepted, a place in a trial match for selection to the 'Southern Country Week' team which was due to play, as the name suggests, in 'Country Week' in Sydney in late November. He performed well, and selection duly followed. Thus it was that Don made his first appearance – for the Southern Country Week against Riverina – on 22 November 1926 at the SCG in front of a Sydney crowd. By the end of the week he had been invited to play for the St George Cricket Club in the south-eastern suburbs of Sydney – all expenses paid.

23

It was the first time he had encountered a grass wicket but on the Saturday, using the new bat acquired from his mother, Bradman scored 110.

From then until his move to Sydney in September 1928, Bradman's life was nothing if not busy. Each Saturday during the season meant a 5 A.M. start for the early train to Sydney – a match for St George and return at midnight; the rest of the week meant work in the estate agency and cricket practice whenever possible in the evening. There was little time for anything else. But the onward march was irresistible: a final 320 for Bowral, an average of 48.16 in his first season with St George, and the great reward at the beginning of the 1927–28 season: selection to the New South Wales team to tour the southern States, with two Sheffield Shield championship matches among them, against South Australia in Adelaide and Victoria in Melbourne. 'Don Bradman's success in his initial effort in . . . cricket,' intoned one journalist, 'is yet another instance of the opportunities which await persistent effort in this sunny land.'[15] The march from small-town hero to national star was well under way.

There was a 'Reception and Dance' for the 'Bowral Boy' in Bowral on a Friday night at the end of the 1927–28 cricket season. It was, for the young Don and his family, a great occasion. The attendance, it was said, was 'exceptionally large'. Bradman was presented with a gold watch and chain after 'dancing had been indulged in for some time'. There were speeches – notably, and at some length, by Alf Stephens, by now the Mayor of Bowral. It was no mean achievement, he said, for a country boy to go to Sydney and in his first season win second place in the Sheffield Shield averages and second place in first-grade averages in Sydney. 'The great wish of his Bowral admirers,' the report of the Mayor's speech continues, 'was to see him in an Australian team. (Applause).'

The young Don was 'evidently overcome by the extreme cordiality of his reception'. His speech was made with difficulty, but was noted for the 'modesty of demeanour that explains the rapid progress he has made in the affections of his new associates in the game'. Percy Westbrook pointed out that Don Bradman had endeared himself 'not only by his cricket but by his character, which was the same in private life as on the cricket field'. The report of the event concluded by remarking that 'an excellent supper was served by the ladies'.[16]

The young man was suitably flattered. But he was by then on the point of the first big decision in his life. In September 1928 Don Bradman left his father and mother, his family home in Bowral, his friends and schoolmates, and moved to the great city of Sydney.

2

'A POOR WANDERING DREAMER'

IT WOULD BE ABSURD TO IMAGINE that the Sydney of 1928 bore much resemblance to the Sydney of today. The natural beauty of the place has not changed – indeed, it has been enhanced over the years by the bridge and the Opera House, and the grand colonial buildings on Macquarie Street, the barracks and the Cathedral next to Hyde Park, all still stand. But to the student of Australian history – in all its forms, political, social or sporting – the Sydney to which Don Bradman moved nearly seventy years ago presents a stark, and sometimes depressing, contrast to the modern, confident and thrusting city of the new millennium.

To start with, there was the aftermath of the First World War. Australia, like the other belligerents, could not escape the period of confusion which characterised its aftermath. Anzac troops, grown hard and cynical through experience, had returned to find themselves competing for jobs with those who had stayed at home. The transition to a peacetime economy was far from a smooth ride along a straight and even road. Indeed, it was little more than an uncomfortable series of forward lurches on a bumpy track. Furthermore, there were some very clear class and sectarian divisions, already present but given sharper overtones by the War, and made even sharper by the two referenda on conscription held in 1916 and 1917. The Irish Catholics, for instance, whose leader was the aggressive Archbishop Daniel Mannix of Melbourne, had been opposed to the whole endeavour, largely on the grounds of their support for Irish Home Rule and the British treatment of what they perceived as the heroes of the 1916 Easter Rising in Dublin. Following this logic, they continued, in the post-War period, to oppose the very Empire for which Australian troops had been laying down their lives.

Then there was the rise of the Australian Labor Party – itself anti-War, and largely influenced, and indeed penetrated, by Catholics – which succeeded against expectations in winning power in the early 1920s in a number of States. This success in turn sparked both the ex-soldiers and the Protestant bourgeoisie into fierce reaction. Dubious secret societies and paramilitary groups were founded. The existing masonic lodges spawned numerous daughter lodges, their membership carefully chosen. Indeed, in the early 1930s Bradman himself was persuaded by the captain of St George to join the craft in Sydney, and became an active member.

There was perhaps good reason, since the situation in New South Wales was particularly tense. In Sydney, unlike in Melbourne, there was, after all, a Protestant majority, which ran most of the businesses and created the wealth of the city. With the arrival of a Labor Government in 1920, there was a general feeling among the influential that the State was slipping steadily but inexorably towards bolshevism; and for their part the Protestant establishment, supported by the Diggers, did not like it. These antagonisms soon led to violence. The Moore Park riots of May 1920, for instance, saw 150,000 people, mainly Catholics, protesting against the deportation of a Catholic priest, confronted by some 20,000 Diggers shouting Loyalist slogans such as 'God, King and Empire' and waving the Union flag. The resulting punch-up was, it was said, 'a wonder to behold'.

The political and sectarian contrasts may have been sharp, but they would not have erupted into such violence if the prosperity of the business class had spread downwards to those below. In fact, the reverse was the case. The conditions in which the majority of Sydneyites in the inner city lived were hardly imaginable. The urban slums were disgusting beyond modern belief, and there was gang warfare, organised by groups known as 'pushers'. The influenza epidemic of 1919 had caused dreadful misery – New South Wales was declared a quarantine area and all theatres, cinemas and dance halls were closed. The wreckage of the War was everywhere to be seen – men whose lives had been broken in the trenches lay in the streets and wept. Drunkenness, too, seemed to be a particularly Sydney disease. With the pubs closing at 6 P.M. the 'six o'clock swill' left droves of inebriates vomiting and urinating on pavements as they were thrown out of the overcrowded bars. Nor were the morals of the city underclass anything other than dismal: crime, frequently violent, seemed unstoppable, and the back seats of taxis were said after midnight to be 'brothels on wheels'.[1]

At the other end of the scale, however, it was the 'jazz age', the age of optimism. There was a building boom, spilling into suburbia 'a litter of bungalows ... scattered for miles and miles'.[2] The measures of respectability were the front lawn, the motor car, the wireless aerial, the ebony elephant sitting on the mock-mahogany coffee table in the front room next to the cocktail cabinet. Dance halls flourished as never before, and the flappers flapped as energetically as their sisters in London or New York – provoking a pastoral letter from the Catholic Archbishop Kelly to the effect that clothing was given 'for our necessities not for our vanities' and that it was 'to hide the shameful members'.[3] It was the time of 'Everything good-oh', of the extravagant annual Artists Ball, of Dulcie Deamer ('a poor wandering dreamer'[4]) Anne Brennan (the 'Gutter Venus') and Jack Lindsay (the 'Spirit of the Roaring Twenties'). The revellers called it the Golden Decade.

All this was a far cry from the starchy rectitude of Bowral, and it is no surprise that the parents of the twenty-year-old Don Bradman were reluctant to relinquish their parental responsibilities for the young man. It was unusual in those days for young men of twenty to leave home – twenty-one was still the approved threshold of independence – and Don's elder brother Victor was staying safely at home in Bowral, so why, they asked, should Don head for what looked suspiciously like a pit of uncompromising iniquity? Quite apart from the principle, the young man was far from robust in his physique. At a height of no more than 5'8" and with the fresh face of a country boy, he did not even look his twenty years, let alone seem able to defend himself in the street fights that were common currency in the Sydney of the day.

But his parents had by now come to understand the streak of stubborn and single-minded determination which was part of the character of their younger son. Besides, there were three things working in his favour. First, the journeys from Bowral to Sydney and back to play Saturday matches for St George had become wearisome, and there were longer absences in the latter part of the summer of 1927–28 when the 'Bowral Boy', as he was by then known, had played several Sheffield Shield matches for New South Wales. Second, his Bowral employer, Percy Westbrook, had set up an estate agency in Sydney and had offered Don employment as secretary to the new firm. Finally, a friend of the Bradman family, a country inspector for a large and respectable insurance company, had volunteered to act *in loco parentis* in Sydney and to lodge the young man, at least for the first six months, at his home in the relatively sanitised suburb of Concord West. In the end, and after a good deal of argument, the deed was done. It was decided that Don Bradman's first residence in Sydney was to be with Mr and Mrs G. H. Pearce. Mother and father had been won over, and off the young Don went – not, it should be imagined, without some trepidation.

Bradman had visited Sydney many times over the previous two years, but visiting a city for a day's cricket is quite different from taking up permanent residence. In fact, he had probably learnt more about the strains of urban life from his new colleagues in the State cricket team than he had from his journeys to Hurstville Oval for the relatively gentlemanly Saturday matches. His selection for the New South Wales side, as twelfth man for the tour of the southern States in December 1927, had brought with it triumphs and hardship, but also some idea of the harshness of the urban character as against the open friendliness of the countryman. A 'cordial kid' and 'a bright-faced boy'[5] he might have been, as the press saw it; but he was teetotal, self-assured and perhaps rather too quick to point out the deficiencies of others – not through malice but through failure to understand the hierarchy of the group of young male sportsmen of which he was now part. Nor did it help that Bradman's response to any teasing – as it was to any nervousness when he went into bat – was something that looked suspiciously like a cheeky grin. As a result, he had been subjected to the usual rituals which such groups employ. He had been given a nickname ('Braddles') and made to play the piano, whenever one could be found, well into the night – 'Give us a tune, Braddles'[6] – had had beer poured over his head, and so on. There was ample opportunity for such fun and games. In those days State sides for the Sheffield Shield championship matches seemed to spend almost as much time travelling as playing cricket. It was not until after the Second World War that Shield and Test teams travelled by air. The trains were slow. Journeys were long – sixteen hours from Sydney to Brisbane and a good two days from Sydney to Adelaide. Stops to take on water were frequent; dining cars were rare; the track gauges varied from State to State – therefore there were frequent changes on interstate journeys. It was impossible to open carriage windows without getting covered in coal smuts; and the carriages themselves were insufferably hot in the summer, just when the cricket sides were travelling.

It is little wonder that the young Bradman's health had suffered. On the first leg of the southern States tour, on their way to Adelaide for the Shield match against South Australia, the New South Wales team stopped at Broken Hill, a silver-mining town on the western edge of the State where they were due to recuperate before the run along the Main Barrier Range down to Adelaide, some 250 miles to the south-west. Bradman had hardly slept during the journey from Sydney. Nor for that matter had his fellow 'colt' Archie Jackson, who had developed a boil on his knee, while Bradman had caught a bad cold which affected the sight in one of his eyes. Both were sent to bed for the rest day, but it was Bradman, the twelfth man, who was considered the fitter to play in the game against the Barrier team on the following day. It was not the easiest of appearances for the new recruit. The pitch was made of concrete; the heat was stifling and a dust storm blew up during the day. Wearing ordinary walking shoes – the studs on cricket boots were quite unsuitable for concrete – Bradman made 46, uncomfortably and, for the latter part of his innings, with a badly bruised finger.

Nevertheless, the train carrying the New South Wales team – including the somewhat battered young Don – had rumbled on, down into South Australia to arrive in Adelaide at about 10:30 on the morning of 15 December 1927. It must have been a strange sight for the newcomer. Adelaide was, and still is, quite different from the cities of what was then called 'the east'. Founded in 1836 as a settlement for the tenants of the South Australia Company – and originally a 'paradise of [religious] Dissent' which had decided to 'have no connections with any persons of dissolute habits or immoral principles or whose former actions could not undergo a strict examination'[7] – it was both beautiful and prim. There had been a regrettable period when the Aboriginal population was pushed off the coastal havens and into the dry hinterland, but after that the quiet of Adelaide had not been disturbed. The social tone – quite different from that of the convict colony of the east – was that of the guardians of morality, the puritan clergy or laity, who protected their Sundays not just by going to church or resting from work but by abstaining from looking out of windows, since that might lead to the risk of 'beholding vanities abroad'. It is not for nothing that at least one visitor to Adelaide has christened the city 'Greater Cheltenham'.

Jackson's knee had still been causing him pain, but Bradman was by now sufficiently recovered from the bruise on his finger to play in the game starting the following day, his first Sheffield Shield match and his debut in first-class cricket. As if that were not enough, South Australia were fielding the one bowler a debutant batsman would have chosen not to face, the New Zealand – by then South Australian – leg-spinner Clarrie Grimmett.

It seemed to make no difference whatsoever to the 'Bowral Boy'. In spite of going in just before tea on the first day (at no.7), Bradman hit two fours off Grimmett in his first over, reached 50 in sixty-seven minutes, and was 65 not out at the close of play. On the following morning, a cloudless summer day, he went out to complete his innings. 'Good luck Don hope finger better: May' was the telegram from his sister that sent him on his way.[8] He did not disappoint her: just before lunch he was out for 118. In his first Shield match, in his first innings in first-class cricket, he had made his century. Only nineteen batsmen before him had achieved the same feat.

The telegrams rolled in. 'My heartiest congratulations on your great innings; everybody Bowral delighted: from Uncle'; 'Hearty congratulations from all your Bowral friends and well wishers'; and so on. Don wrote back to a Bowral newspaper: 'I would like to convey my sincerest thanks and appreciation to those people who have sent me messages of congratulation . . . it is very gratifying to know that one's efforts are . . . appreciated by the people of Bowral.' It was not very elegant, but it had to do. The press, too, was hyperbolic: 'brilliant debut' and 'smacking boundaries with a delightful abandon' were two of the more restrained comments.[9] But the one solid result was that Bradman immediately became a permanent member of the New South Wales team. Indeed, with another century at Sydney in the final match against Victoria his record for his first season in first-class cricket, at the age of nineteen, had been: 10 innings, once not out, total runs 416, average 46.22. The real argument for his move to Sydney had been made.

IN ONE RESPECT THE young Don's move was badly timed. Apart from the social unrest in the city and the continuing sectarian divide, the economic climate in late 1928 was turning towards severe low pressure. Australia in general, and New South Wales in particular, had over-borrowed in the London market throughout the 1920s, and the London bankers were beginning to doubt the credit on which they had lent. A British Economic Mission had arrived in 1927; its report had been pessimistic and unfriendly. Public works had to be cut back, but even then the City of London was unimpressed. A loan issue for the Commonwealth of Australia in January 1929 was a flop – with 84% left with the underwriters – and the underwriters themselves refused any commitment for the future until Australia had put its house in order. What was meant by that, of course, was a drastic deflationary fiscal and monetary squeeze. 'Everything good-oh' came to an abrupt end.

Bradman could take out some sort of an insurance policy against the social problem by enrolling, as he did, in the new militia which was being formed. The Don Bradman of new cricketing fame became a modest Private Bradman in the Illawarra Regiment (New South Wales). The duties were not onerous, but the mere fact of his volunteering both showed his hand as a supporter of the conservative Protestant supporters of Empire and ensured protection from the right-wing – legitimate and paramilitary – organisations, should trouble arise.

But from the economic troubles there was no obvious safe haven. The real-estate explosion of the 1920s had finished in a puff of smoke, and the firm of Deer & Westbrook was one of the first to be blown away. Another job had to be found. Fortunately a safety net was to hand. Bradman's sporting reputation was now such as to attract the attentions of a firm selling sporting goods – the bolthole for unemployed sportsmen down the ages. In February 1929 he was offered a job in the public relations department of Mick Simmons Ltd, an old established firm selling a variety of sporting equipment. Again, the duties were not onerous – running coaching sessions for schoolboys, signing autographs and even teaching the rudiments of fishing (Bradman had rather taken to fishing as a boy in Bowral). He was allowed time off, it was understood, for cricket.

In another respect, however, Bradman's arrival in Sydney was well timed. Immediately south of Concord, the suburb where Don lodged with Mr and Mrs Pearce, was the outer suburb of Burwood. There was not much to choose between the two suburbs, except that in the one lived Don Bradman and in the other lived Jessie Menzies, who had been to business college in Sydney and who had now found a job in the Commonwealth Bank – her uncle was a former governor of the institution. One thing, in the end, led to another – but not for what would seem today to be a very long time.

But in the context of the collective life of Australia the timing of Bradman's move could hardly have been more dramatic. It coincided not only with the arrival of the British bankers to tell Australians that there was no more money, but also with a general collapse in morale. There was a moment in late 1928 when, in the words of one, 'all of a sudden everything seemed to stop'.[10] The prices of wheat and wool were falling sharply. Unemployment was rising – by the spring of 1928 seasonal employment had virtually petered out. Crowds marched through Sydney in support of striking timber-workers singing not just 'The Red Flag' but also, and with more sinister motive, the 'Internationale'.

In this situation, it was not enough just to elect a Labor Government for the Commonwealth. Nor was it enough for the Labor Premier of New South Wales, Jack Lang, to repudiate the interest payable on the State's debt in London, hitting back, as it were, at the anonymous financiers who seemed to control the lives of people who lived on the other side of the planet. As self-doubt crept in, what Australians were looking for was a new hero, a young Siegfried, with a sword of magic potency, who would slay the dragon and bring back the hope that they had lost.

Of course, there were no dragons immediately available for slaughter. But such as there were arrived in Western Australia in mid-October 1928, on the liner *Otranto*. The dragons in question were cricketers, the MCC touring side which, unveiling their disguise to become 'England' for the Test matches against Australia, were there – as far as England was concerned – to defeat Australia and retain the Ashes, the ultimate trophy between the two countries, which had been so decisively lost in the years after the First World War but had been won back in 1926. The English line-up was certainly impressive – 'the strongest since the War', it was said.[11] Captained by A.P.F. Chapman, the side included Walter Hammond, Jack Hobbs, Maurice Leyland, Herbert Sutcliffe, Maurice Tate, Jack White and, as an omen of things to come, Douglas Jardine and Harold Larwood. These were dragons indeed, and cricketing Australia – which included most Australians – were anxious to see how, and by whom, these dragons could be slain.

Don Bradman had little opportunity at the start of the season to demonstrate his conviction that he was the young hero who should at least face up to – and perhaps even slay – the dragons of England. He had no doubt whatsoever in his own ability or determination. Indeed, he had difficulty in understanding why other young men did not aspire to, and attain, his already high level of achievement. Like the young Mozart, he could not appreciate the special nature of his own genius.

But to prove it was another matter. In the early season, in late September, he had, it is true, performed spectacularly well for St George. But this was not first-class cricket.

His first opportunity came in the Test Trial at Melbourne in mid-October. On the strength of his previous year's performance he was picked to play for the Rest vs. Australia. The result was a desperate failure – scores of 14 and 5. Fortunately, redemption came swiftly. Only a week later, at Brisbane in the Sheffield Shield match between New South Wales and Queensland, Bradman made a century in both innings. But these were not just ordinary centuries; for the first time he totally demoralised the opposition bowlers. They simply did not know how to bowl to him; he could score apparently at will. Further redemption came in the game in the following week between New South Wales and the English tourists: Bradman 87 and 132 not out, facing Larwood for the first time. There was now little doubt about his Test place, and on 20 November 1928 he duly received a telegram – oddly enough via the Adelaide Stock Exchange, where Jeanes, one of the selectors, had an office – instructing him to report to Brisbane on the 27th. Don Bradman was to play in his first Test match, and against England at that.

Yet the Brisbane Test, starting on 30 November 1928, was a disaster for both Bradman and Australia. On the opening Friday, Bradman had plenty of time to devote to watching England bat. True, he had one success, running out Hobbs, normally the best judge of a run, with a bullet-like throw from the boundary. On the Saturday, the Australian fielding 'fell off a lot, a few of the men moving very slowly under the stress of the long outing'.[12] The English batsmen took advantage, Hendren anchoring the innings with a patient 169 and sharing a partnership with Larwood of 124. By the time the Australians went in to bat they were tired and disgruntled, and in that mood Larwood was too much for them. On the third morning of the match Bradman found himself in at 71 for 5, and out for 18 half an hour later (lbw to Tate in a decision he was prepared, even sixty years later, to describe as 'dubious'[13]). The first innings scores read: England 521; Australia 122.

The second innings went no better. Chapman decided that England would bat again and so they did, finally declaring at 342 for 8, with Jardine not out at 65. England had all the luck as well. Australia soon lost Ponsford to Larwood, after which it rained. In the days of uncovered wickets, especially at Brisbane, rain inevitably brought disaster. Bradman had never seen a rain-affected wicket before and, as he said later, he asked 'one of my team-mates what the ball would do on such a pitch'.[14] Answer, apparently, came there none; Bradman was out second ball to the spinner Jack White. Australia went down to their greatest defeat ever – by a margin of 675 runs.

For the next Test Bradman was dropped down to twelfth man, but, as luck would have it, Ponsford broke a finger while batting in Australia's first innings and the twelfth man found himself fielding throughout England's innings of 636. Hammond made 251 of them ('probably the best I'd seen up to that time', Bradman recalled, '. . . Walter was then at his peak'[15]). England went on to win the match with ease.

Recalled for the Third Test at Melbourne, Bradman established his place in the Australian side for the next twenty years. Seventy-nine in the first innings was followed by 112 in the second, on 3 January 1929. He was at that time the youngest player ever to score a century in a Test. Almost bowled by White when he was on 7, he settled down with Woodfull 'to grind out the runs'.[16] After the tea break, Bradman started to drive White more aggressively. By the time Larwood and Tate were brought back into the attack they were met with strokes of huge confidence – Bradman's second 50 was scored in only 83 minutes.

As Bradman approached his century the crowd at the Melbourne Cricket Ground swelled rapidly, although it was late in the day. All over Australia radios were switched on. In Sydney the excitement was so intense by the scoreboards which newspapers had erected outside their offices – to flash up the score as it was telegraphed through – that trams were stopped to allow people out into the already crammed streets. When Bradman finally reached his hundred – with an all-run four – the reception was spectacular: there were prolonged cheers at the ground itself, but at Sydney there was little short of delirium. 'One could see nothing,' wrote the journalist A. G. Moyes, 'but a mass of hats, umbrellas and handkerchiefs in the air, while their owners jumped up and down, clapping and yelling with joy.' The Sydney *Sun* was even more lyrical: 'Some pictures on life's canvas

are quickly obliterated. Others, like this one, are unforgettable.'[17]
Sydney, and perhaps Australia too, had found its hero.

Between the third and fourth Test matches there were two
Sheffield Shield games to be played, against South Australia in
Adelaide and Victoria at Sydney. In the first, Bradman was given
his one and only trial as an opening batsman. 'I rather fancied
opening,' Bradman recalled. 'The man who got me out was Tim
Wall and I just couldn't cope with him.'[18] The result was 5 and
2 in the two innings. It may have been a freak result, but it tends
to confirm the view that throughout his batting life Bradman was
at his least secure in his first ten minutes at the wicket. He was
not a 'good starter', in the words of one his greatest admirers.
That was why he cultivated a forward push wide of mid-on for
a single to get him off the mark. Once he was past the first ten
minutes, in the words of the same admirer, 'the door was shut'.[19]
There was no getting him out, other than to an untypically lax
stroke or bad fortune.

The story was different in the second Shield match. New South
Wales batted first, and Bradman went in first wicket down, just
before lunch on 24 January 1929. New South Wales declared
soon after tea on 26 January at 713 for 6. Bradman was 340 not
out. It was the longest innings ever played for New South Wales
in a Sheffield Shield match; the highest score by an NSWCA
player in any Sheffield Shield match; the highest first-class score
ever made at the Sydney Cricket Ground; the highest first-class
score ever made by a batsman under twenty-one; and he was the
youngest Australian to make 300 in first-class cricket.

The fourth Test match, in early February 1929 at Adelaide, saw
Archie Jackson, the other 'colt' from New South Wales, make his
first Test century. It was a most elegant performance. In the words
of one writer, comparing the two 'colts', Bradman had 'forced his
way to the top by sheer natural ability, a straight bat, cool cheerful
temperament, determination and enterprise', but Jackson was (at
the age of nineteen) 'the finished batsman, the batsman who
knows the one stroke for every ball . . . executes that stroke
with an artistry that has no parallel in the present day'.[20]

It was a reasonable assessment. Don Bradman, even then, made
no pretensions to style – he just wanted to make runs. Jackson, on

the other hand, was first and foremost a stylist – a younger version of Hobbs or Kippax, or even Victor Trumper. But Jackson was the shooting star of cricket: he died four years later of tuberculosis at the age of twenty-three.

At Adelaide Bradman was caught off Tate for 40 in the first innings and run out for 58 in the second (later claiming that the English wicket-keeper, George Duckworth, had dropped the ball before breaking the wicket, and that he was therefore not out). The large Test score that would have confirmed his position as one the world's greatest batting prospects still eluded him. So, for that matter, did success elude Australia. Although they only lost the Adelaide Test by 12 runs, it was still lost, and Australia faced the prospect, if defeated yet again in the last Test at Melbourne, of the humiliation of five lost Test matches out of five. It was little wonder that the gale of public emotion had reached storm force by the time the two sides reached the great amphitheatre of the Melbourne Cricket Ground to open, on 8 March 1929, what turned out to be one of the most exciting cricket matches of all time. It was to last eight days.

At first, everything went about as badly as it could for Australia. Hobbs, at the age of 47, made 142, his twelfth century against Australia and his fifth on the Melbourne ground. Hendren followed with 95 and Leyland with 137. Then Grimmett injured his knee and was unable to bowl on the second day. By tea-time on the third day England were all out for 519; Australia were already expecting another heavy defeat.

But fortune turned in their favour. First Woodfull made a stolid 102, putting on 54 with Jackson for the first wicket, 88 with Kippax for the second and 61 with Ryder for the third. Bradman came in just after lunch on the fourth day, but Woodfull was out immediately. Bradman's partner from St George in Sydney, Alan Fairfax, came to the wicket. Australia were 203 for 4. The crowd of over 40,000, the English team, Bradman and Fairfax all knew that this was the critical point in the game. If the English bowlers – Larwood, Tate, Geary and White – could break through again, the game, with Australia more than 300 runs behind, was as good as won. If, on the other hand, Australia could hang on and get near the English total, there was every chance that the hot north wind – gusting across the ground as it was – and the fearsome barracking of the Melbourne crowd could tip the balance in Australia's favour.

The challenge was met. Bradman and Fairfax were still together at the close of play. The crowd had shouted themselves hoarse once they realised that the two young batsmen were starting to dominate the English bowling – 'old Yarra must have trembled in her banks', wrote one journalist ecstatically. 'Some men were so hoarse they could yell no more and, leaping up in their seats, they were crouching like bookmakers before the last race on Melbourne Cup Day.' When Bradman reached his century, after eight minutes short of three hours at the wicket, '[there was] cheering round after round . . . rolling away in great waves, while hats waved in the air with parasols and handkerchiefs.' It was all too much for one writer: when the two came in at tea, he wrote, 'Great Pompey in his passage of Rome had nothing on them.'[21] His meaning may not have been entirely clear, but in the excitement of the moment that hardly mattered.

On the following morning, Bradman and Fairfax continued their partnership. Bradman was out for 123, after the two had put on 183 for the fifth wicket. Australia came within 28 runs of England's first innings total. It had been a desperate war of attrition. The bowling figures tell the story: Larwood 1 for 83 in 34 overs; Tate 0 for 108 in 62; Geary 5 for 105 in 81; White 2 for 136 in 75. Only Larwood had conceded more than two runs an over.

England, as many had predicted, performed badly in their second innings, only Hobbs, Hendren and – surprisingly – Tate getting past 50. Their total of 257 left Australia 287 to win – not by any means easy, but not wholly out of reach. As it turned out, both Larwood and Tate were badly out of form and only Hammond, at best a part-time bowler, took wickets. For Australia, Oldfield, Woodfull, Jackson and Kippax all made runs, without any of them making the match-winning innings that was required. By the time Bradman went in for his second innings, on the eighth morning of the match, Australia were 204 for 5 – still needing 83 to win with only five (rather doubtful) wickets left.

Bradman's partner at that decisive moment was Jack Ryder; and the two held out to win for Australia. Writing later Bradman claimed: 'My one desire was to see Ryder make the winning hit, for he had been a wonderful fellow in the previous matches . . .'[22] Be all that as it may, it was indeed Ryder that performed this duty, but not before a false alarm had led Maurice Tate to grab two stumps as a souvenir – to be replaced when he realised that his enthusiasm had been premature. Ryder it was who then made the necessary runs, and found the pitch invaded by the crowd determined to carry both Ryder and Bradman shoulder-high to celebrate the famous victory. Bradman managed to escape to the pavilion, only to be mobbed as he left later to catch the train back to Sydney. In the end, he, together with the other New South Wales heroes, Kippax, Jackson and Fairfax, fought their way through the crowd, found an old hansom cab and, 'hanging on like grim death', arrived at the Melbourne railway station just in time for the Sydney train.

The arrival at Sydney was just as hectic. The crowds – the unemployed, the drunks, the old soldiers, the young boys – were all there to greet their heroes at the railway station when they arrived; and they chased them, particularly Bradman, to their taxis for autographs. The verdict of the Sydney press was clear; it opined that 'the Bowral boy, Don Bradman, is on a pinnacle . . . paralleled only by the immortal W.G. Grace of England'.[23] There were ceremonies. The St George Club gave a dinner for Bradman and Fairfax; all present and past members were invited. Bradman was presented with a gold fountain pen. Buttons depicting Bradman's face were sold for a shilling each.

And yet there were those even then who thought that the whole thing was getting out of hand. One of those was Don Bradman himself. He knew perfectly well that, the cricket season now over, he would have to return to his lodgings in Sydney. He had had to change lodgings so as to continue to qualify for St George. Fortunately, another relatively well-off patron appeared – none other than the Secretary of the club, Frank Cush. Thus, in the early part of April 1929 Donald Bradman moved his still meagre belongings to the substantial Cush house in the plush suburb of Rockdale.

He also started his new job. It could hardly be called either exciting or challenging, but the truth was, however unpleasant, that the young Don badly needed the money. Cricket only paid subsistence during the season and in spite of the fact that he neither drank nor smoked, nor joined in the expensive business of young social life in the city (his life was of great simplicity, enlivened only from time to time by 'musical evenings' with the Menzies family at nearby Burwood) there was not much left over.

So, the boring job it had to be. True, there were one or two short, up-country tours in the autumn of 1929, but the winter was to be spent in the drudgery of what were known as 'familiarisation tours' around the commercial territory of Mick Simmons Ltd, purveyor of sporting goods. Oscar Lawson, who was in charge of advertising and public relations for the company, was assiduous in making sure that their new acquisition should be kept hard at work. Bradman was sent with Simmons' salesmen to visit retailers all over New South Wales, to tell them about the big world of cricket that he had seen and to persuade them that the goods they would buy from Simmons were unparalleled in their quality. There were lectures, too, to the up-country lads, and demonstrations of the 'art of batting, by Don Bradman'.

It was not much of a life for a young Siegfried, and there was obvious relief when the cricket season came round again at the end of September 1929. There was an element of luck as well, since the financial crash of the following month, together with the subsequent free-fall of wheat and wool prices, wrought havoc with the Australian economy, as with others, and brought the future of the Mick Simmons business into question. Australia suffered badly. Export revenues of £139 million in 1929 became £99 million in 1930. That fall was magnified in turn for the domestic consumer, both by the fact that around half of those revenues were required simply to service foreign debt and by the understandable move by the banking system to restrict loans to only the most creditworthy businesses. It was certainly not a time to go out and buy a new set of golf clubs, and Mick Simmons' business suffered accordingly. But for his cricket, Bradman might have been out of a job yet again.

It was not only young Don who might have been out of work, and for others it became a reality. Apart from the misery which this brought to the families affected – a misery common to all countries in the capitalist world at the time – there was a special effect in Australia. For Australians, the rest of the world seemed so far away, and their country so isolated from the economic and political mainstreams, that on top of economic misery was piled a sense of inadequacy, of inabilty to influence events. The election of the Labor government under James Scullin at the end of 1929, and the subsequent efforts of that government to respond to the crisis, illustrate the point. Nothing in Scullin's previous experience had prepared him for the tidal wave which was now hitting him. The result was little short of chaotic. Taxes on non-essential items – golf clubs, for instance – were increased. External tariffs were raised repeatedly to try to correct the foreign deficit. Begging was now seen openly on the streets.

It is small wonder that Australians started to look not only for heroes but also for scapegoats. Labor spokesmen referred darkly to 'the manufactured depression that high finance has engineered'.[24] It was clear who was the villain. The City of London was the only possible candidate; and, it should be added, by its behaviour in the months at the end of 1929 and the beginning of 1930, the City duly played the role – of the Victorian pantomime villain – to perfection.

These leitmotifs were quickly picked up by the popular press, and became established wisdom in the minds of those whose lives were being wrecked by the economic circumstances of the moment. In later years, the rebellious mood turned to violence, but in 1929 it was more sullen than aggressive. Nevertheless, as the winter of 1929 gave way to the summer of 1929–30, the national mood had quite clearly sharpened; and, as it did, the need for a genuine all-Australian figure to respond – in whatever field – to the perceived threats from outside grew. In the circumstances, it should come as no surprise that the crowds turning up for the appearances of the young Don Bradman increased both in numbers – by then many of them had nothing else to do – but also in the volume of their vociferous support.

For Bradman himself, there were three major tests in the

summer of of 1929–30, each of which he passed with ease. In late November a scratch MCC side called in at Sydney on its way to New Zealand. 'Scratch' it may have been, but its members were formidable cricketers: not least Woolley and Duleepsinhji. Bradman passed this test in style – making 157 in his only innings – while Woolley, in the MCC first innings, marked his last appearance at the Sydney Cricket Ground by making Bradman field to his own score of 219. 'It remains,' Bradman said later when talking about Woolley, 'one of the most majestic and classical innings I have seen, with every stroke in the book played with supreme ease.'[25]

The second examination was the Trial Match on the same ground ten days later. The Australian selectors pitted a 'J.S. Ryder's XI' against a 'W.M. Woodfull's XI' as a way of deciding who should be selected for the tour of England in 1930. For Bradman the start was gloomy – Jackson and Ponsford put on 278 for the first wicket for Ryder's XI, who finished 663 all out. The response from Bradman was immediate. He made 124 out of 309 in the Woodfull XI's first innings and, when the follow-on was enforced, made a further 225 in the second innings, sharing a partnership with Kippax of 218 for the second wicket. Of the runs he made, 275 were made in one day. Australia had never seen anything like it.

The last serious examination of the season was the proof that Bradman was now to be placed in the highest class; in other words to prove that he could be consistent in his run-making as well as brilliant when he was on form. Again he passed without difficulty. By the time the team to tour England was announced, he had scored 1,400 runs in thirteen first-class innings with an average of 127.27. The next best average was Jackson's 75.87.

The average, of course, had been helped – to say the least – by his score in the second innings of the Sheffield Shield match between New South Wales and Queensland at Sydney in early January 1930. On the first day the two sides were more or less even, with New South Wales 235 all out (Bradman – opening the batting again disastrously – out for 3) and Queensland nearly managing to reach 200. On the following day, 4 January, Queensland finished their first innings 8 runs behind. New

South Wales batted again, and soon after lunch, now batting first wicket down, Bradman was in with the score at 22 for 1.

By the close of play, he had batted three and a quarter hours for 205 not out. On Monday 6 January, he reached his 300 before lunch and went on to his 400 ninety minutes later. By now it was clear to the crowd that the young 'colt', as they still called him, was out to beat the record set by Ponsford in 1928 of the highest score in first-class cricket: 437.

In a few more moments it was done, and the now customary pandemonium broke out. Yet again, Australia was claiming a hero. Even at the end of his innings, when Kippax declared at 761 for 8 (Bradman 452 not out), neither the crowd nor the Queensland players would let him go. There was a moment of farce when one of the Simmons salesmen ran on to the field to try to carry Bradman off on his shoulders – only to fall down in the attempt with his quarry on top of him. But the honours were done by the Queenslanders themselves, picking him up and taking him on their rather broader shoulders into the pavilion. Don Bradman, it need hardly be said, was still grinning. He knew as did everybody else, that, in the words of one newspaper: 'Today he can, with safety, pack his bag and label it – D. Bradman, Australian Eleven, England.'[26] He was twenty-one years and four months old.

3

BOWRAL vs. ENGLAND

THE CRICKET TOURS OF THE 1930s, like much else in that decade, were leisurely affairs compared with the scrambles of today. For a start, there were no regular aeroplanes to ferry players – and their accompanying camp followers – speedily across time zones and climate changes without pause for rest or even breath. Furthermore, there were fewer countries whose cricketing abilities merited a full tour by the leading countries of the time, England and Australia. The result was that those tours that did take place were regarded by press and public as much more important events than are the present hurried scuttles around whole continents by players already exhausted by their previous season in the opposite hemisphere. This was particularly true of the tours, either in England or in Australia, which were to determine the immediate destiny of the Ashes. The excitement generated was intense. The prospects for both teams were analysed extensively in advance, the games followed with the passion that only large crowds can ignite and the results dissected minutely to find pointers which would help predict the outcome of the next encounter.

The Australian tour of England in 1930 was a good example of this steady rise to climactic excitement. First of all, the touring team was selected – fifteen players in all. That was at the end of January, and created its own spurt of interest. Then there was the build-up to the departure of the tourists. For the players this was accompanied by a gradually heightened sense of anticipation as the reality came closer. Admittedly, the administration prior to departure was complex and time-consuming. Confusing instructions came from the Australian Board of Control about how suitcases should be painted (with bands, one inch wide, of the Australian colours – green and gold); about where to order trousers, shirts and – for some unknown reason – pyjamas (from Viyella, who were handing them out free); and, more fiercely, about how to get a Certificate from the Taxation Department, which was a necessary prelude to obtaining a passport. But, in its own way, all this added to the sense of excitement.

On a more celebratory note, albeit with a certain sadness at the thought of an absence from home of some seven months, there were the farewell parties. For Bradman, of course, there was a particular significance to the formal leave-taking of his family and friends at Bowral. This time it was not just a matter of moving from a small town to a larger; it was truly a matter of leaving for good the country town of his childhood and taking his place on the wider stage of world cricket. The send-off was all the more emotional, and consequently all the more elaborate. In his honour the Empire Theatre had been booked, and on the evening was apparently 'crowded with youth and beauty'.[1] Don arrived with his father and mother. They stood outside the theatre for a few moments after most of the guests had taken their places, while the Bowral Band played 'Advance Australia Fair', and only when the company was settled did they walk into the theatre. The entry was well-timed. They were greeted with rumbustious cheers, singing by the crowd – by then obviously well fortified with beer – and a number of sincere but lengthy tributes from local grandees. Bradman replied with a speech of equal banality (he was a long way from the ease in public speaking which he later attained), after which 'dancing was resumed and supper partaken of'.[2] It needed five sittings to feed all those who had come to see Don off.

For the press and the public, the excitement lay in the analysis of the team and its prospects. The general consensus had it that the players were on the young side – England still had the advantage of experience – but that there were one or two bright Australian youngsters, as well, of course, as the potentially match-winning leg-spinner Clarrie Grimmett, who might just, if all went well, make it into a reasonable contest. Of the youngsters two were considered especially promising: Jackson and Bradman. They were put in that order because it was believed that Jackson's more classical style was better suited to the softer English wickets which they were to meet. Bradman's play was too unorthodox, even cross-batted – very good on firm Australian wickets but doubtful in England. The experts were agreed on this, particularly since they were supported in their views by authorities as distinguished as Frank Woolley, Percy Fender and Maurice Tate. The press agreed with the experts. All they needed to do now was to sit back and watch their predictions fulfilled. It need hardly be said that they were in for a very rude shock.

On 7 March 1930 the Australians set off on their odyssey. As it turned out, the first leg of the journey turned into something of a nightmare for Bradman. It was the first time he had ever boarded a ship, and the steamer that transported the team across the Bass Strait to Tasmania, the customary first port of call for Australian touring sides before the long voyage to Europe, pitched uncomfortably in the rough seas. He was sick all the way to Tasmania and all the way back. It would ever be thus. 'I never became used to sea travel,' he said in later life. 'If the sea was rough on the last day of a voyage, I could be just as seasick as I was on the first.'[3] After two matches in Tasmania (and one Bradman century) the team sailed back to Melbourne, this time on a more comfortable ship, the Orient liner *Orford*, took the train for the long overland haul to Perth, played a final match against Western Australia and, at last, embarked again on the *Orford* at Fremantle. The liner sailed for England on 24 March.

In many ways, the players and their managers must have been relieved that the journey had at last started. They were, after all, leaving behind them a country now in acute economic distress. The signs of poverty were everywhere – in rural areas as well as in the big cities. More personally, cricketers were all amateurs, and the prospects of finding or holding on to a reasonably permanent job were rapidly diminishing. Even a good job brought in an average wage of less than £5 per week. True, even as amateurs they received some pay – Bradman, for instance, was paid 10s. per day when playing Sheffield Shield cricket for New South Wales (although he had to pay for all his equipment himself); but it was not much. Yet Bradman was one of the lucky ones. He at least had a contract with Mick Simmons which would see him through his return to Australia. Others were less lucky.

The £600 which each player received for the 1930 tour, plus the £50 apiece for equipment, 30s. per week for 'incidental expenses' – not to mention free accommodation and travel, made them, at least in their own eyes, comparatively rich. For some of them, of course, the financial problem was simply postponed until their return. But in return for such riches, the contracts that had to be signed were severe. No wives, children or relatives could accompany them; strict standards of behaviour were to be observed, to be reported on by the manager at the end of the tour; there was to be no employment on the side, in particular no broadcasting or writing for newspapers; and at the end of the tour not only was there no guarantee of future work but there was the threat of a fine if the manager's report was unsatisfactory or if, in the sole opinion of the Board, they had in any way failed to carry out their contract to the letter.

Nevertheless the immediate future was one of hope, and as the *Orford* sailed on its way northward the members of the team had time to get to know one another. This, however, also posed problems. Of the fifteen players, six were from New South Wales. But of these, three were 'colts', as they were still known: Jackson, Bradman and McCabe. That in itself was an uneasy mixture. From Victoria came the captain, the stolid and gentle Woodfull, and the experienced Ponsford. South Australia sent the vice-captain Richardson and Grimmett. The Queenslanders in the side seemed to be there mainly to preserve some sort of balance between the States. It was difficult to mould these very disparate elements into a coherent group; nor was Woodfull much good at it. Bradman had special difficulties, partly because of his seasickness but more because his upbringing had not given him the social skills for the sort of life he was expected to lead. Besides, he was teetotal – he just could not see the point of drinking alcohol, or of smoking for that matter – and tended to lecture his colleagues on their regrettable habits. They in turn took their revenge by making him play the ship's piano for hour after hour.

In spite of the initial tensions, however, it seems that the tourists adapted smoothly to the life of luxury that was to be theirs for the next few weeks. In truth, it was as though they were living in an isolated but immensely opulent hotel. Most large liners of the day were richly equipped, but the London–Sydney run was one of the most profitable and prestigious for the operators, and hence the most modern ships and the most experienced crews were employed on it. Since the Orient Line had won the contract to transport the Australian tourists – against severe competition from their rivals P & O – they were determined to give of their best, and thereby maximise the publicity value of the contract.

First-class accommodation was provided for the players and the two managers. This in turn allowed access to the huge ornate art deco public rooms, their walls panelled with gilt inlay and their floors covered with lushly coloured thick carpets; to the carefully prepared meals served by stewards in starched white uniforms; to the full range of swimming pools, deck games, dancing at tea or after dinner (black tie was the required wear); and to concerts given by an orchestra specially recruited for the voyage. Bradman's own diary records these events in the style – understandable, given his age and background – of an awed schoolboy. 'Draw for deck games out and everyone crowding around the notice board. I played in the various games as drawn with the following results' (each game is carefully noted – needless to say, Bradman won them all); 'Swim in between times. Carnival night. The boys all dressed up and had a fine night.' Or again: 'Usual routine on board. Concert in the lounge at night. Wonderful sunset in the evening.'[4]

The *Orford* completed the journey of just over 3,000 miles from Fremantle to Colombo, in what was then Ceylon, in eight days, and dropped anchor in Colombo harbour on 1 April. It was Bradman's first visit to a foreign country, and the diary takes on an excited, staccato quality. 'By cars to Mt. Lavinia, Galle Face Hotel. Rickshaws, cars honk honk, oxen, policemen, bungalows, squirrel, native quarters, people. Buddhist temple, shoes off. Orchids and perfumes.' It was obviously quite strange to the young man, and full of bewildering surprises. He even bought a 'topee' at 'Millers'. There was, nonetheless, time for a more familar activity: a match against the 'natives' – in reality mainly expatriate English dressed for some unexplained reason in black and white traditional Sinhalese costumes. 'Made 40 . . . Standard of cricket quite high.'[5] A rainstorm, however, washed the game out half-way through, and the players adjourned for dinner, after which the Australians took the launch out into the harbour and from there boarded their luxurious home. The *Orford* weighed anchor and set course for Aden and the Red Sea.

By now the Australians were fully rested, had got to know one another and were all fit. Some were even losing weight, owing to the strenuous exercise they took in the unrelenting heat. Bradman himself had lost half a stone. But, most important, they had all lost the pale, somewhat pinched look – clearly the result of the poor diet of the Australian Depression – which is evident in the photographs taken before departure. The healthy Orient Line food was having its effect.

The long journey continued. From Aden the liner sailed up the Red Sea ('Miss Staley and I beat Miss Harrison and Alec Hurwood 9–7, 2–6, 6–3 in the final of the mixed doubles ball tennis. Wringing wet at the finish') and arrived at Suez ('Town visible. Bad smell'[6]) on 12 April. A special train took the Australians to Cairo and a visit to the pyramids and the Sphinx, to be followed by dinner at Shepheard's Hotel ('Wonderful Hotel. Native employees. Bright costumes. Meals peculiar'). From Port Said they sailed to Naples, where the team were to leave the ship, after suitable farewells to fellow passengers, and travel the rest of the way by rail and Channel ferry. There was more sightseeing to be done – Bradman records one of the sights as 'the Fascist police' – above all a visit to Pompeii ('Inspected it all'). Strangely enough, a photograph of the Australians at Pompeii still survives. But for the sheepish smiles the group, in regulation trilby hats and sober raincoats, strolling with hands in pockets down a ruined street in the old Roman town, could be taken for a gang of Chicago mobsters. It was enough, however, for a journalist to caption the photograph, in perhaps the worst pun in cricket history: 'Have they gone for the Ashes?'[7]

The train took them up to Rome, to northern Italy, through the Alps – stopping for a sight of snow and a funicular ride up a mountain ('Snow fight, Australian XI vs. The Press. Great fun') – over the border into France and across the Burgundy plain to Paris. The first stop was the Folies Bergères, to be followed on the next day by a coach tour of the city. There was more entertainment in the Latin Quarter in the evening ('Strange customs. Shows open all night') and then, exhausted with all the jollity, to bed. Next morning it was the coach to the Gare du Nord, train to Calais, boat to Dover, and on to London. The party arrived at Victoria Station at 7:35 P.M. on 23 April, to an official welcome by the Lord Mayor of Westminster and the President of the MCC, and a large crowd waiting to catch their first glimpse of the tourists. Unsurprisingly, it was raining.

The journey from Australia had taken the best part of two months; but there is no doubt that, in terms of the education of the young Don Bradman, it was two months well spent. He had seen wonders which he could only have half imagined during his Bowral childhood. He had learned, not without difficulty, to mix with fellow Australians from very different backgrounds; and, however naïve it may appear today, his diary shows a developing ability to observe his surroundings and to ask himself – and indeed others – why they were as they were. Having found out some of the answers, he seems to have been apt to inform his less curious colleagues what he had discovered, and in doing so may have shown less tact than would have been appropriate for a junior member of the team. But single-mindedness, and a consequent difficulty in understanding the sensitivities of others, was by now ingrained in his character, as, indeed, was what some perceived as his lack of hearty masculine sociability. He often preferred to stay in his room and write letters – for instance, he wrote a regular weekly letter to his mother throughout the tour – rather than drink with the boys. That was part of his character too. None of this is particularly surprising, given his own origins and background. What is perhaps surprising is that during the two-month journey there is no record of any shipboard romance, nor even of a mild flirtation with the ladies with whom he played deck games so assiduously. Perhaps there was; but if so, it has been hidden in the web of discretion which Bradman has always sought to weave around his private life.

★　　★　　★

THE FIRST MATCH OF the tour was, as was customary for overseas tourists, at Worcester. There had been no more than a week between arrival in London and the start of the Worcestershire game, but almost every minute had been taken up. There had been the official welcome at Australia House, net practice at Lord's, collecting clothes and equipment from Viyella and Stuart Surridge, a succession of press interviews, and a visit to the FA Cup Final at Wembley (Huddersfield Town vs. Arsenal) where the Australian cricketers were introduced to King George V. For Bradman in particular there had been dinner – at the National Liberal Club – with the bat-maker William Sykes, and a trip to Leeds to stay with Sykes and sign bats for his firm. More important for the future, however, Bradman had been approached by the literary agent David Cromb, who had suggested that he write a book about his cricketing experiences and who had assured him it would not be difficult to find a publisher. Bradman's contract, of course, forbad him any writing about the tour while it was still on, but he agreed to start on something which could be published when the tour was over. As it turned out, it was a decision that was to have unforeseen, and unpleasant, consequences.

April is usually a harsh month for cricket in England, and 30 April at Worcester was no exception to this rule. The trees surrounding the cathedral which overlooked the ground were still as bare as in mid-winter; there was no protection from the cold wind. Shower clouds scudded across the pale blue sky, frequently blocking out the weak spring sun and threatening at any moment to unload more rain on the already damp wicket. It was a world away from the hot sun of Sydney or Melbourne. The Australians, losing the toss, huddled in their sweaters while Worcestershire struggled to a total of 131 by mid-afternoon. Woodfull and Jackson opened for the Australians, but Jackson was out soon after tea with the score at 67. Bradman made his usual slow way to the wicket for his first innings in England.

By close of play, after ninety minutes' batting, he was 75 not out. The next morning he reached his century in a further thirty minutes, and then proceeded to put the Worcester bowling truly to the sword. In spite of the unfamiliar slow pitch he was particularly severe on any loose ball, whether short or of full length (or, indeed, later in his innings, on good-length balls as well). Both the pull and the square cut were used with venom. The Worcester bowlers were the first to find out that in this mood there was no way this small, almost birdlike figure could be contained, such was the astonishing range and power of his shots.

Bradman ended on 236, scored in four and a half hours. It was the highest score ever made by an Australian in his first match in England, and the highest by any batsman playing his first innings in another country. The Worcester crowd had never seen a performance to compare with it. They cheered him all the way back to the pavilion. They were still cheering him at the end of the match, after Worcestershire had gone down by an innings and 165 runs.

But it was not to be an isolated event, a sudden shooting star which quickly burned itself out. The story was repeated at Leicester in the following match. After Leicestershire had been bowled out cheaply by Grimmett, Bradman went in at 18 for 1 and was 185 not out when rain finally stopped all further play in the match – and incidentally deprived him of a second double century – at 5:30 P.M. on the second day. Bradman was again applauded generously by the Leicester crowd; only the most gloomy reflected on the fact that the new star in the cricket firmament was only 21 years and 251 days old. If this was the performance of the boy, they thought, how much suffering would the man inflict on English cricket?

As May went by, still in wet and windy misery, Bradman's runs piled up. Seventy-eight against Yorkshire, 9 and 48 not out against Lancashire, 66 and 4 against the MCC, 44 against Derbyshire, a thumping 252 not out against Surrey at the Oval – his response to the Surrey captain Fender's criticism of his batting technique – and 32 against Oxford University left him only 46 runs short of any batsman's dream: 1,000 runs in May in first-class cricket or, to be more accurate, 1,000 runs before the end of May. Only four players had managed it before: W.G. Grace (in 1895 – at the age of forty-seven), Hayward of Surrey (in 1900), Hammond (in 1927), and Hallows of Lancashire (in 1928). No Australian had ever done it.

On 31 May the Australians started their match against Hampshire at Southampton. Hampshire won the toss and batted. It looked for a time as if Bradman would never get to the wicket on that day to make the runs he needed. But he himself ran out Hampshire's opening batsman when he was well set, by throwing down the wicket from thirty yards or more – 'the greatest fluke of my career'[8] he called it – and the Hampshire batting collapsed soon afterwards to Grimmett. Bradman, sent in by Woodfull to open the Australian batting, was at the wicket by 3:30 P.M. and had made 28 by tea. During tea the rain started. It seemed to have set in for the evening, putting an end to all hopes of further play and depriving Bradman of the chance to make his final 18 runs. Miraculously, at about six o'clock, the rain let up and the players went back out on to the pitch. Bradman made a further eleven runs before the rain started again in earnest. It was now pouring. Lord Tennyson, the Hampshire captain, decided to stay on the field for one more over, tossed the ball to the bowler with a quick instruction and stood back to watch his bowler bowl one full pitch and one long hop, which were duly despatched to give Bradman the runs he needed. The players bolted off the field. In five minutes the ground was under water. But the deed had been done.

By now, of course, there was hardly anybody in England who had not heard of this new Australian phenomenon. The English cricketing public was in a state near to catatonic shock. It was mesmerised by the skill of the man, but deeply fearful of the havoc he might wreak. More important, however, was that he was recognised openly in the streets of English towns; that he was continually followed by a posse of small boys demanding autographs; that in the world of cigarette cards – those cards in cigarette packets which were the favourite collector's item for boys in the 1930s – his picture was traded in school playgrounds at a substantial premium over not just other cricketers but footballers, golfers, tennis players and even film stars.

Bradman's fame in England was established. But news there could be, and was, immediate. More interesting, and in the longer run more important, was the speed with which his successes in England enhanced his already high reputation in

Australia. That this was so was in some measure due to the invention of the radio telephone. The first London–Sydney link was opened, fortuitously, at the end of April. The news from England was relayed in a flash on live programmes to the 350,000 radio receivers scattered around the major cities of Australia from which programmes were broadcast. The equipment was, of course, primitive: cumbersome valve radio sets with high and ugly aerials. But at least the sound came through, albeit of varying quality, and Bradman's scores were relayed throughout Australia almost as he was making them.

The radio telephone had the incidental effect of allowing the players to keep more directly in touch with home. Some of the players made use of the new invention by making a call to their families towards the end of May. The first effort, earlier in the month from Liverpool, seems to have failed. The second, from London, was, after some delay, successful and the connection was established. The players stood nervously in a studio, while their families and friends stood or sat together, equally nervously and dressed smartly as though on their way to church, in an office in Sydney. The players took it in turn, with both rooms listening to whatever was said. Bradman spoke to his mother, father and sister, and to Mr and Mrs Cush; the others spoke to their wives or families. The voices were heard clearly but distantly ('Uncanny feeling'[9] he reported in his diary).

The radio telephone really came into its own with the Test matches. The technique used by the broadcasting companies was nothing if not ingenious. The English commentaries were picked up in Sydney on earphones, and an Australian commentator relayed them in his own words – and sometimes with his own interjections – to the listening audience. It was quite a new experience. It was as though Australians were listening to a direct broadcast from England on the progress of their heroes. Given the time difference, broadcasts were in the middle of the night, and parties were regularly assembled around the primitive receivers to listen in. It only served to heighten the sense of drama.

It is difficult to exaggerate the effect of the new technology. Suddenly all Australia, in the middle of its economic travail, could focus on events thousands of miles away in all their immediacy. In its own way, and in spite of the limitations in technique and in the size of its audience (although with an average of five listeners to every receiver the broadcasts would have reached nearly one third of the population of the country), it was as powerful an invention as television was to be later in the century. Heroes, instead of being words in a newspaper, suddenly came alive in sound.

The Test series started in earnest at Nottingham on 13 June. True to his promise, Alf Stephens, the former Mayor of Bowral and one of Bradman's early mentors, had arrived a few days earlier to see Don's first Test match in England, and joined the crowd that filled the Trent Bridge ground to capacity. England started clear favourites but, after winning the toss and deciding to bat, wickets fell regularly to Grimmett. By the end of the first day they were 241 for 8. Rain, however, fell overnight, and by the time Australia batted the wet wicket made Maurice Tate and Dick Tyldesley almost unplayable. In less than an hour, Woodfull, Ponsford and Bradman were out to Tate, Bradman for an unhappy 8, and Australia ended all out for 144. Back home there was a collective night-time sigh of the deepest disappointment.

England, thanks to Hobbs and Hendren, added to their first-innings lead and left Australia with 432 runs to win – a virtually impossible feat. Woodfull went early to Larwood, but Bradman played out the rest of the third day and went on into the fourth. By lunch he was 88 not out – he was once missed by Tyldesley off Tate – and reached his hundred at 2:45 P.M. after batting for three and a half hours. It was a cautious innings, but it was not the time to take risks. Bradman was finally bowled by Robins for 131, and Australia lost the match. As he went out he passed Robins, who mumbled 'Bad luck, Don' – not wholly convincingly. Don's reply was absolute: 'Just you wait till Lord's.'[10]

Between the two Tests there was the now-familiar round of social engagements: at the Albert Hall to see the Australian singer Harold Williams as 'Hiawatha' ('We had the Royal Suite'); at a lunch at Grosvenor House given by the Dowager Countess of Darnley ('. . . gave us a dinner. Very distinguished gathering including Stanley Bruce, Madame Melba, many Lords etc.'[11]), whose menu started with 'Melon frappé Woodfull' and ended bizarrely with 'Café Wallaby'; at the Houses of Parliament for lunch at the Commons; and at Wimbledon to see Tilden and Helen Wills, the champions of their day. There were visits to the theatre, too, and, if there was any spare time, rounds of golf.

Bradman had told Robins to wait until Lord's, and Lord's was indeed worth waiting for. In fact, it was the Lord's Test match of 1930 that set up Don Bradman as the clear and bright new star of the cricketing firmament. Responding to an England first-innings total of 425, of which Duleepsinhji made 173, Woodfull and Ponsford put on 162 for the first wicket. Bradman came in next, and immediately started to treat the Lord's crowd to an exhibition of the kind of batting with which Australians were familiar. His first ball was from Jack White, the slow left-arm bowler who had proved so difficult to score off in the 1928–29 series. Bradman, with obvious and deliberate intent, danced out of his crease and hit it on the full to deep long-off. It was a sign of what was to come. He and Woodfull took the score to 393 before Woodfull was out for 155. Bradman and Kippax then added a further 192 before another wicket fell. Bradman's first 50 took him only 46 minutes, his first century only 106 minutes. By close of play he was 155 not out.

On the following day he took his score to 254, batting in all for 339 minutes. There was nothing the English bowlers could do. The loudest round of applause for them came when Tate managed to bowl a maiden over to Bradman. Records went down one by one: highest score ever in a Test match in England; highest score against England in any Test match; youngest batsman to score a double century in a Test match for Australia; record score for two consecutive Test match innings (385). Furthermore, it was all reported lovingly to the Australian public through the radio-telephone link. There was little sleep that night. 'Local wireless fans,' reported the *Sun*, 'are beginning to look very heavy under the eyelids.'[12]

In the second innings Bradman was out to Tate for 1, but Australia's first innings total of 729 for 6 declared gave them enough of a margin to allow them, after some alarms, to win the game. For Bradman there was now a match against Yorkshire (in which he made only 1) and then a rest from cricket until the next Test. The holiday was both deserved and needed, and he used it to return to Wimbledon for the finals, to cruise up the Thames to Richmond, and generally to 'have a look round London'.[13] In the second week of July he drove in a leisurely manner up to Leeds.

By the time the Third Test got under way, at Headingley on the morning of Friday 11 July, the cricketing public in both England and Australia was in a state of high fever. It was a question, as one newspaper remarked, of 'Bradman versus England'. A full 33,000 filled every available space in the ground. In the event the public were not to be disappointed. The weather was again miserable, with a strong, cold wind and the threat of rain, but the weather was ignored in the excitement of the day. Woodfull won the toss for Australia and chose to bat. Again Jackson failed, out for 1 in Tate's first over, and so Bradman made his way to the middle, the collar of his shirt turned up against the breeze. Once there, he showed even less hesitation than at Lord's, setting about the English bowling with such venom that by lunch he had made 105 not out. Only Trumper and Macartney before him had scored centuries before lunch in a Test match against England.

But worse was to come for England after the interval. The onslaught was even fiercer: between lunch and tea Bradman made a further 115, and capped that with a final 89 between tea and the close of play, to complete his third hundred and to leave him 309 not out – ready for the following day. By the time he was out on the next morning, for 334, there was hardly a record left standing. One by one they fell again: the highest score in Test cricket; the youngest batsman to make 2,000 runs in an English season; the highest number of runs in a day's play in a Test match; the fastest first hundred in a Test match – in 99 minutes; two double centuries in consecutive Tests; and the largest margin in Test matches between his score and the next highest (Kippax with 77). His whole innings had taken him only 383 minutes, and, significantly in the light of what was to come, Larwood had been hit for 139 in 33 overs. 'How came this Bradman,' wrote Neville Cardus in the *Manchester Guardian* the next day, 'to expel from him all the greenness and impetuosity of youth while retaining the alacrity of youth? How did he come to acquire, without experience, all the ripeness of the orthodox – the range and adaptability of other men's accumulated years of practice in the best schools of batsmanship?'[14] There was no answer to the question, but all who were present at Headingley, like those who had been at Lord's, were unanimous in recognising that, in its own way and in its own field, Bradman's innings had been a revelation of genius equal to any in the more traditional performing arts.

As it turned out, the match itself was washed out by rain, but in the excitement that hardly seemed to matter. There was, however, a fallout that was personal. Bradman's performance had, of course, delighted the Australians, both the team itself and those, by now many thousands, who were 'listening in' at home. It had also commanded the respect of the Yorkshire crowd – ready to recognise and applaud genius when they saw it – and the English press. But there was one sour note. The Australian players expected him to join them in the bar of their hotel for a celebration; but Bradman himself preferred to stay in his room, writing letters and listening to music. He was equally reluctant to show himself to the applauding crowd, or, at the weekend, to walk through the streets of Leeds. 'Don Bradman is the most elusive man of all,' wrote one English newspaper, '. . . preferring to write letters in his room or get away to a show.' He also has a habit of going off sight-seeing alone, or with only one companion. A more level-headed man or one less likely to become spoiled by admiration never wore flannels.'[15] True, but his dislike of publicity, which was to become more intense as the publicity developed into adulation, was to create problems for him in the future.

Bradman was also £1,000 richer. While he was in the field at Headingley a telegram arrived for him from an Australian expatriate businessman asking him to accept the gift 'as a mark of his wonderful performance'.[16] At first Bradman thought it was some sort of joke, but, on being assured by Woodfull that it was genuine, quietly pocketed the telegram (and subsequently the money). It was a generous gesture – the equivalent of £25,000 today – but it did not go unnoticed by his colleagues. Yet again the occasion was turned by some into sourness, particularly when they asked him to celebrate the gift by entertaining them to dinner – a suggestion which Bradman coolly declined to take up.

From Leeds the touring party went to Scotland for two matches, both of which were ruined by rain. Bradman did have, however, a chance to visit Gleneagles ('finest hotel I have ever been in,' he wrote in his diary, '[but] tariff very high'[17]) and to play a round of golf on the King's course. But that night he went to bed with bad stomach-ache, was sick during the night and, indeed, was ill enough to miss the next tour match at Durham. When news of his illness leaked out to the press there was, as might be imagined, consternation, since the Fourth Test – at which everybody was expecting another Bradman spectacular – was due to begin in a few days' time.

By the time the match got under way, Bradman was fit again. But on this occasion, whether owing to the after-effects of illness or not, luck deserted him. The pitch was soft and still damp from rain, and the light was bad. He had also had to wait while Woodfull and Ponsford put on over 100 for the first wicket. After an uncomfortable thirty minutes at the wicket he had only managed 14 runs, before being caught off the young leg-spinner Ian Peebles. The relief of the English was immeasurable. 'Bradman, after all, is human,' sighed the *Observer*.[18]

The relief did not last long. The Test was yet another victim of the rain, but in the next game, against Somerset, Bradman made yet another hundred, his eighth in the tour so far. The rain intervened further in the succession of county matches which followed, and there was no play at all in the Warwickshire game at Edgbaston. It meant low scores on uncertain pitches at best, and long waits in the pavilion at worst. There was, however, plenty of time for activities off the cricket field. By the end of July, Bradman had delivered the first part of his book to his literary agent, had filmed an interview with British Movietone News (describing his strokes in detail 'in a clear, hard voice'[19]), had visited the Welsh National Eisteddfod in Llanelli and a hospital in Northampton. It seemed that he would never be allowed to stay still.

The series of Test matches came to its climax in mid-August. With England and Australia level at one victory each, the deciding match, according to the rules of the day, would be timeless. It would start on 16 August and continue until there was a conclusion one way or another; and the place where this final confrontation would take place was the Kennington Oval in London.

England changed captains for the match, dropping A.P.F. Chapman and appointing R.E.S. Wyatt. This was generally interpreted as a defensive move. From the Australian camp, on the other hand, there was a hint that Bradman would use the occasion to improve on his 334 at Leeds. Indeed, the idea was by no means implausible. The tour had demonstrated that, although Bradman had shown he was vulnerable early on in an innings, once he had passed 20 or 30 'the door was shut'.[20] In a timeless Test there was no reason why he should ever stop.

On the morning of 16 August the match began. England won the toss, and Hobbs and Sutcliffe opened the batting. The day went slowly ('very dull batting',[21] one newspaper remarked), and on the second day rain held up play. England ended with 405, a total which started to look slender when Woodfull and Ponsford put on 159 for the first Australian wicket. By the time Woodfull was out, there was only an hour left for play, during which Bradman cautiously moved to 27 not out. There was rain again on the third day, allowing only four hours play. Bradman moved steadily on, reaching 130 not out at the close, his partner by then being Jackson. At this point the English journalists started to become depressed. 'There is nothing to say about this match,' opined the *Daily Mail*, 'except that Bradman is a great menace to English cricket . . . We shall have great difficulty in avoiding defeat.'[22]

The fourth day, however, produced the most interesting cricket of the match. The wicket was by now drying out, and, unusually for the Oval in the 1930s, turned into a dangerous 'flier'. The ball kicked and lifted unpredictably. Larwood, not unnaturally, took advantage of it with a burst of sustained short-pitched hostility. Both Bradman and Jackson were hit, Bradman in the chest and on his wrist, Jackson under the heart. Both were badly hurt, and at one point it seemed as though Jackson would be physically sick from the pain. Australian spectators, said the press, watched 'with tears in their eyes'.[23]

Some say that Bradman was frightened by this assault. 'There is no doubt that Bradman showed signs of disliking the short ball intensely,'[24] Wyatt was to say later; and Larwood himself was to claim that that morning proved the genesis of the tactics used by England in the 1932–33 tour of Australia. Be that as it may, Bradman certainly resisted with great courage and determination, as did Jackson. Their partnership, which put on 243 for the fourth wicket, was the decisive moment of the match. Bradman himself went on to make 232 and Australia ended their innings at 695. This was too much for England, whose batting collapsed and who lost the match by an innings. Australia had won the series and with it the Ashes.

Once the Test series was over, the rest of the tour came as something of an anti-climax. There were certainly some tense matches, and Bradman made his sixth double century of the season. He also became the highest scorer for the Australians on a tour of England, passing Trumper's 2,570 runs of 1902. But the main business, after the final match in Scarborough, was the succession of farewell parties given for the victorious tourists. By this time the young Bradman had become quite familiar with London life. In his diary he notes, for instance, that on 20 September he did 'jobs in London'; visited Elstree Studios, where he met a number of film stars; had tea at his hotel; went to a reception; to dinner with other friends; then to the Theatre Royal, Drury Lane and afterwards to the 'Kit Kat' club.[25] It was a full life for the new celebrity.

By the time Don Bradman left London on 27 September for the long journey home he was far from being the coltish innocent who had started out from Bowral seven months before. He had travelled across seas and continents, had made many friends (as well as a few enemies), had seen the life that big cities like Paris and London had to offer, had shaken hands with royalty, and had learned that with success came adulation. By the end of the tour he was already taking stock – not just of his cricketing ability but of how he could use it to material advantage. 'When I first met Bradman, during the 1930 Folkestone Cricket Festival,' wrote R. C. Robertson-Glasgow some time later, '. . . he was fresh from triumphs against England at Lord's and at the Oval. And now, quiet and calculating, he was, he told me, trying to capitalise on his success. He has since told me that his business efforts on that evening . . . were not in vain.'[26] The boy of the Depression was by now determined to use his genius to achieve a financial security that neither he nor his family had ever known. This ambition, pursued as it was with the same single-mindedness as in his cricket, was to lead him along strange paths. But first he had to understand, and to cope with, the adulation with which Australia was preparing to greet her new hero on his return home.

4

FOR BETTER OR FOR WORSE

'EIGHT MONTHS AGO DON BRADMAN WENT away a smiling boy. Now he has come back thinner, maturer and much more serious.'[1] So ran a report on Bradman's return to Australia in October 1930. In fact, not only was he more serious but he was much more wary of those around him. It is not difficult to see why. The truth is that he was wholly unprepared for the reception that awaited him at his homecoming. Indeed, none of the Australian players were aware of how closely, and how passionately, their progress in England had been followed at home through the radio-telephone link, or how deeply the continuing Depression had nurtured the desperate need for good news from somewhere – almost anywhere – to alleviate the seeming hopelessness of daily life. Besides, to a large extent the tourists had been insulated from the realities of life at home by the continuing round of sporting and social events that had made up the tour – and by the comfort in which they had lived. It was all the more shocking, therefore, to return to a homeland in such obvious distress.

Bradman himself was perhaps more aware of those realities than were some of his colleagues. He had, after all, been planning his financial future even while touring; he knew that his contract with Mick Simmons Ltd would expire in February 1932, and that he had therefore only a year or so to make arrangements for a new job. Besides, he was by now seriously contemplating marriage with his childhood friend Jessie Menzies, and they were both sensible enough to know that marriage in the middle of the Depression was full of danger. As one who lived through that period put it: 'The only way to survive in those days was to be on your own – married people, oh, married people . . .'[2] Certainly he was better off than many, and his income from sponsoring cricketing equipment helped, but the young man was by now far too shrewd to take anything for granted. 'Maturer and much more serious' just about describes his state of mind.

Indeed those economic realities, and the human misery which accompanied them, were almost beyond modern comprehension. By most reasonable estimates, from the middle of 1930 until the last months of 1934, more than a fifth of wage- and salary-earners were out of work. To these should be added school leavers, who often never bothered to enter the workforce, and others, mostly women, who gave up in despair. The Australian census of 1933 showed that two-thirds of all breadwinners had received an income of less than the basic wage in the year 1932–33. Nor was there any co-ordinated support for those who were unemployed. They had to live on charity and very basic sustenance allowance in the form of ration orders exchangeable for food – known as 'susso'. 'Susso' amounted on average to less than half the basic wage that purported to represent essential requirements.

Bradman had, perhaps more than his team-mates, understood the problem. He realised that, however well he and his family had managed to avoid the worst effects of the Depression (he had sent money back to his mother from England during the tour), the economic world in which he lived was a dangerous place. On the other hand, he does seem to have been completely taken aback by the way in which the despair induced by economic hardship had fomented a need for hero-worship amounting to near hysteria, and even more taken aback to find that he was the hero who was to be worshipped. 'My preference [was] for the more homely and peaceful side of life,' he commented in later years.[3] Furthermore, he had enjoyed the 1930 tour. Although there had been occasional difficulties with his fellow players and the manager William Kelly, these were minor squalls in what had been a successful and interesting – indeed fascinating – experience. The boy from Bowral had, after all, met royalty, and at the age of twenty-one at that. But the enjoyment of the tour was to turn to bewilderment on the return, and eventually to sourness. By nature given to bouts of reserve, which on occasion turned to self-deprecation, and by upbringing quite untrained for the role in which he was suddenly cast, he found himself in a situation with which he was almost unable to cope.

The situation can be quite easily described. He was now commercial gold dust. As such, he was to be ruthlessly used both by his employers and the American company General Motors, who quickly barged in on the act, as a publicity stunt to promote their respective businesses. To some extent, he was given early warning. It all started with a message from Oscar Lawson, a journalist – of no great reputation, it must be admitted – in charge of the public relations at Mick Simmons, requesting him to leave the party at Perth and travel separately to Adelaide by train. The message arrived as the *Oronsay*, the liner ferrying the Australian team home, docked at Colombo. It had been a pleasant enough trip, apart from the odd day of bad weather ('Stayed in bed all day,' reads his diary. 'Not too good'[4]), and the reception in Ceylon had been warm, the people of Colombo presenting Bradman with a silver model of the great Buddhist temple at Candy. So far all was harmony. When Lawson's request arrived, however, Bradman was obliged to transmit it to the Australian Board of Control, who in turn allowed it. By then it was obvious to Bradman's team-mates that he was to be given royal treatment on his return. As one newspaper put it when the news got out: 'From that moment [the team] will become a comet with a long tail – Bradman being the head and the rest of the team the tail.'[5] The last leg of the journey was far from harmonious.

The *Oronsay* docked at Fremantle on 28 October. Even before she docked, the welcome for the homecomers had started: the other ships in Fremantle harbour greeted them with a cacophony of horns and cheers from the crews. As soon as they had disembarked, the players were whisked off by car to Perth – to a ceremonial welcome at the Prince of Wales Theatre, then on to lunch at the Palace Hotel with the State Governor, followed by a visit to the Diggers' Hospital, another celebratory dinner at the Esplanade Hotel and a final special appearance at the Theatre Royal. But wherever they went, there was only one person the crowd wanted to see, and at the Theatre Royal the applause that greeted Bradman when he appeared by himself on stage was quite noticeably louder than the applause for the whole team together. Throughout the day, he had to struggle his way through the crowds. He was mobbed by autograph hunters – many of them women and girls. Bradman himself believed that he signed more than five hundred on that one day. He had to put up with the coy gossip of the Perth press: 'Don Bradman paid duty on . . . two beautiful silk shawls. One was for his sister. The other? He wouldn't say.'[6]

'I didn't like it,' Bradman later said tersely.[7] It was obvious already that he was embarrassed and upset by the adulation which was poured over him by the thin and raggedly clothed crowds that now attached themselves to his coat-tails. The contrast between the glamour of the new star and the poverty of the country could hardly have been more stark. They mobbed him again at Perth station when he caught the Transcontinental Express for Adelaide, and again at the small mining town of Kalgoorlie and at the little railway halts along the way across the vast Nullarbor Plain ('Crowds of boys everywhere,'[8] his diary reports). Just before arrival in Adelaide there was a civic reception at Port Augusta. At Adelaide station movement was almost impossible, so many enthusiasts had gathered to meet him.

Throughout Bradman's confused and noisy overland journey Woodfull and the rest of his team, having re-embarked on the *Oronsay*, were wallowing in the Great Australian Bight on their way to Adelaide by sea. As might be expected they were not altogether pleased when the reports came in of Bradman's triumphal progress. Some were unemployed outside cricket; others had their own businesses. But all wanted at least a share of the publicity that Bradman was now getting by himself, if only to help them find a job or some better business when they arrived home. By the time they reached Adelaide, Bradman was well into the programme that Lawson and General Motors had arranged for him. He broadcast an account – suitably embellished by his sponsors – of the excitements of the 1930 tour, and went on stage by himself in front of a Saturday night audience at the Regent Theatre. It is hardly surprising that when he drove down to Port Adelaide to meet his former colleagues from South Australia, just coming off the *Oronsay*, he found the atmosphere far from warm. Indeed, within the week, Richardson, the vice-captain, was to say publicly: 'We could have played any team without Bradman, but we could not have played the blind school without Clarrie Grimmett.'[9]

None of this was Bradman's fault. In everything he said he was meticulous in awarding full share of the credit to his fellow players – particularly the captain, Woodfull. But all that passed unnoticed. What was noticed was the next leg of his bizarre homecoming. This consisted of a much-publicised flight from Adelaide to Melbourne. The aircraft was, of course, primitive – a three-engined Fokker monoplane – and flying in any case was a perilous activity in those times, when there were no reliable navigational aids. But there it was: Bradman was under contract to allow himself to be exploited in whatever manner Lawson and General Motors required.

The journey to Melbourne got off to a bad start. The motorcade taking the party to Adelaide airport went smoothly enough – Bradman in front in a car decorated with streamers and a sign saying LORD MAYOR'S RELIEF FUND on the side (General Motors had donated several cars to the fund for the poor of the Depression). But such was the confusion at the airport that the plane took off late; not only that but Shortridge, the pilot (who in fact disappeared only four months later on a regular Sydney–Melbourne flight) went off course, to the point where the crowd waiting at Essendon aerodrome in the suburbs of Melbourne began to fear the worst. Fortunately, Shortridge found his way back to his proper course and landed the Fokker only two hours late. By that time, however, the 10,000 enthusiasts who had made their way out to Essendon to greet their hero had diminished in number to around 5,000. Nevertheless, the remainder put on the now customary hysterical performance when they saw a badly airsick Bradman extracting himself from the cockpit, where he been sitting with Shortridge. He 'hesitated in the doorway of the plane amazed', one newspaper reported, 'and for a few seconds it seemed he could not face the hero-worshipping crowd.'[10]

Once more Bradman had to make an impromptu speech – from the back of a truck, draped with an Australian flag, to which he had been escorted by police on horseback – and once again he gallantly paid due tribute to Woodfull and the other players on the

1930 tour. But it was to no avail. The crowds only wanted to see Bradman, and he rolled in yet another motorcade to the centre of Melbourne – all the other cars on the road simply stopped to let him go by, the occupants greeting him by blowing their car horns and cheering – and yet again there were the receptions and the crowds. The 'Mothers of Melbourne' presented him with a bouquet of roses for his mother; there was a cheque for £100 from a group of anonymous admirers, presented at the Tivoli Theatre; and finally there was an official welcome at the Theatre Royal – also attended by Woodfull and Ponsford, the two Victorian Test players, who had by then completed their slow journey home to Melbourne by sea on the *Oronsay*. However generous they were, it is hard to believe that the reunion of the players was wholly cordial.

The next morning saw Bradman climbing back into the 'Southern Cloud', as the uncomfortable aircraft was known, for the journey to Goulburn in his home State. Shortridge was told by Lawson to fly low over every town on the way, so that the inhabitants might know that the hero was in the air above them. Such was the weather, however, that the hero himself was doubled up in the back of the plane, cold to the marrow and retching painfully. At Goulburn airfield he was met by his father and his brother Victor, who had come by car from Bowral. He was offered a cup of tea in town by the Mayor – and accepted 'providing there was no reception'.[11]

It was not until they arrived at Bowral that Bradman visibly perked up. It may have been another platform (this time a makeshift bandstand), and yet another speech; but this time it was, as he said, to friends – harder to speak to, he claimed, than any other audience. Yet the figure had regained some of its perkiness. His face, which at times had seemed pinched and unhappy, became fuller and more relaxed; his hair was smartly brushed, with its natural front wave firmly in place; his tie was smart, the collar of his raincoat was turned up as usual and his hands rested lightly in its pockets. He looked brisk and confident, even though his surprisingly small frame was overshadowed by the two policemen who stood on either side of him.

The Bowral band, such as it was, was much in evidence. The

hit tune of the moment was 'Our Don Bradman'. It did not achieve any particular height of lyricism ('Our Don Bradman, and I ask you is he any good . . . as a batsman he is certainly "Plum Pud" ') but it was nonetheless a catchy little number. The band played it when he arrived, adding particular verve when Don stepped out of his car and embraced his mother, going on to present her with the 'Mothers of Melbourne' bouquet. The subsequent official ceremonies were long and exhausting, finally coming to a close well into the evening.

'Left Bowral 9:45. Raced to Sydney with Wizard Smith,'[12] reads Bradman's diary for the following day ('Wizard' Smith being the racing driver hired by General Motors for the occasion). 'Did 82 mph at one stage of the trip' – Bradman had recovered his boyish excitement. At Liverpool, some twenty miles out of Sydney, Smith dropped him off at the Cross Roads Hotel, where a bright new Chevrolet was waiting, a gift from General Motors. The car was, by all accounts, somewhat flamboyant. 'A cheeky-looking sports roadster,' the press called it, 'upholstered in pig-skin, maroon in colour and a mass of silver plating.'[13] Bradman drove himself into the centre of Sydney with as much panache as he could muster – in the first car he had ever owned. The reception when he arrived at Mick Simmons' was 'magnificent'. ('Received by all and sundry.')[14]

The usual ceremonies followed. General Motors provided a lunch at the Royal Automobile Club ('Lord Mayor, Chief Secretary and others there'[15]) and in the evening there was a musical programme at the Sydney Town Hall, during which the keys of Bradman's car were formally presented to him on stage by Mark Gosling, the Chief Secretary of Jack Lang's newly-elected New South Wales Labor government. Gosling, somewhat oddly, baptised Bradman as the 'Phar Lap of cricket' and went on: 'Mr Lang . . . [is] looking for new taxation schemes, and I would suggest that they might impose a tax on centuries, and make Don pay a super-tax on every second century.'[16] Bradman replied that he had made up his mind to score a century in the Sheffield Shield match due to start the following week, but that if he was out for a 'blob' they would have to blame Mr Gosling. The jokes were perhaps not very good, but they would have to do. By this time everybody was getting rather tired.

Bradman duly made his century (61 and 121) in the Shield match, his first innings since he had left England and with no practice in the meantime. He was cheered all the way to the wicket by his South Australian opponents and a crowd of 12,000 – not, perhaps, a large number for the Sydney Cricket Ground, but unemployment was biting hard – before being dragged to yet another ceremony, this time at St George, where his club had rented the Victory Theatre at Kogarah. This time he and Fairfax, the other St George Test cricketer, were formally presented with club blazers. St George, in fact, had every reason to be grateful. 'Crowds at our games,' the club's history recalls, 'grew in numbers to reach record proportions for attendances at grade matches, so great an attraction was the magic of Don Bradman.'[17]

The magic of Don Bradman, however, was starting to provoke a reaction. There were those – not least some of his colleagues on the 1930 tour – who were still muttering about the social distance he had put between himself and his colleagues; there were also those who were openly saying that Bradman was not as good as all that, and that Grimmett had been the real winner of the Ashes for Australia, whatever anyone might say. Petrol was poured on the flame by a journalist, Geoffrey Tebbutt, who claimed, in a book about the tour, that Bradman was, in the eyes of the others, 'rather less than human in the way he took success' and that one of the Australians had said to him of Bradman: 'He is not one of us.'[18]

Tebbutt may well have been quoted out of context, but he made the mistake of adding to the controversy by claiming that the tour manager, William Kelly, 'lacked the firmness to take the situation in hand before it got beyond him'. This was too much for Kelly, who riposted in a statement that 'Mr Tebbutt is quite wrong'; that there had been 'no breach between Bradman and the other members of the team, and Bradman did not lead a life aloof'. This in turn provoked another broadside from Tebbutt, to the effect that '. . . since I claim that . . . I have written the whole truth, I mentioned the fact that Bradman was aloof. I stick to that. He certainly was.'[19]

All this would no doubt have passed on its way as an insignificant ruffling of feathers had it not been for the timing and the place of Tebbutt's pronouncements. The first news that the Australian public had of Tebbutt's strictures came on the morning of the first day of the opening Test match in Adelaide, against the new tourists to Australia in 1930–31, the West Indies. They were not considered a strong side, and Learie Constantine, one of the West Indies' strike bowlers, said that they 'accepted Bradman's customary century. It was the dismissal of the other batsmen on top of this which was the problem.'[20] As it turned out, Bradman failed at Adelaide, caught at third slip after batting an uncomfortable quarter of an hour for only 4 runs. It was left to Kippax and McCabe in the first innings, with 146 and 90 respectively, and Ponsford and Jackson in the second, with 85 and 65 – both not out – to save Australia's dignity.

As if that was not enough, the place where Tebbutt pursued his case was in the London evening newspaper, the *Star*. As it happened, the *Star* had a particular reason for keeping the controversy alive, since it was to the newspaper that Bradman's literary agent, Cromb, had sold the serial rights of his book – now known simply as *Don Bradman's Book*. The first article had appeared on 4 August 1930, while its author (give or take some help in drafting from the journalist Ben Bennison) was still a member of the Australian touring team and therefore under its restrictive contract. The book itself was published in November 1930 – with an introduction from 'Mr P. F. Warner' – after Bradman's return to Australia. But this was not the point. The point was that articles had been published under Bradman's name while he was under contract, and the Australian Board of Control could not simply ignore the matter.

Inevitably the row engendered great heat. It might have been calmed down at the outset, but the Australian Board of Control were not exactly nimble on their feet. A statement was issued, mumbling that nothing could be considered until Kelly's report on the tour had been received and discussed on 29 December. This was certainly not enough to stop the press, who by now were well informed of the affair, from breaking down the fences. 'Will Don Bradman be bossed by the Board of Control?' shouted

Smith's Weekly. 'Manager Kelly cannot chain young Napoleon,' it went on. The *Referee* joined in: '. . . a man only has to win eminence in any sphere to invite and encounter blasts of criticism from men of smaller mould.'[21] So it went on. The milder Adelaide *Chronicle* quoted approvingly from Pelham Warner's introduction in its issue of 27 November: 'Mr P. F. Warner refers to Bradman's feet as "small and beautifully neat, which Pavlova might have envied".'[22] The Melbourne *Argus* noted on 21 November that Bradman had dedicated the book to 'My dearest father and mother'. There was by now no doubt where the loyalties of the press lay.

The matter came to a head at the by now heavily advertised meeting of the Board of Control on 29 December 1930. The meeting, at the Board's offices in Melbourne, lasted two days. It so happened that Bradman was in Melbourne at the time, playing in a Sheffield Shield match against Victoria. He had arrived from Adelaide, where he had made 258 against South Australia in 282 minutes. In Melbourne he was out for 2. On the morning of 30 December Bradman attended the offices of the Board of Control, was kept waiting for two hours, and went in to be asked a few questions but, more important, to hear the Board's verdict. It was unanimous. Bradman had broken his contract and (this time on a majority vote) it had been decided that £50 of his good conduct fee would be withheld and that he would be censured. There was no right of appeal.

Bradman emerged from the meeting wearing his habitual smile. But the truth was that neither Bradman nor the Board had understood the nature of publishing. Bradman was perfectly in order in writing a book about the tour. Grimmett had, after all, done the same. He was then entitled to sell the rights to an agent. The agent was within his rights to sell the serialisation of the book to a newspaper without further reference to the author other than to accede to Bradman's request that, in the words of Bradman's subsequent statement, 'nothing whatever relating to the tour in progress must be published in any shape or form prior to my return to Australia'.[23] This condition was, in fact, met. But once Bradman was on the return boat, his comments on the tour would be published by the *Star*, as indeed they were.

It was an unhappy episode, the result summed up by the London *Daily Herald*: 'Bradman is apparently suffering from a combination of hero-worship and official irritation. The fact that one half of Australia expects him to score centuries without effort, and the other half thinks that he is a bad boy, must have an adverse mental effect on one who, after all, is little more than a schoolboy.'[24] It was a fair verdict, but the Sydney public thought better. As he walked out to bat in the second Test match against the West Indies at the SCG, 22,000 rose and cheered him to the wicket. At least they knew where they stood.

'I know that my concentration during that season fell away because of these extraneous matters,' Bradman was later to say.[25] It is certainly no less than the truth. Leaving aside the difficulty of adjusting again to the pace of Australian wickets after the soft English pitches, it is difficult to deny that his form, in his own word, was 'patchy'. The term, of course, is relative; he still averaged 74.50 in the Test matches of that summer. But he was not pleased with his performance. The West Indies had three fast bowlers of international class – Constantine, Griffith and Francis – and Constantine's fielding and Headley's batting were outstanding, but the general standard of the side was mediocre and, apart from the last Test at Sydney in late February 1931, where the West Indies caught Australia twice on a sticky wicket, Bradman only batted once in each Test. His scores were certainly 'patchy': 4, 25, 223, 152, and 43 and 0 (bowled by Griffith – his first Test match 'duck').

At the end of the first-class season, Bradman joined a tour of Queensland led by his New South Wales captain Alan Kippax. It was not a particularly serious event in cricket terms – the object being to encourage young cricketers in the outlying areas in the north of the State; but it did have one serious outcome for Bradman. The start of the tour was easy enough, by sea from Sydney to Cairns past the islands of the Great Barrier Reef. But when the side reached Rockhampton in mid-April to play Central Queensland, Bradman met with disaster. Turning quickly in the field, he tripped in a hole in the rough outfield and broke his ankle. The 1930–31 season was well and truly ended.

By the middle of 1931, Bradman was facing a number of difficult problems. It was not just that he had to hobble around on crutches – his injury proving worse than had at first been expected. Nor was it that his job with Mick Simmons was becoming repetitive and boring, or even that he still had to attend lunches and dinners, and write articles for local newspapers. All these were difficult enough, and he still resented the way he had been used by the Simmons and General Motors publicity machines the year before. Nevertheless, he quite fairly recognised the security that his job had given him, not to mention the Chevrolet (now christened 'The Red Peril') which had become a frequent sight on the Sydney streets.

The real problem was the future. The Depression was, in mid-1931, threatening to engulf not just those who were already out of work but those in work as well. Bradman knew that his contract with Mick Simmons was coming to an end on 1 February 1932. As he said himself later: 'It was not the time to be out of work.'[26] Whatever small nest-egg he had built up as a result of gifts from cricket lovers, it certainly was not enough to see him through what threatened to become a sustained period of unemployment. Besides, he was becoming more and more determined that he could not, and would not, depend on cricket – and its spin-off jobs – to provide him with a living for the rest of his life. He was conscious, too, that as yet he had no skill or trade other than cricket. He had, after all, left school at fourteen, and had never had the opportunity to serve a further apprenticeship before being swept up in international cricket, and he was far too intelligent not to have noticed the eclipse suffered by former cricketers once their career was ended.

The matter was not only of concern to Bradman himself. His relations with the Menzies family had become closer with his move to Sydney in 1928, and became closer still after his return from England in 1930, when the Menzies family home provided a shelter from unwelcome media attention. It was now assumed by both families that it was only a matter of time before Don and Jessie would announce their engagement; indeed, the matter had been discussed in earnest prior to the 1930 tour. The problem, however, was one of Don's future financial security.

Furthermore, neither Don nor Jessie wished to see their whole future mortgaged to the game of cricket.

There were two possible solutions. The first was to leave cricket altogether and learn a trade. The difficulty with this was that there was no conceivable prospect of employment in the foreseeable future for anyone without a skill. Indeed, there were many with a high degree of skill who were begging on the streets. The other alternative was to try to use his cricket to make enough money quickly to see him, and his wife, through the gloomy times in which they lived. The hope would then be that by the time he had done this the prospects for permanent employment would look better. It was not much, but it seemed the best bet.

It so happened that the opportunity to make money presented itself precisely at that moment. An approach came – indirectly through Learie Constantine – to Bradman with an offer to play in the Lancashire League. The League (with its Yorkshire equivalent) had been, and to some extent still is, the English equivalent of Grade cricket in Australia – in other words, of a high standard but just below first-class level. Besides, the clubs in the League were each allowed to engage one professional player. Since the clubs were backed not just by faithful and enthusiastic crowds but also by the textile magnates of the north of England there was money to spend. The President of the Lancashire League at the time, for instance, was Edward Crabtree, the owner of a textile mill in Todmorden. In fact it was he, it is said, who put out feelers to Bradman on behalf of one of the League's clubs, Accrington.

Exactly who first approached whom is obscure. The truth is that Bradman and Constantine had discussed the Lancashire League during the West Indies' tour of 1930–31, not least because Constantine himself had played for a League club in the summer of 1929. Constantine, informed of Bradman's financial ambitions, probably talked over the possibility with Claude Spencer, a devoted supporter both of the game of cricket and of Don Bradman personally. By August 1931 matters had gone far enough for an offer to be put on the table. Accrington were prepared to offer Bradman a contract for three seasons at £500 per season, and passage both ways.

There is no doubt that Bradman was tempted by the Accrington offer. He was not particularly enthusiastic about leaving Australia, but the financial terms were attractive. They became even more attractive when Spencer, on Bradman's instructions, managed to negotiate better terms: a two-year contract at £600 per season. On top of that, he could expect to make further money from writing for the English newspapers, as well as from sponsoring any and every form of sporting equipment. It was even suggested, for instance, that there might be a 'Bradman billiard table'. In total, he would make well over £1,000 a year.

Needless to say, news of the negotiations leaked out. The London correspondent of *Truth* (perhaps a strange name for a Sydney newspaper) cabled his head office, and on 6 September 1931 the paper screamed: BRADMAN IS GOING TO ENGLAND! At that point, the press in England and Australia both became desperate for follow-up stories. The inventions multiplied. The proposed salary was inflated – the figure being 'understood', for instance by the *Manchester Chronicle*, to be £1,300. The length of contract was extended; and Bradman had already accepted.

Throughout September and October seemingly everybody in the cricket world discussed the matter except Bradman. When asked for comment he made some evasive response or just said nothing. What he did do, however, was to ask the Australian Board of Control whether acceptance of the Accrington offer would violate his contract for the 1930 tour, one of whose clauses had expressly stated that players should not return to England to play cricket 'within two years from the completion of the official tour'. The tour had officially ended in September 1930; Accrington wanted Bradman to start in the spring of 1932. The Board's reply was unambiguous. 'If the Clause were broken by any member,' it pronounced, 'the Board would not approve of his selection for Australia.'[27] In other words, if Bradman went to Lancashire his Test career was finished.

BOARD'S BLUSTER WON'T BOUNCE BRILLIANT BOWRAL BOY shouted the *Truth*. But if Bradman was not bounced, his supporters certainly were. By late October a trio of Sydney businessmen had hatched a plan to keep him in Australia. Again, Spencer was the intermediary. The plan was simple: three business groups, the Sydney *Sun*, the radio station 2UE and the retailers F.J. Palmer & Son would club together to offer Bradman a two-year contract. He would write for the *Sun*, broadcast for 2UE and promote Palmer's sports goods. The deal was quickly done, and on 30 October Bradman cabled Accrington: 'Regret decline your offer'. His published comment was: 'I am delighted that I am staying here. I did not want to go away or to lose touch with Australian cricket, nor become a professional cricketer if I could avoid it.'[28]

In fact, Bradman had done just the thing he had not wanted to do. For a start, the contract was for only two years – and on terms less generous than those Accrington had been prepared to offer. He had also committed himself to dependence on cricket for his livelihood – there was no prospect whatever of him 'learning a trade' in his new employment. Perhaps worst of all, however, he had signed up to write articles for a newspaper, which, in the eyes of the Australian Board of Control, was something close to an unforgivable sin.

But the deed had been done. At least the matter was settled for the moment, and it was against this somewhat more stable background that Don and Jessie announced their formal engagement in November 1931. There was, as might be imagined, more publicity to be faced. Telegrams of congratulation arrived from all over Australia. The Commonwealth Bank in Sydney, where Jessie worked, became an object of simpering interest from the gossip columns of the Australian – and indeed the English – press. It was discovered that the two had been at the same school together in Bowral, that she had won a gold medal for needlework, that she was fond of tennis and music, and that she was a horsewoman and a good driver. She was 'of medium height', it was reported (although she was several inches shorter than her future husband), 'with wide-apart hazel eyes and a brown wavy shingle'[29] or, according to another source, 'a young and pretty brunette, with vivacious blue eyes and wavy hair'[30]; and her engagement ring was reliably said to be of platinum, set with a large diamond in the middle surrounded by smaller ones.

In reality, Jessie Menzies showed herself, then and subsequently, to be shrewd, reliable, selfless and, above all, uncomplicated. She was not above the occasional prank, and her face became alight when she laughed out loud, or when her normally rather square jaw split into a wide smile. But her devotion to Bradman was evident, and she was the perfect foil to his concentrated, and occasionally mercurial, character. As for Bradman himself, he never failed to acknowledge his debt to her in the stability she brought to his turbulent life. Jessie has been described by one of her friends as a 'star'; and the description is fair. Without her, Bradman himself has admitted that he would not have come through the challenges which he was to face during the long period of their married life.

Before they could get married, of course, there was work to be done. It was not just a question of fulfilling his new contract of employment; Bradman had to play cricket as well. He still played for St George; he went on up-country charity tours (in one, at Blackheath, he scored 100 in just three eight-ball overs, hitting 10 sixes, 9 fours, 1 two and 2 singles); he was selected – unsurprisingly – for New South Wales both for the Sheffield Shield matches for the season and to play against the touring South Africans; and for Australia in the Test matches against South Africa.

It was in the Australian summer of 1931–32 that Bradman was probably at the peak of his early career. It was the touring South Africans who suffered worst. Yet the tour itself almost never took place. Nobody could now ignore the Depression, which was affecting both Australia and South Africa in equal measure. As late as early July 1931 the tour was in doubt. There simply was not the money to pay the necessary expenses, let alone any guarantee that those expenses would be recovered by attendance at the matches. The unemployed on 'susso' could not afford to watch cricket, and the South Africans anyway did not have the attraction of an English Ashes tour. There was even talk, in early 1931, of the direction of the tour being changed entirely. It was felt that, with Bradman, an Australian tour of South Africa would be a much more appealing proposition.

In the end, it was South African business that came to the rescue, and the tour went forward as planned. But the South African cricketers could have been excused for wishing that it had been cancelled, such was Bradman's domination of the series.

He averaged 201.50 in Test matches but, as he wrote himself, 'this in no sense reflected the skill and quality of the South African bowlers'.[31] Certainly there were some bad fielding lapses, not least in the First Test at Brisbane in late November, when Bradman was dropped in the slips at 11 and 15. With Bradman in his best form such chances had to be taken; he went on to make 226 – in four hours and thirty-seven minutes. A further 219 for New South Wales against the tourists was only a prelude to his 112 in the Second Test at Sydney – in two hours and twenty-seven minutes. The Third Test at Melbourne saw a rare failure in the first innings (caught at the wicket for 2); but that was followed in the second by 167. Then, in the Fourth Test at Adelaide in late January 1932, he destroyed all previous records for Test matches in Australia with 299 not out, the last batsman in being run out in the attempt to get Bradman to his triple century. Fortunately for the South Africans, he fell in the dressing room just before the Fifth Test started, strained a ligament in his ankle and was unable to bat.

'To bowl to him is heart-breaking,' wrote the South African fast bowler Sandy Bell. 'When batting Bradman always seems, to the weary bowler at any rate, to assume a sort of cynical grin, which rather reminds one of the Sphinx . . . Another remarkable thing about Bradman is that he never seems to perspire . . . At Adelaide the temperature was 108 in the shade. Don was in the course of making 299. We were all just about exhausted, but Don – he was as fresh as a new pin. The only sign of his 180 runs was a tiny little damp spot in the middle of his back.' Off the field, however, it was quite a different matter. 'Imagine our surprise on seeing a tiny fellow in a neat grey suit, and then finding him to be the redoubtable Don Bradman . . . he is a good conversationalist, obviously out to learn all he can, and he gives one the impression of being an astute business man . . . he neither smokes nor drinks. He keeps reasonably early hours and looks after himself very carefully. He does a course of physical training, and combines it with wrestling . . . He plays the piano remarkably well, and plays most tunes he is asked either from ear or music.'[32]

It is a fair summing up of the Bradman of early 1932, just before his marriage. What it leaves out, of course, is the extent

Donald George Bradman, aged two, in 1910.

Don (right), aged about eight, with his brother Victor.

Bradman's parents, George and Emily.

With his dog, Teddy, in about 1917.

Bradman in 1920.

The young busines[s]
Bradman in about 1[ ]

Jessie Menzies, later Lady
[B]radman, in the late 1920s.

Batting during his first Test match
at Brisbane in December 1928.

On the way to 452 not out
for New South Wales against
Queensland, January 1930.

The front page of the Sydney
Daily Telegraph Pictorial after
his record-breaking innings.

Packing before the 1930 tour.

Batting at Trent Bridge during the First Test of the 1930 tour.

The Second Test, 1930: Bradman acknowledging the applause of the Lord's crowd after reaching 200.

The Third Test, Headingley, 1930: on the way to 334.

Practising before the Fifth Test, the Oval, August 1930.

The Fifth Test: Jack Hobbs, in his last Test, applauds Bradman's innings of 232.

An unusual bulletin board gives the score from the Oval.

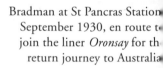

Bradman at St Pancras Station
September 1930, en route to
join the liner *Oronsay* for the
return journey to Australia

Speaking from Bowral bandstand
to the welcoming committee on
his return to Australia.

At the wheel of the
'Don Bradman Car'.

to which Bradman had become a national hero. When he was introduced in March 1932 to the listeners of Station 2UE (as 'Our Don', broadcasting together with 'Uncle Lionel and the Listerine Serenaders' – Listerine being even then a popular mouthwash), the listening figures for the station rose almost exponentially. Nor was there any peace for him in public, or even in his own home. 'The ordinary citizen has not the remotest idea what it feels like to be a public figure,' he wrote later. 'Remember, you can't turn this thing on and off like a tap . . . The sentimental folk will say "What a compliment." That is probably so, but try it yourselves for twenty years and see what it does to your nervous system.'[33]

The publicity which was by now Bradman's constant companion reached a climax with his wedding on 30 April 1932. The church of St Paul's in suburban Burwood was under siege all through the day by a crowd which had come out from central Sydney to see the event. 'Hero-worship,' one newspaper wrote, 'seemed to develop into a positive frenzy.'[34] The police tried to keep order by putting up barriers outside the church, but these were soon broken down and many of the crowd found their way into the building alongside those who had actually been invited. There was some irritation when the uninvited guests stood on chairs and pews to get a better view of what was going on, and some discontent when those who had been formally bidden found their places taken; but by the time the principal actors arrived there was at least a reasonable degree of calm.

The service took place in the early evening. Bradman was there on time, with his brother Victor as best man. Jessie arrived soon after on the arm of her father, with her sisters, Jean and Lily, as bridesmaids. The men, as was the fashion of the time, wore dinner jackets with high starched collars and black bow ties, with carnations in their button holes; Jessie wore a dress of white and silver brocaded satin, with a long veil of tulle which served as a train, while Jean and Lily wore silk eau-de-nil dresses with smart orange velvet caps. All in all, they made a good-looking, if somewhat conventional, group. The service was taken by a 'cricketing parson', Canon Hughes of Melbourne's Anglican cathedral, a choice that was generally regarded as thoroughly suitable. Everything, it was said, was as it should be.

81

Apart from a few days at a friend's house in Melbourne, there was not much of a honeymoon for the newly-weds until the end of May. It so happened that Arthur Mailey, an old journalist friend of Bradman – and a distinguished former Australian Test cricketer – had agreed to assemble a tour to the United States and Canada. It was to be a light-hearted affair, and many of the participants were expected to pay their own way – not, of course, Don and Jessie Bradman, whom Mailey had invited (not least for their publicity value) and whose expenses he himself was prepared to meet.

It was Bradman's first visit to North America, and Jessie's first foreign trip of any kind. Admittedly, the standard of cricket was mediocre, but there was every opportunity for the young couple to enjoy their joint excitement. The tourists worked and played their way across Canada, travelled down to New York, back to Chicago, up to Winnipeg, over to Vancouver, down to Seattle and then San Francisco and Los Angeles, before returning home via New Zealand. The whole trip took nearly four months, and in that time the two Bradmans saw everything they could cram in. Their curiosity was unbounded, and very flattering to Americans and Canadians who were happy to satisfy it. 'For my wife and me,' Bradman wrote later, 'cricket had thus provided the opportunity of seeing the New World – an opportunity unlikely to have occurred through any other medium. It had been far too strenuous, but nevertheless it was placid compared with the storm which lay ahead, and of which at that time we had scarcely heard the rumblings.'[35] It was the truth, for even as the Bradmans' ship steamed into Sydney Harbour on 23 September 1932, the English touring side for 1932–33, under the captaincy of D.R. Jardine, was nearing Ceylon on their way to Australia. The storm clouds were gathering, and before long thunder would echo around the highest hills of English and Australian cricket.

5

UP CAME THE TROOPERS

THE 1932–33 MCC TOUR OF AUSTRALIA could hardly have come at a worse time. To start with, relations between Britain and her distant dominion were traversing a period of severe strain. The Depression was taking its toll, not only on those who suffered directly, but on governments throughout the world trying to mitigate its effect on those of whom they had charge. Protectionism was in the air. Finance from London was hard to come by, for the States and even for the Commonwealth of Australia itself. Australians, not unnaturally, felt badly let down. New South Wales suspended interest payments on its overseas debt, and now could rely only on domestic sources of finance. In turn, this led to intense friction between the States. The Labor Party itself started to break up, with the expulsion of the New South Wales branch and a series of electoral defeats. A movement which skated along the edge of fascism, the New Guard, had grown rapidly in strength in the early 1930s and was said in early 1932 to have many thousands of armed volunteers on whom it could call.

The climax came in New South Wales, and in dramatic fashion. The Sydney Harbour Bridge was to be opened on 19 March 1932 by the Labor Premier of New South Wales, Jack Lang. On the day appointed, however, before Lang could get to the tape to cut it, there was an unseemly scuffle. Francis de Groot, a Sydney antique dealer, had donned a borrowed uniform, mounted a horse and moved forward through the barrier of police, which gave way in front of him. Arriving at the tape, he tried to slash it with his sabre, but his horse reared at that moment and he was left hanging on grimly. Finally, he managed to grab the ribbon and with 'several upward sawing motions' severed it. He then waved his sabre in the air and pronounced the bridge open 'in the name of the decent and respectable citizens of New South Wales'.[1]

By this time the astonished police had regained some form of composure, and de Groot was arrested. It was difficult to find a precise charge; 'maliciously damaging a ribbon valued at £2' was the police's first effort – but it sounded very far from convincing, and they settled for 'offensive behaviour on Bradfield Highway'. De Groot was tried and convicted, and fined £5 plus £4 costs. A commemoration fund sponsored by the New Guard and the *Sun* newspaper raised £550, which was promptly given to the heroic criminal.

The aftershocks from the incident were far-reaching. The Lang government subsided into confusion, and such was the threat of armed confrontation – let alone financial chaos – that the British Governor of New South Wales, Sir Philip Game, finally decided to sack Lang and replace him with a Premier at the head of a loyalist United Australia Party/United Country Party coalition. Elections in June confirmed Game's decision and gave a majority to the coalition – by now heavily supported by the New Guard. The same coalition had won power in Canberra eighteen months earlier under Joseph Lyons. The shift had been decisive; the 'empire' party was now in charge. The opposition was left sullen and discontented.

There was little doubt on which side of the argument the Bradmans came down. Neither of them had any interest in party politics, but their conventional, country background led them naturally into support for the Empire and stability. Indeed, this was the view taken by most of the cricketers and administrators of the day, apart, perhaps, from Jack Fingleton, who was himself the son of a New South Wales Labor MP. The crowds, however, were another matter. If the views of the rural communities and the suburban middle class were predominantly pro-British and conservative, this was by no means true of the urban working class, which was vociferously hostile to Anglo-Australian imperial patriotism. The reactions to de Groot's antics at Sydney Harbour Bridge illustrate this clear class divide: one letter from a 'Disgusted Digger' told him: 'If you're not satisfied with Australia why not take your hook back where you came from. The police done the right thing when they placed you in the "Giggle House". You, a dirty, low down pommy, had the audacity to come to this fair land and be cowardly enough to do such a despicable thing as you done on Saturday'; while another congratulated him for doing 'just what one would expect from a loyal British soldier . . . let us hope this is the beginning of the end of that political inebriate [Lang].'[2]

Into this maelstrom of class antagonisms sailed the liner *Orontes* with the visitors from England. In the circumstances, the MCC could hardly have made a more provocative choice as captain, and it was the combination of circumstances of the time and the personalities of the leading figures that was to leave a stain not just on cricket but on relations between Britain and Australia. As Rockley Wilson remarked on hearing of Jardine's appointment: 'We shall win the Ashes but we may lose a Dominion.'[3] Such was the explosion of Australian anger over what came to be known as 'bodyline' that Wilson's prediction came disturbingly close to the mark.

Douglas Robert Jardine had been born in Bombay in 1900. The son of a Scottish lawyer who had gone out to India six years earlier to practise law – and who ended up as Advocate-General of Bombay – the young boy was sent back to Scotland at the age of nine, to stay with his Aunt Kitty in a cavernous Scottish mansion and to work his way through the educational system then appropriate for a member of the Scottish upper-middle class. Preparatory school led to Winchester – in those days a terrifyingly harsh and monastic establishment. Jardine was not particularly adept intellectually but he was good at sport, and that earned him the respect of his peers. He was also outstandingly courageous, particularly in a bizarre game known as 'Winchester football'. Among other strange activities in this so-called 'recreation', those who played in the scrum, or 'hot' as it was known, had to stand still while an opponent booted the ball at them from point-blank range. Those who flinched were treated as shameful outcasts. Jardine never flinched.

It was perhaps impossible for anybody to survive the rigours of a Winchester education during the First World War without developing some abnormal character traits – or at least eccentricities – and Jardine was no exception. By the time he went on to Oxford University he was tall, rather stiff-legged and unathletic, with a thin face and a sharply beaked nose. But, more important, he had developed a manner of behaviour which seemed – to those who did not know him, including the Australian public – to be one of quintessential English arrogance. His voice was an upper-class drawl. The word 'off' was pronounced 'awff', 'gone' was pronounced 'gawn' and so on. In fact he could be particularly charming to his friends, but, partly through shyness and partly through the unbending discipline of his education, he rarely appeared so to strangers.

It need hardly be said that Jardine's politics were conservative. His upbringing in India had seen to that. But it also seems to have induced a contempt for 'lesser breeds without the law' as the hymn has it – which included anybody who was not British. On the 1928–29 tour of Australia he had performed well, just missing his century in the fourth Test match, but his habit of wearing a multi-coloured Harlequin cap and a white silk 'choker' while in the field was a gift to the Australian barrackers, who accepted it with pleasure. Jardine did not take kindly to such treatment. Thenceforward, Australians were known collectively as 'bastards'.

The two other senior amateurs in the MCC party were, in many ways, figures of lesser consequence. G.O. Allen was from the same educational drawer as Jardine, only from Eton – where he had developed into an athletic fast bowler – rather than Winchester. The son of the Commandant of the Metropolitan Special Constabulary, his attitudes, and his political views, were to the right even of Jardine's. On the other hand, he was evasive in character, and frequently indecisive to the point where, to others at least, he appeared devious. The third, R.E.S. Wyatt, was socially of a somewhat lower rank. As his cousin observed of the Wyatt family in the twentieth century: 'There has been little from my family to excite the eye or the mind.'[4] Grammar-school educated, Wyatt had been projected into cricket almost as an afterthought. But he was a fine batsman, and although it was a surprise, his appointment as captain of the England team in the last Test in 1930 added discipline and courage to the side.

The last two gentlemen of influence, as it were, Pelham Warner and R.C.N. Palairet, occupied the positions of manager and treasurer respectively – though their functions were not defined with any precision. Warner was a mild man, born of an old English settler family in the West Indies, and Palairet almost without any identifiable character traits other than an elegant charm and an obvious desire to keep as far as possible from any trouble that might be brewing. But, to be fair, it is difficult to see, given the dominant role of the captain and the subsidiary role of management in those days, what either could have done when the fur started to fly. What is clear, however, is that neither Warner nor Palairet were strong enough characters even to begin to deal with a determined Jardine.

It is only in such descriptions that the class basis of the MCC touring party can be properly illustrated. Of course, it is little more than a reflection of the way cricket was organised in those days. Amateurs were regarded as quite a different race to professionals. Not only were there dressing rooms on most English grounds reserved for amateurs and distanced from professionals, but the two groups would, on some grounds, also walk on to the field through different doors in the pavilion. Wyatt, for example, once found himself required to walk out at Lord's accompanied by nine other amateurs – with the one professional solemnly walking out of a different gate. Nothing could have been more absurd, but it was the rule. 'Professionals of those days,' Wyatt subsequently remarked, 'were a [different] type of chap.'[5]

The professionals knew their place, if they had not done so before, when Jardine introduced them to the captain of the *Orontes* on her departure from Tilbury. A large crowd had gathered, having not much else to do, to hear Jardine make a rather lofty and cool speech and to watch him present his team. Allen, an amateur, was introduced as 'Mr Allen'; the Yorkshireman Bowes – admittedly a dour and humourless character – was simply 'Bowes'. Of course, these distinctions were part of the English cricket sociology of the time, and were accepted as such. Nevertheless, they had a practical importance, which was to emerge as the tour progressed. Amateurs, like Allen, felt themselves to be on equal terms with their captain and could speak to him 'as officer to officer'. Professionals, on the other hand, were expected to do what they were told, without discussion. Herbert Sutcliffe was a case in point. As a batsman he was without any doubt superior to both Jardine and Wyatt, but since he was designated as 'senior professional' he certainly did not believe it was his role, or in his interest, to challenge decisions made by his captain in the way in which both Allen (during the tour itself) and Wyatt (subsequently) felt able to do.

Jardine's whole strategy for the tour, such as it was, depended on his professional colleagues doing what he asked. Above all, it depended on his three professional fast bowlers, Larwood, Voce and Bowes, doing what he asked of them. Of the three, Larwood was the finest. He was without a doubt one of the finest natural cricketers of all time – as indeed was Bradman. Summoned from a Nottinghamshire coal mine, he had changed from being a miner to being a fast bowler almost overnight. But it was not just that he could bowl fast; many could do that. What made Larwood such a fearsome weapon was that he was not only fast – very fast – and temperamentally fiery but, above all, he was accurate. He was not tall, but he was thick-set, with a miner's powerful shoulders and buttocks; and he had a naturally endowed rhythm, timing his run-up and his bowling stride to ensure both maximum pace and maximum concealment from the opposing batsman of the flight and pitch of the ball. Even now, sixty years on, to watch Larwood in action on film is one of cricket's greatest sights. To have been at the receiving end must have been truly terrifying.

Voce was not nearly so frightening, but in the Nottinghamshire side of the period he complemented Larwood in the same way that the Australian fast bowlers of the early 1920s had complemented one another. But even the two of them together would not have been such a powerful force had it not been for the influence of their county captain, Arthur Carr. Carr has been described as 'really a dreadful man'.[6] It is said that he used to take Larwood and Voce out in the evenings during matches and, not to put too fine a point on it, fill them up with beer. Indeed it was common knowledge that during tea intervals at the Nottingham ground of Trent Bridge pints of beer would be lined up on a ledge for the two bowlers to refresh themselves before returning to a final assault on the opposing batsmen after the interval.

Jardine's strategy for the tour, once he had accepted the captaincy – about which he had doubts, as it happened, which took some time to overcome – was quite simple. It was to contain Bradman. Bradman had, after all, during the 1930 tour of England, changed the nature of the game. He had shown, even on soft English wickets, that he could dominate any English bowling attack, even one including Larwood, to such an extent that, on the harder Australian wickets, he would be invincible. Unless some chink in the armour could be found, Bradman would be able single-handedly to humiliate England and, to put it in its crudest form – since such was the thinking at the time – the mother country would yet again be defeated by a mere dominion.

There is little doubt that Jardine set about his task with the concentration that his Scottish ancestry, Indian childhood, legal background, Winchester education and, not least, his own temperament demanded. He studied the film records of Bradman batting in 1930; he read the accounts of Bradman's matches; he discussed the problem with those who, like him, had seen Bradman in action; he noted that Australian batsmen had over the years changed their technique against fast bowling, tending to make their first movement backward and across their wicket rather than forward and straight as was the English practice. In short, it was a thorough, and in modern terms a truly professional, piece of research. But in the end, according to his daughter, it was the film of Bradman – and Archie Jackson – at the Oval in the last Test of the 1930 series, when they were facing Larwood on a rain-affected wicket, that put an idea into Jardine's mind. 'I've got it,' he apparently said 'He's yellow.'[7]

That said, or perhaps not said, it would be wrong to imagine that 'fast leg theory' or 'bodyline', as it came to be called by the Australian press, emerged fully formed from Jardine's head at that precise moment. Certainly Larwood and Voce were sounded out by Jardine in early August 1932, at a dinner in the grill-room of the Piccadilly Hotel, on whether they could bowl accurately at the leg stump, 'making the ball come up into the body all the time,' in Larwood's own words, 'so that Bradman had to play his shots to leg . . . we thought Don was frightened of sharp rising balls,' but there was apparently no suggestion that the attack should either be very short, or aimed at the batsman's head, or supported by a packed leg-side field. Subsequently, Jardine discussed field placings for a normally-pitched leg-stump attack with Frank Foster, who had bowled 'leg theory' in Australia in 1911–12, but there is no evidence that even by the time the MCC team arrived in Australia the full concept of 'fast leg theory' – of fast, short and intimidatory bowling to a field of seven men on the leg side – had been fully developed or, indeed, that the players were aware of what Jardine had in mind. What was abundantly clear, however, on the boat going out to Australia was Jardine's insistence on a policy, quite simply, of hate. The Australian opponents were to be hated, and none more so than Bradman. Indeed, on one occasion Jardine summoned his players and told them solemnly that from then on Bradman would not be known as 'Bradman' or 'Don' but as 'the little bastard'. It was hardly an announcement of future sporting friendship.

The object of this attention was, on his return from Mailey's tour of the New World, going through what he himself described as 'a very serious, a very difficult period'. Marriage was a new venture, and he had 'the job of settling down to find a home, to make a home for myself, my wife' and then he added 'and so on'.[8] A home was not too difficult to find, and was indeed duly located in Lower Bayview Street on McMahon's Point – a pleasant enough place with a good view, as the name implies, over the harbour and the bridge. There were, of course, snags: once it was known that this was the Bradman home, the couple were hardly ever left in peace, to the point where Bradman was forced to apply for an unlisted telephone number – almost unheard of in those days. At the same time, he had severe dental problems, which required a series of long and painful visits to his dentist.

But it was the 'and so on' that was the real problem. Bradman had signed a two-year contract to write for the Sydney *Sun*. He had known that the Australian Board of Control had a regulation that players who wished to be considered to play for Australia could not write for the press without the consent of the Board.

It was all quite clear. But Bradman was still a young man and, on his own admission, somewhat naïve. He was therefore 'absolutely dumbfounded' to discover, when he wrote what he thought was a purely formal letter to the Board explaining his contract, to receive a reply from the chairman to the effect that the Board could not give him permission to write, since journalism was not his sole occupation. Bradman's response was immediate and angry. 'I have signed a contract to write articles,' he announced to the press, 'and I must keep it. I cannot let cricket interfere with my work.'⁹ He went on to tell the Board that, if that was their last word, then he would honour the contract and 'stand out' of Test cricket for two years.

The thought of even one Test series – and one against England at that – without Bradman was enough to send the press into hysteria. The Board of Control was isolated in defending its position. It was, of course, blackmail, but none the less effective for that. Furthermore, Bradman rubbed it in by accepting an invitation to play against the tourists in their second match, for an Australian XI at Perth. His progress across the continent was nothing if not royal. Together with Fingleton and McCabe, he boarded a train at Sydney in late October for the five-day journey. As Fingleton reported, 'When the train was on its long run across the Nullarbor Plain, lonely men and women of the outback travelled many miles to catch a glimpse of this cricket magician. Piping little voices travelled the length of the train calling "Bradman, Bradman, Bradman", when infrequent stops were made at night along that desolate dreary line.'¹⁰ By the time the train arrived at the small mining outpost of Coolgardie, Bradman had had enough, and locked himself in his cabin. But the Coolgardie miners were determined to see him, and set about ransacking the train. Windows were broken and doors wrenched off before the conductor decided it was time to move on.

Bradman's arrival at Perth was no different. 'No prince,' Fingleton goes on, 'could have had a more regal entry . . . thousands crammed the station, the adjoining roofs and buildings, the exits and the streets outside. Police had to force a passage for Bradman, and the Palace Hotel, where we stayed, was in a constant simmer day and night.'¹¹ Many in the crowd sported lapel buttons with the simple message 'Bradman must play'. There were even those who called for a cricket strike or at least a boycott unless and until the Board climbed down. Bradman himself held out a compromise offer, saying publicly that he would not write any articles before the Board met again – just before the second Test match. In other words, he would be eligible for the First Test.

As it happened, the Perth crowd – some 20,000 in the ground, many having travelled hundreds of miles to see their hero – were to be deeply disappointed. Not only did the English fail to choose their main fast bowlers, Larwood, Voce and Bowes, but Bradman had to bat on a rain-damaged wicket and was out to Verity for 3 in the first innings and to Allen for 10 in the second. Worse still, it all happened in a single day.

One week later, however, Bradman was back on his pedestal. On 5 November, in a Sheffield Shield match against Victoria at Sydney, he made 238 in only three hours and twenty minutes in front of a crowd of 25,000. 'Those present at the time,' one newspaper reported, 'will agree that nothing finer in batting has ever been seen on the famous ground ... Bradman has developed into a greater batsman than ever, with his on-side battery absolutely bewildering to bowlers and captains in placing the field.'[12] The gauntlet had been well and truly thrown at the Englishmen's feet.

The first confrontation came at Melbourne on 18 November, when the MCC played an Australian XI. Jardine, perhaps for tactical reasons, had decided to take time off to go trout-fishing (at which he was something of an expert), and Wyatt was left in charge. According to Wyatt's own account, Larwood and Voce opened the bowling with orthodox fields, but as the shine wore off the new ball Wyatt moved Larwood's slips one by one from the off side to leg. By the time Bradman came in Larwood was bowling to three short legs and a man back on the boundary for Bradman's hook. The first casualty, however, had been Woodfull, who had been struck just above the heart by a short, fast ball from Larwood – bowling, it should be noted, to an orthodox off-side field.

Bradman's approach to the wicket heightened the excitement

of the crowd and the players. Larwood seemed to put on an extra yard of pace; the English fieldsmen were ready on their toes. 'They attacked him remorselessly,' said Leo O'Brien, the batsman at the other end, 'and he was certainly upset; there was no doubt about that. The wicket was a bit on the green side and they had him in a bit of trouble.' Bradman was in for an hour and only then, in his own words, did he believe that 'I was just getting on top of that attack.'[13] He had played what for him were some extraordinarily bad strokes. Indeed, at one point he sat down in trying to cope with what he thought would be a bumper from Bowes. As Hobbs described it: 'Bradman sat on the wicket with his bat somewhere over his left shoulder and the ball hit it, going for a single between the umpire and mid-on.'[14] In the end he was out lbw to Larwood for 36 ('a very bad decision', he later said). But he fared no better in the second innings, when he was bowled, again by Larwood, trying to cut a ball, just short of a length, from the line of his off stump.

By now it was clear that things were going wrong. He had failed four times against the English attack, and there were those – including Larwood – who thought that his confidence had been permanently damaged. They were confirmed in their belief when it was learned that Bradman had complained to the Victorian cricket officials about the English tactics and predicted trouble for the future if they were not curtailed. But worse was to come. In the next game, for New South Wales against the MCC at Sydney, Bradman was out to Tate for 18 in the first innings and then, after spending a day in bed with an infected throat, was bowled by Voce in the second innings for 23. It was this event that pointed up Bradman's obvious discomfiture. Voce, now using a full 'bodyline' field of four to five short-legs with two men covering them in the deep, bowled a short ball. Bradman expected it to rise. He went over to the off ('near the wide mark', Fingleton, batting at the other end, wrote); and looked back to see his middle stump out of the ground behind his back. The English thought that he was 'finished' and that he 'would never be the same man again'.[15]

Things had now arrived at a point where Bradman's health started to break down. It was not just that he was 'very tired, very run down' after the American tour.[16] The dispute over his journalism, the constant and unrelenting publicity, the feeling that the hopes of all Australia were on his shoulders, combined with the perception, finally confirmed in the New South Wales game, of the malice behind the English tactics, began not just to take its psychological toll but to affect his physical well-being. He was tired, battered and, in the end, ill. In public he maintained a robust front, but at home it became obvious to Jessie that her husband was far from able to cope with the stress which would inevitably come with the first Test match. His illness was immediately reported to the Australian Board of Control.

As it happened the Board were far from upset at this turn of events. They were still in dispute with Bradman over the matter of his writing and they could see no easy way out of their dilemma. His illness, if it was confirmed, would buy them a little more time. They were therefore quite prepared to request two doctors to conduct a formal medical examination and to report. The doctors duly conducted their examination, and found that Bradman was basically healthy but had had a bad attack of influenza, was run down and needed a period of complete rest to regain match fitness. The Board announced that he was unfit to play – with something less than perfect timing – on the day before the first Test match was due to begin.

The public reaction was one of stunned disbelief. 'It might have been the fall of an Empire,' reported Reuters' representative in Sydney. 'Bulletins were posted in the shop windows, and no one could talk, think or speak of anything else.' It was rumoured that he had had a nervous breakdown – perhaps not too far from the truth; but, worse still, it was claimed that he was suffering from pernicious anaemia, that his career was over. Indeed, one London newspaper had an obituary already lined up. Some even said that his illness was 'diplomatic', so frightened was he of Larwood.

In fact, two or three weeks' rest was all that was needed, and he was well enough to watch the first Test match at Sydney (and, incidentally, to broadcast his usual evening comment on each day's play). The match finished – with Australia defeated but saved from humiliation by a brash but effective 187 from McCabe – the Bradmans set off for the rest cure, to a cottage on the coast south of Sydney owned by the New South Wales Cricket Association's physiotherapist. While there, and at rest, Bradman was able to give his full mind to the problem: how to defeat the 'fast leg theory' attack. The analysis was sharp and persuasive, and shows Bradman at his intellectual best. He reasoned that conventional shots had effectively been ruled out by Jardine's field placing. A defensive prod risked giving a simple catch to the array of short legs – the 'leg trap'; while a hook shot, which McCabe had used with great effect, but with astonishing luck, at Sydney, would give a catch to the deeper fieldsmen behind; and a pull shot past mid-on, one of Bradman's most prolific strokes, was too dangerous to a bowler of Larwood's pace.

The conclusion was logical. It was to take a leg-stump guard, step back as soon as the pitch and direction of the ball was established, and attempt to hit it through the off side. If the tactic succeeded, the bowlers – particularly Larwood, who was the major problem – would be forced to switch their field from leg back to off, and Bradman could then proceed to play as he had always done.

On his return to Sydney, Bradman tried out his theory on his old mentor A.G. ('Johnnie') Moyes. It was open, Moyes said, to a number of risks, not least that Larwood would bowl a full-length ball and leave Bradman stranded outside the leg stump. Bradman answered these and other objections with intelligence and deliberation; he had, indeed, thought of them all himself. His answer was that his reflexes were sharp enough and that he was quick enough on his feet to wait until Larwood bowled, at which point he could formulate his stroke accordingly.

The solution was typical of Bradman in three quite different respects. Firstly, he had a totally clear perception of his own ability. He knew that he was able to stand quite still until Larwood (bowling at some 90 miles per hour) had committed himself to a particular length and direction and then – only then – decide what shot to play and, if necessary, to skip back outside his leg stump to play the ball to the off. Secondly, he also knew that the Australian public relied on him to make runs against the English, and, fickle as crowds are apt to be, would not take kindly to seeing their hero either fail or simply stand there and allow himself to be hit. Thirdly, he was quite impervious – indeed it probably never occurred to him – to the criticism that would surely be levelled against him, that he was running away from Larwood, playing only for himself and not for his team.

In the end, Moyes was convinced, and Bradman started to put his plan into action. It was not, of course, necessary in the Shield match against Victoria on Boxing Day, when, after a careful start, he slaughtered the Victorian bowling to score 157 – completing his 10,000 runs in first-class cricket (in his 126th innings, against Ponsford's 161). But at least he had recovered his form, and was now ready for the second Test match, due to start at Melbourne two weeks later.

There was still, however, the matter of Bradman's dispute with the Board of Control over his journalism. Right up until the day before the start of the game, the Board insisted that he should not write, and Bradman insisted that in that case he would not play. The impasse was only broken when R.C. Packer, the editorial director of Associated Newspapers, offered, perhaps on the prompting of members of the Board, to release Bradman from his contract. That might have worked had Bradman not insisted on honouring it. He even made a counter-offer to Packer, to the effect that he should drop out of the Tests, write for a London newspaper and hand the fee over to Associated Newspapers.

At this stage it is difficult to believe that Bradman was not just being awkward. Admittedly, the Board had manoeuvred itself into a collective corner, and both the Board and Bradman were still smarting from the row over *Don Bradman's Book* two years earlier. Even so, at the age of twenty-four Bradman was proving not just intransigent, but impertinent to the governing body of Australian cricket. Of course, he knew, as did the Board, that he had the public and the press on his side, but his response was hardly a model of reason.

Bradman's hot temper still showed when the matter was finally settled. In the end, he accepted Packer's proposal and agreed to play in the Test matches, but immediately issued an angry statement. 'The Board of Control continues to prevent me from earning an honourable and permanent living from journalism . . . the difference between journalism and radio work is so small as to make any distinction appear ridiculous . . . their legislation means they are able to dictate to players the means whereby they shall earn their living . . . I must emphatically protest against the Board of Control being allowed to interfere with the permanent occupation of any player.'[17] It was hardly a message of peace and harmony.

But there it was; and Bradman turned up at the Melbourne Cricket Ground on 30 December 1932 to play in his first Test match against England since the triumphs of 1930. It was a blazingly hot day, and the Australians were delighted when Woodfull won the toss and decided to bat. Unexpectedly, when Woodfull posted up his team's batting order in the dressing room, Bradman's name came at no.4 rather than his usual no.3. O'Brien, who was down for no.3, was putting his pads on and saw Bradman, who had not looked at the list, also padding up. 'You don't seem to have much faith in me, Leo,' Bradman remarked. 'Well, I wouldn't say that, Don, not by any chalk.' Bradman went over to have a look at the batting list, came back, took his pads off and went out to watch the game. He 'never said a word, no,' O'Brien went on. 'He was sort of like that, Don: no comment.'[18]

Runs came very slowly against the England all-pace attack. Woodfull was bowled by Allen for 10, but Fingleton and O'Brien took the score to 67 before O'Brien was run out. It was two minutes to three in the afternoon when Bradman started his walk to the wicket to join Fingleton. Some 64,000 were watching him in the ground – further countless thousands listening to the radio or watching the big scoreboards that dotted the city centres – all willing their hero to success. As he passed Herbert Sutcliffe, Sutcliffe said to him: 'Wonderful reception, Don,' to which Bradman replied, 'Yes, Herbert, but will it be so good when I'm coming back?'[19]

As he came out of the shadow of the pavilion into the glaring sunshine, Bradman made a wide semi-circular approach to the wicket to accustom his eyes to the light. The crowd cheered every step, and continued to cheer as he took guard to Bowes. There was nothing to do but to wait for the noise to die down. Eventually, Bowes was able to start his run-up but, as he did, the cheering started again. Bradman moved away from his stumps and waited again for the noise to stop. Again Bowes started his run-up and was half-way to the bowling crease when the noise started afresh. Bradman again turned away, Bowes stopped, went back to his mark and, as he put it, 'for the sake of something to do' moved a fieldsman. Finally, Bowes was able to bowl Bradman his first ball. As it happened, it was a harmless enough delivery, a short ball – some would call it a rank long-hop – just outside the off stump. Bradman stepped outside the line of the ball and went to hook it. 'If the ball had bounced as high as he expected,' Bowes later said, 'it would have been going yet.'[20] As it was, the ball took the bottom edge of Bradman's bat and cannoned on to the base of his leg stump. Bradman had been bowled first ball.

'A hush fell on the ground,' Fingleton reported, 'an unbeliev-able hush of calamity, for men refused to believe what their eyes had seen.'[21] Bradman walked back, past Sutcliffe, in complete silence. It was then that Bowes noticed Jardine. 'Jardine, the sphinx, had forgotten himself for the one and only time in his cricketing life. In his sheer delight at this unexpected stroke of luck he had clasped both hands above his head and was jigging around like an Indian doing a war dance.'[22] As Bradman came into the Australian dressing room, O'Brien was coming out of the shower. 'What the devil happened to you?' O'Brien asked. 'I got bowled first ball,' Bradman replied.[23] No more was said; and, in truth, there was nothing more to say.

Fortunately for Australia, O'Reilly bowled to the top of his form and England ended their first innings 59 runs behind. Bradman went in again to bat at five minutes to one on the third morning, with Australia at 27 for 2. Another failure would have meant the certain loss of the Test – they would then be two down in the series. But this Bradman was quite different. Again the large crowd – this time of 68,000 – cheered him all the way to the wicket. But this time there was to be no wild swing at the first ball. 'It was as if he had slept upon his seven consecutive failures against the Englishmen and had decided that they were more than enough.' Fingleton went on: 'The stumps on this occasion were always behind his body or his bat, and he made a century, not like the old Bradman, for there was an absence of the spectacular; but a century rich in the honesty of purpose.'[24]

It was also rich in the new method of coping with the English pace attack. '[Bradman] ran to the off or out to leg to get away from those head-high whistling balls,' Walter Hammond later wrote, 'and he played golf shots and overhead lawn tennis shots, and from one after another the ball went crashing to the pickets . . . That was sheer courage . . . Those who said that Bradman was afraid of "bodyline" don't know cricket as it was played on that tour.'[25]

Bradman carried the Australian innings. The crowd were just preparing to celebrate his hundred when the ninth wicket fell, and to their dismay Bert Ironmonger came to the wicket. It was the same Ironmonger of whom the story was told that he was playing in a match when a woman rang up the pavilion and said: 'Oh, it's Mrs Ironmonger here. I'd like to speak to Bert, please.' The reply came back: 'I'm very sorry, Mrs Ironmonger, but he's just gone in to bat.' To this Mrs Ironmonger answered: 'That's all right. I'll hold on then.'[26] In view of Ironmonger's reputation, Bradman thought it wise to go to meet him as he made his way to the wicket. But Ironmonger was up to the task. Before Bradman could get in a word Ironmonger brushed him aside, saying: 'Don't worry, son, I won't let you down.' Nor did he. After taking guard, Ironmonger simply kept his bat firmly in the block hole. As luck would have it, Hammond, the English bowler at the time, bowled the last two balls of the over just outside the off stump, missing both bat and wicket by no more than a hair's breadth. Bradman completed his hundred, and the Australian lead was enough to allow O'Reilly and Ironmonger to bowl England out for an Australian victory by 111 runs.

The reaction to Bradman's century was one of desperate relief and unfettered hero-worship. As he returned – bare-headed – to the pavilion, the reception was ecstatic. Spectators, it was reported, overran the ground and used knives and pins to dig souvenir pieces of the Melbourne turf 'as though they were diamonds'. 'Women,' it was said, 'threw their arms around him and kissed him . . . later in the day a shilling fund was opened by the Melbourne Cricket Club committee for the purpose of presenting to Mrs Bradman a memento for her husband's remarkable performance.'[27] The memento, surprising as it may now seem, was to be a grand piano.

It was at this point that Bradman made his protest direct to the Australian Board of Control. He knew that the Board did not regard him as their favourite son. His statement was therefore released to the press – again, not, in the circumstances, a wise manoeuvre. 'On account of his great speed, Larwood' – there was no mention of Voce or Bowes – 'is able to pitch the ball short and make it fly rather dangerously . . . Only those who have played against bodyline bowling are capable of understanding its dangers. I do not know of one batsman who has played against fast bodyline bowling who is not of the opinion that it will kill cricket if allowed to continue.'[28]

The statement had no apparent effect. The Board, no doubt encouraged by the Lyons government in Canberra, wanted no disturbance with the mother country. Besides, it was rumoured that there was dissension even in the English team, about tactics which were more and more regarded as Jardine's own. Allen would have none of it, and had taken full advantage of his amateur status to quarrel with Jardine on the matter before the Melbourne Test. Bowes and Voce, on the other hand, said that Allen could not have bowled bodyline even if he had tried, such was his inaccuracy, and that he was just using the row to keep his own place in the Test side. Wyatt in later years said that he was inclined to agree with them, but at the time he wisely kept his own counsel.

Be all that as it may, the interval between the Melbourne Test and the next Test at Adelaide, due to begin a fortnight later, saw a steady crescendo in the volume of the debate. It is true that there were those in Australia – since the matter was discussed at length in most households, let alone on the streets and in the pubs – who thought that Bradman had found the answer to bodyline at Melbourne and had neutralised the threat. There were others, however, many of them unemployed, who recalled the almost contemptuous attitude of the Bank of England to Australia's economic plight, and the sacrifices which Australians had made in what became known as 'England's War' of 1914–18.

Indeed, war seemed now to be in the air. It was not war in the conventional sense, but it was war nonetheless, and the battle ground was to be none other than the peaceful and benign turf of the Adelaide Oval.

6

ONE – TWO – THREE

'WE PLAYERS DIDN'T REFER TO IT as "bodyline",' Bill O'Reilly said later. 'That was a term that was coined during the Test series, but we were referring to it long before the fracas really started in Adelaide. We were referring to it as the "scone theory". "Scone", of course, was the colloquialism used for your head; and one that bounced, we used to call it a "sconer" and, if you got hit, you said you were "sconed". We'd sit in the dressing room and a batsman would pick up his bat and you would say to him with all the tenderness, the sentimentality of a chap who was going to walk in and face up to something where you might never see him again. That was the feeling you had.'[1]

O'Reilly's sentiments, however syntactically inelegant, found their echo in the public mood. Even in Adelaide, that most sedate of cities, the Depression had brought violence. There had been a fierce street battle two years earlier between the police and a large crowd of unemployed who were protesting at a cut in their 'susso'. The South Australian government were so frightened that a state of revolution was upon them that they kept a heavy police presence on the wide Adelaide streets throughout the following months. The arrival of the English cricketers for the Third Test in the second week of January 1933 revived the government's sense of panic. If Australian batsmen were going to be bombarded by these terrors, they thought, the spectators would certainly riot. The morning of 13 January, therefore, saw the quietly picturesque Adelaide Oval under what can only be described as a police siege. Mounted officers lined up along the banks of the gentle river Torrens, which ambles along past the main entrance to the cricket ground, and groups of foot police, armed with batons, were at every gate.

The authorities' fears were far from ridiculous. The crowd of just over 30,000 – the full capacity of the Adelaide Oval at the time – arrived in a mood of mixed excitement and apprehension. There was excitement at the thought of the institutionalised violence which they were expecting to see, apprehension at the thought that the sufferers would be the Australian batsmen and, in particular, their hero Bradman.

The match got off to a quiet start on the Friday, England losing early wickets but then recovering to bat through the day. By the Saturday afternoon they were all out for 341. The crowd held its collective breath as Woodfull and Fingleton went out to face Larwood. Fingleton was quickly out to Allen, and Bradman came out of the pavilion, at his usual slow pace, and with his collar turned up – also as usual – to join his captain. But hardly had he settled down and played out the rest of the over when Woodfull, facing Larwood at the other end, was hit by a short and very fast ball which kicked unpleasantly into his chest. It was almost an exact repeat of the incident at Melbourne in mid-November: again, Larwood was the striker; and Woodfull, the Australian captain, the victim. Woodfull, now as then, dropped his bat and staggered away from the wicket, clutching his chest as though he had been shot.

This was what the crowd had been waiting for. There was an eruption of shouting and booing, and fists were waved in the air. But the situation might still have been saved, once an appropriate pause had intervened – and a proper amount of concern shown – to allow Woodfull to resume his innings in a calmer atmosphere. Jardine aggravated the problem by walking up to Larwood and saying in a loud voice, within Bradman's clear earshot, 'Well bowled, Harold,'[2] an obvious attempt to explain to Bradman that this was the treatment he could expect in his turn.

Even that, however, might have passed by. What really poured petrol on the smouldering fire was Jardine's decision, at the start of Larwood's next over, to stop him in the middle of his run-up for his first ball and to call the off-side field to move over to the leg, to form what was by then seen to be the classic leg trap. The implication of the move was clear, and was certainly not lost on the crowd. It was only Larwood's third over of the innings; the new ball was still moving in the air; it had up until then been an accepted principle that Larwood would bowl his natural out-swinger to an orthodox off-side field while the ball was still new. What Jardine was now doing was serving notice of his determination to finish Woodfull off by what were, on any analysis, intimidatory tactics. Furthermore, he knew, as did everybody else at the ground, that Bradman was at the other end. It was no longer a game. It was open physical and psychological warfare.

When Woodfull faced up to Larwood's next ball he was, understandably enough, 'as white as a sheet of paper'.[3] Equally unsurprisingly, the crowd barracked Larwood all the way up to the wicket. As it happened, the ball – another Larwood express – kicked again and knocked Woodfull's bat out of his hand. The noise from the crowd moved up several decibels in volume. The police thought that the pickets would be stormed, and moved in. An English fieldsman said to one of the umpires, George Hele: 'George, if they come over the fence, leave me a stump.'

'Not on your life,' replied George. 'I'll need all three myself.'[4]

It could hardly be said to be ideal circumstances in which to be batting at the other end, and it is little surprise that Bradman was badly rattled. A few uncomfortable overs followed before he was out in the manner which 'fast leg theory' had always planned: caught in the leg trap off a rising short pitched ball from Larwood, trying to fend it away from his body. McCabe followed in the same manner, and Australia ended the Saturday well behind in the match. The English tactics, however unpleasant they were, seemed to be working. Jardine was convinced that he had 'got the bastards on the run'.[5]

What turned a dispute about cricketing tactics into a major international incident occurred over the weekend of 14–15 January. After close of play on the Saturday evening, according to the eye-witness account of Leo O'Brien, the Australian twelfth man, Woodfull took a shower and, as he came out, 'towelling his hair', O'Brien asked him: 'How are you, Bill?' Woodfull replied: 'Leo, there's some awful things going on out there.' Just then O'Brien heard footsteps and turned round to see Warner and Palairet.

'Bill looked at them, and Warner said to Bill, "We called in to see how you are, Mr Woodfull," and Bill just looked. He said "Mr Warner," he said, "there are two teams out there on that field," he said, "and one is playing cricket and the other is not," he said. "That's all I have to say. Good afternoon." They turned on their heels and walked out.'

Leaving aside the syntax and the repetitions, there seems little doubt that O'Brien's account of the incident – of which there are many versions – is at least close to the truth. But more important is O'Brien's sequel. 'Within a minute or two I went and had another yarn with Bill; and . . . the only other person in the room was the old rubber-down, an elderly gentleman, and he was stone deaf – well, we know he was deaf – and so he couldn't have heard what was said. So I went out and told the boys. They said, "What happened, d'you know?" I told them. I said, "Only half a dozen words spoken and that's that."'[6]

The story broke in Sydney on the Sunday evening and was on the front page of every paper in Australia on the Monday morning. As O'Brien said later: 'They've been trying to find out ever since who spilt the beans.'[7] Most at the time believed it was Fingleton, who was, after all, a professional journalist, and Warner was said to have offered a sovereign to anyone who took Fingleton's wicket cheaply in the second innings. Fingleton in turn claimed that the leak came from Bradman, and later elaborated the story by relating a secret meeting which had taken place between Bradman and the Sydney sportswriter Claude Corbett. Bradman always denied Fingleton's allegations, asserting his belief that '[Fingleton] leaked the story and he was blaming me as a smokescreen for himself.'[8] The only other evidence comes from O'Brien: 'Someone was seen talking to a Sydney journalist, who printed or forwarded the information.' In itself, this seems to support Fingleton, but O'Brien was himself an Irish Catholic like Fingleton, and would tend to support his friend and colleague, particularly since both he and Fingleton were speaking years after the event and in the light of the continuing distrust between Bradman and the Irish Catholic cricketers which marked the later 1930s.

Whatever the truth of the matter, the outcome was explosive.

When play resumed on the Monday morning, the Adelaide crowd was in a cantankerous mood. The future Prime Minister Robert Menzies recalled sitting with another spectator who, on the Saturday, had been 'quietly-spoken, cultured and most interesting' – up until the Woodfull incident. On the Monday the same spectator was 'a changed person. He was on his feet and his face was choleric. He shouted, he raved and he flung imprecations at Larwood and Jardine . . .'⁹ Matters got much worse when Oldfield, the Australian wicket-keeper, tried to hook Larwood and was hit on the head. On any dispassionate analysis, of course, the ball was perfectly legitimate and was bowled to an off-side field; Oldfield simply played a bad shot. But this was not a moment for dispassionate analysis. The crowd again burst into rowdy temper, and there was another near riot as Woodfull marched out of the pavilion, walking determinedly and angrily upright, and strode to the place where Oldfield had fallen to help him back – and, as it turned out, to hospital.

Matters had by then been made worse by a press statement from Warner to the effect that 'Mr Woodfull has expressed regret for Saturday's incident to Messrs Warner and Palairet. The incident is now closed and we are now the best of friends.' In the event, and under the new circumstances of Oldfield's injury, Woodfull's riposte was understandably brutal. 'I did not apologise to Mr Warner for any statement I made. I merely told him that there was not anything personal between himself and myself. I strongly repudiate any suggestion that I tendered any apology to Mr Warner for any statement I made.'¹⁰ So there it was.

By now the point of no return had been passed, and a new set of characters came on stage. The members of the Australian Board of Control who were in Adelaide – only five out of fifteen of them, in fact, were there – decided to contact the Chairman in Melbourne with a view to sending a protest to the MCC in London. A cable was duly drafted and approved by the Chairman, subject to the agreement by other members of the Board. There was a hurried consultation by telegram to members in various parts of the country – the text of the proposed cable, by an absurd oversight, was not included in the telegrams, which simply contained a request to authorise the despatch of a protest to London – and a slim majority agreed.

Several things went wrong. For a start, the text of the cable was, by any reasonable standards, exceptionally maladroit. It said that 'bodyline' – and by implication those who sponsored it – was 'unsportsmanlike'. As Bradman later said, 'I was not surprised at the English reaction to the thing.'[11] Then there was the matter of the press. The Board released the text immediately to Reuters, who wired it express to their London office, while sending the cable themselves by ordinary rate. It was therefore published in the London press before it arrived at the MCC. Lastly, the Board had completely misread the mood of the English. Their victories in Australia were a matter for celebration; Jardine and Larwood were heroes. When Oldfield was hit, for instance, Movietone News pointed out that 'Larwood was again the unlucky bowler.'[12] There were only three correspondents – all from evening papers – covering the tour; the dailies relied on Reuters. Newsreels arrived in England several days after the event. The English public were not bothered with the details, even if they had been available. Celebration was in the air.

Of course, had the Board acted earlier in the tour, when Bradman had suggested it, and when the series was even at one match each, things might have been different. From Adelaide, however, where Australia showed every sign of losing the match, it sounded to the English suspiciously like whining. Bradman himself thought that they had acted 'a little unwisely'.[13]

As it happened the game ended reasonably quietly. In their last innings Australia needed 532 to win and never came within sight of the target. Bradman made a hectic 66, stepping back to leg to hit Larwood and Voce through the off side, before being caught and bowled by Verity; but Australia duly lost by 338 runs. Jardine's speech afterwards was typical of the man: 'What I have got to say is not worth listening to. Those of you who had seats got your money's worth and then some. Thank you.' Woodfull was more diplomatic: 'This great Empire game of ours teaches us to hope in defeat and congratulate the winners if they pull off the victory. I want you to remember that it is not the individual but the team that wins the match.'[14] As a piece of verbal fencing, it could hardly have been surpassed.

The Board's cable was considered by the Main Committee of the MCC when it finally arrived in London. The Committee was of quite a different social composition to the Australian Board of Control. It was headed by the Viscount Lewisham, elder son of the 6th Earl of Dartmouth, educated at Eton and Christ Church, Oxford, former Conservative Member of Parliament for West Bromwich. Although he listed his recreations as fishing, shooting and golf, he became, apparently without effort and without much interest in cricket, President of the MCC. He was also Lord Great Chamberlain of England and, consequently, a personage of influence at Buckingham Palace. Nobody could have represented more accurately the *mores* of the MCC in the early 1930s. Furthermore, there were on his Committee members of equal, or nearly equal, social distinction – half a dozen peers, the Lord Mayor of London, the Speaker of the House of Commons and an ex-Governor of Bengal.

The reaction of this Committee to the Board's cable was one of deep affront. Englishmen, it was said, were being accused – by mere colonials at that – of behaving in an 'unsportsmanlike' manner. Besides, the cable had mentioned 'bodyline' as the main source of complaint, and nobody on the Committee had any clear perception of what this meant. Furthermore, the Board seemed to be suggesting that the MCC should disown the tactics of their own appointee, a public-school boy of impeccable credentials, just because Australia had gone 2–1 down in the series. It was all too much. The Committee's view was conveniently reinforced – if reinforcement was needed – by the English press, which had gone on the rampage. 'Undignified snivelling,' said the *Daily Herald*. 'Cheapest possible insult,' said the *Star*. 'It is unthinkable,' thundered *The Times*, that an English captain would permit a form of bowling attack 'which was not cricket'.[15]

Thus fortified, it is hardly surprising that the MCC Committee accepted, almost without discussion, an uncompromising riposte – drafted, it is said, by Lord Lewisham himself, with the assistance of his colleague Sir Kynaston Studd. 'We deplore your cable,' it announced. 'We deprecate your opinion,' it went on, 'that there has been unsportsmanlike play. We have fullest confidence in captain, team and managers . . .' And so it continued. But it was in the last paragraph that the MCC delivered what was tantamount to a nuclear strike. 'If,' they said loftily, '[the situation] is such as to jeopardise the good relations between English and Australian cricketers and you consider it desirable to cancel remainder of programme we would consent, but with great reluctance.'[16]

Lewisham was no fool. He knew perfectly well that, in the hard times of the Depression, no Australian Board, whatever the provocation, would forego the financial benefits, not just to cricketers but to the whole Australian economy, of an England tour – particularly one which had aroused such controversy, amounting, on both sides, to something near to blood lust. To that extent, Lewisham had trumped the Board's ace. Although they were anxious to pursue the controversy, the Australian press realised that there was not much to cling on to, and contented themselves with seizing on the press release made by the English players expressing loyalty to their captain 'under whose leadership they hope to achieve an honourable victory'. Knowing of Allen's dissent, they produced the mocking headline OH WE'RE ALL SO HAPPY TOGETHER.

But it did not really work, and in the three-week interval between the Adelaide Test and the Fourth Test in Brisbane, the main issue was the serious one of whether the remainder of the tour would or would not be cancelled. There were some diversions, such as the letter from a distinguished judge to the Sydney *Morning Herald* claiming that any bowler injuring a batsman could be liable for prosecution for grievous bodily harm. There were also some inconsequential tour matches, not least against New South Wales in Sydney when, although Bradman turned out managing only 1 and 71 neither Jardine, Larwood nor Voce played, and the whole thing was regarded as something of an irrelevant sideshow.

There was doubt, right up until the last moment, whether the Fourth Test at Brisbane would take place at all. The night before the match was due to start Jardine told Larwood that he was not at all certain there would be a game. (Larwood replied: 'That's good then.'[17]) The reason for Jardine's doubts was quite clear. The whole dispute had left the bounds of cricket and become a matter of high politics. On 30 January the Australian Board of Control, sitting now in the calm of their Sydney boardroom rather than in the heated excitement of the Adelaide Test, had sent a mollifying cable back to the MCC. Although it did not retreat from the position that 'bodyline bowling' was '. . . opposed to the spirit of cricket and unnecessarily dangerous to the players',[18] it did draw back, as Lewisham had expected, from cancelling the rest of the tour.

At this point the Governor of South Australia, Sir Alexander Hore-Ruthven, intervened. It was all perfectly natural. Hore-Ruthven came from the same stable, as it were, as Lewisham, and the two men knew each other, not least because both were members of the MCC. Hore-Ruthven had managed to avoid getting embroiled in the disputes over the Depression – being conveniently unobtainable when the big 'susso' riots occurred – but he had also been on leave during the Adelaide Test. It was during that Test that he had been contacted by three prominent South Australians, including the editor of the *Adelaide Advertiser*, and told that he was faced with nothing less than a serious political crisis. The hostility towards Britain in the press and in the street, even among the greatest Anglophiles, was borne in on him with force. As a result, the Australian case was put by him in London with greater authority, and with a good deal more subtlety, than had been apparent in the Australian Board's cables.

The machinery of the British Dominions Office was then cranked into action. J.H. Thomas, the Secretary for the Dominions in the National Government of the day, summoned a delegation from the MCC to a meeting at the Dominions Office on 1 February with himself and Sir Thomas Inskip, the Attorney-General. As a result a further soothing cable was sent by the MCC the following day, 'noting with pleasure' the lifting of the threat to cancel the remainder of the tour. The MCC, however, still insisted on raising the matter of the original allegation of 'unsportsmanlike' behaviour. 'May we accept this,' their cable went on, 'as a clear indication that the good sportmanship of our team is not in question?'[19]

By now the waters had been muddied by the English cricketers themselves. Unless the allegation of unsportsmanlike conduct were withdrawn, they said, they would not play. They would simply down tools. This, of course, was a much more serious threat than any conveyed in an exchange of communications between the game's governing bodies. If the cricketers would not play cricket, then no cricket would be played. It was as simple as that. Now in a state approaching despair, Warner got hold of E.T. Crutchley, the head of the British Mission in Canberra, and pleaded with him to use what influence he had with Joseph Lyons, the Australian Prime Minister, to get him to ensure that the necessary retraction was produced. Similar messages were coming to Lyons from London, and it was even said that there was a telephone conversation between Lyons and the British Prime Minister himself, Ramsay MacDonald. London was leaning heavily on Canberra. There could only be one result: Canberra leaned equally heavily on Sydney and on 8 February the Board of Control sent its last cable of the series. 'We do not regard,' it said handsomely, 'the sportsmanship of your team as being in question.'[20] The MCC had won the battle. The Brisbane Test started on schedule – on 10 February 1933.

As it turned out, the match was played in a much friendlier spirit than the previous three. It almost became a game again. There was tacit acceptance that Jardine would persist with 'bodyline' tactics, but the wicket was benign, the weather was hot and sultry and Voce was unable to play; the tactics were very much less effective than they had been in Adelaide. Besides, the Australian batsmen had started to work out answers to the English attack, ranging from body-padding — including cork heart-protectors – to different techniques of batting (including ducking). Bradman, of course, had his own answer – stepping to leg and hitting to off which he employed to great effect on the first day, ending the evening on 71 not out – out of an Australian total of 251 for 3. There had been some hooting at Larwood but, as the press reported, 'the demonstrations were mild'.[21]

The following morning Bradman was soon out, drawing away to leg to cut a ball from Larwood which kept lower than he expected and hit his leg stump. He was out in the second innings to the same shot, again drawing away to Larwood and hitting hard and high to a deep cover-point – the only fieldsman on the off side. But by now there was some muttering about his style of play. Although he made strokes which, in Kippax's words, 'no other living batsman could have made' there were those – not least the veteran Australian captain Warwick Armstrong – who thought that he showed 'unmistakable signs of fright when facing every ball from Larwood'. Armstrong went on to write that Bradman's last shot in the first innings was 'shockingly bad' and that he had not steeled himself to play 'the right type of innings for his side'.[22] Woodfull and the other members of the team, it was said, were 'very dissatisfied' with his tactics. After Australia had lost the match, and with it the Ashes, there was even talk of dropping Bradman from the side altogether, although it is doubtful whether this went much beyond dressing-room gossip.

The Fifth Test at Sydney saw no let-up in the English tactics, even though the Ashes had been safely won. Warner had asked Jardine to abandon 'bodyline' for at least this match as a gesture of good will, but Jardine refused. 'We've got the bastards down there,' he said, 'and we'll keep them there.'[23]

Voce was fit again, but by now Larwood, who had been the spearhead of the attack throughout the tour, was desperately tired and having trouble with his feet. In Australia's first innings a number of batsmen were hit, particularly McCabe, but the Sydney crowd were surprisingly muted in their protest. There was more hooting when Bradman himself was hit painfully by Larwood on the upper arm – the first time he had been hit in the whole series – but at least it seemed that the Australians were getting the measure of the English bowling in scoring 435 (Bradman himself being out for 48, bowled by Larwood trying to glance him down the leg side). England just managed to do slightly better, scoring 454 thanks to a century from Hammond and a surprising 98 from – of all people – Larwood. It was a sign of the lowered tension, as well as of the generosity of the Sydney crowd, that they gave Larwood a standing ovation on his return to the pavilion – applauding the very man who had until so very recently occupied such a prominent place in their demonology.

In the second innings, Bradman carried his tactics to their most thrilling point, pulling away and cutting to the off from well

outside the leg stump, and eventually forcing Jardine to switch
fieldsmen back to the off side – to the cheers of the Sydney
crowd. It looked as though Bradman was finally winning the
battle, particularly when Larwood, after bowling only ten overs,
broke down in the middle of the eleventh. He asked Jardine if
he could go off. Jardine not only refused to let him go while
Bradman was still in, but insisted that he field at cover-point, a
position which requires great mobility – but is also in full view
of the batsman. Jardine was determined that Bradman should be
aware that the main threat was still there – and able to bowl again
(which was untrue in practice, since Larwood had broken a bone
in his foot – but Bradman was not to know that). When Bradman
was finally out to Verity, for a brilliant if hectic 71, Larwood was
at last allowed by Jardine to leave the field.

England won the Test match, in the end quite comfortably
by eight wickets. The tour dribbled to its unhappy conclusion;
when the English players set sail from Sydney (without the
crippled Larwood) for the last few, meaningless games in New
Zealand, not one Australian cricketer turned up to see them off.
On the other hand, when they finally arrived back in England,
they were greeted as conquering heroes. English nationalism had
re-asserted itself. When Jardine appeared at Lord's in the early
match of the 1933 season against the West Indies, he was given
a standing ovation.

When Jardine, Larwood (now almost completely recovered)
and Voce appeared at the Trent Bridge ground for a ceremonial
presentation, the compliments were flying in all directions and
the crowd was both large and ecstatic. The bands were playing
and the crowd numbered in thousands. Larwood – hitching up
his trousers with embarrassment as he came to the microphone,
and then reading from a script claimed that Jardine was 'a
magnificent captain, a great sportsman and a true friend'[24]
(although the two had had some ferocious rows during the tour).
Everybody agreed and cheered as Jardine presented Larwood
and Voce with a cheque representing, as he said, 'tangible
appreciation' of their achievement in Australia. The applause
was thunderous, and, without doubt, quite genuine. Arthur
Carr had his own malevolent comment to make – revealing

yet again the class antagonisms which lay deep below the whole controversy: 'I know plenty of professionals,' he wrote, 'whom I would delight to have as guests in my own home, but I am afraid I cannot say the same thing about most of the Australians whom I have met.'[25]

The truth is that the gap in perception between the English and the Australians of the nature of the dispute was now so wide as to be virtually unbridgeable. To the English, the combination of Jardine's intellectual brilliance and Larwood's fierce skill had overcome the menace of Bradman and won for England an Ashes series for only the second time since the First World War. The subtext was, of course, that they had put the whining colonials in their proper place. To the Australians, on the other hand, the English had used tactics which were not just contrary to the spirit of the game but also wholly unethical. The subtext here was equally uncompromising: the imperial masters had shown themselves to be cheats.

In the long run the Australians were to have the better of the argument, and for a very simple reason. The problem with the bodyline attack, as O'Reilly later pointed out, was that 'if it was permitted in Test cricket, then it would be used in all forms of cricket: Saturday afternoons and concrete pitches with coir mats . . . and the casualties would be enormous.'[26] On the softer English pitches, of course, the problem would not be nearly so great, since it required bowlers of the pace and accuracy of Larwood to make it work. On the harder Australian pitches, let alone concrete wickets, almost any bowler of reasonable pace could make the ball fly dangerously.

In practice, Jardine's tactics achieved their immediate aim – and the immediate aim was all that Jardine was worried about. Bradman had had an uncomfortable tour. He may well have scored 396 runs in four Tests at an average of 56.57, a record which any other batsman of the time, or any modern batsman, would have considered a triumph. (Indeed, it was Jardine, in *his* moment of triumph, who said to a commentator: 'You know, we nearly didn't do it. The little man was bloody good.'[27]) But his unorthodox counter–attack had provoked the criticism that he was only playing for himself – a criticism that has perhaps some truth in it. In an article about Bradman's answer to 'bodyline', Moyes wrote that at the start he 'was howled down in every city' – something of an exaggeration – '. . . was accused of flinching from fast bowlers . . . in [the] face of it all he carried on and triumphed'[28] – again, something of an exaggeration. He was also under continual nervous strain, being forever in the public eye (and the public were never slow to stop him in the street and engage him in debate) and forever conscious of what was expected of him. He said later that he had leaned heavily on Jessie for support. She accompanied him everywhere, sat through the Test matches, and was always ready with an encouraging word. 'If it had not been for her,' he went on, 'I could not have played in a single Test match that season.'[29]

At this point, there were in Don Bradman's life two separate but related problems. The first was the resolution, if that was possible, of the dispute between England and Australia over the matter of 'bodyline'. If there was no resolution, Bradman's future career as a cricketer would be stunted if not brought to a complete halt, since he knew, as did the rest of Australia and the world, that while he was still in the game the same tactics would be used against him wherever he went. The second problem was to decide the pattern of his future life. He was, after all, a married man, with all the responsibilities which the conventional morality of the day and his strict family unbringing laid on him. There was a duty to maintain his wife and, in the future, their children. Certainly, he had long held the belief that he would at some stage have to escape from the prison of cricket; but there was the question of how it could be done, which alternative, if indeed there was any, he should work at and, not least, how he could explain to his adoring public, who continued to pester him on every occasion, that he was no longer prepared to continue as their chosen icon.

As for the resolution of the 'bodyline' controversy, it was no easy matter. Firm stands of principle had been taken – admittedly not always wisely and sometimes in the heat of very difficult moments. For either side to retreat would be seen, rightly, as a climb-down and would bring with it great loss of face. All authorities like to avoid loss of face, but in this case the two authorities in question, the MCC and the Australian Board of Control, had reached heights of pomposity which made their ability to compromise even more doubtful.

Yet unless a solution was reached, it was not just the future of Anglo-Australian cricket which was in doubt – the Australians were already threatening not to send a touring side in 1934. The political tensions within the British Empire, aggravated as they had been by the Depression and the arrogant behaviour of the Bank of England and some of the imperial Governors-General, were in danger of snapping – to the point, some said, of rupture.

In the event, the dispute between the mother country and its troublesome dominion was settled during the autumn of 1933. It was a difficult and tortuous process. The MCC were in no mood to admit anything which could be construed as guilt, while the Australian Board were not prepared to send players to England unless there were bankable assurances that they would not be subjected to what they considered as unfair play. There was a bad-tempered – and fruitless – exchange of cables between the two authorities, culminating in the MCC's missive on 12 June 1933 to the effect that the Committee 'have no reason to give special attention to "leg theory" as practised by fast bowlers'. It was hardly a helpful contribution to the debate, although, to be fair, it certainly reflected the opinions both of the cricket establishment and of the now vehemently anti-Australian English press.

But at this point a fresh actor appeared on stage: no less than Viscount Hailsham, the newly-elected President of the MCC. His was a powerful new presence. Hailsham was, after all, Secretary of State for War and Leader of the House of Lords. If ever there was a man with authority to settle the matter, Hailsham was he. Furthermore, although his relations with the Prime Minister were distant, he was on very good terms with his Cabinet colleague 'Jimmy' Thomas, in spite of their opposing political views. The way was now open for a carefully crafted solution.

Even so, it took a summer of discontent before the English were ready to settle. Two West Indian bowlers, Constantine and Martindale, both very fast, adopted similar 'bodyline' tactics against England in 1933. Furthermore, in a county match in June at Trent Bridge, Leicestershire used the same tactics against, of all people, Arthur Carr, prompting him, in cricket history's greatest *volte-face*, to condemn 'head-high bowling' and to go on to say that 'somebody is going to get killed if this sort of bowling continues . . .'[30]

When it came, the English surrender was complete. The capitulation came in the MCC's cable of 9 October 1933. '[The MCC Committee] agree,' they announced solemnly, 'and have always agreed that a form of bowling which is obviously a direct attack by the bowler upon the batsman would be an offence against the spirit of the game.'[31] By December the capitulation was confirmed in a second cable, which assured the sceptical Australian Board that their October cable had meant what it said. But, as in any surrender, there were casualties. Jardine, selected as England's captain for the winter tour of India, announced that he never wished to play against the Australians again. Larwood was asked by the Nottinghamshire chairman to sign a letter apologising for the way he had bowled in Australia on the 1932–33 tour. Faced with this request, Larwood, deeply affronted, reluctantly agreed to take the letter and show it to his father and mother. When she saw the draft, his mother pushed her spectacles down to the bottom of her nose and said: 'Harold, if you sign this you will never see me alive again.'[32] Harold, it need hardly be said, did not sign – and never played for England again. Lord Hailsham, on the other hand, is reported as having 'rather preened himself' on achieving a settlement.[33] The way was clear for the Australian tour of England in 1934 – and the political dust settled.

While all this was in progress, Bradman himself was struggling with the second problem. His three-way contract in Sydney was due to expire in February 1934; and although the unemployment rate had started to turn down, the prospects were still grim. He was offered an extension to his contract by the Sydney *Sun*, but this would have locked him into cricket – and Sydney – for the rest of his career. At the age of twenty-five, it was not a prospect he looked forward to with any pleasure.

Fortunately there was no tour during the Australian winter of

1933. It was a welcome break from cricket, not least because it allowed time for the Bradmans to be together at their house on McMahon's Point without having to pack every other day for another cricket match. Besides, Don was starting to have trouble with his back. Not only that, but he had to go back to his dentist to have a number of teeth taken out, and he was suffering from recurring headaches and sporadic pains in his lower stomach; all of which made him more than usually tetchy.

But he did his work conscientiously for his employers and, after three months' study, surprised everybody by taking, and passing 'with great credit', the New South Wales Cricket Umpires' Association 'Examination on the Laws of Cricket' in early August. It was not, as he himself pointed out, that he wanted to stand as an umpire. It was simply that, with characteristic thoroughness, he wished to be fully familiar with the laws of the game so as to make sure that he never lost his wicket, as many have before and since, through ignorance of the laws.

The 1933–34 season came and went. In spite of his uncertain health, Bradman's performance was spectacular. In the Sheffield Shield season – shortened because of the need to send a team off to England in early 1934 – he averaged 184.40 over seven innings, including two double centuries against Queensland and two centuries against Victoria. It was as though, now free from 'bodyline', Bradman was starting to enjoy his cricket again. The press returned to its former lyrical tone. 'He is not the purposeful plodder,' wrote an admirer about one of Bradman's innings against Queensland, 'but rather the gay cavalier, his bat a banner waving in the air as he ventures forth to run a course with the unhappy bowler.'[34] That was one of the more restrained press comments.

Yet there remained for Don and Jessie the decision about where their future lay. Almost providentially, an answer presented itself in the form of an Adelaide stockbroker by the name of Henry Warburton Hodgetts. Hodgetts was, in some ways, an odd figure. In appearance he was not much different to many South Australians of his day, or, indeed, of today: square-jawed, greying hair parted down the middle, large ears and nose, and a thick neck which gave the impression of resolution and honesty.

He was also a jovial enough fellow, and cut something of a dash in the generally somnolent Adelaide society. On a closer view, the alignment of his eyes was rather strange – the right slightly lower than the left and half-closed in face-to-face conversation – and to the suspicious might have led to doubts about his motives. At all events, he was a single-minded supporter of South Australian cricket; indeed, as a member of the Australian Board of Control he had been one of the authors of their hasty cable to the MCC after the Adelaide Test of January 1933. He also had a nose for business; even business, as it later turned out, that led to trouble. One thing, however, he did know: if Bradman could be lured to Adelaide, it would be good for Hodgetts' business; and what was good for Hodgetts' business was good for Henry Warburton Hodgetts.

Hodgetts' offer to Bradman was simple. It was a six-year contract at £700 a year, reducing to £500 when Bradman was playing overseas, to take the young cricketer into his firm and teach him the profession of stockbroking. He would be allowed time off to play for an Adelaide club, Kensington District, for South Australia and, of course, for Australia herself.

The offer was difficult to resist. Nevertheless, acceptance meant virtual exile from the life in which both he and Jessie had been brought up. They were rooted in the suburbs and near-suburbs of Sydney; their friends were there, and it was only a short distance from Sydney to their joint homeland in the Bowral/Mittagong district of New South Wales. Although Sydney itself was a rough place in those Depression years – there were still sporadic riots over 'susso' and the persisting unemployment – the cricketing public had remained faithful; whenever he played at Sydney Cricket Ground, or even with his new club of North Sydney, attendances were markedly above the average. It was difficult to leave.

The discussion in the Bradman household was intense. Jessie was doubtful. A move meant leaving family and friends. The gap between Sydney and Adelaide was more than one of geography or, indeed, culture; it was the equivalent today of moving from one continent to another. Don was more positive, pointing out that this would mean security in their still uncertain world. In the event, in Bradman's own words, 'my wife behaved as a dutiful wife, supporting me as she always has'.[35] At the end of the long discussion, the deed was done. On 14 February 1934 Don Bradman formally informed the New South Wales Cricket Association that he was taking up residence in South Australia. The Association replied, equally formally, on the 20th, regretting his decision but wishing him 'success in his new sphere of life'.[36] Reflecting on the loss of attendance at Sydney Cricket Ground, the treasurer of the Association, it is said, burst into tears.

7

IN HEALTH AND IN SICKNESS

T HE ENTRY OF THE BRADMANS INTO Adelaide can hardly be described as triumphal. Indeed, it might almost be said that they slipped in by the back door. The reason for this is not hard to see. Had they arrived at Adelaide railway station in the open light of day in their true names they would have been mobbed by an adoring crowd. In his current mood that was the last thing that Don wanted; nor was Jessie any more enthusiastic. Thus it was that in late February 1934 the pair travelled from the Bradman home in Bowral, where they had been taking a few days' holiday, first by car to Goulburn and then on by train to Mount Lofty in the Adelaide Hills – under the pseudonyms of 'Mr and Mrs Lindsay' – and from there were taken by car to Hodgetts' home in the suburb of Kensington.

It was to be a quick visit. The Australian cricket team to tour England in 1934 had already been announced shortly before, and Bradman was the surprise choice for vice-captain – at the age of twenty-five. The South Australians were, of course, delighted, and wished to celebrate in an appropriately riotous manner. But this was not on Bradman's agenda. Of much greater interest was that he had to establish residence in the State as quickly as possible, to allow him to play in the Sheffield Shield games of the following season, 1934–35. Regulations had it that even though he was away in England the time spent on tour would count as 'residence' in South Australia. It was important to put in the necessary appearance in Adelaide – and perhaps more important to sign a six-year contract with Hodgetts before minds could be changed.

It was not an easy time for either Don or Jessie. Added to the difficulties of leaving their home State for a strange and distant environment, there was the further problem of another seven months' estrangement when Don left for England. Jessie obviously could not, or would not, set up home in Adelaide by herself, and was due to return to her parents' home in Mittagong while Don was away playing cricket. Furthermore, Bradman's health was again causing both of them concern. He had been quite obviously affected by the whole 'bodyline' affair. Not only did he appear to others to have developed 'a slightly different outlook on the game'[1] but both physically and psychologically he was very run down. He suffered from 'continual headaches day and night'; he was very 'lackadaisical' and 'didn't know what was the matter'.[2] Indeed, even after he had been selected for the 1934 tour and had passed examination by the Board of Control's doctors, Bradman himself felt that his state of health was so bad that he was simply not fit to go.

In any case, the tour was not going to be easy. The row over 'bodyline' between the two countries was simmering down, but nobody knew what sort of reception the Australians would receive when they finally arrived in England and had to play in front of English crowds. There were, of course, reassuring noises coming from the MCC: the Earl of Wemyss had promised the Millions Club in Sydney in January that 'you need not be nervous about the reception your team will get in England. It will get a heartier welcome than any team ever received and need have no fear of a smashing [from] bodyline bowling.'[3] Lord Hailsham, too, sent encouraging messages. But the MCC could not control the English crowds – or, indeed, the Nottinghamshire Cricket Club, where tempers still ran high.

Bradman's own problems were compounded by his appointment as vice-captain of the Australian team. It was certainly a great honour, but it had been achieved at the expense of Kippax, a player of great distinction who was coming to the end of his career and who had been Bradman's captain in New South Wales – the State which Bradman at that time was just leaving (or, as some would say, abandoning). Furthermore, Fingleton had been left out of the side. Since his omission followed an article written by Bradman for the Sydney *Sun*, complaining about Fingleton's running between the wickets, and since Bradman had openly said that he thought W.A. Brown would make a better batsman on

English wickets, it was naturally assumed, at least by Fingleton, that Bradman should carry the blame. There was perhaps a small degree of truth in this; Bradman himself later admitted that 'my opinion might have had some bearing on it' and that 'this, of course, was why Fingleton conducted this vendetta against me'.[4] Fingleton wrote a furious letter to Woodfull, a selector for the first time, claiming 'I am sure that you are not only wrong but inconsistent, for you have chosen chaps who obviously do not like fast bowling . . .'[5] The implication was clear.

All in all, it is reasonable to suppose that Bradman would have preferred to settle down in Adelaide and to learn his new business of stockbroking – and, incidentally, spend the months with Jessie setting up home and making new friends – to sailing across the world towards a tour of uncertain temper, with the extra burden of the vice-captaincy on him, in doubtful health mentally and physically, and with the loyalty of his colleagues yet to be tested. In fact, in spite of the verdict of the Board of Control doctors, he took the unusual step of asking Hodgetts to arrange a further opinion from a leading Adelaide doctor. The opinion, when it came, was hardly a model of decision. Doctor Hone, apparently a physician of great distinction, was unable to find anything wrong with the young man. All he could say was that Bradman was 'very run down'; and he ordered a complete rest from cricket until the team's arrival in England.[6] The recommendation was accepted – meekly enough – by the Board of Control. At all costs they had to keep Bradman on the tour.

The upshot was that the Australian team, from various parts of the continent, went off to play the usual warm-up games in Tasmania, came back to the mainland for the long overland train journey to Perth, and played their last match on Australian soil – all without their vice-captain. Bradman, on the other hand, duly seen off by the affectionate Jessie, sailed in the *Orford* – again – round to Fremantle, where team and vice-captain finally met up. What his team-mates thought of this procedure has not been recorded, but their reaction could certainly not have been one of undiluted pleasure.

Bradman was, as usual, seasick on the leg from Fremantle to Colombo, and on arrival looked to a journalist from the London

Daily Express, who had known Bradman in 1930, 'tired and much older than his years'. The journalist was 'genuinely astonished'.[7] Word, of course, filtered back to England, where the press were now openly speaking of Bradman's ill-health; and from there to Australia, and to Mittagong and to Jessie Bradman. She, of course, had no immediate means of verifying the stories and could do no more than wait in patience. In fact, the stories were largely true. Such was Bradman's depression when the *Orford* reached Colombo that he was unwilling to go ashore at all, let alone play in or watch a cricket match. So low did he feel that, in an effort to cheer him up, Dr Roland Pope, who acted as self-appointed medical adviser to the players, persuaded him to come ashore and have a drink. It was the first time Bradman had tasted the stuff, and he was not much impressed. Certainly it did not seem, from all accounts, to have lifted the gloom. As so frequently happens, however, once the *Orford* reached calmer seas, and Bradman was able to engage again in defeating his colleagues at deck tennis, his health improved; and so did his morale. The Australian Davis Cup team were also on board, and there was a good deal of light relief – although the vice-captain still distanced himself from the more robust parties. Fortunately, the Davis Cup players did not compete in the deck tennis tournament, but their manager did – and was just able to prevent Bradman repeating his triumph of 1930.

It is hard to resist the conclusion that this journey was much less happy for Bradman than the same journey in 1930. There are no breathless diaries; no first sight of Suez or Naples Bay; no camel rides in Egypt; indeed, there was to be no grand European tour. Instead of following some of his colleagues who went overland, Bradman stayed on the *Orford* all the way to England. There was, of course, lunch at Government House at Gibraltar, when Bradman announced to the assembled journalists: 'After this long rest I am a different man . . . I am feeling as fit as ever.'[8] But that was more for consumption in Australia than an assertion of reality. In fact, the weather turned very unpleasant in the Bay of Biscay and seasickness overtook him again. Altogether the voyage seems one of wearily attempted convalescence than of excited exploration.

There were, undoubtedly, serious problems with Bradman's physical health. Nevertheless, it seems clear that at least part of his psychological problem of those days – and there is little doubt that there *was* a psychological problem (one of his friends has drawn attention to the suicide rate among cricketers of that era, and in doing so expressed the thought that the Bradman of 1934 could have joined the longish list) – arose from the change in the nature of cricket which 'bodyline' had wrought. Before 1932–33 it had been a game. Admittedly it had been a game which was fiercely played, but there is no harm in that – as long as all the participants recognise that it is a game and not an extension of war. Even after the dreadful batterings suffered by the English batsmen from Gregory and Macdonald in 1921, there was no suggestion of direct personal malice.

Jardine had, in 1932–33, introduced a note – indeed a whole theme – of direct personal malice into what had hitherto been a game; and that malice had been focused on Bradman. Furthermore, the 'bodyline' tactic would possibly never have emerged had not Bradman overrun the English bowlers in 1930. The result was twofold: first, that Bradman himself, and because of him his colleagues, found themselves subjected to direct and frightening physical attack, the like of which they had never seen before; second, that Don Bradman, who, as a 'country boy' had always believed in the Empire and the honour of England (he had, after all, met the King and Queen), had now to come to terms with the knowledge that the English were not as honourable as they had seemed, and that Gallipoli – to use the symbol yet again – might all have been a con-trick.

By the time the *Orford* reached Southampton on 25 April 1934 – Anzac Day, as it happened – everybody had made a great effort to persuade the world that normality had returned. The effort was helped by the sun, which broke through the lowering cloud as the ship approached the quay. The players lined the deck; the Mayor of Southampton went on board, accompanied by Sir Russell Bencraft (representing the MCC) who 'briefly and cheerfully'[9] welcomed the visiting team in the ship's lounge. While the gangway was being lowered the vice-captain, D.G. Bradman, so it was reported, 'entertained the team in the music room at the piano, playing popular tunes to which the cricketers sang'.[10] It was all very jolly. But a different note was struck by Bradman later. 'When I got to England,' he confessed, 'I was still no better.'[11]

There followed the usual ritual events. Immediately on arrival at Waterloo Station from Southampton, Woodfull and Bradman drove to the Cenotaph in Whitehall to lay a wreath. Attendance at the FA Cup Final was also obligatory – the crowd being invited to sing 'for they are jolly good fellows', which they did with something less than total enthusiasm. Lord Hailsham went out of his way, amid all the cares of state, to make them feel welcome. After all, he had brokered the deal which had got them there in the first place, and it was no less (and no more) than his duty to follow up the successful negotiation – although his interest in cricket was only 'keen but sporadic'.[12] There were, as well, the customary receptions and shows of imperial solidarity. All in all it was a reasonable attempt to show that 'bodyline' had never happened.

But, of course, it had; and the Australian cricketers were in doubt about how to respond to the – somewhat affected – jollity which they encountered on their arrival in England. They had been carefully prepared for the event. On no account, they were told, should they speak to the press about the unpleasant incidents of 1932–33 or about any difficulties which might occur during the tour. In fact, they were informed, it would be better if they did not speak to the press at all. It is hardly surprising that they were soon dubbed by the English cricketing journalists 'the silent sixteen'. Bradman was quite happy with this position. He had come to the view – as have many others in all walks of life – that unless he could speak to the press on his own terms it was better not to speak at all. What was never mentioned, for example, was the number of abusive and threatening letters he received early on in the tour, many of which threatened violence and at least some of which bore a Nottingham postmark.

The first match at Worcester set a pattern for the rest of the tour. Bradman told Woodfull that he did not feel up to playing and that he would prefer to sit the match out. Woodfull's response was uncompromising. 'Now if you do that,' he replied, 'it'll only add colour to what is being said in the English press. They are saying that you are a sick man and that you won't be a force on this tour. And so psychologically I want you to play in this match and I want you to do well; that is to undercut what the press are saying.'[13] It was plain that what was being played was the first move in the elaborate game of psychological chess. Bradman was the Australian match-winner; it was no good going into the opening moves without your Queen. Woodfull being Woodfull, it was said in the nicest and most gentlemanly way; but the message was clear.

'When Bradman emerged from the pavilion,' a local Worcester paper wrote, 'the excitement was terrific; he might have been the Loch Ness monster. Even the refreshment bars were temporarily deserted.'[14] Bradman went in after Ponsford was out at 29 for 1, and after Worcestershire had been bowled out – mainly by Grimmett – for 112. It was just before tea on the first day. By close of play he was 112 not out, and on the following day gave his wicket away for 206, scored in under three and a half hours at the crease – in other words, at a run a minute. The bowler to whom he gave his wicket, Howorth, one of Worcestershire's most successful left-arm spinners, ended the innings with an analysis of 4 for 135; G.W. Brook likewise ended with 1 for 114. Bradman had cut and hooked them to pieces. The performance – for that was what it was – attracted more than a hundred journalists and some fifty photographers. Nobody had seen anything like it since Bradman in 1930.

'It took a very heavy toll on me,' Bradman said later about his innings at Worcester. But, as if that was not enough, Woodfull asked him to captain the side in the next match against Leicestershire. 'And that,' continued Bradman, 'was the start of the downward slide for me on that tour, because I was very sick and I felt very exhausted and yet I couldn't tell what was the matter with me.'[15]

At Leicester Bradman made a fitful 65. By comparison with his double century at Worcester – and by Bradman standards – it was a poor effort. He seemed to have lost his appetite for runs, but nobody, least of all he himself, could understand why. All batsmen have lean periods, but Bradman was so far in front of his contemporaries that nobody imagined it could possibly happen to him.

In the three weeks after the Leicester match he made what in a Bradman context can only be described as the pitiful total of 42 runs. There was no particular pattern; sometimes he was out through carelessness; at other times through over-ambition. What was clear, however, was that – for one reason or another – he had lost that power of concentration, almost of dedication, which had up to then made him so difficult to get out after the first few overs, and then so difficult to contain. It was only when the Australians arrived at Lord's to play Middlesex at the end of May that there was any relief from what Bradman himself called his 'slump'.[16] His innings there of 160 has often been described as one of the most brilliant ever seen on a cricket field. 'Well,' wrote C.B. Fry the following day, 'we have seen an historic innings. We'll talk about it for years.'[17] 'It was supreme; it was epic,' echoed William Pollock. 'All the shots were his, the whole field his kingdom.'[18] Bradman's version is – characteristically – more prosaic: 'I felt unwell . . . so I decided, well, this is an occasion where one of us has got to win and I decided that I would attack; and I did and it just simply came off.'[19] Indeed it did; and the crowd, like C.B. Fry, were enthralled. But Bradman, setting himself as always the highest standards, regarded it as no more than 'an oasis at that time on the tour'.[20]

This hectic brilliance was repeated in both the first and second Test matches. In the first, at Nottingham in miserable weather, it was taken almost to the point of irresponsibility. When Bradman went in with Australia at 88 for 2 just before lunch on the first day, Bill Brown was at the other end.

'Ken Farnes was the bowler . . . and about . . . I think it was the first or second ball . . . was a half-volley about the leg stump; and Don took an almighty swing. If he had hit it he'd have hit it for six clean out of the ground, but he missed it and it just missed the leg stump; and he looked at me and gave a broad grin as if to say "Well, you know that's the way I play the game these days."'[21] Bradman was out for 29 in as many minutes after hitting six fours – on the first day of his first Test match as Australia's vice-captain. The critics started to mutter. But his second innings was little better: 21 in the half-hour before tea and a further 4 afterwards; and then – out. Fortunately, thanks to McCabe and Chipperfield's batting and Grimmett and O'Reilly's bowling, Australia won the game quite easily. But the Sydney *Referee* reported that 'some critics say [Bradman] is sacrificing accuracy for showmanship'.[22]

The Second Test at Lord's saw almost a repetition of the First. England batted first, and, thanks to centuries from Leyland and Ames, made 440. Bradman went in at 68 for 1 on the Saturday evening. Again his innings was spectacular, an innings as one commentator said 'of terrible power and splendour'.[23] He hit Farnes for 14 in one over, and then 'took to Hedley Verity like I have never seen anyone taken to before . . . He played absolutely brilliant cricket.'[24] But this brilliance had caused unease in the Australian dressing room. Woodfull sent out a message begging his vice-captain to cool it a bit. It was, after all, a Test match. Bradman promptly jumped out to drive Verity, remembered Woodfull's instruction, stopped his shot and spooned an easy catch back to the bowler. (Bradman never changed his view that it was really Woodfull who got him out.)

There was heavy rain over the weekend, with a drying sun on the Monday morning. The wicket was perfect for a finger-spin bowler, and Verity took full advantage of it. He finished off the Australian innings with 7 for 61, and when they followed on took 8 for 43. Fourteen of those wickets fell in one day. Bradman was one of the victims, out to the classic left-arm slow bowler's trap – on a turning wicket, with no outfield, tempting the batsman to try to hit him back over his head. Bradman fell for it but only succeeded in hitting the ball off the top edge high into the air. Almost anybody could have caught it, but it was the man with the gloves, the wicket-keeper Ames, who quite rightly claimed the catch as his. 'Critics,' it was said, 'shook their heads as Bradman departed.'[25]

'I was not well,' Bradman later said. 'I didn't feel I had the stamina to play a big innings, my mental outlook on the game was wrong . . .'[26] When King George V went on to the field to meet the players, the best he could do, on shaking hands with Bradman, was to comment on the strength of Bradman's hand muscles.

By the end of June Bradman had made only 760 runs, compared with 1,000 before the end of May in 1930. At the end of twenty innings he was averaging less than 50. But things went from bad to worse. A throat infection swept through the Australian team in early July – known as 'Wimbledon throat', since it was believed that they had caught it on a visit to Wimbledon. The symptoms were very unpleasant: a combination of biliousness, headache, high temperature and a painful throat. Some thought that it was diphtheria. For a time it looked as if the Australians would have difficulty in putting out a team for the Third Test at Manchester on 6 July. In the event a team was mustered, but once England had won the toss and had started to amass a large score – in blazing heat – Bradman and Chipperfield, both of whom had been well the previous evening, had to leave the field. It was straight to bed for the rest of that day and all of the next. By the Monday morning Bradman was feeling a little better, and at half-past three in the afternoon went out to bat – at number six rather than his usual number three. 'It was unfortunately all too obvious,' one press report said, 'that he is an ill man. His cheeks are very drawn and never before have I seen him look so thin. The smile that for so long has been planted on his face was completely absent.'[27] His innings only lasted an hour, and had none of the fiery recklessness of Nottingham or Lord's. He went tamely, as indeed did the match, since once the Australians had saved the follow-on, thanks to a century from McCabe and a tail-end 30 from O'Reilly, there was nothing left to play for other than a draw.

At this point several stories were circulating about Bradman's health. He was, it was said, 'a wraith of the greatness we once knew'[28]; he was suffering from pernicious anaemia (again); he was about to visit a heart specialist; he was in the middle of a nervous breakdown. He was also reported to be anxious for Jessie to join him on the grounds that he needed 'special nursing and care'.[29] Inevitably these stories found their way to Mittagong. A story, almost certainly apocryphal, ran that Jessie sent an anxious cable of inquiry. Don cabled in reply that she must not believe any such reports, and that if she waited until the next Test match at Leeds he would 'show them'.

The reply came back immediately: 'Go to it, Don; I believe in you.'[30]

Whatever the truth of the story, at that point the tide seemed to turn. Going in against Yorkshire on Monday 16 July Bradman took time to score his first 50; but then, in the words of Bill Bowes, 'all of a sudden he seemed to go off like a firework. He cut and drove all round the wicket and in twenty-five minutes he'd put on another 50 runs ... This was the old Bradman back with us, in the twinkling of an eye, almost.'[31] He added another 40 in twenty minutes before throwing his wicket away. In terms of technique, the press thought his innings 'one of the greatest exhibitions of his career' (*The Times*) or, alternatively, 'one of the most magnificent and spectacular innings ever played at Sheffield' (*Daily Mail*).[32] It was certainly a good augury for the following week's Test at Leeds. Cricketing Australia – as well as Jessie Bradman – was in good heart again.

The Fourth Test opened on 20 July. The series was level at one-all; the Headingley ground carried happy memories for Bradman; and Bradman himself 'after failing in the other Tests ... was very anxious to make amends'.[33] England won the toss, chose to bat and on the first day limped to a total of 200. Before the close of play, however, Bowes took three Australian wickets without conceding a run. The day ended with the match evenly balanced – and with Bradman about to come in. That evening he declined an invitation to dinner from Neville Cardus, explaining that he had to make 'at least 200 tomorrow'. Cardus pointed out that according to the law of averages Bradman had no chance of getting anywhere near 200. The answer was abrupt: 'I do not believe in the law of averages.'[34]

As it turned out, Bradman was right, and cricket was about to see one of his greatest innings. He started flamboyantly, hitting Bowes' first two deliveries off the back foot past the bowler for four. It is one of the most difficult shots in cricket; Bowes had taken three wickets and was bowling with pace and skill; and Bradman was fresh to the crease. By normal standards Bradman's start was outrageous. But 'I knew he had got me'[35] Bowes admitted later; and indeed he had. The innings continued more sedately, building steadily rather than attempting the pyrotechnics

131

of the last few months. But sobriety brought its reward. Ponsford, too, was on his best form, finally treading on his wicket just before close of play for 181. The partnership had lasted nearly all day; together they had put on no fewer than 388 runs. Bradman went on to make 271 by the time play finished and a further 33 in fifty minutes on the following morning.

It was the first time the two great Australian batsmen – the solid run-getter of the 1920s and the fierce youth of the 1930s – had ever shared a major partnership. The old superlatives were dusted down by the press and brought out again. The Ponsford–Bradman partnership was described as 'a double concerto of classical cricket woven [sic] like a superb counterpoint in the texture of Australia's innings'. Bradman's own innings had 'the vitality of brain, blood and nerve; every part of it throbbed with a consciousness that was of the spirit'. It was 'a creative innings which took its shape hour by hour according to the will of a cricketer playing for Australia'. Bradman, himself, was 'the champion of champions . . . a text-book of batting come to life with never a mis-print or an erratum'.[36]

The hero himself was more modest. He described his innings as 'a very severe strain indeed'.[37] But it is no less than the truth. He had been unimpressed when the whole Australian team had gathered round him after his first day's innings with a bottle or two and a toast 'to Don'.

'I am listening to one toast,' he replied – rather dismissively, perhaps – 'and that is "to victory".'[38] His colleagues had been put in their place. But he needed them when he was out for 304, since he was unable to field with his usual agility and fell badly, tearing a muscle in his right thigh. McCabe and others ran up to help him limp off the field, obviously in great pain. There was no question of him taking further part in the match, which, fortunately for England, was washed out soon afterwards.

Bradman's injury was serious enough to put him out of cricket for a month. But at least he had re-established his position as Australia's hero. Indeed, Jessie told him as much on the radio telephone while his injury was mending – like others she had been listening to the commentaries coming over the airwaves and, also, like many others, had been gathering the opinions

132

of the Australian press and public about her husband and his performance. Apart from that, there was nothing for it but to rest, listen to the popular music of the day and wait for fitness and the Fifth Test – due to start on 18 August at the Oval.

Bradman's fitness for the Test was a matter of doubt right until the last minute. He had had, after all, to spend some days in hospital with his leg in plaster, and there had been talk of more serious problems during his convalescence. He had even been taken in hand by no less a figure than Sir Douglas Shields, a consulting surgeon from Melbourne University who had migrated to London and founded a private hospital at the lower – and opulent – end of Park Lane. Shields not only insisted on treating Bradman personally, but also offered the hospitality of his country home in Berkshire while the injury healed. His house was part of a sizeable estate, around which Bradman was fond of walking. The experience revealed an unexpected trait in Bradman's character. 'Just at the back of [Shields'] charming home,' he later wrote, 'was a small natural wood. I delighted in walking through there each morning – to see the squirrels and birds in a setting which had remained unchanged for centuries. Nothing in this world has ever appealed to me more than England as nature made her.'[39] The determined and concentrated hero was suddenly shown to be a romantic at heart – and an Anglophile to boot.

Of course, Bradman's injury was not without its repercussions. For a start, none of his colleagues saw their vice-captain for three weeks (apart from the occasional visit) during what was a particularly difficult stage of the tour, with Woodfull out of form and even talking of dropping himself from the Test side. It was not a particularly happy period for team spirit. Then there was a resurgence of rumours about Bradman's general state of health. Anaemia was mentioned yet again; and even Bradman admitted to 'sudden spells of lassitude and loss of energy'.[40]

Nevertheless, when the day came for the final and decisive Test at the Oval on 18 August he was ready. Australia batted first and, in what was almost a repeat performance of their partnership at Leeds, Bradman and Ponsford put on an even larger score – this time 451 runs for the second wicket. It was a world record, and still remains the Test record for Australia for any wicket. By the time they were out, Ponsford had made 266 and Bradman 244. Australia's total of 701 was far too much for England and, although the follow-on was not enforced, a further 327 in Australia's second innings – Bradman making 77 before being bowled by Bowes – ensured an easy victory and the recapture of the Ashes.

By now Bradman appeared to be back to his form of 1930. His success in the last two Test matches seemed to have lifted the cloud of depression. He was no more gregarious with his colleagues – or anybody else for that matter – than he had been, but at least he had emerged from what had seemed to be a long night of gloom. By way of demonstration he went on to complete the 1934 tour with two dazzling displays: 149 not out against an England XI at Folkestone, and 132 at the Scarborough Festival – in ninety minutes before lunch (Bradman thought it 'the most exciting innings I ever played in England'[41]). By the time the Australian team arrived back in London in the third week of September he could look back on a tour which had in many ways been unhappy, but which had at the end proved to be a triumph of will-power over mental and physical frailty. His standing as Australia's hero had been reasserted. Furthermore, he had overcome the self-doubt that seemed to have been with him since the 'bodyline' assault. But so far was only so good. He was not to know – nor indeed was anybody else – that within a few days he would be in the shadow of an early death.

ON SATURDAY 22 SEPTEMBER the Australian team, in the Langham Hotel in Portland Place, were preparing for the ritual farewells and the long voyage home. At about 4:30 P.M. a guest arrived to see Bradman – a former Bowral school friend who had come to London to make a career as a concert singer. The talk over tea, as might be expected, was all of Bowral and the old days. But, even during the conversation, Bradman started to feel pains in his lower stomach. By the time his guest left, he was so ill that he told Woodfull he simply did not feel up to going to the dinner which had been arranged for the evening. With that, he went up to his room to rest.

It was no good pretending that this was just another minor ailment. Woodfull was by now badly worried, and asked an English surgeon, John Lee, who happened to be dining with the Australians that night, to go and have a look at the vice-captain. Lee went upstairs to examine Bradman. As it turned out, although the patient – for that was what he had now become – was in acute pain, there was no easy diagnosis. In other words, and not to put too fine a point on it, Dr Lee was baffled.

Bradman had a bad and painful night. Nothing was getting any better, and by the time Lee came back to see him on the following morning he was still in obvious distress. But there was still no clear indication of what was causing the distress – let alone how it should be dealt with. At that point, Lee decided he needed time for reflection, undisturbed by other matters which demanded his attention. His solution to this problem was to jump into his motor car and drive off. Unlike today, of course, the car was one place where the driver could be free from the attentions of the outside world. Fortunately for Lee, since it could hardly be said that his full concentration was given to his driving, it was a Sunday and the streets of London, and indeed the roads of Berkshire – where he apparently went – were free from traffic.

In modern terms, it seems an odd way to arrive at a diagnosis, particularly since the patient was by then back on his feet and had resumed his packing for the journey back to Australia – still suffering from a steady, and now increasing, abdominal pain. Indeed, Lee's odyssey revealed no further clarity, other than that the symptoms were those of appendicitis. By the Monday morning the situation was such that Lee felt it necessary to seek a second opinion – not, it might be said, before time. Sir Douglas Shields was called in, and in the afternoon Bradman was taken by ambulance to Shields' hospital in Park Lane. The diagnosis was now clear – acute appendicitis. Within the hour, Bradman was on the operating table under general anaesthetic – unprepared, in those days. He was operated on immediately.

When Bradman's abdomen was opened, it was quickly discovered that the medical condition was serious. It was so serious, indeed, that Bradman himself wrote later, with poetic and perhaps somewhat portentous solemnity, that 'there can be no doubt that for some time I hovered on the brink of eternity'.[42] It was discovered that the appendix had not only become infected but was not in its normal position. It was found deep in the pelvis. Furthermore, it had become acutely inflamed and had adhered to the neighbouring bowel.

Surgically, this posed a problem: how to remove the appendix without collateral damage to the intestine and to the peritoneum – the layer of tissue which lines the abdominal cavity. At first, it seemed as though the surgeons' efforts had overcome the problem. The infected appendix was taken out and the intestine left intact. But by the evening of the following day it was clear that all was not well. Bradman had lost a great deal of blood, although the reason for this is still not entirely clear; his temperature refused to go down; and, although the original incision had been sewn up satisfactorily, he was in inordinate internal pain. It seemed that the worst had happened, and that peritonitis, infection of the peritoneum, had set in. In most circumstances of those times, when penicillin and sulphonamides were at best in an experimental stage, the condition was usually fatal. At 8 P.M. on the Tuesday evening the Park Lane hospital issued a bulletin. Bradman was struggling for his life.

The effect of the announcement was little short of spectacular. The press immediately assumed that Bradman was either dying or, indeed, dead. Neville Cardus was cabled by the editor of the *Manchester Guardian*, while on a cruise at sea, with instructions to write an obituary without delay, as were other journalists less far afield. The King, while not wishing to disturb a shooting holiday at Balmoral, sent messages of sympathy and asked to be kept informed. There were daily reports in the newspapers. When it became known that Bradman had lost a great deal of blood during the operation and that the hospital was planning to replace the lost blood by the – then new – technique of transfusion, many donors came forward. The Park Lane hospital was unable to cope with the number of calls enquiring after Bradman's health, and closed its switchboard. Even government ministers were refused permission to see him.

By now the news had reached Jessie Bradman in Mittagong. In the circumstances, there was only one thing for her to do. Bradman had sent a cable just before his operation urging her to come to England. It was an imperative: she had to go to her husband as soon as possible. She replied immediately by cable: 'It's all right, Don, I'm coming.'[43] With the help of the Sydney *Sun*, arrangements were made with the greatest despatch: to travel by rail across the continent, to catch the Peninsular and Orient liner *Maloja* at Fremantle. From Naples, she was to take the overland route through Italy and France, and the sea crossing from Calais to Dover. It was no more than coincidence that that was the route which Don had taken in the heady days of 1930.

When she reached Melbourne, she was told that Don had died. Nothing could have been more depressing, and for moments she felt that there was no point in continuing her frantic journey. Fortunately, the radio telephone was still working – which was a piece of sporadic good luck – and a call to London told her that he was still holding his own. So on and on she went across Australia. At Perth Railway Station she was met and rushed to Fremantle where the *Maloja* was waiting. The sailing was delayed for her, and she climbed aboard. It had all been hectic and unplanned. 'My luggage was in an awful muddle,' she later recalled. 'I had neither heart nor time to think about picking frocks.'[44] But by then at least she had received news that Don had survived and was – gradually – on the mend.

It had taken Bradman three days to overcome the crisis. Indeed, Lee said that Bradman might not have come through but for Jessie's cable, which 'meant a great deal to the patient at a critical stage'.[45] By 29 September, the hospital's bulletin was optimistic. Their man had pulled through. But there was to be no immediate release. It was not until three days before Jessie's arrival at Dover, on 27 October, that Don was allowed out of the Park Lane hospital; and then he was told to take six months' rest – and play no more cricket for twelve months. By the time husband and wife finally met, it was clear that they would have more time to spend together than they had had so far during their whole married life.

That was no bad thing, and the couple took full advantage of it in a way that they had been unable to do in the 'honeymoon' cricket tour of North America immediately after their wedding. They were entertained, too, wherever they went. Bradman's illness had somehow converted him from an Australian hero to an Empire hero. A car and a chauffeur were put at their disposal by a group of English well-wishers; hotels were only too happy to have them as their guests; Bradman was able to show his wife 'some of the beauties of England'.[46] They stayed with the Duke of Portland at Welbeck Abbey in Nottinghamshire, drove to Scotland, visiting Edinburgh and staying with the Bell family (of the eponymous whisky – which Bradman did not touch) in Perth, before reversing their tracks and going down to Devon. On return to London, they were taken on a guided tour of the capital by a Cabinet Minister, and on their departure from Victoria Station they met Winston Churchill. All in all, it was not a bad trip for a country boy from Bowral.

From there it was to Switzerland, to Christmas on the French Riviera and then ship from Toulon – again on the *Otranto* – on 22 January 1935 to head for home. By now, Don was well restored from his illness and able to enjoy himself. He knew that no permanent damage had been done and that he would be able to resume his cricket in due course. Nor was his other – budding – career in danger. The Hodgetts contract had held firm in spite of Bradman's prolonged absence from the stockbroking business in Adelaide, and would be waiting for him on his return. Furthermore, the Bradman name had retained its particular magic, and his revenues from sponsoring sporting equipment – not least the Sykes cricket bats – could now be described as comfortable.

All in all, the barometer for the two Bradmans in early 1935 could be said to stand at 'Fair'. True, Don still had to learn his new business, and they still had to make their home in Adelaide. But these were minor problems; indeed, they were to be mitigated by the new sense of optimism that was running through Australia as the Depression started to run its course. Unemployment had been falling slowly but consistently for nearly two years, and at least some confidence was beginning to return to business. 'Everything good-oh' was perhaps on the way back.

Nevertheless, doubts still remain – to this day – about the

real state of Bradman's health at the time. The received view was that he had been suffering from an unidentified malaise for nearly two years, which was attributable to the latent appendicitis and which reached its crisis in September 1934. Modern medical opinion would find it difficult to sustain this view. Indeed, there are a number of reasons why it cannot be sustained. Appendicitis is an inflammatory, infective condition; it blows up when it blows up. It is clinically quite unlike, for instance, many cancers, which may be slow growing, and consequently debilitating, over long periods. Furthermore, there is no evidence that appendicitis – or, indeed, peritonitis – would have as after-effects a deterioration in eyesight. Yet Bradman found his eyes 'troublesome', and 'for a brief period . . . had to resort to glasses'.[47] Finally, the 'headaches' and 'lassitude' about which Bradman complained in 1933 and 1934 are not usually associated, at least in current medical experience, with a condition, however grave, of the appendix.

It seems reasonable to suppose that Bradman's illness of September 1934, severe and life-threatening as it was, was only one of a number of similar and related events that were to mark his cricketing career. Indeed, it is notable that after retiring from cricket Bradman enjoyed generally robust health. The reasons for what is by any standards a complex phenomenon are perhaps to be found in Bradman's own character. Determination and concentration, such as Bradman applied when batting, leave their after-effects: psychosomatic ill-health may well be one of them. If that is so, then the picture of Bradman so far put forward – as one who plumbed the depths of ill-health in 1934, to recover thereafter until muscular problems attacked him some years later – now has to change. The picture becomes one of a Bradman whose psychology was so dedicated to the work in hand that it continually neglected his own physique. If that in turn is the case, Bradman becomes in one medium, like Mozart in another, a genius whose unique ability imposed an intolerable strain on his body.

8

'FINGLETON WAS THE RING-LEADER'

O N 25 APRIL 1935, ALMOST A year to the day after his arrival in England for the 1934 tour, Don and Jessie Bradman finally arrived to take up permanent residence in South Australia. The intervening year had been a long – and at times painful – pilgrimage; but it had not been without its benefits, not least, in its later stage, in providing shelter for Bradman from the constant and blinding light of publicity. On Don's return from England, he and Jessie had spent a further three months at Jessie's father's farm in Mittagong. As it turned out, for them, as for their two families, it had been a particularly happy time. It was not just a matter of being among relations and friends. Nor was it even the freedom from the stress of the previous few years, welcome though that was. What had mattered most was the space which the young couple could now enjoy to think about themselves, their future in Adelaide and, no doubt, the question of whether and when to start a family.

At a different and more public level, there were questions about Don's future, in particular whether he would ever be fit enough to play Shield or Test cricket again. He had, after all, been forced to miss the 1934–35 domestic season in Australia. Although his golf was certainly improving and he was playing tennis again, this was hardly the point. The press were interested in his cricket future and – reasonably enough – unable to restrain speculation about his motivation to re-enter the arena, in other words to resume a full national and international cricketing career. In truth, there were grounds for such speculation; Bradman seems at times to have thought that enough was enough, and that it might be right to concentrate wholly on his new career as a stockbroker. The fear of poverty and the sense of responsibility to his wife were competing in his mind with his ambition – and the knowledge of his own ability – as a cricketer. It was a delicate balance. In the end, the uncertainties were cleared up. But such had been the speculation that Bradman felt obliged to issue a statement to the press denying that he was considering retirement. The statement was accepted for what it was, but there is little doubt that retirement had not been rejected without a good deal of thought.

It was probably the move to South Australia that made the thought of returning to first-class and Test cricket more palatable. Admittedly, the Bradmans were not moving to the centre of the city or to an up-country retreat. They were moving, as it were, from suburb to suburb, and to that extent from one suburban culture to another. Nevertheless, the whole social atmosphere of South Australia was quite different to that of New South Wales. Adelaide was, after all, the home of the 'wowser' – the teetotal puritan; its *mores* were predominantly those of the German Lutheran and English Nonconformist traditions, even if the religion of the upper class was the Church of England of the 1662 Book of Common Prayer. As such, it was monarchist, Protestant, and deeply disapproving of the 'convict' city of Sydney and the Irish Catholic disloyalty of Melbourne. In that sense, it was familiar territory for the boy from Bowral and the girl from Mittagong.

When they arrived, Don and Jessie rented a house in Holden Street in the suburb of Kensington Park. It was a pleasant enough house – something, in fact, of a colonial villa – in the low hills a few miles away from the city centre. The street was not of any particular distinction in itself, but it was to assume a special importance, since they set about buying a plot of land and building a house in the same street, this time to their own specifications, which was to be their home for the rest of their lives. Bradman had also to set about learning his new job. He appears to have taken to it easily. True, Adelaide was not a major Stock Exchange to rival Sydney or Melbourne, let alone London or New York, and there were no great fortunes to be made; but there was enough business in Government Bonds and shares in some of the smaller firms which were locally based for a broker to make a reasonable living. Bradman was prepared to work hard, and his previous job as an estate agent had given him a good feel for figures. He had a sharp and questioning mind, and was never afraid to pursue points he was unsure of or to challenge unproved assumptions. Given his character, it is not surprising that he was a success at business; nor was it a requirement to be an active Freemason, as it had been in Sydney, and he was able to slip into inactive membership. Furthermore, he had used his year of convalescence to his intellectual profit – reading a great deal, particularly books on history or travel. Not, however, that it was all drudgery; he was, after all, a young man. Although he very rarely had a drink – an occasional glass of sherry, but mostly nothing stronger than ginger beer – and never smoked, he enjoyed dancing and was fond of playing on the piano what, in the language of the day, was called 'honky-tonk'.

Nevertheless, the outer skin which he had developed in the rough world of Sydney and cricket never left him in the more relaxed world of Adelaide and stockbroking. 'He decided,' said an acquaintance, 'to remain encased in a shell that any oyster would have envied. With Don it was a case of so far and no further . . .' And yet the same acquaintance saw two young men one evening in Adelaide, 'obviously completely sober . . . joking to each other and roaring with unrestrained laughter'. To his amazement one of the young men proved to be Bradman. 'Bradman,' he thought to himself, 'with someone he trusted, and out of the public eye, could clearly be as friendly and unreserved as anyone could wish.'[1] It was a perceptive thought, and as a summary of Don's character at the time it can hardly be faulted.

Of course, one of the disadvantages of the move to Adelaide, as yet unperceived, was precisely the reverse side of that particular coin: his further detachment from the more cosmopolitan society of Sydney. Where Sydney was kaleidoscopic, Adelaide was monochrome. The more the Bradmans became embedded in South Australian provincialism – which even led at times to talk of secession from the Australian Commonwealth – the more distant to them became the cultural clashes which enlivened the big city. In particular, it was easy to forget the religious sectarianism that was so much a part of the cities of the east. If there was one serious consequence of the distance that Bradman had put between him and the east it was this, since, as it happened, religious sectarianism was to become a major element in the personal disputes and wrangles which plagued Australian cricket in the second half of the decade.

It was not until September 1935, a full year after his last match at Scarborough, that Bradman was ready to appear again on a cricket field. Much had happened in the meantime. He had ruled himself out of selection for the tour of South Africa in 1935–36 on the grounds that his health was still too fragile to stand up to a long and demanding tour. Vic Richardson, the then captain of South Australia, was chosen to lead the Australian touring side. This being so, it was natural – particularly since Richardson was coming to the end of his career and Bradman had been Australia's vice-captain on the 1934 tour – that Bradman should be appointed in Richardson's place as captain of South Australia for the 1935–36 Sheffield Shield matches. Natural, however, it might have been, but the South Australians understandably needed a little time to adapt themselves to the newcomer, and the transition was not without difficulty.

After a few games for Kensington to get himself back into trim, Bradman took the field in a first-class match on 8 November 1935. By an odd coincidence, the opponents were English – an informal MCC XI which had stopped off in Adelaide on their way to New Zealand. Needless to say, the cricketing world was agog to see how Bradman would perform. His march to the wicket, when it came, was reported as 'the signal for a great outburst of enthusiasm from the crowd, and hand-clapping from the Englishmen'.[2] But, in cricketing terms, it was not a happy occasion. One cover drive for four, a straight drive for three and then a ferocious hook for four all promised well. But he was quite obviously badly out of practice against bowlers above club level, and his timing of the ball was uncharacteristically awry. In neither innings, apart from those three strokes, did he even resemble the Bradman of old, twice being out lbw (a very unusual form of dismissal for a Bradman on form).

It was not until the Sheffield Shield matches started in earnest that Bradman began to show that he had lost none of his former ability. Indeed, once he had assumed the captaincy of South Australia, and conscious of the responsibilities that entailed, he had spent as much time coaching the young side as he had on his own batting. Batsmen were told to refrain from over-ambition; bowlers were instructed to concentrate on line and length and not to 'give away runs with rubbish'[3]; and the fielding was sharpened up. Further, it was noted by the *Sporting Globe* that Bradman had a 'wonderful cricketing brain'.[4] Indeed, such was the enthusiasm generated by the new captain that people even started to talk as though South Australia, under Bradman's leadership, might win the Shield itself.

Bradman being Bradman, however, he was far from neglecting his own preparation. He trained himself to field as well as he had always done, and practised for hours on end to bring his batting back up to what he regarded as its proper standard. It was hard work, naturally, but Bradman never was one to shy away from that. The rewards soon came. In the first Shield match of the season, against New South Wales at Adelaide just before Christmas, he made his first century for his new State, and South Australia won by an innings. In the second Shield match, against Queensland, again at Adelaide, just after Christmas, he made 233; and, again, South Australia won by an innings – and 226 runs. In the third Shield match, against Victoria at Melbourne, he made 357 in seven hours and one minute. There followed something of a pause: South Australia beat Queensland at Brisbane, but this time Bradman made no more than 31. Then there was a drawn match against New South Wales at Sydney – in which Bradman was out for nought – the match being abandoned because of the news, on 20 January 1936, of the death of King George V; and a further personal failure at Adelaide against Victoria – out for 1 – but a further victory for South Australia. Finally, in the last match of the season, against Tasmania at Adelaide at the end of February, Bradman completed his season with a typical flourish: 369 in only four hours and thirteen minutes. South Australia won by an innings and 349 runs.

Bradman's batting average for the Shield matches had been 130.33. It had been an astonishing comeback, as well as a triumph for South Australia – hitherto always an outsider – to win the

Shield. Bradman himself had made several points clear beyond doubt: his health was recovered; his form was beyond question; his concentration was as complete as it had ever been; and, as a captain, he was possessed of one of the most acute cricketing brains, both in terms of strategic planning and of immediate tactical perception, that Australia had seen.

There were, of course, the snipers. The cream of Australian bowling, it was said, was away in South Africa; Bradman had had a free run. Besides, the critics went on, if Bradman was in such marvellous health and form, why had he not agreed to go to South Africa with the others? In truth, there were several possible answers to the carping. The first, and easiest, was to assert that medical advice was against his going on the South African tour. This was true, but would not by itself answer the argument about Bradman's form in the concurrent domestic season. The second, and more difficult answer – but perhaps nearer the truth – was to claim that he needed a period of rest from the stress of international cricket if his ability to play long innings for Australia in a Test match was to be restored without his health breaking down again. The third, and even more difficult answer – but perhaps even nearer to the truth – was to state quite frankly and without any equivocation that he was sick and tired of the constant aggravation which seemed to accompany him just because he was good at cricket; that he wanted to enjoy the game which he loved without the pressure; that he wanted to spend time with the wife whom he loved in a home which, like millions of people throughout the world, he was building; that he wanted to get on with his job and make himself enough money to remove for ever the country boy's fear of poverty; and, finally, he wanted to be who he was and not some figment of journalistic imagination.

Whatever the truth, there is little doubt that Bradman's refusal to go to South Africa led him into one of the happiest periods of his young life. In his mid–twenties, after a precocious youth and an uncertain adolescence, he had achieved something of a balance of personality. That this was so was in no small measure due to Jessie. She was, of course, immensely supportive; but, more than that, she was not afraid of Don – or of his incandescent talent.

145

She would always support him, but equally would tell him – with some firmness – where she thought he was wrong, and in what particular; and she had the confidence to do this since she knew how much Don depended on her – not least to help him with the angularities in his own personality, of which, at this time, he was only dimly aware.

The winter of 1936 was one – give or take the odd domestic dispute and the usual problems of running a home in a strange town – of general contentment in the Bradman household, perhaps even happiness. Don was getting on with his job; the house in Holden Street was now his home, and his accumulated cricketing paraphernalia installed. Golf was going well – Don was now champion of the Mount Osmond Golf Club. Friends came in to visit 'the little couple', as they were known. But, above all, Jessie had become pregnant, and all the excitements of expectation of a first child – as well as the anxieties of a first pregnancy – dominated home life. The couple had almost become – as perhaps they always would have wanted – an ordinary, down-to-earth, suburban pair, with a pleasant house, in an agreeable neighbourhood, with a family and a selection of interesting and sympathetic friends, and reasonable financial security.

The fly in this otherwise pleasing ointment was, however, Bradman's cricketing genius. The result of the 1935–36 season was to show Australia, and indeed the world, that the Bradman of 1930 – and of parts of 1934 – was back. Don could no longer remain in the agreeable obscurity of the Kensington suburb of Adelaide, playing cricket as and when he wanted, stockbroking during the winter and entertaining his friends as he wished. Nor indeed could Jessie, even in her pregnancy, retire to her home and cultivate the garden which she loved. The outside world was about to intrude. As it happened, with the start of the new cricket season in September 1936, two new challenges were thrown down to Bradman which he was unable to resist.

The first was the arrival at Fremantle, on 13 October 1936, of another England touring side. This was to be the 'tour of reconciliation', and the MCC tourists were led by G.O. Allen who, apart from his credentials as a cricketer, was known to be a strong supporter of the Empire (perhaps relatively stronger of the white nations of the Empire than of the coloured ones), was Australian by birth and, much more important, had refused to have anything to do with Jardine's 'bodyline' tactics. He would certainly, it was said, play the game like an English gentleman.

He would also probably lose like an English gentleman as well, since the side which had been chosen was considered to be inferior to anything the Australians could put out – particularly with Bradman back in action. Hammond and Leyland were formidable batsmen, and Farnes and Voce formed a strong opening attack, with Verity to follow with spin. But there was no Larwood, and the general view was that 'the Tests would be fair if it wasn't for Don'.[5] The truth was still that nobody was at all certain how they were going to get Bradman out. Furthermore, after his huge scores of the previous season – including the two triple centuries – Australia had again become 'Bradman mad', as the journalist William Pollock noted. 'You hear his name all day long in the mouths of men, women and children. Everything he says or does – or is supposed to say or do – is seized upon . . . most of them idolise the little champion of cricket.'[6] Indeed, the first shout that the Englishmen heard at Fremantle when their liner docked came from a tugboatman: 'Have you heard Bradman's latest score? It's 212.'[7]

It was only a slight elaboration of the truth. Bradman had indeed scored 212 – four days earlier – in the match that was the second challenge of the new season. Richardson's Australians had arrived back after a triumphant tour of South Africa to find that Bradman had been appointed a selector for the national team, and would certainly become captain for the Ashes series against England. The news was heard with some dismay, since Richardson had proved to be an astute and gentle captain in South Africa, carrying on the Woodfull tradition rather than introducing a somewhat harsher regime. It was suspected – rightly, as it turned out – that Bradman's style of captaincy would be much tougher. The riposte of the returning Australians was to participate in a testimonial match for the benefit of two former Australian Test cricketers, W. Bardsley and J.M. Gregory. The match was played at Sydney, and the tourists, under the guise of 'V.Y.

Richardson's XI', were to play the rest of Australia as 'D.G. Bradman's XI'. It was assumed that, with McCormick, O'Reilly and Grimmett, the Australians would easily bowl out the Rest while, with Fingleton, Brown and McCabe, they would easily cope with the Rest's bowling. As it turned out, the opposite happened, thanks to Bradman. Although he was at first wary of O'Reilly's medium-pace leg spin – understandably, since O'Reilly was regarded by many as the best bowler in the world at the time and was bowling to the top of his form on that day – and took two hours and ten minutes to score his first century, he cut loose thereafter and took only one hour for his second. He finished with 212, and O'Reilly finished with 1 for 96 in 22 overs. The Rest 'went on', Bradman recalled later, 'to beat the [returning] tourists quite comfortably, and I don't think they were very happy about that. They thought they were a great side until we beat them.'[8] The truth was that Bradman had deflated the reputation of his future colleagues. Furthermore, he knew it, and seems not to have been too shy in pointing it out. However much that reflected the reality, it was to make Bradman's task as captain that much more difficult.

It is perhaps reasonable to imagine that the hostility towards Bradman in a section of the Australian team dates from this point. Certainly Fingleton had been furious at his omission from the 1934 tour, but others had not shared his disappointment or his insistence on blaming Bradman, and Fingleton had remained a lone figure – apart, that is, from the professional jealousy that was felt at the press attention given to Bradman, and the general feeling that he was not somebody who would easily buy a team-mate a drink. What was important about the South African tour and the subsequent events of October 1936 was that a group of players, Fingleton, O'Reilly, O'Brien, McCabe and McCormick, had been to South Africa and had formed something of an alliance. Of course, as their names imply, they were all of Irish origin, all Roman Catholic and mostly Labor in politics because of it.

'Fingleton,' said Bradman much later, 'was the ring-leader,'[9] and it is easy to see why. McCabe, on the other hand, was the least hostile of the group. Indeed, Bradman has been noticeably sympathetic to McCabe's memory, going to some lengths to cast doubt on the circumstances of McCabe's subsequent apparent suicide, asserting his belief that McCabe's fall from a cliff was accidental. But about the others, Bradman has been less tolerant. 'When they arrived at Melbourne Railway Station,' he continued, 'they were met by a bunch of priests in cassocks.' The seeds of one of the most divisive rows in the history of Australian cricket had been sown. But, if the truth be told, the row was no more than a reflection of the deep divisions within Australian society at the time; and if personal dislike and religious sectarianism were not enough, the death of King George V and the subsequent dispute over the future of the English – and Australian – monarchy in the hands of a King apparently having an affair with a twice-divorced American only added fuel to the fire.

As yet unaware of the problem to come, Bradman suffered another terrible personal tragedy. On 28 October 1936, the day before South Australia, under Bradman's captaincy, were due to play against the MCC, Jessie Bradman gave birth to a son. The congratulations poured in. But there had been complications, and the prognosis for the baby was at best doubtful. Throughout the day, Don kept the doubt to himself – as his 'oyster-shell' required. In the evening, as though by way of release from the tensions of the day, he went to the Adelaide hotel where Neville Cardus was staying and asked him to spend the evening with him. He drove Cardus to his home in Kensington. There was dinner, and a discussion of the Test series to come and how O'Reilly could control Hammond – and so on. Driving Cardus back to his hotel, Bradman stopped off for a moment at the hospital for news of Jessie and the baby. It was not good. When he came out, Bradman told Cardus: 'I'm afraid the poor little chap will not pull through.' The baby died a few hours later. Bradman pulled out of the game against the MCC; the flags at the Adelaide Oval flew at half-mast. Don went back to the hospital and, apart from a token attendance at the Oval – 'to pay his respects to the visitors'[10] – played no further cricket until Jessie was out of hospital and until, as a couple, they were on the mend.

A fortnight later, Bradman made 192 in three hours in a

Sheffield Shield match against Victoria at Melbourne. In itself the fact is not remarkable; Bradman's career was so full of centuries that one more seems of little consequence. Nevertheless, he had been off the field with gastro-enteritis on the previous day – perhaps even a nervous reaction to the death of his first child – and, even when he went in to bat, looked anything but fit. His innings, by all accounts, was ferocious. His last 89 runs were scored in 46 minutes. Towards the end he hit 14, 13 and 19 off different overs, and all against a bowling attack which was near to Test standard. Certainly, behind the 'oyster-shell' there was deep grief and anger at the death of his first-born son.

THE MAIN OPPONENT, OF course, was England; and that was not to be forgotten. Nevertheless, a change had taken place in the Australian attitude to the mother country. In political and economic terms, England was, in the view of many, not the enemy she had seemed during the years of the depths of the Depression. True, England – or rather Britain – was still the Imperial Power, mighty in majesty, and the stranglehold had not relaxed: the Bank of England still held its vice on Australia's finances; and those whom an American sociologist described as the 'owner-producers' of Australia, almost entirely British or of British origin, were still the dominant economic power. But the bitter anti-British movements of the early 1930s, bred in the trough of the Depression, seemed to have lapsed into incoherence.

To some extent, however, the decline of the perceived external enemy had served to throw into sharper relief Australia's own internal problems. Australia herself, in the eyes of the rest of the world, seemed to be no more than marking time. 'Australia was an advanced country forty years ago,' wrote the same American sociologist, 'but, perverse though the world may be, it has moved forward and overtaken Australia in many directions.'[11] It was, of course, noted by foreign diplomats that Australians were a free-and-easy people, fond of outdoor leisure and sport; and, indeed, this was certainly true. Football, cricket and racing were among the few interests that spanned the classes and the geographical distances of the day to excite a common enthusiasm. But the implication – however offensive it might be – was that Australia should not be taken seriously other than as an appendage of the British Crown; and one, moreover, which was riven by dangerous and bitter internal socio-economic conflicts.

Whatever the truth of this analysis – and whatever the additional impact of the British Abdication crisis of late 1936 and early 1937 – there is little doubt that the underlying social currents of Australia flowed again – as they had during the First World War – in the direction of two extremes. There were those, predominantly Irish by origin, Roman Catholic, Labor and Republican, who resented the resumed dominance of what they regarded as the English Empire. There were others, predominantly English by origin, Protestant (and in many cases Freemason), Liberal-Country and monarchist, who were irrevocably attached to the Empire and the Crown. The two extremes did not sit easily together at the same table.

It is hardly surprising that the underlying tensions came to the surface in Australian cricket. Cricket was, after all, since the death of Phar Lap, the main common Australian interest of the day. At first the 'dissidents' if they may be called that, kept relative peace. The team for the First Test against England was announced on 25 November – Bradman, of course, being one of the selectors. The main surprise was the omission of Grimmett, who had performed well in South Africa. The truth was that Grimmett had not been on top form in Australia for several years, that he was now forty-five, and that two new spin bowlers had appeared, Ward of South Australia and Fleetwood-Smith of Victoria. Besides, Grimmett had been dropped from the Australian side in 1932–33, after three unsuccessful Tests. But Grimmett's friends, including those who had been with him in South Africa, took the news badly. So, for that matter, did the press.

The First Test started at Brisbane on 4 December. There had been no rain there since Easter, and the weather was stiflingly hot. Everything went just about as badly as it could for Australia. Bradman lost the toss, was out for 38 in the first innings, saw England pile up a lead of 380, and then watched while the heavens opened at the beginning of the fifth day. 'A wet wicket in Australia,' Bradman himself has said, 'is very, very much more difficult than a wet wicket in England. In matches over there you'll frequently get rain and the pitch is not more difficult after rain than it is when it is dry; it doesn't get sticky and the ball doesn't fly as it does in Australia.'[12] Indeed not, and a sticky wicket at Brisbane is one of the most difficult. It was also true that wickets were covered in the Shield matches and left uncovered for the Test matches. The Australian batsmen had had no serious practice on wet wickets. But nothing can mask the extent of the Australian humiliation. Voce and Allen shot them out for 58 in their second innings – Bradman was out second ball to a stroke 'as purposeless as a man flicking at the gyrations of a wasp or a mosquito'[13] – and England won by 322 runs.

The press reaction was surprisingly muted, as though normally voluble journalists had succumbed to collective shock. When the selectors chose the same team for the Second Test there were no complaints; they realised that it was the strongest side that Australia could put out, and that there was no point in change at this stage. But, if Brisbane had been bad, Sydney, where the Second Test started on 18 December, was even worse. Allen again won the toss and, thanks to an innings of 231 not out from Hammond, was able to declare at 426 for 6. At that point the rain came, and again Voce and Allen did the damage, helped this time by Verity. Only O'Reilly put up any sort of a fight, hitting three sixes in succession off Sims in an innings of 37. In truth, the wicket was not nearly as difficult as at Brisbane, and the Australian performance that much feebler. Bradman was out for nought again – this time off the first ball he faced from Voce, with a stroke that Cardus described as 'not fit for public consumption'[14] – and Australia were all out for 80. This, of course, ruled out all hopes of winning the match; the only possible course of action was to pray for extended rain. In fact, in their second innings the Australian batsmen made a better fist of it. Fingleton and Bradman put on 124 for the second wicket, and McCabe made runs as well, but none of them managed to make the large score which was required. The innings petered out, to leave England winners by an innings and 22 runs. Bradman himself was bowled by a slow long hop from Verity. 'The greatest run-getter in the history of cricket,' wrote C.B. Fry, 'has made the worst stroke in the history of cricket. A wild hook with his eye off the ball.'[15] England were now two up in the five-match series. Allen was beside himself with joy. Bradman made no statement.

The press were much less kind than before. The English were patronising: 'I came 12,000 miles to see England win the Ashes,' said one. 'I want to see them won on their merits, but I hate victory when the other side capitulates.'[16] The Australians were no less scathing: 'It looks very much as though we have developed a crop of "cream puff" batsmen' was one comment.[17] But for Bradman the situation was worse: he was not able, it was said, to combine the role of selector, captain and main run-getter. Furthermore, there was talk of dissent within the Australian team. The Sydney *Sunday Telegraph* was clear on the matter on the morning following the ignominy of the second Test match. 'Selectors and the Board of Control,' it claimed with authority, 'are disturbed at the suggestion that the Test teams are not pulling together, and that Bradman has not had the support generally given to an Australian captain . . .' But the second barrel of its assault was more revealing: 'Some members of the team have not been giving Bradman the co-operation that a captain is entitled to expect . . . There is definitely, and has been for some time, an important section of the team that has not seen eye to eye with Bradman, either on or off the field.'[18]

It was not difficult to guess which players might form, and certainly did form, the section which the *Sunday Telegraph* referred to. They were those who had resented Bradman in the first place, either through envy of his position or because of their political and religious background. Fingleton, for example, 'your typical Irish-Australian', as he has been described, wrote later that Bradman was 'a little, churlish man'[19]; O'Reilly also said later that 'I am inclined to think that in a lot of ways Bradman did a tremendous amount of damage to Australian cricket. He didn't ever come clean as a personal member of the side, he was always a far-distant relative.'[20] What was said openly later was, of course, said in loud but unattributable stage whispers at the time. Moreover, there were those who opined that Richardson should be brought back as Australia's captain, and others who thought that McCabe should be given the job.

Both Bradman and McCabe issued statements repudiating all suggestions that there was less than whole-hearted support for Australia's captain. 'The statements that there has not been complete harmony amongst the members of the Australian XI,' Bradman's statement read, 'are, in my opinion, completely without foundation.'[21] McCabe was equally forthright. Nevertheless, the rumours would not die down, and it was a discontented Australian side which went into the Third Test at Melbourne on New Year's Day 1937. Four changes had been made: Brown for O'Brien, Rigg for Chipperfield and Darling for Badcock were straight swaps, but Fleetwood-Smith for McCormick was to strengthen the spin attack at the expense of speed.

As it happened, the fortune which had favoured England in the first two Tests now turned round to favour Australia. Bradman won the toss and decided to bat first; but the Australian batting was so poor that only McCabe made much of a showing. Bradman himself failed yet again, out for 13, bringing his total for the first five Test innings of the season to no more than 133. However, the rain came when the score was 200 for 9, and Bradman promptly declared. England, in their turn, were caught on a wet wicket. 'It was a terrible pitch,' Bradman later commented. 'England had got to 68 and they had lost three wickets. Now that, I believe, was the crucial point; if Allen had closed at that point – and there was still some considerable time to play that day, we would certainly have lost three or four wickets before play ended that night.'[22] Allen, however, continued England's innings – to no great effect, since they lost a further six wickets for eight runs in spite of Bradman's instructions to his bowlers. 'I don't want you to get another wicket,' he told them. 'I don't want you to get anybody out.'[23] But the tactics soon became obvious to Allen, who declared when England were 76 for 9.

Bradman's response was a classic in Test match tactics. Realising that there was still some time to play before the close, Bradman sent in two tail-enders, O'Reilly and Fleetwood-Smith. Understandably, they were both bemused, particularly Fleetwood-Smith, who was playing in his first Test match and was

154

billed to go in at number eleven. Bradman was unsympathetic. '"Chuck," I said, "put the pads on." And he said, "Why me?" And I said: "Well, the point is this: you can't get out unless you hit the ball. Now," I said, "you can't hit the the ball on a good wicket, so you've got no chance of hitting it out there."' Needless to say, Fleetwood-Smith, who was after all going out for his first innings in a Test match against England, understandably 'didn't relish the remark too much'.[24] Bradman, on the other hand, thought it very funny.

As it turned out, the tactic worked to perfection. O'Reilly got out, but Fleetwood-Smith, and then Ward, managed to miss the ball until close of play. The following morning saw a dry wicket, and although rain interrupted play during the day the wicket remained reliable. Fingleton and Bradman put on 346 for the sixth wicket and, after Fingleton was out for 136, Bradman went on to make 270, without giving a chance. He batted for seven hours and thirty-eight minutes of relentless concentration and application – in front of a crowd of nearly 88,000. By the time he was out, not only had Australia made the match safe but they were in a winning position. He was Australia's hero again. England's batsmen were both bemused and demoralised and, in spite of a century from Leyland, were unable to rescue the game. Australia won by 365 runs.

And yet, although Bradman had won the Melbourne Test decisively – both by his batting and by his captaincy – his troubles were far from over. He may have been back on his pedestal with the Australian public, but there were further shocks to come from the players. The Board of Control had finally decided to take action in the face of the rumours of unease and dissent between some of the Australian players and their captain. The action they took can only be described as tactless almost beyond measure. Without Bradman's knowledge, they summoned, on the very day the Melbourne Test ended, the four players who they thought were giving the most trouble, McCabe, O'Brien, O'Reilly and Fleetwood-Smith. All four, of course, were of Irish Catholic origin, and it comes as something of a surprise to find that Fingleton's name does not appear among the four. Be that as it may, the four listened while a typewritten document was read out to them, in which unfitness and insubordination were alluded to but not specifically alleged, until O'Reilly lost his temper and expostulated: 'What's this, a game of tiggy-touch, is it?'[25] The Board members present were dumbfounded by this impertinence, but had no answer – nor indeed any specific charges. The meeting then broke up in confusion.

The result could hardly have been worse. When Bradman heard of the meeting he was understandably furious. He complained bitterly to two members of the Board, who replied '[We] didn't tell you because we wanted you to be completely innocent and at arm's length so that you knew nothing about it.' Bradman's riposte was direct and brutal: 'You can't possibly expect them to believe that.'[26] Nor indeed did they. All four thought that Bradman had set the whole thing up, and found it intolerable that Bradman himself had not been at the meeting to face them openly. 'I never really forgave him for it,' O'Reilly said just before his death. 'I still haven't forgiven him now.'[27]

The Board had thus achieved the worst of all possible worlds. They had launched an ineffective assault on one section of the team without telling the captain; they had failed to tell the players that the initiative was taken without the captain's knowledge; they had exacerbated the undoubted tensions which already existed, largely owing to jealousy of Bradman's supremacy mixed with a hostile cultural and religious background; and they had, in doing all this, undermined their own authority. To cap it all, they failed to make any sort of public statement to clear the whole thing up. In truth, it was a wonder that the team held together at all.

Salt was rubbed into an already painful wound by Alan Fairfax who, although now resident in England, had been back home during the Sydney and Melbourne Tests. 'The boys in the Australian team feel that they are not getting a fair break from the crowd. Bradman, Bradman, all is Bradman . . . Some of the trouble is caused by Bradman being captain . . . You have to mother a cricket team, and Bradman is no mother. He is too brilliantly individual. Armstrong, Woodfull – they were the skippers to study the players' interests and get the best out of them. Don simply does not come up to that. He is a pleasant little chap, hard-headed, shrewd. I played with him for ten years.'[28]

It was not a helpful contribution to the debate. But there were two factors which contributed to mitigate the damage which the incident might otherwise have caused: first, the English press was so preoccupied with the Abdication crisis that it had little time or space for anything else; and, second, whatever anyone might say, Bradman's popularity remained undiminished. 'I heard people say,' wrote Pollock, 'that Bradman's popularity was in the balance at this time. I didn't believe it. I should say that quite ninety per cent of those who follow cricket in Australia – which is approximately ninety-nine per cent of the total population – were with him.'[29] Besides, even if it had come to an open row, there was simply no one who could possibly replace Bradman as captain. He himself knew perfectly well that he was short on experience, but he was certainly not going to give up because of a minor storm. His only comment, made fifty years later, was that he believed that 'what it did in the long run was to improve relationships between me and the players, because they recognised that I'd been placed in a very embarrassing position and it wasn't my fault'.[30] That may be so, but the effect in the short run can easily be imagined.

But there was still work to be done. For the Fourth Test at Adelaide the Australian selectors retained all the four players who had been reproved – so it seemed – by the Board of Control, and Fingleton as well. It was obvious that Bradman, as both captain and selector, was determined not to bear grudges. As it happened, this tactic worked perfectly, partly because Fleetwood-Smith turned out to be one of the match-winners and partly because of Bradman's own performance. Australia batted poorly in their first innings, on a fine day and a true wicket, for 288, only McCabe playing with distinction. England, however, did little better, finishing with a first-innings lead of 42. When Australia batted a second time, the match had reached a point where a major score was needed. Bradman provided it: he made 212 – again slowly, in seven hours and seventeen minutes. Allen tried the technique of restraining Bradman by allowing him to take singles almost at will; the idea was to stop him hitting boundaries. The result was not only that Bradman scored slowly but that his innings included 99 singles and only fourteen boundaries. 'It was,' Bradman recalled, 'a very difficult innings – one of the longest I ever played.'[31] England needed 387 to win in their last innings. It was not impossible, and at the beginning of the last day they needed no more than 244 runs with seven wickets standing. It was here that Fleetwood-Smith, bowling his left-arm wrist spin, proved his worth, bowling Hammond with what Bradman described as 'one of the most beautiful balls I have ever seen delivered',[32] and ending with an analysis of 6 for 110 in 30 overs.

The series was now balanced at two-all. The deciding Test was to be played at Melbourne, starting on 26 February. By now, the emotional temperature was well off any reasonable thermometer. The first spectators arrived at dawn to take their places in the queue to get into the Melbourne Cricket Ground, waiting five hours for the gates to open.

Over 80,000 crowded in to see Bradman win the toss and choose to bat. The weather was hot, fine and clear; there was no suggestion of rain. Going in at 42 for 1, Bradman played what Arthur Mailey described as 'one of the greatest innings I have ever seen him play'.[33] Gone was the cautious Bradman of the previous Tests. England's fast attack failed entirely to make any impression; Bradman reached his century in two hours and five minutes. His partnership with McCabe for the third wicket was worth 249. Bradman was finally out for 169 – in three hours and forty-three minutes; McCabe made 112 in two hours and forty minutes; Badcock added to the English misfortunes by making 118 in three hours and twenty-five minutes. But by then almost nobody noticed. Australia ended with 604 – a total well beyond England's reach. The English were tired and without discernible ambition; they collapsed to 239 in their first innings and, following on, could do no better than 165 in their second. Australia had won by an innings and 200 runs. It was one of the most emphatic victories in the history of Ashes cricket.

There was pandemonium at the ground. The players raced to the pavilion gate as soon as England's last wicket fell. McCabe, clutching a stump, managed to make it unscathed, but Fingleton was caught by the invading crowd and subjected to merciless back-slapping. The crowd swarmed over the wicket and threatened to storm the pavilion; they were urged to go back to their seats by officials with loudspeakers, but it was no good. Bradman had to make a speech – in which he tactfully thanked 'my team-mates for the magnificent support they have given me right through the series'[34] and Allen replied in a suitably sportsmanlike manner. It was all quite different to the end of the 1932–33 series. Even the new King George VI sent a message to Bradman, saying he had followed 'with the closest interest' the progress of the Test matches in which 'Mr Bradman has once more given evidence of his predominant skill as a batsman'.[35] Lord Gowrie – formerly Hore-Ruthven as Governor of South Australia but now promoted in both position and style as Governor-General of Australia – had his say as well: 'Hearty congratulations on winning the Ashes and on the splendid way in which you all demonstrated what is commonly known as playing the game.'[36] It was perhaps a little too obvious, but the reference to previous events was clear.

Bradman had much to reflect on at the end of the 1936–37 season. He had gained valuable experience as a Test captain and had shown himself to have an agile and perceptive cricket brain, not least in the Third Test at Melbourne when he had out-manoeuvred Allen. He had retrieved Australian fortunes after the first two disasters, largely by his own batting performances. Most important of all, he had survived the criticism and the hostility which had been directed at him. He had been attacked with venom, particularly after the Second Test when the cause seemed lost, but also, though with less venom, when Australia were winning – on the grounds that he was only interested in his own personal records. Both lines of criticism were unfair, and it is a sign of Bradman's growing maturity (he was still only twenty-eight) that he could take the criticism without losing his temper. Equally, there was no sign of personal conceit. If he occupied the crease it was because he knew that he was the only player on the side who had the ability to win matches on his own. This was no more than realistic self-knowledge, which had always been a feature of his character. What he was acquiring with the passing years was a more developed understanding of the merits and demerits of other players. He was no longer the young lad of 1930 who could not understand why everybody was not as good as he was.

Nevertheless, Bradman still had not developed an easy relationship with his team-mates. As Pollock wrote, 'people told me that he was a go-getter and not a good mixer, but even if this was true there were things in him that interested me. I could see that he was intelligent, and, I thought, shy. I nearly always come to like shy people; there is usually a lot in them.'[37] Perhaps he pressed his colleagues too hard in his anxiety to win, where Woodfull would have coaxed them. But that, again, was probably due to his shyness. The fact that his colleagues resented him more than they might was due, quite simply, to envy. In truth, there was no denying the reality; he was worth, in cricketing terms, more than any of them. Woodfull had been right when he said, before the 1936–37 series began: 'If I were a selector I should count him as two batsmen if he was playing in form.'[38] Furthermore, the crowds came to see him bat in a way in which they would come to see no one else. People who knew nothing about cricket, especially women, turned out to watch him, and when he was out they went home. Of course, it was never easy for Bradman to fully come to terms with this stardom. Even O'Reilly was sympathetic. 'Poor old Don,' he said, 'we watched it more in sorrow for him than in anger . . . he was never able to do anything, go anywhere.'[39] It must have been with the greatest relief, but also with justifiable pride, that Don returned in March 1937 to his wife and home in Adelaide for what he hoped would be a quiet winter's stockbroking.

Don and Jessie on their wedding day, 30 April 1932.

Harold Larwood
in action during the
1932–33 'bodyline' tour.

Bill Voce.

Bowled first ball by
Bill Bowes during
the Second Test,
Melbourne,
December 1932.

Bradman aiding Woodfull, who had just been struck by a ball from Larwood. The Nawab of Pataudi stoops to retrieve Woodfull's bat while Jardine looks on.

Woodfull again, this time ducking under a bouncer from Larwood during the Fourth Test, Brisbane, February 1933.

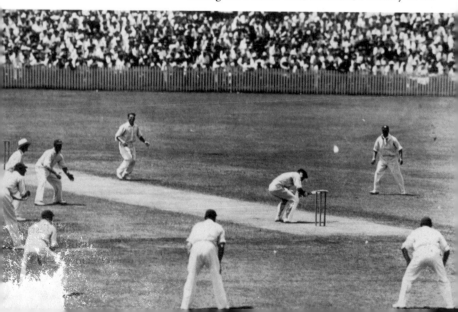

Douglas Jardine.

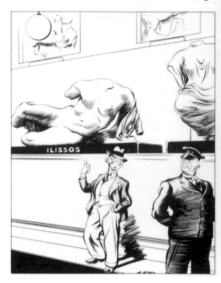

ILISSOS

Members of the 1934 touring party, together with Australian Davis Cup tennis players, aboard the SS *Orford*.

Bradman, at the piano, entertaining Chipperfield (left) and Fleetwood-Smith in 1934.

Bradman and the team are met at Waterloo Station by MCC
President Lord Hailsham, at the start of the 1934 tour.

Choosing bats and other equipment at the factory of
Stuart Surridge & Co., April 1934.

Batting at Worcester, 3 May 1934. As in 1930,
Bradman started the tour with a double century.

Sydney radio station 2BL reporting on the 1934 tour via cable from England.

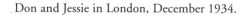

Don and Jessie in London, December 1934.

Don and Jessie outside the Kensington Park home of Harry Hodgetts, in about 1935.

Dealing with correspondence, 1936.

9

THIRD TIME ROUND

O N 27 AUGUST 1937 DON BRADMAN celebrated his twenty-
ninth birthday. There was certainly much to celebrate. In
the short space of ten years or so he had shown himself to be
not just a freak from up-country New South Wales, as some
had originally thought, but a batsman who had overtaken almost
all previous records and, in doing so, had attained the supreme
honour of the unchallenged captaincy of Australia. All this was
to the good. On the other hand, in spite of all the success, and
however contented life was on the surface, it is not difficult
to detect at this time a certain restlessness and, at times, even
depression.

There are, as always with complex characters, several possible
explanations for this. One, at least, might be his relations with his
employer. For instance, although his contract was of undoubted
financial satisfaction, he was never invited by Harry Hodgetts
to become a partner in Hodgetts & Co., nor, apparently, was
the suggestion even hinted at. Odd as it might seem, given the
commercial possibilities which he brought with him, Bradman
remained an employee throughout his career with Hodgetts,
while the firm itself remained under Hodgetts' single ownership.
Quite why this is so is not altogether clear. The firm, by the time
Bradman had learned his trade, was expanding its business fast;
the name of Bradman was a marketing asset of great potential;
and Harry Hodgetts and both the Bradmans were on excellent
terms. Indeed when Don was away playing cricket Hodgetts and
Jessie Bradman sometimes sat together listening to the cricket
commentaries, Hodgetts sitting in an expansive armchair placidly
smoking his pipe and Jessie perched on another, half concentrat-
ing on her knitting. Perhaps Hodgetts felt that the Bradmans,
for all their national fame, were not sufficiently recognised in

the upper echelons of Adelaide society, or that Bradman himself was too young; perhaps he thought it inconvenient to have a partner who would be absent for long periods; perhaps – and this, on reflection, seems the more likely explanation – he just wanted to keep all the profits to himself.

Whatever the reason, it seems clear that Bradman in mid-1937 can be described as a keen but somewhat semi-detached member of Hodgetts' team of employees. As it turned out, in the long run this was to be an advantage. But even at the time the arrangement had its merits. It allowed Bradman to keep regular office hours and to avoid the social life of a stockbroker, such as it was, which Hodgetts was used to but which Bradman would certainly have found irksome. It also allowed him time to enjoy his new-found domesticity, to take up squash (to which Allen had introduced him during the 1936–37 tour), to improve his golf handicap, to play the piano or billiards, to go to the theatre, to garden, to look after their dogs, cats (and even 'canaries in open cages',[1] it was reported) – in other words generally to spend the hours in a way which suited him and his wife rather than dictated by outside circumstances. Bradman also had time to write the larger part of a book, subsequently completed by the journalist William Pollock and published during the 1938 Australian tour of England in serial form by the *News of the World* in London under the title *My Cricketing Life*.

All in all, then, the winter of 1937 was, on the face of it, placid and contented. Significantly, too, Bradman's health was giving him no trouble. Certainly there must have been times when life seemed a trifle dull, but at the time that was perhaps true of Australia generally. It was not just that Adelaide was boring. The pioneering spirit of the whole of Australia seemed to have lapsed into inertia. 'In what, at present, can we take pride?' asked the writer P.R. Stephensen in 1936. 'In our cricketers, merino sheep, soldiers, vast open spaces?' It was a fair question, even if put by a writer known for extreme views. Sheep were, after all, just sheep; vast open spaces were no more than that; soldiers were part of history. 'Until we have a culture of our own,' he went on, 'a quiet strength of intellectual achievement, we have nothing except our soldiers to be proud of.'[2] He ought, of course, to have added 'and our cricketers' but he was certainly right in saying that there was not much else. Intellectual life suffered from the sterility of censorship imposed by the United Australia Party/Country Party government in Canberra – and supported by Liberal/Country League Premier Butler in South Australia. Even if the Bradmans had wanted to – which is itself far from clear – they would not have been able to read Joyce, Defoe, Hemingway or George Orwell, or a further 5,000 books which were declared 'prohibited publications'. Nor had Butler himself achieved power in South Australia to overthrow the restraints on what others would regard as innocent social enjoyment which dated mostly from the previous century, and which had become an integral part of the Adelaide ethos. Bradman would certainly have had to be careful how loud he played his grand piano late in the evening or on a Sunday. The general peace – however suffocating – was not to be disturbed.

The fact that Australia's cricketers were considered by an intellectual to be one of the few major sources of Australian pride is in itself interesting. It goes a long way in explaining Bradman's status as a national figure, at a level of idolisation which he would not have achieved (or, to put it in his terms, to which he would not have been subjected) in a country which had heroes in other walks of life or, indeed, which had other values. The truth is, of course, as Stephensen pointed out, that there was simply nobody else. This truth, unwelcome to Bradman as it was, sheds at least some light on the complexities of his character. Reflecting as he must have done, as he approached the age of thirty, he would have concluded that, although he was ambitious, his ambition was neither unreasonable nor abnormal. He had not wanted greatness. All he had wanted to do was to play cricket. If he had set himself to write poetry or practise law, and if he had shown the same genius for either activity as he had at cricket, he might have risen, in the course of time, to some sort of fame, but few would have asked for his autograph, and he certainly would not have been incessantly mobbed in the street before he had reached the age of thirty. But it is equally fair to say that once greatness was his for the taking he was unremitting in its pursuit. It was in that continuing determination, despite his domestic contentment, that Bradman's restlessness at this time can best be detected.

On his birthday he would have reflected that, in that early Australian spring of August 1937, he was growing to full maturity. In anybody else's terms, of course, he had already completed a spectacular career. Nevertheless, he knew, as did others, that, as a cricketer, he was only now approaching his prime, since it was held then – as now – that a batsman is at the height of his powers in his early thirties, when youthful ability and speed of eye is accompanied by the experience – and the caution – of maturity. But even before arriving at his prime, he had already broken most cricketing records. In Australian cricket, for instance, he had already made 1,000 first-class runs in the domestic season no fewer than eight times, a feat which the nearest contenders, Woodfull and Ponsford, had only achieved twice in their respective careers. Internationally, he had not only reduced English bowlers to despair; he had forced them to devise a new tactical method to cope with him – otherwise they knew that they would never get him out. In short, he seemed to the world to be next to invincible. It is little wonder that when a school inspector visited a small school in the outback of New South Wales in 1936 and put a question to the class 'Who is the greatest man alive today?', one boy immediately answered 'Don Bradman'; and when the inspector followed with the instruction 'Stand up all who had that answer', all but one of the children stood up straight away.[3] Stephensen's complaint, if that was what it was, stood justified. In no other developed – or half-developed – country of the day could cricketers have occupied the status which they did in the Australia of the 1930s; but the plain fact is that there was no other icon for Australians. Cricket was the one thing they were good at, against the rest of the world. And of their cricketers, Bradman was the best.

By any reasonable standard, it was a heavy burden to lay upon anybody, let alone somebody whose upbringing had ill-prepared him for what was, in some respects at least, the role of demi-god. For a start, his origins were against him. The 'boy from Bowral' was far from being able to claim antecedents or education which would endorse him as Australia's Siegfried. Furthermore, his physique was hardly of heroic stature. He was by his own account 5′8″ (his height seems curiously to vary according to the source); his limbs were in proper proportion, in other words small; and he took shoes of what have been described as 'a ladylike size – 6 or 6 and a bit'.[4] The significant features were his shoulders, square for a man of his size, and – above all – his arms and wrists, both of which were powerfully muscular beyond the size normal to a man of his height. All that, however, could have been, and probably was, due to the exercise which he had taken from childhood onwards.

What were distinctive were the contours of his face. The photographs of the time show a reasonably ordinary frame for the centre of the face: a small head, but not too small for the size of the body; a forehead whose hair was starting to recede, not uncommon at his age and certainly less pronounced than his contemporaries O'Reilly, Chipperfield and McCabe; a parting on the right as the conventions of the time dictated; and, lower down, the suspicion of a double chin. His eyes were close together – the eyebrows slanted downward – over what appeared to be a slightly long nose. Below that, the lips of his mouth were thin and his jaw had a tendency to harden. Smiles, when they came, seem to come uneasily. It was certainly, on the photographic evidence, a face of suspicion and defence. Even at rest, it seemed either to be in search of something or trying to ward something off.

Nor is it difficult to see, from the same photographic evidence, the determination and single-mindedness of the character. It is even possible to detect the ruthlessness in the gaze of his fierce blue eyes. What is more difficult to appreciate is the Bradman in relaxation. If there is to be an immediate assessment of the near thirty-year-old, it would be that the look of total concentration was enough to burn not just outwards but inwards through the slight physique of the man and exhaust it. And yet, it is, from all the evidence, equally clear that in the company of his wife and friends he was relaxed, charming and, above all, courteous. Bradman himself has claimed that he owed much to his wife, and indeed one of their friends has insisted that 'she is a star'.[5] Although she never lost, any more than her husband, her respect for the values with which she had been brought up, and, although her dress sense, again like that of her husband, was on the conventional side – he in his double-breasted grey suit and trilby hat worn at a slight angle, she in the rather lumpy dresses of the day with the customary 'permanent wave' – she was not only devoted to Don and sensitive to his moods but also self-sufficient enough to be able to endure his long absences without, as yet, having children to look after. If Don's strength was outward and easily perceived, Jessie's was inward and deep.

By the time the 1937–38 cricket season started Bradman was in a more confident frame of mind than perhaps he had ever been. He was able to say that he had acquired a skill outside cricket which would stand him in good stead when his sporting career came to an end, that he had formed a good working relationship with Harry Hodgetts, to their mutual financial advantage, and that he had achieved personal security in a home which he loved and with a wife to whom he was deeply devoted. It was in this spirit that he felt ready to confront the challenges of the new season and, looking beyond it, to the burden and the honour of captaining Australia for the first time in a tour of England, due to take place in the English summer of 1938.

Bradman's confidence was well rewarded. In the 1937–38 season he yet again made more than 1,000 runs. He went past Clem Hill's record of 6,274 runs in Sheffield Shield cricket for South Australia and Warren Bardsley's total of 17,461 runs in all first-class cricket. By the time the season ended he had played three years for South Australia, had taken his aggregate to 2,138 runs at an average of 101.80, and had become the only player to score a century in each innings on two occasions. But in all this plethora of runs perhaps the most piquant confrontation of the season came in the match at Adelaide between South Australia and New South Wales. Bradman was, of course, the leading batsman for South Australia and O'Reilly the leading bowler for New South Wales. 'When Bradman batted,' reported 'Johnnie' Moyes on the confrontation, 'there was no relaxing. Every ball was charged with hostility, filled with venom and calculated to destroy . . . Sometimes the batsman prevailed; sometimes the bowler won the duel . . . It was a battle for mastery, one champion against another.'[6] O'Reilly took 9 for 41, but the one wicket that escaped him was Bradman's. 'O'Reilly would have given the other nine for the one the batsman's skill withheld from him,' remarked Moyes. Given the hostility between the two men – at least on O'Reilly's side – it is fair comment.

The great interest of the season lay, of course, in the performance of the various candidates for selection to tour England in 1938. Bradman was one of the selectors, along with two non-players appointed by the Board of Control, 'Chappie' Dwyer and Bill Johnson. It was not an easy side to pick. One innovation was, however, welcome: the manager of the team was to be the Secretary of the Board of Control, W.H. Jeanes. The idea was to improve communications between players and Board once the tour was in progress. In practice, nothing much changed, but, as Bradman said later, rather acidly, 'I am sure in later years the Australian Board has been very grateful for the useful knowledge brought back by their Secretary.'[7] As far as players were concerned, the problem lay in the bowling. There was only one fast bowler who measured up to Test standards, E.L. McCormick of Victoria (another Irish Catholic). Cotton of South Australia was fast, but his action was suspect, and the risk of taking him to England was too great. On the other hand, there was a surplus of competent spin bowlers. Apart from O'Reilly, who could not possibly be left out, there was Ward, who had bowled well against England in 1936–37, Fleetwood-Smith, who was a match-winner if he hit his true form, and, of course, Grimmett. It was Grimmett who was the major problem. Although he was a fine bowler, and had been the mainstay of Australia's spin attack before O'Reilly's arrival on the Test match scene, he was forty-six, a poor fielder and no more than a marginal contributor with the bat.

In the end, and after much deliberation, it was decided to omit Grimmett. The decision was widely derided. Ponsford, now retired, called it 'sheer lunacy'.[8] O'Reilly put it down to Bradman's personal hostility towards Grimmett as the result of an unpleasant dressing-room incident, which Bradman has claimed never took place at all. In fact, Grimmett had not been particularly successful in Test matches against England; he had been dropped during the 1932–33 series and not even been considered for the

1936–37 series. True, he had been spectacularly successful in South Africa, but his place as Australia's second spinner had by now been decisively taken over by Fleetwood-Smith. But Grimmett's omission was much welcomed by the English, as was that of Oldfield, the veteran wicket-keeper. All in all, the verdict of Pelham Warner was probably fair. 'I have never known,' he wrote, 'an Australian team who were not good. Obviously these are, but I hope and believe that they are not invincible.'[9] Perhaps so; but, as everybody admitted, the English still had to devise a way of getting Bradman out.

The long trip to England started as others had before it. There were matches in Tasmania and at Perth, and the *Orontes* was once again waiting at Fremantle on 21 March 1938 to take the tourists onward to Colombo and Europe. Bradman, ominously enough, was 'very tired on leaving Australia'.[10] The season which had just finished had clearly done his health no good. He spent the first part of the journey in bed with a sore throat and a bout of 'flu. Besides, he was seasick again. He did not play in the usual match at Colombo, but face was saved when Lindsay Hassett scored a century – batting in place of Bradman, whose name was on the scorecard, and giving every impression of being Bradman himself. At least the crowd seemed to be taken in.

Bradman was rather more cheerful on the way across to Aden, and even managed to turn out, in suitably ludicrous dress, for a fancy-dress party. It was certainly not in character, but it showed at least that he was taking his responsibilities as captain seriously. He also played in a match against 'Egypt' in Cairo, while the *Orontes* was slowly making her way through the canal; 'Egypt', of course, being a side of British servicemen with, as the reports had it, 'maybe one or two Egyptians'.[11] From there it was on to Naples, where, Bradman noted in his diary, 'We saw about 36 destroyers, 8 cruisers and 72 submarines. They looked very ominous.'[12] Further, as he wrote in a letter to Hodgetts, 'I guess they were not built to rust.'[13] Indeed, what was now borne in on the Australians, as their journey brought them steadily into Northern Europe, was the latent sense of menace. This was no longer the world of 1934 which, though poor, had been peaceful. Now, as they sailed across the Mediterranean from

Naples to Toulon, they became suddenly conscious of the news that Germany had, only a few weeks before, annexed Austria (the plebiscite confirming the incorporation of Austria into Greater Germany took place only three days before the *Orontes* arrived in Naples). Mussolini's Italian Empire was now covering large tracts of North Africa, and Spain was convulsed by a hideous civil war. The peace of Australia seemed suddenly to be a very long way away.

It came as something of a relief to be greeted by British normality at Gibraltar, albeit normality tempered by a wary caution about the effects of the Spanish Civil War. It was not difficult to imagine a Franco government laying forceful claim to the Rock. The garrison was kept on alert. Nevertheless, there was time off for the customary welcome for an Australian touring side on their way to England, even if Barnes, a newcomer to the side, slipped on the deck of the *Orontes* and broke his wrist. By now, of course, Bradman was learning quickly the art of captaining a touring side. He was noted for his 'debonair cordiality to all and sundry, including the journalists' – not a characteristic that had been previously marked – '. . . in contrast with some earlier Australian cricketers'.[14] Admittedly, when invited by General Sir Charles Harington to accompany him in taking the salute at the march-past of the King's Liverpool Regiment, which formed the garrison at the time, he stood firmly to attention with his hat in one hand and his other hand at the salute, but it was pointed out that his only previous military experience had been with the Bowral school cadet corps, and that he could hardly have been expected to master there all the demands of British Army protocol.

The *Orontes* docked at Southampton on 20 April 1938. There was an official welcoming party, as might be expected, and it was two hours before the tourists could get away on their special train. The reception at Waterloo was similar – but perhaps of higher tone. Lord Hawke, Sir Pelham Warner, Sir Stanley Jackson were all there, as were 'Allen, Holmes, Robins . . . and others'. ('To the Victoria Hotel. Interviewed pressmen. Got 2 Gunn & Moores and saw hosts of people.'[15]) From there, later on, Bradman went to call on Sir Douglas Shields. It was perhaps more than a courtesy call. It was in large measure due to Shields that Bradman was fit enough to be there in the first place.

There were then the familiar ceremonies, which Bradman remembered from 1934: the Cenotaph, lunch at the Royal Empire Society and so on. There were old friends to be visited and new acquaintances to be made. There was at least time for a visit to the theatre (*Bluebeard's Eighth Wife* at the Plaza), before setting off for the serious business of the tour, starting, as always, at Worcester, on Saturday 30 April. Those who thought that Bradman's batting might have suffered as a result of his health problems or the responsibilities of captaincy were immediately in for a nasty shock. In front of a crowd of some 11,000 which had elbowed and trod its way into the ground to see him bat, on a day which was clear and cold ('cold as charity',[16] his diary reported), and on a perfect wicket, Worcestershire won the toss and put the Australians in to bat. Bradman responded by making 258, without giving a chance.

It was the third time Bradman had opened an English tour with a double century. Nobody else had ever done it more than once. This time it was the highest score ever made on the opening day of an English season. Although he took just over two hours to score his first fifty, his second was made in thirty-eight minutes. In all, his innings lasted just under five hours. 'The Worcestershire captain's resignation,' wrote Cardus, 'apparently achieved a philosophy so profound that he declined the new ball at 200. Probably he was right; a new ball costs money, and Worcestershire is not a wealthy club and every little counts.'[17]

On the Tuesday of the Worcestershire match, Bradman visited the Royal Worcester Porcelain factory, where he was shown the first of many trophies which he was to receive during the tour. It was a porcelain urn, designed by the company's art director, decorated in the royal blue of Worcester porcelain tradition, with a painted panel in front depicting the Worcester cricket ground, with Bradman batting. The company wished to give it to him to commemorate his three double centuries there of 1930, 1934 and now 1938. Bradman described it as 'lovely' – not the most ecstatic of epithets; but he did go on to buy a set of coffee cups, or, as he wrote in his diary, to get 'some pottery for Jessie'.[18] It is another example of how much his wife was in his thoughts. The matrimonial cord, so it seemed, stretched easily over 12,000 miles.

The Worcester match was the start of another remarkable cricketing May. Bradman reached his 1,000 runs on the 27th, again at Southampton. It was done in no more than seven innings, at an average of 170.16. Furthermore, he had not been bowled out in any of those innings, and apart from his dismissals had never given another chance. The high point had been his 278 against the MCC at Lord's (his highest ever score there), of which 257 were made on the Saturday, 14 May, in five hours and twenty-six minutes in front of a crowd of some 30,000. It is little wonder that one writer commented that 'he has upset the balance of the game as it has never been upset before by the genius of a single player'.[19]

There were two snags in this otherwise triumphant progress. The first was, again, Bradman's health. The official version was that he had started to feel muscular pain in his back. In itself, this was not perhaps unusual for a cricketer, but for one with Bradman's health record, particularly – and uniquely – when he was subjecting his body to the physical and mental strain of playing long innings, it was worrying. Others, however, said that he had a chill, and that doctors had recommended a rest. Indeed, so worrying was it that he felt obliged to miss the games immediately prior to the first Test match, which was due to start on 10 June at Nottingham. As it happened, he took the opportunity of watching part of the England Test trial at Lord's, where he saw the medium – and sometimes rather more than medium – leg-breaks of the young Kent novice D.V.P. Wright. Bradman was immensely impressed – to the point where later in the year, after his return to Australia, he described Wright as 'the discovery of the year'.[20]

The second snag lay in Bradman's relations with the Australian Board of Control, which had, to be sure, been troublesome on a number of occasions over the years, but which were now about to enter yet another period of what can only be described as extreme turbulence. The matter concerned the position of players' wives. At the end of the 1934 tour, the Board of Control had allowed

Mrs Woodfull to join her husband at the end of the tour and sail back to Australia with him – at his expense, of course. The 1938 tourists, like the 1934 tourists, had been required to sign a contract, to all appearances drafted with great care by the Board's lawyers, covenanting that they would not be accompanied by their wives or relatives for any part of the tour and, furthermore, that neither wives nor children would be in England when the team were touring there. The clauses may have been carefully drafted, but were by any standard virtually unenforceable in law. Moreover, the contract only mentioned 'England or elsewhere outside Australia where the Team from time to time may be touring'.[21] Wives and relatives could easily go to France, for instance, or even to Wales or Scotland when the team were not playing there.

But that was not the issue, since Bradman, having signed the contract, was not the sort of person to take advantage of any sloppiness in its drafting. Equally, he asked for no preferential treatment. Any member of the team was, in his view, entitled to make the same request. At the same time, if any member of the team objected to his proposal, he would drop it. Thus it was that during their first week in England he summoned a team meeting and told them of his proposed request. All he wanted, he said, was what Woodfull had been granted four years earlier. Nobody had any particular objection; indeed those who were married put in their own requests that their wives be allowed to meet them in Colombo on the return journey. It was all perfectly reasonable, and Jeanes was asked to write to the Board accordingly. They then sat back and waited for the Board's response – expecting, they assumed, easy concurrence.

Even with the new seaplane service from England to Australia, letters took ten days in transit, and the players were reconciled to a month or so of waiting to allow Jeanes' letter to arrive, and to be considered, and for the Board's response to be sent back to England. In the meantime the tour continued. Bradman, even during the rest to allow his back to recover in time for the First Test, still had a busy schedule. There were lunches and dinners and receptions, at all of which he was required to make a speech of some sort. There were fan letters to reply to, and invitations to open fêtes, judge beauty contests, and attend dogshows, agricultural shows or regimental dinners or other events customary in the social calendar of the English middle class. It was all hard work. But it had one, perhaps unexpected, benefit. Surprising as it seemed to those who had heard his earlier efforts, Bradman by this time had become something of an expert at public speaking. He had overcome his initial shyness, and, although he still prepared what he had to say with great care, and was reluctant to speak extempore, he was fluent and witty, and was able to catch the sense of occasion which each event generated, however different each might be.

Nevertheless, the main business was cricket, and, in particular, the First Test, starting on 10 June. It was far from being a happy occasion for Australia's new touring captain. He lost the toss on a perfect wicket, on which, quite naturally, Hammond, the English captain, decided to bat. There were two important newcomers to the English side: Hutton of Yorkshire and Compton of Middlesex. In the event, Hutton made 100, Barnett made 126, the ageing Paynter made 216 not out, and Compton made 102; and England declared at 658 for 8. Australia's response to this huge total was hesitant. Bradman himself was in bad trouble against Wright and, although he survived a difficult period, was out for 51. The onus of defending fell on McCabe, the vice-captain. In fact, McCabe not only met the challenge but played one of cricket's greatest masterpieces, scoring 232 out of 300. Cardus described it as 'one of the greatest innings ever seen anywhere in any period of the game's history'.[22] So powerful was his stroke-play that even Bradman thought that it was the finest innings he had ever seen. 'Come and watch this,' he said to his team-mates in the dressing room. 'You'll never see anything like it again.'[23] Later he wrote: 'Towards the end I could scarcely watch the play. My eyes were filled as I drank in the glory of his shots.'[24] It was perhaps the greatest compliment Bradman ever paid a fellow batsman.

Despite McCabe, Australia were forced to follow on 247 runs behind England. It was obviously not a time for fireworks. Brown and Fingleton survived the crowd's heckling to put on 89 runs in two and a half hours. When Fingleton was out, Bradman

173

came to the wicket, and played an innings the like of which no commentator had seen from him before. There was no flamboyance; there were no flashing strokes; there was no attempt to dominate the bowlers psychologically; above all, there was no cocky smile. 'His nose was on the pitch,' wrote Moyes, 'and the enemy was the clock ... No mother-in-law could have been more firmly entrenched, no star boarder or squatter could have made himself so much at home or have shown a greater reluctance to leave the scene.'[25] Bradman stayed for six hours and five minutes for his 144 not out, and never gave a chance. At the end of his innings, when he had declared with the game saved for Australia, Bradman was limping from a strained thigh muscle and had one eye almost closed from the dust that the pitch had thrown up. But he had saved the First Test and, by way of celebration, on the following day made a century in two hours against the Gentlemen of England at Lord's. It is little wonder that he was now being talked about as the greatest player the world had ever seen.

There is no doubt that Bradman's achievements in May and early June would have attracted even greater attention from both press and public than they did, had the worries of the world been less intense. It was, indeed, a worrying time. The crisis over Czechoslovakia was reaching one of its many climactic points. Czech reservists had been called up; their frontier posts were manned; and on 20 May the Czechoslovak government announced that Hitler had been on the point of launching a surprise attack against their country. In fact, the information was wholly inaccurate, but that did not prevent it spreading alarm in those countries which were, at least in theory, committed to the defence of Czechoslovakia's territorial integrity. There was near panic in Britain at the thought of an imminent war.

In these circumstances, it is hardly surprising that some commentators thought they might be witnessing the last Test series for many years. Indeed, plans for a 1939 season were already being – at least temporarily – shelved. This lent a certain *fin-de-siècle* poignancy to the second Test match, which started at Lord's on 24 June. As it turned out, the pessimists were right, since this was to be the last England–Australia Test to be played at Lord's for ten years. Oddly enough, as though in keeping with the threatening background, the match itself turned out to be damp and depressing. True, fortunes swayed from one side to the other: Hammond put England on top in the first innings, and when Bradman was out for 18 it looked as though England could not lose and would probably win. But Brown saved the Australian first innings, and England's declaration set Australia a target to win the game which was well beyond their reach. All that could be done was to bat out time. This Australia did quite comfortably, with Bradman ending at 102 not out. But it had been an unsatisfactory game; indeed the only feature of the whole occasion which Bradman felt worth recording was the arrival of a television set – 'this new scientific marvel'[26] – in the Australian dressing room to allow the players to watch the tennis at Wimbledon.

If Lord's was damp, the next Test at Manchester was a complete wash-out. It rained for four days almost without stopping. The two captains, Hammond and Bradman, did not even bother to go out to toss up, and the match was called off without a ball being bowled. But Bradman had arrived in Manchester in a very snappy temper. The trouble had been the response of the Board of Control to Bradman's request for Jessie to be able to join him in England at the end of the tour. The answer arrived while the players were staying – in some elegance – at a country hotel at Grindleford in Derbyshire, preparing for games against Derbyshire and Yorkshire. The Board's reply was categoric: 'No'.

Bradman was both offended and hurt. He was offended because he was not being accorded the same privilege as Woodfull four years before; and he was hurt because it looked like a personal slap in the face. He was pressed to make a statement, but his contract was specific: he could only make a statement with the permission of the manager. But since Jeanes was himself the Secretary of the Board he was obviously not going to agree to Bradman issuing any statement which was critical of the Board's decision. Needless to say, Bradman and Jeanes had a row (Bradman records it as a 'dust'[27]). Finally, Bradman hit upon a stratagem. He drafted the equivalent of a statement, but, as it were, in indirect speech. He proposed to use his friend, the journalist 'Johnnie' Moyes, as his mouthpiece. Moyes, of course, would pass it all on to the English press, which was waiting, as might be imagined, with its collective tongue hanging out. The draft emphasised that Bradman could not talk without permission, that permission had been refused, that if he could have talked he would have said that he was distressed by the decision, that it was in direct contrast to the treatment accorded to his predecessor, that it was a slap in the face, and that never again would he play in a match under the jurisdiction of the Australian Board of Control.

It was certainly heady stuff. It meant quite simply that Bradman would no longer play for Australia if his request was refused. He would retire from Test cricket. Moyes, of course, showed the draft to Jeanes, who was by now feeling the pressure of what can only be described as Bradman's blackmail. Jeanes asked Moyes to hold the whole thing up for a few days while he cabled the Board. That was agreed. But by that time the scene had moved to Manchester. The Australian team held a meeting on the matter – without Bradman. The decision was unanimous: they were 'heart and soul'[28] behind Bradman's request and, furthermore, they would cable the Board and tell them so. Even Fingleton and O'Reilly were in Bradman's camp.

Bradman was immediately told of the meeting and of the team's unanimous support. Fortified by this show of solidarity, he went to Jeanes and discussed the whole matter. 'Finally,' Bradman's diary notes, 'we agreed on a cable to be dispatched to the Board.'[29] The cable pointed out, in direct language, both the extent of Bradman's anger and the consequences of refusing his request a second time. Australian Test cricket without Bradman – while he was merrily playing in Sheffield Shield games – was unthinkable.

The press piled on the pressure. The *Daily Mail* called Jessie in Sydney, where she was staying with Mrs McCabe, and pronounced that 'there was no mistaking the note of indignation in her voice'.[30] In England, it was predicted that Bradman would 'defy the Board' and that he might withdraw from the remainder of the tour. There were renewed offers from the Lancashire League; Moyes reported that several clubs would virtually allow Bradman to 'write his own ticket'.[31] It was said that a leading newspaper was prepared to pay Jessie's passage to England and 'fight the Board in the courts'[32] on the legality of the players' contract. The Board were described as 'Fascist dictators', 'sporting Hitlers' or 'Little Tsars of Sport', according to taste. In short, the press were thoroughly enjoying themselves.

By now most of the Australian Board were able to recognise defeat when they saw it, although there were some who were still more than usually myopic. At a further – heated – meeting, they reversed their previous decision by eight votes to five. But there was a sting in the tail. They allowed not just Bradman's wife but any wife, including Jeanes' wife, to join their husbands at the end of the tour. The captain and Australia's hero, it seems, was not to be given any special treatment – even the treatment which they had given Woodfull on the earlier tour. It was perhaps fortunate that the Third Test was rained off without a ball being bowled. Bradman was still angry, his team was upset, and the manager was still suffering from the crossfire. It was far from the happy body of men needed to engage with the enemy in what could have been the decisive Test match of the series.

Once the matter had been resolved – in other words, once the Board had completed their rather ragged retreat – Bradman resumed his now customary cricket form. There were two matches between the abandoned Manchester Test and the Fourth Test at Leeds; against Warwickshire at Edgbaston he made 135, his last 85 in sixty-one minutes, and against Nottinghamshire he made 56 and 144, reaching in the process 2,000 runs for the season in only twenty-one innings. The stage was therefore set for Headingley. But the stage, unfortunately, was disconcertingly wet from the recent heavy rain, and due to get wetter if the forecasters were to be believed. The conclusion was clear. It was certainly going to be a low-scoring match. There was no question of Bradman making a third triple century.

As it turned out, he did almost as well. England were out for 223 – Hammond scoring 76 and O'Reilly taking 5 for 66. Bradman went in when Australia were 87 for 2 on the second morning. The light was as bad as it could be – Cardus described the Australians as 'lost souls in a November fog, being led about by Bradman and his torch'. Hobbs wrote that 'Bradman is in such form that he could have played by candlelight'.[33] In the event, Bradman made a chanceless 103, his sixth century in successive Tests and by general agreement the finest of the six. There was certainly no question of Bradman playing for himself or for the record book; he was playing for his side, shepherding his fellow batsmen until he was eighth out at 240. The Australian innings closed soon after at 242.

England's second innings was also played in the deepest gloom. Few of the English batsmen could make headway against O'Reilly, who again took five wickets, this time for 56 runs in 21.5 overs. Australia went in for the last time, and managed, after many alarms, to knock off the 107 runs needed for victory. Bradman could hardly watch – he had been out early. Jeanes actually went for a walk outside the ground, such was the tension. But in the end the deed was done. Australia won the match and retained the Ashes. 'Tonight,' Moyes reported, 'the Australian captain is wearing a smile that will not come off.'[34] It had been an extraordinary match. 'What I shall remember longest of the match,' wrote another journalist, 'is, I think, the picture presented by Bradman and Bowes as they faced each other. Bradman was all intense concentration, motionless for a full seven seconds as he watched Bowes turn, run up and shoot the ball. Very, very rarely was he puzzled. His footwork was beautiful. He kept the secret of his stroke to the last half-second. There, beyond all question, was a captain of men.'[35]

It was a further four weeks before the two countries met in the last Test match. In the intervening period, Bradman made 202 at Taunton against Somerset, but failed against Glamorgan at Swansea, and then took a rest from the two games the Australians played in Scotland. He rejoined the side for the match against Kent at Canterbury, making 67 before lunch before giving his wicket away and then fielding to Frank Woolley's last innings – 81 at the age of fifty-one.

From there it was back to London and to the last Test match at the Oval on 20 August. It was a disaster for Australia. Bradman lost the toss again, for the fourth consecutive time in Test matches. England batted, and Hutton passed Bradman's Test record by making 364. Leyland made 187 and Hardstaff was still there at the end on 169. The Australian bowling attack had completely collapsed. O'Reilly could do no better than 3 for 178 in 85 overs, but Fleetwood-Smith took the wooden spoon – 1 for 298 in 87 overs. Not unnaturally, frustration in the Australian team gave way to irritation and anger. O'Reilly was furious at Fleetwood-Smith, whose behaviour was certainly eccentric. 'He [made] peculiar noises in the field,' O'Reilly complained. '"Gee up, Bess! Gee up, Bess! Come on, Port Melbourne! Hi there!" . . . and I'd meet him somewhere about the middle of the pitch, changing over, and I'd rip into him.'[36]

In the end, to relieve his hard-pressed bowlers, Bradman put himself on to bowl. However kindly meant, it turned out to be a mistake. 'I busted my ankle,' he wrote in his diary, 'and was carried off . . . X-ray revealed flake fracture . . . Bad night.'[37] O'Reilly was less sympathetic. 'You'd swear I was an opal miner,' he said later. 'I was going down, down and down, and he stepped into that and did his ankle and was carried off. And the crowd that came out to cart him off, you'd have reckoned it was an aeroplane disaster . . .'[38] Bradman was taken to St Thomas' Hospital, spent the next day in bed, went back to the hospital on the following day for further X-rays and then spent the rest of the day in his hotel. In the Test, Australia collapsed twice, to lose the match catastrophically by an innings and 579 runs. 'Well,' O'Reilly went on, 'we didn't see Bradman again on the tour. We waved him goodbye as he left the field, never laid eyes on him again until we got on the ship to come home.'[39]

Factually, O'Reilly was right. Bradman spent the rest of the tour recovering at the home of Walter Robins, where he was joined by Jessie. But it was not just his ankle that was troubling him. He was worried about the recurrence of back pains. Furthermore, he had found the whole business of captaining a touring side quite exhausting. 'There had been times,' he wrote later, 'when I found it difficult to keep going, and although not old in a cricketing sense I did not feel capable of standing the strain on another occasion.'[40] He was still tired when, against the advice of his friends, and indeed his travel agents, he and Jessie decided to travel across France to Toulon to join the ship which was to take the whole party back to Australia. The threat of war was real; air-raid shelters were being cobbled together in London itself; the tone of international politics was becoming ever more despondent.

The Bradmans, together with their friend Moyes, travelled by train from London to Toulon. They were crossing the plain of northern France when they heard banging on the door of their compartment. It was the guard, shouting happily '*Pas de guerre!*' ('No war!') and dancing with joy. The Munich agreement had been signed. That may have been so; but on that journey, the talk was all of the future after Munich, and about the future of cricket. Bradman was pessimistic. He expected a war, which would be long and bloody. As for himself and his future in cricket, he had doubts about his health; he had found the whole business of touring England as captain too great a strain. More than once, on the journey, he simply threw himself on to a bed and dropped straight off to sleep. The conclusion was clear: he was not prepared to face it again. It seemed that Don Bradman had toured England for the last time.

10

THE BUSINESS OF WAR

A LONG SEA VOYAGE, IT USED to be said, is the one truly effective remedy for the pain of an unhappy love affair. Distance, isolation, fresh air, the gentle rhythms of the sea and carefully organised idleness combine to distract the mind and mend, albeit slowly, the emotional bruises of the spirit. True, the 1938 Australian tour of England can hardly be said to have been a love affair, even at the start. There had been too much friction for that, both among the Australians and with the English; and in no sense can it be said to have been happy at the end. There had been division, and even bitterness; most of the players were tired, and many were angry as well; and, as a menacing backdrop, there had been the sense of danger from the threats of war in the Old World. A long sea voyage was almost a necessity, and as the *Orontes* edged her way southwards, leaving the Mediterranean autumn behind and heading into the warmth of the Southern Hemisphere, the healing magic started to work.

For Bradman and the other married men, the journey was made more pleasant by the company of their wives and, in Bradman's case, the idleness was all the more marked in that he was still convalescing from the fracture in his ankle. Furthermore, as the *Orontes* went on her way, the news seemed to improve. In the latter months of 1938, after Munich, the international clouds appeared – however deceptive the appearance – to lift. Not to be outdone by Britain's new accommodation with Germany, France signed 'a declaration of friendship' with Germany. It did not amount to much, but it did contain an agreement that the two countries would confer together if international activities should arise in the future, and each recognised the other's frontiers. The British, too, followed their Munich initiative with a series of trade missions to the country, on the grounds that a prosperous

Germany would be less politically rumbustious. They followed these up with new overtures to Mussolini, in the hopes that he would act as a moderating influence on Hitler. Whatever the merit of these moves, and the policy which lay behind them, there is no doubt that the British – and therefore the Australians, not least those who were returning to their country on the *Orontes* – were lulled, as these pieces of news filtered through, into what turned out to be a wholly false sense of security. Indeed, so secure did the Australian government feel that in the financial year ending in April 1939 it allocated only £13 million for the armed forces.

It is therefore understandable that the players, on their arrival in November at their respective destinations, found the talk turning not to war or rumours of war but to the new domestic cricket season. The Board of Control were already laying plans for the next Ashes series, due in the summer of 1940–41. The relative performance of the players in England was combed over by the press and assessments made of the chances of each State in the coming Sheffield Shield competition. The threat of war was consigned to its proper place on the other side of the world. But before a start could be made on the serious business of playing Shield cricket, there was an important event which required the attendance of anybody of cricketing importance – the game to celebrate the centenary of the Melbourne Cricket Club. It was certainly not an occasion to be missed, and the players duly turned up – to be confronted by a major surprise. There was, it was known, a vacancy for the job of Secretary of the Club. The surprise was that one of the leading candidates for the job of Club Secretary was none other than the current captain of Australia, Don Bradman.

From Bradman's point of view the idea made a certain amount of sense. The job was one of the most prestigious in Australian cricket. The previous Secretary, Hugh Trumble, had died in August 1938, and Melbourne was looking for a figure of substance to replace him. The salary was no less than £1,000 per annum, and, barring upsets, it was a job for life. True, Bradman would have had to give up stockbroking, his new house in Kensington and his widening circle of friends in South Australia. These were formidable obstacles, and Bradman certainly did not seek the job out. It was only after a great deal of persuasive argument by a Melbourne Club committee member that he allowed his name to go forward as a candidate. Interestingly enough, one thing that did not deter him was the thought that, if he took the job, his days of Test cricket would virtually be over. Whatever cricket he might have been able to play – and at the age of thirty he would still want to play cricket – there would be no question of any future tours of England and, for that reason, an end to his captaincy of Australia and probably to selection for domestic Tests as well. Nevertheless, the Secretaryship of the Melbourne Cricket Club was, and indeed still is, one of the most attractive jobs in the world of Australian cricket, and it would have brought Bradman both financial security and a continuing connection – at a high level – with the game he loved.

As it turned out, there was no shortage of applicants for the position – more than one hundred and fifty, it is said. A sub-committee of the Club was convened to draw up a short-list. So long was the process that it was not until mid-January 1939 that the full committee of the Club sat down to consider its final choice. The meeting lasted some three and a half hours. There was, as is normal on such occasions, much debate. As the debate progressed, it became clear that there were only two serious candidates – Bradman, and a long-standing member of the committee, Vernon Ransford, himself a former cricketer of distinction, both for Victoria and for Australia. In the end, it was the casting vote of the chairman that decided in favour of Ransford. Bradman offered his congratulations to the successful candidate and, when asked whether his candidature had meant that he would welcome a move away from South Australia, replied laconically: 'I am quite happy in Adelaide.'[1] It was probably a fair statement of the truth: Bradman was 'quite happy' in South Australia. But it is nevertheless significant that he considered taking the job in the first place.

By January 1939, of course, the domestic cricket season was well on its way, and Bradman was leading the South Australian challenge for the Sheffield Shield. He had already scored 118 in the centenary game at Melbourne. Now there was no stopping him. He scored 143 against New South Wales, 225 against Queensland at Adelaide, 107 against Victoria and then 186 against Queensland – again – at Brisbane. Just at the time when the Melbourne Cricket Club were debating his candidature he was completing his sixth first-class century in a row, with 135 not out against New South Wales at Sydney – in his first six innings of the 1938–39 season. Seemingly without effort, he had equalled the record of six successive centuries in first-class cricket set by C.B. Fry in 1901.

Unsurprisingly, the Adelaide Oval was full to capacity for the following match against Victoria, starting on 25 February 1939, to witness Bradman's conquest of Fry's record. In the event, he was out for 5, caught – unlikely as it must have seemed at the time – by the normally butter-fingered Fleetwood-Smith. Bradman disguised what must have been his genuine disappointment by grinning all the way back to the pavilion. The crowd was furious at Fleetwood-Smith. Fry, on the other hand, was perhaps rather relieved that his name still stood in the record books. He cabled Bradman: 'Genuinely sorry. Superlative skill merits absence of bad luck. Fry.'[2]

Despite his failure to beat Fry's record, 1938–39 was a glorious season for Bradman. He was now batting as well as ever. His average for the season was 153.16; his average for the twelve months of 1938 itself was 112.88; and his average in Sheffield Shield matches was 160.20. As if this was not enough, South Australia won the Shield for the second time in four years under his captaincy. It was, as Bradman himself wrote, 'my most successful season in domestic cricket'.[3] It was also, as it happened, the last before the outbreak of war.

But the whole thing had been tiring, and the winter of 1939 brought a welcome respite from cricket. Bradman, like others on the 1938 tour of England, had been playing almost without a break from November 1937 to February 1939, since, in addition to his appearances for Australia and South Australia, he had a full programme of club cricket with Kensington. Not that his batting became stale; far from it – he seemed to get better with each month that passed. Nevertheless, the incessant travel, as well as the cricket, was exhausting. Besides, there was too little time left for his new career or, indeed, his wife. Fortunately, he was able to spend a few months at home during that autumn and winter. It was doubly fortunate, in fact, since on 10 July 1939 Jessie gave birth to a son, John Russell Bradman. It was said by some that this new arrival served at least to mitigate the pain of the loss of their first child in 1936; perhaps so, but such sorrow is not removed easily, and certainly Jessie still felt it acutely. But the new baby was strong and healthy and the birth had been without complications. The Bradmans were at last, after eight years of marriage, a family. Nor was sport wholly ignored – it never would be with Bradman. He went in for the South Australian squash championship, just to keep himself fit. Needless to say, he won. But, as he later wrote about the hour-long final, 'it was more exhausting than a full day's batting'. After that, 'I never played competitive squash again.'[4]

On 3 September 1939 the whole world changed. The Prime Minister, Robert Menzies, announced at 9:15 P.M. Eastern Australian time, in suitably melancholy tones, that it was his duty to confirm that Britain was at war with Germany and 'as a result, Australia is also at war'.[5] It was not altogether logical, and there were many, particularly in the Irish Catholic community, who had difficulty in seeing why it should be so. But Menzies, who had become Prime Minister only five months earlier after the death of Joseph Lyons, was fulsomely loyal to the mother country. He had followed Britain uncritically down the road of appeasement and had supported the belated (and ultimately futile) guarantee of Polish independence – in spite of his private conviction that 'nobody really cares a damn about Poland as such',[6] and he pushed Australia into the Second World War as quickly and as unquestioningly as his predecessors had rushed into the First. But there was now an extra dimension: in 1914 Japanese ships had escorted Anzac troops across the Indian Ocean; now Japan was threatening aggression in South-East Asia and, by extension, towards Australia herself. In view of this there was no question of sending an Anzac expeditionary force to Europe; they might be needed at home. Menzies made that much clear to the British.

In practice, in the immediate aftermath of Australia's declaration of war, very little happened. The government took

185

powers under the Defence Act to call up a militia for home service and to raise volunteers for overseas. The response was, to say the least, muted. Not only was the pay of an infantry private – quite astonishingly, under the circumstances, and for no apparent reason other than a perceived need for financial restraint – reduced from 8s. a day to 5s., but a number of volunteers were refused because they worked in essential skilled jobs. Menzies himself suggested that Australia should get on with 'business as usual',[7] and, indeed, the amount wagered on the result of the Melbourne Cup of 1939 turned out to be an all-time record. Furthermore, the government formally requested the Board of Control to ensure that the full Sheffield Shield programme was completed as normal. This, it said, would be good for morale – although, again, nobody quite understood why.

Thus instructed, cricket went on in the normal pattern of a domestic season; and, in the normal pattern, the season was dominated by Bradman. Starting with 188 in two and a half hours for his club, Kensington, in late October, he went on to make 251 not out against New South Wales, 138 against Queensland, 267 against Victoria and 209 not out against Western Australia (his thirty-fifth double century), finishing the season with a first class average of 132.75 and, for the first time, over 1,000 runs in Sheffield Shield cricket alone. Only Ponsford had done it before him. Furthermore, he drew in what by today's standards would be considered enormous crowds – simply to see him bat, and melt away if he was out: 78,000 at Melbourne, 75,800 at Sydney, full houses in the smaller Adelaide Oval. His drawing power was put to good use in late February when, right at the end of the season, Bradman captained the Rest of Australia against New South Wales, the winners of the Sheffield Shield, to raise money for 'patriotic funds'. The match raised over £1,000.

Meanwhile, the War had been moving lazily along. But even Australia was shocked by the fall of France in June 1940. Recruitment to the armed forces took a sudden lift; government spending on defence rose to £170 million in 1940–41; and aliens were interned. Nevertheless, in spite of this increased surface activity, the War still seemed a long way away. It turned out that, many, perhaps most, of those who volunteered were formerly unemployed. Nor had civilians as yet been asked to make sacrifices; indeed, such was the economic effect of the War that there was something of a boom both in industry and in agriculture. Australian youth, which had lived through continuous economic gloom since their schooldays, were little inclined to respond to imperial rhetoric. Their country, they were inclined to say, had not needed them in the past few years; they did not see why they were now being told that their country's need should be taken seriously. Furthermore, a large section of the population – those of Irish origin – were certainly not going to support the British War. O'Reilly, for instance, refused to enlist. He recalled the First War: 'I can remember those boys going away and getting farewelled, and then the news would come back: Killed in action . . . If I'm going to war, I'm the man who's going to decide. I couldn't give a damn what anybody else thinks at all.'[8] All in all, it is not surprising to find a survey of public attitudes in 1941 recording 'a sense of disillusionment, disappointment, futility, distrust, disgust, diffidence and indifference which so many possess with regard to politics and society in general and the War in particular'.[9]

Bradman, on the other hand, did enlist. As he later wrote, 'I felt the urge of all patriotic citizens to do my duty in a sterner sphere.'[10] This, more than anything, illustrates Bradman's deep underlying loyalty to King and Empire. The difference with O'Reilly, and indeed with many of his fellow countrymen, could hardly be more marked. Thus it was that on 28 June 1940 Australia's captain of cricket enrolled in the Royal Australian Air Force reserve at their recruiting station in Adelaide. He passed his medical examination, took the oath and was assessed as an air-crew member with the role of observer. As it happened, he was only just under the age limit of thirty-two. There was, of course, an immediate press release about the new recruit; the authorities were certainly not going to let this important catch go unnoticed. Congratulations came in from all over Australia; and the Mayor of Adelaide pronounced that 'it should be an inspiration to all sportsmen. Let us hope now that Don will get centuries in the air as readily as he got them on the ground.'[11] 'It was with pride and admiration,' wrote one of his fellow

Australian selectors, 'that I read of your joining-up. I am sure that your action will be an inspiration to all South Australian and Australian cricketers to fall into line.'[12] But after this spurt of activity there followed a long pause. The flow of recruits into the RAAF was too much for the crumbling official machinery to cope with – out of some 120,000 applicants they only managed to absorb some 5,500 as air-crew and 18,000 as ground staff. Bradman attended training classes but, apart from that, he was left, like many others, on a rather uncomfortable shelf. True, he let it be known that he would only play cricket for patriotic purposes (whatever that meant) and he broadcast in September in support of the War Savings campaign. But that was all there was to relieve the frustration.

In the meantime, the subtle skirmishing of inter-service rivalry had started in earnest. The Army could not see why they should not benefit from this big catch, since the Air Force were quite obviously doing nothing about it. Negotiations were opened between the two services for Bradman's transfer to the Army. Bradman himself was naturally consulted, but was undecided. He sought the advice of no less a figure than Lord Gowrie, by then Governor-General of Australia. Gowrie's advice was that Bradman should accept the transfer, on the grounds, apparently, that the job the Army was offering – as a supervisor of physical training – would suit him better than being an observer in an aeroplane. As it turned out, Gowrie's advice, though well meant, was wholly misguided. What he had not realised was that Bradman's health had started to collapse again, as he thought it might during the homeward trip from the 1938 tour of England. While he might have been able to continue service as an observer in an aeroplane, his body was simply not up to the pressure of a hard course in physical training.

Nevertheless, Gowrie's advice was accepted and the transfer effected in October 1940. Bradman duly joined the Army School of Physical and Recreational Training, with a view to becoming an instructor. On the last day of that month, now with the rank of Lieutenant, he was posted to the Army School of Physical Training at Frankston, Victoria. The regime was physically demanding, since the school was modelled on the British Army

School at Aldershot, but, once there, Bradman found himself among friends. Fleetwood-Smith was there, oddly enough as a sergeant-major – an unlikely rank for such an eccentric; and there were two wrestlers, King Elliot and Bonnie Muir (also sergeant-majors) and the rugby player Max Carpenter. Everybody seemed, in one way or another, to have had a previous place in Australian sport.

When the transfer, and Bradman's subsequent posting, was announced, it raised in the public mind all sorts of embarrassing questions. He had volunteered, it was noted, for active service in a fighting force; yet here he was, within three months or so, transferred to a branch of the armed forces which, by the very nature of things, would rarely, if ever, face enemy bullets, and, at the same time, he was given the King's commission as an officer. The conclusion of the cynics was quite clear. Someone in authority had decided that Bradman was too great an asset to be risked on the battlefield, and that he was to be given, in the jargon of the day, a 'cushy' job well away from the firing line. It was to counter such comment that the Army issued an announcement to the effect that, after his training, Bradman would stay in Adelaide for six months before being posted to the Middle East as divisional supervisor of physical training with the Australian Imperial Forces in that war theatre. It was a good try, but, in the event, failed to satisfy the cynics who – then as now – thought that Bradman was being protected 'from on high'.

The course at Frankston was certainly as physically demanding as would be expected. There were physical jerks 'that limber up every part of the body',[13] long jumps, high jumps, wrestling, boxing, medicine ball, shot-put and, of course, running. All that started at 9 A.M. and went on until 4:30 P.M., with short breaks for rest and lunch. After that students had to study anatomy, physiology and hygiene, and to learn how to arrange and conduct every kind of sporting event from a wrestling match to a sports meeting. In addition, they had to learn to cope with injuries by passing the St John's Ambulance course (Bradman came out top) and to understand the essentials of army discipline.

There was little cricket. Bradman refused to play for the Melbourne sides which were chasing him, and only played, in early December 1940, for the Army Physical Training Corps against the Fire Brigade because it was sponsored by five firms in aid of the Soldiers' Cigarette Fund – to the extent of 2/6d. for every run he made. Bradman obliged by scoring 109. But this was an isolated case. And, yet again, his small and seemingly fragile physique was about to betray him. The intense physical activity of Frankston, together with the psychological effort required to keep up with younger men – Bradman was never one to be beaten – turned out to be too much. As he wrote himself: 'My 1934 troubles recurred with greater severity.'[14] Worst of all, his eyesight started to fail.

It was at Frankston, in December 1940, that an Air Force ophthalmologist, researching ways of improving pilots' vision and speed of reflex, wanted to test Bradman's eyes. He was, after all, a natural choice for speed of reflex. The tests were made; but the results were wholly unexpected – except by Bradman himself, who suspected that the '1934 troubles', stress-related as they had been, had badly affected his eyesight then, and that the physical and mental stress of Frankston was having the same effect now. Strange as it now seems, Bradman's eyesight, much to everybody's embarrassment, was declared to be well below par.

This surprising news was confirmed when Bradman played at Adelaide against Victoria over the Christmas holiday, in a match designed to raise funds for the War. He was out first ball in the first innings, caught in the slips, and in the second innings misjudged his first ball to such an extent that he fell over and nearly sat on his wicket. After a further difficult ten minutes he was bowled for 6. It was the same story in a 'Patriotic Match', played – again to raise money – at Melbourne in the New Year. Bradman was out first ball in the first innings and for a miserable 12 in the second. His first-class average for the 1940–41 season therefore went down, as a result of these two matches, which were the only ones he played, as 4.50. The simple fact was that he had been unable to get the ball into focus.

But this was not the only problem. Shortly after the Melbourne match, the muscles of his back became inflamed and frequently went into unpredictable spasm. For a physical training instructor this obviously would not do. He went into the Repatriation

General Hospital at Keswick in South Australia for treatment, but all the doctors could do, with the knowledge of muscular trouble and psychosomatic illness at the time, was to diagnose something known as 'fibrositis'. In layman's language, this meant no more than 'something wrong with your back'; but there it was. Discharged from hospital, Bradman took part in the Australian All-Services Athletics meeting at Melbourne on 14 February. He won his own race, led the winning team and was at the head of the Army team of competitors in the final parade. But the effort proved too much for him. It was back to hospital. But, again, nobody could diagnose the true nature of the illness. He was discharged, but there was no improvement. Twice more he had spells in hospital, but to no greater effect; and on 1 May it was announced that he had been recommended for discharge on medical grounds. In June he was formally invalided out of the Army. The greatest cricketing hero Australia had ever seen had been declared unfit to defend his country. It was a humiliation that Bradman felt deeply. 'I am only good for a job as an ARP warden,'[15] he wrote sadly to Moyes. Officially, he was a semi-invalid.

There was nothing for it but to return to civilian life – and to try to live down the suspicions of cynics, who again whispered that the whole thing had been fixed. In some depression he went back to his father-in-law's farm at Mittagong to try to get his health right. Jessie went with him, but she had become a mother again in April, with a new baby girl, Shirley June. Yet again, however, there was sadness, since the baby showed early signs of cerebral palsy. Jessie had now a whole series of problems to cope with: a sick and depressed husband – unable to work – a young son and a new baby. It could easily have been a recipe for her own stress breakdown but, as throughout her life, she met the challenge with courage and good sense. There is no doubt that, in those dark days, she pulled Don through.

It took nine months for Bradman to return to full health. Although his illness was diagnosed as 'fibrositis', that was only because medical opinion of the day was far from understanding the true origins of muscular illnesses. In fact, from all the evidence and from Bradman's own description, he had quite clearly developed what is now known as a 'frozen shoulder'. He became unable to lift his right arm – to the point where he could not shave himself or brush his hair, and he lost all feeling in the thumb and index finger of his right hand. All that, of course, was quite apart from the excruciating pain. Jessie, as Bradman was first to admit, had to become expert in the use of a razor and a hairbrush.

Nowadays, of course, a frozen shoulder is properly diagnosed and is treated by a course of steroid-based injections. It is still an extremely unpleasant and painful condition, but not one which is cause for major medical concern. In 1941, however, there were no steroid injections; without them, modern medical opinion holds that it can take anything from three months to two years for the condition to subside, and that even then there may be painful and dangerous recurrences. It is therefore hardly surprising that it was April 1942 before Bradman, now accompanied by his wife and two small children, felt able to return to Adelaide and civilian life. He then did his best to overcome the burden of disability and the disappointment of remaining no more than flotsam on the beach of the Second World War. It was, of course, the worst time to be out of it. Menzies ('Pig-iron Bob', as he was known, after breaking a strike against exporting pig-iron to Japan before the War) had been forced to give way to Labor's John Curtin as Prime Minister. The Japanese had struck at Pearl Harbor and at the British defences – such as they were – on the Malay Peninsula in the previous December. Most disastrously, on 8 February 1942 Singapore surrendered.

'They grouped together about the chief,' wrote the poet Mary Gilmore, 'and each one looked at his mate/ ashamed to think that Australian men should meet such a bitter fate!/ And black was the wrath in each hot heart, and savage oaths they swore/ as they thought of how they had all been ditched by "impregnable" Singapore.'[16] The literary style is perhaps overwrought and not to everybody's taste, but it sums up the mood in Australia of February 1942. The fall of Singapore was, in truth, a second Gallipoli. Once again, it seemed that the mother country had betrayed its errant, but ultimately faithful, child. The pictures of Australian soldiers – under their British generals – being herded into Japanese prison camps was almost as shocking as the thought that the next target for Japan would be Australia herself. Indeed, the Japanese were already bombing – on 19 February – the northern Australian port of Darwin. The Australians had at last started to feel what the British had felt for the previous two years: that they were the next in line for execution.

Unsatisfactory as it was, in this dark period there was nothing for Bradman to do but to go back to his desk in Harry Hodgetts' business. He felt able to play a little golf in the winter of 1942, and more in 1943, and busied himself with various charitable activities such as, for instance, the secretaryship for South Australia of the Gowrie Scholarship Trust Fund, named as such after the Governor-General Lord Gowrie, whose son had been killed in north Africa (and who had incidentally given Bradman such bad advice two years earlier). But his main occupation was his work on the Adelaide Stock Exchange. It would be wrong to say that the Exchange was a source of great excitement. It was certainly a far cry from the adulation of 80,000 people at the Sydney or Melbourne Cricket Grounds. As the nation limped through the war crisis of 1942, the Adelaide Exchange was fighting its own battle for survival. There were controls on profit margins and on share price movements; for weeks on end trading was at the lowest possible levels; and at many of the three official daily calls there were only one or two transactions. In March 1942, for instance, there were four transactions at the noon call on the 3rd, and one transaction at the 3 P.M. call; on the following day there were four transactions at 10 A.M., none at noon, and two at 3 P.M.; on the following day there were no transactions at all at any of the three calls. It could hardly be said that this was a thriving business from which thrusting entrepreneurs could earn a good living.

Yet that was all there was. Furthermore, there were now the additional irritations of rationing, shortages and preparations for civil defence. In practice, these measures were more honoured in the breach than in the observance. Mrs Newland, for instance, the wife of a prominent stockbroker, declined to go into the trench which her husband had dug in their garden on the grounds that it was dirty; she preferred, she said, to hide under the dining-room table. Fortunately, of course, neither she nor her husband, nor anyone else in Adelaide for that matter, were ever called upon to put their defences to serious use. The air-raid shelters in Victoria Square were, in the end, left to rot.

It was not a comfortable time; indeed it was a frustrating and difficult time. But it is a measure of the character, both of Don and Jessie, that they resolved to make the best of what they had. After all, they had a pleasant home – not, perhaps, to everybody's taste, some saying that it resembled a rectangular two-storey military barracks with a garden tacked on; young children – although Shirley was at a difficult stage and John was showing signs of youthful rebellion; and a secure income – in spite of rumours which even then were starting to circulate in Adelaide society about Harry Hodgetts. But these, in a sense, were peripheral problems. The main purpose of Bradman life at the time, given that Don was excluded from participating in the War as he would have liked, was to make the best of it.

By the beginning of 1943 things were starting to look up. The immediate military danger to Australia seemed to have been averted. This, in turn, led to increased activity on the Adelaide Stock Exchange – albeit still, for the moment, in Commonwealth War Loan – and a brighter atmosphere all round in Adelaide society. There was more entertaining; there was more talk about what would happen when the War had been won; and there was at least some relaxation of the censorship which had prevented the press from reporting the bad news as opposed to suppressing it in favour of anything which could be considered good. On the Exchange, however, there was still a serious problem of membership – and indeed solvency. Members' subscriptions had fallen to a total of £692 in the year to March 1941, and had only reached £932 in 1942; members serving with the Australian armed forces overseas had their subscriptions waived. It was hardly enough to run a proper securities operation.

The extent of the problem became evident during 1943. In January a member was expelled for involvement in a case of forgery of a share certificate. In June came the death of another member who had joined the Exchange in 1896. In August died the most respected member of all, Whitmore Carr, elected as long ago as 1891, who had been a member for almost the whole of the history of the Exchange. It was hard, people said, to imagine the Adelaide Stock Exchange without him. 'His performance of the daily rituals,' they said, 'serving as president and committeeman and descending the stairs to the Stock Exchange Club, were part of its fabric.'[17]

Nevertheless, the future of post-War Australia was on the agenda. It would clearly be a more regulated country, and more centralised; the Commonwealth of Australia had, after all, been able to assume powers over income tax in 1942 in spite of objections by the States in the High Court. It was therefore clear that the Stock Exchanges of Sydney, Melbourne and Adelaide would be much more closely linked in the future. Given the ultimate economic prospects of Australia – which few doubted – it made sense to be involved in that future, and several applicants were in the market for seats on the Adelaide Exchange in 1943. Captain Donald Turnbull, a sporting goods salesman then on service in the north of Australia, was the first to apply, and acquired a seat in late 1942. Two or three others bought seats before Maurice Hamer's seat came on the market. Mr Hamer wrote a letter to the Chairman of the Exchange expressing his deep regret at having finally to sever his links with his much valued colleagues; but he was going to sell, and that was the end of it.

Somewhat to the surprise of others, the Hamer seat was acquired by an employee of another member – one Mr Don Bradman. Mr Bradman was, as was the custom, duly elected a member of the Exchange. It was, of course, noted, although nobody knew the precise figure, that the seat had changed hands at between £300, the nominal price fixed by the Exchange itself, and £350. Neither price bore any relation to the prices paid for seats before the War. The conclusion was clear: there was a shrewd operator about. As it turned out, the conclusion was reasonable enough; but it would take some considerable time before the shrewd operator could realise the benefit of his investment.

In practice, the benefit from any such move would, without doubt, have to wait for the end of the War. Until then, the main business of the Exchange, such as it was, would continue to be in Commonwealth Loans. Business in shares would continue to be confined to distress sales – by trustees of estates or investors selling to meet tax liabilities. All in all, there was not enough business about to justify an investment in a seat. Nevertheless, as time went by, this did not deter another Hodgetts employee, Len Bullock, from buying a seat in May 1945, for £450. But by that time, of course, the War had virtually come to an end, and Bullock's investment was much safer in May 1945 than was Bradman's in May 1943.

Both Bradman and Bullock were to receive a high-voltage shock on Saturday 2 June 1945. On that day, much to the general astonishment, Harry Hodgetts informed the Exchange that he was unable to meet his commitments. In other words, he, and by extension his firm, was bankrupt. Unknown to anybody, as it turned out, he had been propping up his business by a series of dubious deals, stretching back, so it was said, to the early 1940s. He had also relied on a sub-lease on the ground floor of the offices of H.W. Hodgetts & Co. at 23 Grenfell Street, in the centre of Adelaide; the head lease being, for reasons which nobody could make out, in the name of D.G. Bradman.

Whatever the reason for Bradman owning that particular lease, there is no doubt that he had to move quickly to shore up his position. He was, after all, dependent on his stockbroking for his livelihood while there was no cricket to be played. At the same time as the announcement of the bankruptcy of H.W. Hodgetts & Co. came the announcement of the bankruptcy of Harry Hodgetts himself. There was only one thing for Bradman to do: take over as much of Hodgetts' business as he could. He discussed with the Official Receiver the clearing up of clients' open accounts – not least his own, since he was a creditor himself. He further arranged with the Receiver to use not only the ground floor of 23 Grenfell Street, on which he immediately cancelled the sub-lease, but also the furniture – free of charge pending a valuation, at which point he would have an option to buy it. He further submitted a list of outstanding settlements to the Adelaide Stock Exchange. Finally, he applied straight away to the committee of the Exchange to register his new firm's name as Don Bradman & Co. The application was quickly granted. In its issue of 5 June 1945, the Adelaide *Advertiser* announced that 'Mr Don Bradman started in business on his own account in the name of Don Bradman & Company, stock and share brokers, yesterday.'[18] The piece appeared above the *Advertiser*'s daily report on the previous day's fruit and vegetable market.

Bradman – together with Len Bullock – had acted with commendable speed to retrieve a situation of potential personal disaster. But matters became very much more difficult when the Official Receiver's report was submitted to the Bankruptcy Court. Police arrested Hodgetts, now aged sixty-three and suffering from rheumatic gout, at his Kensington Park home and charged him with three counts of fraud. When the case came to court, Hodgetts pleaded guilty to fraudulent conversion and false pretences. The whole thing became more and more murky. It appeared that some £2.5 million had passed through his firm's books in 1939, when he was still solvent, but that even then he had had an overdraft of £50,000 at his bank. His difficulties had increased by 1942, when Bradman had re-joined the firm; his overdraft had grown, and he had had to rely on loans and guarantees from friends. He had even pledged his Adelaide Club debentures as security for a loan. In passing sentence, the judge agreed with defence counsel's plea that Hodgetts had not embarked on a deliberate course of fraud but that he had thought, like so many others, that he would be able to trade himself out of his difficulties. Nevertheless, fraud was fraud and the only possible sentence was a prison term. The judge fixed it at five years; on hearing this, Hodgetts was unable to restrain his tears.

In the prim Adelaide of the day the whole affair caused much sensation, and even drove the news of the final phase of the War off the top of the agenda for society gossip. It was widely reported in the press, Hodgetts being described variously as the 'former debonair man-about-town' or 'the well-dressed Grenfell Street commercial business leviathan'.[19] It was further known that Lord and Lady Gowrie had entrusted their portfolios to Hodgetts, and that they were considering suing their agent, the Commonwealth Bank of Australia, for recovery of their lost assets. In all this chatter, it hardly needs saying that the position of Don Bradman was also much discussed. Given that the staff of Hodgetts & Co. had amounted to a mere five, including a younger Hodgetts, Bullock and Bradman, it seemed to those on the outside that they must have known of their employer's problems.

In fact, Bradman had been caught quite unawares by Hodgetts' bankruptcy, and, indeed, by his long-standing malfeasance. But it was hard to find anyone to believe him. It was harder still to retain Hodgetts' former clients. Nevertheless, and with some support from his bankers, Bradman managed to make a go of it. Enough people trusted him to leave their accounts where they were. Don Bradman & Co. climbed, laboriously and by dint of hard work, into serious business. But the road was certainly uphill; and, indeed, there was a further complication. The publicity given to Bradman's entry into business in his own name had raised the whole matter of stockbrokers' advertising. Other brokers complained that Don Bradman & Co. had deliberately sought, and got, publicity. Under the rules of the Exchange that was strictly forbidden. Bradman was forced into giving evidence to the committee that it was none of his doing – that he had not issued any statement or communiqué of any sort. The committee accepted him at his word, as, indeed, they were bound to, but an unpleasant mist of bad feeling remained.

There had, of course, been compensations for Bradman during the difficult period between his return to Adelaide in April 1942 and the Hodgetts disaster of June 1945. Apart from his continuing interest in the Gowrie Scholarship Trust Fund, he had been elected, first to the committee and then to the Presidency, of the Commonwealth Club of Adelaide. The club may not have had the social cachet of the Adelaide Club itself, but there were a thousand or so members, mostly from the business community, and it was at least one rung on the social ladder. There were dinners, to which distinguished visitors were invited – Dame Enid Lyons, for instance, the formidable widow of Prime Minister Joseph Lyons, and 'Honest John' Curtin, the then Prime Minister of Australia. There were also the pleasures of living a relaxed life with his family. Cricket, as he later wrote himself, 'never crossed my mind'.[20] That may be true, but, if so, it indicates only how far Bradman was able to concentrate on the matter nearest to hand.

By the time the War in Japan came to an end in August 1945, Don Bradman & Co. had started to find its feet. With the arrival of peace, stock markets all over the world were picking up, and Adelaide was no exception. Besides, the restrictions on dealing were relaxed. True, the passage of the Commonwealth Bank Act and the Banking Act in the same month not only turned the Commonwealth Bank into a federal central institution with wide powers of monetary control, but also imposed tighter controls on commercial bank lending. The project to nationalise the Adelaide Electric Supply Company also dampened sentiment. But, all in all, it was not a bad time to be starting a new business. Yet it needed hard work – and sometimes long hours – and secretarial assistance from Jessie.

Gradually, however, the business settled down, and Bradman's daily life became like that of millions of businessmen the world over. At about 8:30 A.M. on weekdays he kissed Jessie goodbye and took the tram from near his house to travel the three miles to his office, leaving his car at home. Once at his office he walked through the outer room, past the young man who acted as receptionist and the shelf of tidily arranged financial papers for visitors to read, went into the inner office and started work at the desk which he had placed strategically facing the door. There was, as one visitor reported, 'a subdued, stable atmosphere about the office . . . it reminds one of a family solicitor's place, except that it is tidier'.[21] Bradman's own room was panelled, carpeted and quiet; his desk was 'immaculate'. On the desk sat two photographs: an Australian Test team of pre-War years and a coloured photograph of his two children – 'both good-looking and more plump than their father'. Bradman dealt quietly and efficiently with his clients who came to see him, but although there was not much laughter or affability, he was able to put them at their ease by his courtesy and, on many occasions, charm. But, as always, he was careful what he said. 'He will either tell you what you want to know or he won't . . . I got the impression that wild horses could not drag an indiscretion from him.'[22]

The working day completed, Bradman left the office at 5:30 P.M. and took the tram home. Evenings and weekends were spent quietly – perhaps a game of golf, some piano-playing or gramophone records or playing in the garden with the children. It was a pleasant enough life, but there was a darker side. It was not just the lingering suspicion, however unworthy, in the Adelaide business community that he had had a greater involvement in the Hodgetts affair than he cared to admit – even as late as 1952 the Melbourne *Truth* ran a series of articles, entitled 'Rogues of the Stock Exchange', the first of which was devoted to Hodgetts (who by then had conveniently died). Peace had brought with it the return of the Australian soldiers, airmen and sailors who had fought overseas. With them in turn came the stories of battles in the north African desert, of comradeship in the skies over Europe, of mates who had not come back and, above all, of the horrors of the Japanese prisoner-of-war camps and the Burma railway. The Australians, rightly, were proud of themselves. As an example of their dash and cavalier spirit, it was said of Keith Miller, soon to be a cricketer for Australia, that after a sortie over Germany he had had to ditch his bullet-riddled aeroplane in an English field, but that when the police searched for the missing Australian pilot they found him joining in a village cricket match more than a mile away. That, they said, had been the spirit of the Australian War. To mark it, they reinvigorated the Returned Services League and forged a lapel badge 'RSL', which they wore with pride, as their fathers had worn the Gallipoli badge in 1918.

Sad – and silly – but true, the pride of the 'RSL' had its reverse side: resentment against those who had not fought overseas. Bradman, of course, was one of those, and it was a reflection of the old jealousies which he had provoked that he was attacked more than, for instance, O'Reilly, who had not even bothered to volunteer for service at all. It was of course all very unfair, since Bradman had done all he could to demonstrate his patriotism, and, indeed, had he not accepted Gowrie's advice to transfer to the Army, might well have continued in the Air Force and have flown missions over occupied Europe just like the others. But, as Bradman knew as well as anybody, fairness is not necessarily part of life.

Peace also brought with it a return to the interests of pre-War. In Australia this meant a renewal of the passion for sport –

and, in particular, cricket. Now that they had got round to it, Australians realised that the major question in the cricket world was whether Don Bradman would play cricket again and, if so, for whom and at what level. In August 1945, even before the peace with Japan had been signed, the South Australian Cricket Association elected him as one of their three members on the Australian Board of Control – ironically to the place formerly held by Harry Hodgetts. He took his seat (at the age of thirty-seven, he was by far the youngest member there) on 6 September. The following month the Australian government announced that an English Test team would be welcome for the 1946–47 season, and the MCC immediately took up the challenge.

There was by now intense press interest. Everybody knew that Bradman had had an acute muscular condition and had not held a cricket bat for nearly five years. It therefore came as a surprise when he turned out for South Australia over the Christmas holiday. As it turned out, he did well: 68 in the first innings and 52 not out in the second. He followed this up with a chanceless 112 for South Australia against an Australian Services side a few days later. The *Advertiser* was also back on form: 'Don Bradman is fit,' reported its correspondent – bizarrely named Harry Kneebone – 'in cricket form and in physical condition . . . played all bowlers with sublime confidence . . . sprinted up the grandstand steps at the end of his innings.'[23]

But it was not that easy. Bradman was, at thirty-seven, at the age when Australian cricketers generally looked to retirement. His stockbroking business was still fragile, and needed to be nurtured. Furthermore, his shoulder was not completely mended, and from time to time still went into painful spasm. He certainly ruled out a late season tour of New Zealand in the autumn of the 1945–46 season, and refused to give any indication to the press of whether he would or would not play again against the English when they came. 'Bradman himself could not be interviewed,' reported one eager journalist. 'He remained detached, unapproachable, uncommunicative,' said another, '. . . his only comment [was] that he did not want to be pestered with posers about his cricket future, and when stirred out of his silence he made only acid reference to inquisitive people who should mind their own business.'[24]

There was no shifting him. His refusal to commit himself was absolute. The answer to the major question Australia was asking would just have to wait.

11

WILL HE OR WON'T HE?

'FOR A FEW YEARS AFTER THE Second World War it seemed possible that Australia was on the brink of self-discovery. As in so many other countries it was an extraordinary time. Past darkness and future brightness came together in startling contrast, and for a moment there was a lapse from passion and prejudice and a glimpse of moral courage and hope.'[1] The sentiment, of course, was by no means unique to Australia. In one way or another, all the belligerents in the Second World War were having to come to terms with the changes in national psychology and consequent political turmoil which were the unforeseen – and unforeseeable – results of a long and bitter intercontinental conflict. The adjustment to peace in 1945 was as hard in its own way as it had been in 1918.

Admittedly, Australia was to some extent on the periphery of the Second World War – at least in the early period. True, troops had been sent to help the British Empire in its time of gravest danger. That was all very well; it was a call to ancient loyalties. But when the Japanese threat became more than just a hypothesis, with the fall of Singapore and the bombing of Darwin, it was no longer a matter of fighting out of loyalty. 'The fall of Singapore opens the Battle for Australia,'[2] Prime Minister Curtin had announced on 16 February 1942. Indeed it had. Australian troops had soon found themselves fighting the Japanese in New Guinea – the last stop, as it were, before Australia itself – and, during March, not only Darwin but the neighbouring towns of Wyndham and Broome had been raided several times. In May, Japanese submarines had forced their way into Sydney Harbour and shelled civilian homes on the surrounding hills. There had followed, as might be imagined, a measure of panic among those affected – even looting in the shops, it was said – and something of a shudder throughout Australia. It was the familiar problem: nobody thought that it could possibly happen to them. But there it was; the enemy was on the doorstep.

The attacks on the Australian mainland, of course, can hardly be compared with the London blitz, the fire-bombing of Hamburg or the nuclear destruction of Hiroshima and Nagasaki. But what became progressively clearer, as the panic started to die down, was that the only power which could possibly act as Australia's ally – indeed as Australia's only effective shield – was the United States. The British Empire was, to say the least, occupied elsewhere and was, as far as the defence of Australia was concerned, completely out of the game. So strong was this feeling that General MacArthur, Supreme Commander of Allied Forces in the Pacific, soon set up his headquarters not in Hawaii, which might have seemed the natural place, but in Australia – first in Melbourne and then in Brisbane. After the New Guinea campaign, Australian forces were assigned to his command, while the Australian government made no effort at all – even had they been capable of doing so – to intervene in the American conduct of the War.

The cumulative effect of these events was, in psychological terms, almost as profound in Australia as in other countries whose territories had been invaded or otherwise devastated in the conflict. The whole question of national identity was raised. The obvious was suddenly discovered: Australia was vulnerable and Britain could no longer be considered a viable protector. Certainly it took a little time for this view to be put forward in strength, and even then it was not shared everywhere or with the same enthusiasm. Nevertheless, however different the answers given, the question itself could not be shrugged off. In essence, it was simple: whether post-War Australia was to revert to the status of a distant appendage of the British Empire or whether there was an opportunity to be grasped as a secondary power in an American-dominated south Pacific.

Of course, as with all such grand and sweeping questions, there were complications at the personal level, which, in the end, had a powerful effect on the outcome. The unfortunate truth was that nobody had much personal liking for American troops. In

Brisbane, there had been an open street battle in November 1942 between American soldiers and Queensland residents, and the same type of incident had occurred in Melbourne in February 1943, and in both Sydney and Perth in the late summer of 1944. As in wartime Britain, so in wartime Australia; the American serviceman was a figure of resentment – and sometimes open derision. An uneasy situation resulted. Australia found itself owing its formal loyalty to Britain, while realising that the British had failed to provide the ultimate guarantee such loyalty demanded, but at the same time was fully aware of the reality of its debt to America, while heartily disliking Americans. It was just at that moment that Australia could be said to have been 'on the brink of self-discovery'.

It was against this complex background that Australians made their choice. It was perhaps not just a matter of nostalgia; there were problems at home, of rebuilding and social welfare, that needed attention. Rather than embark on new and radical adventures in foreign policy, Australians seemed to be in the mood to choose the devil they knew, whatever that devil's obvious deficiencies. Australia turned back to Britain, and back to its old method of self-assertion – sport.

The symbol of this return to competitive sporting normality was, without any doubt, Don Bradman. It was he who had been the pre-War hero, repeatedly and satisfactorily slaying the imperial Goliath. Besides, he was all that Australians thought that they stood for – the 'boy from Bowral' making good. But quite apart from the question over Bradman's future, nearly eight years had elapsed since the last Ashes Test series, and many of the old war-horses were no longer able to respond to the sound of battle. O'Reilly, for instance, had gone on the half-hearted tour of New Zealand in 1945–46; he had finished the First Test more or less immobilised. 'When I walked in off the field,' he said, 'my old knee felt so crook that I thought: "Well, this is it, mate."'[3] And indeed it was. Fingleton, too, had given up; McCabe and Fleetwood-Smith as well. Of the 1938 team, only Hassett, Brown and Barnes were still playing serious cricket. It was all the more obvious that, on any analysis, the only figure of stature who could lead Australia back into the post-War cricket era was 'the little feller', the sick man of Adelaide, the wartime invalid now nearing forty. It is little wonder that all Australia wanted to know precisely what he was proposing to do.

As far as the politics of the post-War period are concerned, Bradman's position seems to be reasonably clear. He belonged, as it were, to the pre-War school. If there was a question of Australia facing a period of renewal, his instinct was to be in favour of any renewal taking place within the context of the British Empire. He had, after all, been entertained by the British Royal Family, and he had been quick to respond, however unsuccessfully, to the patriotic call, and during the 1930s regularly referred to England as 'Home' or 'The Old Country'. Furthermore, he had shown no particular sympathy for Americans during Mailey's 'honeymoon' tour of 1931. Indeed, the widely reported meeting between Bradman and 'Babe' Ruth, the brilliant but louche baseball player of the American 1930s, consisted in reality of little more than a succession of prolonged silences. 'Self-discovery', whatever that might have meant, was not on the agenda in Kensington Park.

What was on the agenda, on the other hand, was whether Bradman could – or would – face up to the challenge of leading Australia out of its post-War vacuum and back into the old pre-War sporting rivalries. He was, after all, quite content making his living as an Adelaide stockbroker – and playing his golf and enjoying his family. One or two reasonably successful innings over the 1945 Christmas holiday had not changed that. Besides, he was still not free from recurrences of muscular trouble, and his general health was still suspect. Nevertheless, he was well aware of the responsibility which was now his. He knew that all Australia was looking to him – the press comment told him that. He also knew that, in his own words, 'cricket badly needed a good start in the post-War era',[4] and that he was the person to provide it. Jessie, too, added her voice. It would be a pity, she said, if their son John grew up without ever having seen his father play Test cricket.

There were, however, two problems which had to be dealt with. The first was his business. It had not been going for long, and still needed his personal attention. If he was to be away for extended periods playing cricket he ran the risk of losing clients. The situation was very much complicated in May 1946 by an offer of £10,000 from a London newspaper to report the Test series against England. 'The financial reward for not playing,' Bradman later said – with delicate understatement – 'was tempting.'[5] Nevertheless it was rejected. Arrangements were made with Len Bullock to look after the firm in his absence, Jessie agreeing to go in and lend a hand. During the winter of 1946 it looked very much as though the decision was sliding in favour of him playing, and leading Australia against the English when they arrived in the spring.

The second problem was Bradman's state of health. This, too, had seemed at one point to be moving towards a solution. During the winter of 1946 he underwent, on the recommendation of his colleague on the Australian selection committee, 'Chappie' Dwyer, extended treatment from Ern Saunders, a Melbourne masseur who specialised in injuries to athletes. He had had another bad attack in his shoulder, again being unable to write or to shave. There was, however, no treatment which was more advanced than before. Fortunately Saunders' manipulation, although extremely painful, seemed to bear fruit. But no sooner did it seem that his muscular problems were at last nearing a cure when he developed gastritis. It must have seemed that his troubles would never end. He had now lost a stone in weight, his face looked pinched and drawn. To cap it all, he went into hospital again, this time for a minor operation.

By then – September 1946 – the MCC team under Walter Hammond was safely aboard the *Stirling Castle* on its way to Fremantle. Hammond, of course, had been one of the great batsmen of the 1930s, but he was now forty-three years old; furthermore, domestic problems had soured his temperament – never particularly friendly – and he was apt to lose his temper easily. But he had had a fine season in England in 1946 and could hardly be passed over for the captaincy. Indeed, he started off the tour with a double century against Western Australia at Perth. With Hammond came much of the pre-War English talent: Hutton, Compton, Wright, Edrich and Hardstaff. On paper it was a good enough group of players, but it was noted that some of them seemed still to bear physical traces of their years of wartime service, and all looked thin and unfit.

Their arrival in Australia was the object of much – rather sentimental – rejoicing, nowhere more so than in Adelaide. When they reached the city they were immediately taken to a reception in the Town Hall hosted by the Lord Mayor. As the players took their places on the dais there was 'prolonged clapping'. The Mayor called Hammond 'one of the greatest sportsmen of all time' and went on to say: 'We want you to remind people at home how proud we are to be members of the great British Empire.'[6] The wish to cling on to Britain's hand could hardly have been more clearly expressed.

Even at that stage it was not clear what Bradman's final decision would be. Those English players who had known the Bradman of 1938 were shocked when they saw the Bradman of 1946. Compton, for instance, recorded later that 'some of us wondered whether or not he was due for a nursing home rather than a cricket pitch'.[7] There was no disguising the fact that he was ill; indeed just before the English team's arrival he had spent a further ten days in hospital with a recurrence of gastric trouble. Nevertheless, only eight days before the start of the MCC vs. South Australia match he had his first practice of the season. His eyesight had completely recovered, and those who watched him thought his form to be good. Two days later he played for Kensington, scored 42 not out – and pronounced himself fit to play for South Australia.

It was a relief to everybody. The press, perhaps unfairly, had begun to get irritated at what they were starting to think was Bradman's hypochondria, and were glad that he had at last made up his mind to play. They also realised that if he was going to play for South Australia he was going to play as well for the Australian team itself. Given what the Australians thought of the power of the English side, the fact that Bradman considered himself fit enough would, in the words of Adelaide's Lord Mayor, 'thereby equalise things for us'.[8]

It was a courageous decision. Now aged thirty-eight, he could easily have decided to rest on the laurels of the 1930s; he could have made himself a great deal of money by writing instead of playing; and, on a more mundane note (but one, as always, important to Bradman) it was most unlikely that he would be able to sustain his career average of 95.82. But, although it is not difficult to believe that Bradman may have been over-anxious about his health, it is without doubt right to take him at his own word. 'The over-riding consideration, which I could not dismiss from my conscience, was that it was my duty to do whatever lay in my power to assist my country in the restoration of a sport which meant so much to Australians.'[9]

As it happened, Bradman spent the first two days of his resumed first-class cricket career in the field, while MCC accumulated 506 for 5 – both Hutton and Washbrook scoring centuries. After a day's rest, Bradman went in before lunch on the Monday with South Australia at 26 for 2. He spent half an hour reaching double figures, was missed at the wicket off Pollard when he was 15, and only then settled down. He was finally out for 76 to his first ball after the tea interval. Nevertheless, he had shown 'the never-to-be-forgotten Bradman strokes, including powerful punches off the back foot on both sides of the wicket . . . He nursed himself wisely,' the journalist went on, 'as he is still short of full health, but he seems likely to be his old dominating batting self by the end of November when the first Test is due. Write him down as a certainty to captain Australia again.'[10]

In fact it was only just about enough, and there was further doubt about his form when he only survived eight balls in the second innings. All doubts vanished, however, when he made 106 for an Australian XI against the MCC, in a partnership of 205 with the young Arthur Morris, and followed with 43 and 119 in a Sheffield Shield match against Victoria. It was no surprise, when the Australian side for the First Test was announced, that Bradman's name was included. Only a few cynics remarked how strikingly his health seemed to improve when he made runs.

Bradman was duly appointed captain of Australia. Whatever the doubts, it was what he had always wanted. To have finished his Test career with the rout of Australia at the Oval in 1938 would have been a personal humiliation. That disaster had to be reversed. So it was that Bradman approached the First Test, starting in Brisbane on 29 November 1946, in a spirit of determination amounting almost to ruthlessness. He always liked winning, but this series, whatever lofty thoughts he might express about his duty to Australian cricket, was to be revenge for the Oval 1938. It only added spice that England's captain was the self-same Hammond who had led England to triumph in that match. Hammond must go down, and England with him.

In the event, that was precisely what happened. A combination of powerful Australian batting and the Brisbane weather brought about the heaviest defeat England had suffered to date, by an innings and 332 runs. But it was not achieved without controversy. Indeed, an incident occurred which caused more friction between the two teams than any single incident since Woodfull was hit over the heart by Larwood in the Adelaide Test of 1933.

The facts, apart from the one main question, are reasonably simple. Bradman, after winning the toss, came in when the score was 9 for 1. A further Australian wicket fell at 46. Bradman himself was in great difficulty with Alec Bedser, whom he was facing for the first time. 'Bradman's survival through his opening minutes,' it was reported, 'was close upon miraculous.'[11] When he had made 28 scratchy runs, Bradman faced Voce, bowling as usual left arm over the wicket. Voce bowled a ball that was of full length – 'near enough to a yorker',[12] Bradman described it later. Bradman tried to chop down on it (with his bat at an angle) to guide it through the slips. The ball flew to Ikin at second slip and was caught at chest height. The English fielders were then astonished – or professed themselves astonished – to see Bradman standing at his crease 'idly looking away over the square-leg boundary'[13] as Hammond put it. 'Somewhat belatedly',[14] there was an appeal, and the umpire at the bowler's end immediately gave Bradman not out.

The main question, of course, was whether the ball pitched before Bradman edged it for a fair catch, as the English fielders contended, or whether it had hit the bottom of Bradman's bat before it reached the ground and was therefore a 'bump ball', as Bradman himself contended – supported by both umpires and Hassett at the other end. The truth of the matter will, of course, never be known. The whole incident was over so quickly, and the difference between the two versions no more than a matter of inches. Certainly nobody who was not on the field – and paying attention – at the time could possibly have judged precisely what happened. This, needless to say, did not prevent commentators and journalists from giving authoritative views on the matter. Fingleton and O'Reilly, as might have been expected, both took the view that Bradman was out, and wrote as much later. O'Reilly was particularly forthright. 'I am quite sure,' he wrote, 'that the Australian captain must have had grave doubts as to the excellence of the decision when he thought over the facts of the case later on. To get a bump ball to go shoulder high at a speed sufficient to spin Ikin side-on needs some uncanny propulsion seldom seen in cricket.'[15] Other press opinion was divided. Of the players on the field, Yardley – fielding in the gully and hence watching the outside edge of the bat as the stroke was made – was clear that it was a fair catch, as was Ikin himself, Wright and Bedser and, of course, Hammond.

In a number of ways the 'Ikin incident', as it is known, was a decisive point in the whole Test series. For a start, Bradman went on to make 187 in a partnership of 276 with Hassett; Australia's grip on the match was, by then, vice-like. A thunderstorm ensured that England would have to bat on a sticky wicket, and they were bowled out twice. That was bad enough; but on top of that Hammond had lost his temper, and at the end of the over had walked up to Bradman to say, in the bitterest of voices: 'A fine fucking way to start a series.'[16] If the incident itself was not enough to sour relations, Hammond's language certainly was. It is difficult to find evidence of the two captains greeting each other with anything but hostility for the rest of the series. Admittedly, at the end of the Test match, Hammond, obviously in order to repair relationships, said (according to Bradman): 'I thought it was a catch, but the umpire may have been right and I may have been wrong.'[17] But neither then nor now does it sound very convincing.

There was, perhaps, a consequence of the 'Ikin incident' which was longer lasting. In interviews with the Australian press Bradman is reported by Yardley as having – apparently – said: 'I did not know I had given any catch. I heard an appeal; the umpire indicated not out; so I batted on. Naturally, if I had thought I was out, I should not have stayed there.'[18] Yardley, without meaning to imply any 'unsportsmanship', threw doubt on the suggestion. The meaning, however, was clear: opponents of Australians always knew that they played 'hard', but fair. Much of the unsmiling efficiency of Australian cricket seemed to stem from Bradman's approach to the game. What was apparently new was the practice of waiting for an umpire's decision before leaving the crease when the batsman knows that he is out. This was clearly not the case in the Ikin incident, since Bradman did not think that he was out and, indeed, may well not have been. But at least one captain of England takes the view that the practice of waiting for the umpire's decision even when there is no doubt and, indeed, of protesting against the umpire's decision, became the fashion that it is today not least because of what occurred in Brisbane on 29 November 1946.

By now, it was clear that Bradman had made up his mind that toughness and determination were the order of the day. There was to be no quarter given, and no hostages taken. It was evident in the Second Test, which started at Sydney on 13 December 1946. Another recurrence of stomach trouble and a strapped thigh did not deter him from his main objective. Although this time England won the toss and batted first, and although Bradman did not field on the second day and put himself down at no.6 in the Australian order, he nevertheless commanded the game – and made 234 himself, sharing a partnership with Barnes of 405. Again – this time without the help of the weather – England were confounded. Australia won by an innings and 33 runs.

Barnes, too, made 234, but was involved in an unpleasant incident which attracted the hostility of the crowd at the end of the second day. There was a heavy shower in the afternoon, and the pitch was playing uncomfortably when Australia opened their first innings. Barnes lost Morris to Edrich at 24, but then proceeded to appeal repeatedly against the light. Each appeal was booed by the crowd, and when the fifth appeal was upheld Barnes was heckled off the field. He later admitted that it was the drying pitch rather than the light which had been the worry, and went on to claim that he was acting under instructions from Bradman. 'Bradman told me,' he said, 'to get my head down, stay there at all costs and appeal against the light at the first opportunity . . . Bradman told me he wanted to bat as little as possible that day.'[19]

It was certainly within the laws of the game, but the intention of the law was equally certainly pushed to the edge. Nobody could quite understand why the last appeal was upheld since, according to one journalist, 'the light did not seem to have grown worse than at the first [appeal]'.[20] Nevertheless, play finished an hour early, Bradman did not have to bat on a sticky wicket and, after a dry weekend, the pitch rolled out perfectly on the Monday morning. As Barnes later said, 'It was a Test match and we just had to win.'[21]

Bradman's innings was, even by his own standards, quite out of the ordinary. As he described it himself, 'I was fortunate to bat at all. On the Friday I tore a leg muscle which prevented me from fielding on Saturday. This was followed by an attack of gastritis which kept me in bed most of the weekend, and I felt far below par on the Monday. Even then my leg was heavily strapped and the whole innings was played off the back foot. I scarcely made a forward shot the whole day.'[22] Indeed, he was 'not feeling too well' on the Monday night when he returned to his hotel after making 52 not out. There was some doubt whether he would be able to play at all on the Tuesday. But play he did, and he and Barnes stayed together until seventeen minutes from the close of play. 'Bradman's batting,' wrote R.S. Whitington about his innings, 'convinces me that if his body was only hanging together by strips of adhesive tape, he would still score a century against any bowling the world can at present put against him.'[23]

All in all, it was confirmation that the Australian attitude to the game was as tough as it could be within the rules. But it undoubtedly worked. As far as Bradman was concerned, in spite of his painful leg and gastritis, he had shown twice that he could play a long Test innings. Indeed, the adulation of the crowds was back to the level of the 1930s. His innings at Sydney, his eighth successive century against England but his first against England at Sydney, was followed ball by ball by the largest crowd ever seen at the SCG on a Monday. When Bradman was out, a large section of the crowd simply got up and left. The next batsman in, McCool, who had sat padded up for two days, had to struggle through the departing spectators to get on to the field. 'If I'd have walked out to the crease wearing a false nose and smoking a cigar,' he reflected later, 'nobody would have noticed.'[24]

Australia had re-discovered her hero. Bradman had scored 421 runs in his first two post-War innings against the mother country. Crowds followed him everywhere. It was rumoured that he would be going into politics, that safe seats were being held open for him by both the Labor and the Liberal parties, that he was going to retire at the end of the Sydney Test. None of this, of course, was true; Bradman never showed any interest whatsoever in party politics. But it is a measure of the general belief in the infallibility of their hero that Australians thought he could not only beat anybody at cricket but that he could run the country as well.

In the event, Bradman only played in four more first-class matches in the 1946–47 season, all of them against the tourists. He stood down from South Australia's Sheffield Shield games against New South Wales and Queensland, taking a three-week rest between the Fourth and Fifth Tests to go back to Adelaide and look after his business. In the New Year Test at Melbourne he was out for 79 and 49, both times to Yardley. Astonishing as it may seem, it was the first time that he had failed to make a century in a Melbourne Test, and his poor form – relatively – was demonstrated by his scoring only two boundaries in his first innings, and being almost lbw to Wright for 3 and missed at the wicket off Bedser when 44. Nevertheless, centuries by McCool in the first innings, and by Morris and Lindwall in the second, were enough to ensure a draw. The Ashes stayed in Australia.

But there were two more unpleasant episodes: both Edrich and Compton disputed their respective lbw decisions. The English press supported them. The London *Evening Standard* declared flatly that Edrich had played the ball on to his pads, and went on to say that 'this unfortunate decision against Edrich may have cost England the Ashes'.[25] The *Star* sniffed that the two decisions 'only serve to show that the Australian umpiring standard is below that of England'.[26] The Australian press hit back. 'The campaign against Australian umpires by a small but powerful section of the English press is sinister,' retorted the Melbourne *Age*. 'It deserves to be sneered at . . . The truth is that the English team is not good enough.'[27] Yet again, what should have been minor events on the field of play became objects of sour comment on both sides. The post-War tour of goodwill was, in terms of relations between the two countries, turning into something near to a fiasco.

The Fourth Test at Adelaide started on 30 January. The weather was very hot and humid, but a large crowd turned out – not least to see Bradman bat. They were to be disappointed. England batted well to make 460 in the first innings, and Australia were 18 for 1 when Bradman went to the wicket eighteen minutes before close of play on the Saturday. Eight balls later he was out – bowled by Bedser for 0. Bradman later described the ball as 'the best ball ever bowled to me'.[28] Be that as it may, the crowd let out a howl of dismay; their weekend had been ruined. 'Depression was written on every face,' Compton noted. 'You might have thought that they had lost their life savings in a crash.'[29] But it could have been worse. In his second innings Bradman only narrowly avoided another duck, nearly playing his second ball, this time from Yardley, on to his wicket. He did, however, go on to make fifty in just over the hour before finishing the game 'in very dull fashion',[30] making only 6 in the final twenty-three minutes. The game itself drifted away into a draw in equally dull fashion.

For Bradman, the last Test at Sydney was little better. He had had no match practice for nearly a month, and looked badly out of touch. Again, 'thousands of people were at the ground specially to see Bradman bat . . . they were unlucky to see him on one of his worst days.'[31] When only 12, after nearly half an hour at the crease, he jumped down the wicket to Wright, hit right across a straight half-volley and was bowled.

But his second innings was altogether a more serious affair. Now it was a question of winning the match, and even though the Ashes were safe, any Test match had to be won. He was lucky to be dropped at slip by Edrich when only 2, but after that played up to his best form against Wright and Bedser on a wicket that was helping both bowlers – particularly Bedser's leg-cutter.

When he was finally out to Bedser after nearly two hours for 63 – slow batting by Bradman standards – he, together with Hassett, had put Australia within sight of victory. It was duly achieved, and Australia had won the series without conceding a match.

'That winning hit closed the nastiest and most acrimonious season I've ever experienced in 39 years of cricket, including 15 years as an umpire.'[32] These were the words of the Australian umpire, Jack Scott, announcing his retirement. It was perhaps overstated, but Scott had been the umpire who had made the decisions against Compton and Edrich which had provoked the English press to fury – Compton was cheated out, they said – and had been attacked mercilessly. 'I'm getting out of the game,' Scott went on. 'I've had it.'[33]

It had indeed been an acrimonious series, played in a manner which was both dour and hostile (although not as bad as the 1932–33 tour). The personalities of Hammond and Bradman seemed antipathetic, and Bradman's determination in his captaincy had made the series into a much rougher contest than was necessary. After all, in announcing that Australia would welcome the tour, Dr Evatt, the Australian Minister for External Affairs, had been trying to be helpful. But as the English players packed their bags for the return journey they were in a sour and resentful mood. Nor were the English journalists any more cheerful. But the truth is that the hangover from the War – not least many years of danger when the thought of Test cricket being played again was almost irreverent – was too much for them. They were, as the Australian press pointed out, not yet good enough; and Bradman was certainly not in a mood to make concessions to weakness. He was, as has been said, 'now a man of vast experience, steeped in the ways of Test cricket and wedded immovably to the concept of Test cricket as a matter of life and death'.[34]

Fortunately, and probably as a result of the effort to create a post-War harmony between the two countries, the acrimony and antagonisms mattered less at the time than they had fourteen years earlier. They seemed to pass away as froth on the sea of the great post-War events that were taking place. Indeed, in terms of Australian 'self-discovery', the 1946–47 tour added nothing. On the contrary, it was in itself a form of retrogression. Certainly there was a genuine attempt to pretend that the War had never happened, to pick up the threads which had been abruptly cut in September 1939. But the world had moved on, and, whatever the nostalgic view of the imperial past, the two countries – Britain as well as Australia – had, however subtly, moved apart. If the tour was acrimonious, it was because the English thought – however subconsciously – to restore their old right to dictate the cultural future of a British dominion, while the Australians were seeking – equally, however subconsciously – a new post-War identity.

Bradman, of course, was caught in the middle. He knew perfectly well, and said so on many occasions, that he felt it his duty, whatever his health problems, to lead Australia back into the game that had been the common denominator of the British Empire. On the other hand, he surely knew that the British Empire was in practice on the verge of exhausted collapse. The result was that by an odd paradox he found himself, in that sense, playing for – as well as against – old England.

The role of imperial cricket's elder statesman, since that is what he had by now become, was evident during the Indian tour of Australia of 1947–48. The MCC tour of 1946–47 had certainly been something of a strain. But Bradman had had a winter of rest in 1947, with his wife and young family and his stockbroking career. Reflecting on the events of the previous summer, it was clear to him that his decision to resume Test cricket had turned out, whatever the risks, to have been the right one. His average for the 1946–47 Test series had been 97.14. Admittedly, his fielding had not been as sharp as it once was, and he had rationed his first-class cricket with great care; but he had still scored 1,000 runs for the season and had headed the averages. The risk to his health had been justified. Indeed, at the end of the 1946–47 season he had looked very much better, in spite of all the effort he put into it, than he had at the beginning.

The Indian tour was an altogether more relaxed affair than the MCC tour of 1946–47. For a start, the Indians represented a country which had only recently come into being – and had been born in conditions which can only be described as murderous. Indeed, one of the team originally picked, Fazal Mahmood, was forced to drop out since, living in Lahore, he was deemed to be Pakistani. Moreover, it was the first tour of Australia by a team from the Indian sub-continent and the first time that they had been faced with a five-match Test series. Finally, Indian cricket was all played on matting wickets because, as one player ruefully remarked, 'we can't afford the water from the more important business of growing food'.[35]

There was obviously going to be no serious contest, and the Indians realised it. Pankaj Gupta, their manager, announced on their arrival that they were in Australia to learn – particularly from Bradman. '[We] would prefer to lose every match and see Bradman play,' he declared, 'than win every match and not see him.'[36] It was hardly the sort of remark to improve the morale of his side; nor did it go down well with the Indian press, who regarded it as 'creeping and crawling'. But it was probably near to the truth.

Bradman, in turn, was at his most mellow; almost – if it dare to be said – representing the old British Empire to encourage the new British Commonwealth. He was by now in what, if he had been a racehorse, would have been described as 'fine fettle'. He had also been made, in September 1947, a life member of the South Australian Cricket Association, and had received 'a gold medallion in token of such membership'.[37] Bradman was understandably pleased; it was, after all, a long way from childhood games in Bowral to life membership of the socially highbrow SACA. Nevertheless, life was not without its irritations. There had been criticism of his captaincy in the press; Fingleton had published a wounding account of the 1932–33 tour; and some journalists had gone so far as to claim that he had covertly written articles for an English newspaper on the 1946–47 Tests. Bradman was able to brush critics aside – albeit rather petulantly. 'It seems,' he said, 'that the open season is here again, and that I am to be the "Aunt Sally" for certain people who endeavour to draw attention to themselves by criticising me.'[38] Yet the mere fact that he felt moved to make a public pronouncement on the matter showed that the critics had found a sore spot.

In announcing his decision to make himself available to play against the Indians in 1947–48, Bradman let two things be known: first, that this would be his last season of Test and first-class cricket in Australia; and, second, that he had made no decision about whether he would be available for the Australian tour of England, due to take place in the English summer of 1948. After that, he allowed himself to relax. He found the Indians 'charming in every respect'[39] not least, cynics remarked, because he knew that they would put up no serious opposition. Furthermore, the Indians had indicated, in the words of one player, that 'Bradman has 97 first-class centuries, and we hope he will get his century of centuries against us'. Few players have received such an open invitation; certainly Don Bradman was not one to refuse it.

Although he had had little match practice up to then, Bradman turned out for South Australia against the Indians on 24 October 1947. He duly scored his ninety-eighth first-class century in his first innings – as it happened, in 98 minutes. He followed with another century against Victoria at Adelaide on 8 November in his only Sheffield Shield match of the season. The stage was thereby set for the event which the Indians had so patently desired: Bradman's century of centuries, to be made in his next match, for an Australian XI against the Indians at Sydney. It was, as Bradman said himself, 'of more than usual significance . . . [I had] set my heart on making that century on Sydney Cricket Ground. Throughout the years no cricket ground in the world had supplanted Sydney in my affections. I always felt that the crowds there were sympathetic towards me . . .'[40] Indeed they were, in spite of his having abandoned Sydney for Adelaide all those years ago.

'I think,' Bradman said later, 'of all my experiences in cricket, that was the most moving one.' The fifteenth of November, the second day of the match, was a Saturday. Even before lunch, the crowd numbered over 25,000, and more came in as word spread that Bradman was batting – and nearing his hundredth hundred. His partner was Keith Miller, content to feed the bowling to Bradman whenever possible. Just before tea, with Bradman 99 not out, the Indian captain, Armanath, gave the ball to Kishenchand – to bowl his first over of the tour. A push to the leg side gave Bradman his 100th century. Both the Indians and the Sydney crowd went wild.

After that, the Test series was something of an anti-climax. At Brisbane, in the First Test, bad weather ruined the game – although Bradman had time to score yet another century. The

Indians were caught on another Brisbane 'sticky' wicket, and only managed, in their two innings, to make 58 and 98. At Sydney, the Second Test was again almost washed out, only ten hours' cricket being played in all. Another two centuries, one in each innings, were racked up by Bradman at Melbourne in the Third Test, and a further double century at Adelaide in the Fourth. In the Fifth Test at Melbourne Bradman tore a cartilage under the rib when he was 57 not out, and retired hurt.

'Australia,' wrote the sports editor of an Indian newspaper travelling with the Indian players, 'cannot go on depending on Don for ever. I believe he will retire from Test cricket after the tour in England.'[41] It was no more and no less than the truth. Having announced that he had played his last Test series in Australia, Bradman announced that he would be available for the 1948 tour of England. There was no longer any doubt about his health; the only question was whether his business could survive his long absence. That problem was solved partly by the acquisition of a reliable chief clerk, but more by his wife's insistence that he should go. In the darkest times, Jessie had learned how to cope with the mechanics of the business, and, in these better times, was able to convince Don that he should make one last – and, as it turned out, glorious – appearance on the world's cricket stage. If this was to be the twilight of old England, and perhaps of old Australia, it was to be a twilight of beauty and style.

12

1948

IT WOULD PERHAPS BE AN EXAGGERATION to say that by early 1948 Bradman's character had taken on the gentle colours of autumn. He was still, after all, the same Bradman about whom Learie Constantine could write, in a book published in that year, '. . . he pities none. If he can make any bowler look foolish, he will do it . . . No room for mercy, no standing back while a disarmed rival picks up his fallen weapon . . .'[1] Nevertheless, the Indian tour of 1947–48 had shown a side of Bradman which had hitherto been hidden from his cricketing colleagues and the press. Not to put too fine a point on it, he had become much less prickly. For instance, during the Indian tour he had made it a practice to visit the Indian dressing room at the end of a day's play and tell them, in the nicest possible way, where they had gone wrong and how their game could be improved. He seemed also to go out of his way to mix with his team-mates, and even to laugh at the – admittedly tentative – jokes made at his expense. He was, in short, quite obviously getting more fun out of life.

This new-found confidence had its foundation in a happy marriage and family life. Furthermore, some of the irritants of the pre-War and War years had been removed. The press were more sympathetic – even, from time to time, reverential. More important, perhaps, the 'dissidents' in the Australian team – particularly Fingleton and O'Reilly – had retired, and he could afford to overlook, in his position as elder statesman, the occasional spasms of temperament of the newer figures in Australian cricket.

But it is perhaps not too much to say that it was in the progress of his business career that Bradman had found most satisfaction. He had taken a risk, and the gamble had come off. His long-term ambition, of finding a life for himself and his family which was not dependent on cricket, had by then almost been achieved. He had a respectable client list. He could now speak with authority about shares and bonds and use with ease the technical jargon common to financial markets. Besides, the Adelaide Stock Exchange, like other stock exchanges throughout the world, was enjoying its freedom from wartime restrictions and looking forward to the boom years of peace. All in all, Bradman could with good reason reassure himself that the sense of insecurity which had cast its shadow since his childhood was at last starting to disappear.

His confidence showed itself in a number of ways. For a start, the trilby hat – judging from the photographs of the period – was worn at a more jaunty angle. The three-piece suit with the tightly buttoned waistcoat remained, of course, but that was part of the uniform of the Adelaide businessman and there could be no question of deviating from that. But there was also much more laughter, particularly when guests came to visit his home in Kensington Park. True, he and Jessie had to cope with the now obvious disability of their daughter; she was clearly severely spastic, to the point where she had lost effective use of her right arm. But, as so often in such situations, the disability of the child, far from diminishing the parents' love, only served to deepen it. A swimming pool, for instance, was added on to the home solely for her remedial exercises.

Together with this greater balance in his life came, as is often the case, a softening of his features. The previously beak-like nose seemed to have retreated as the cheeks fleshed out and a double chin started to appear. His body was just as small and spare as always, but his face gave a less angular impression to the outside world. Whereas nobody had hitherto been quite certain whether his grin had been one of good humour or one of a predatory wolf, his smile now was obviously friendly – and was accompanied by the relaxation of the cheeks and the light in the eyes that are the sign of a well-wisher, rather than the baring of teeth of a potential enemy.

It would, of course, be a mistake to imagine that, as a result, Bradman's critics had mysteriously vanished. The old jealousies ran far too deep for that. On the other hand, and gratifyingly, the party which was selected for the 1948 tour could hardly have been more to Bradman's liking. Hassett, the dapper survivor, not just from the 1938 tour but from service in the Middle East, was the ideal vice-captain – quiet, with a deadpan sense of humour, and, above all, loyal. Brown, another survivor from 1938, was charm and modesty personified – 'a real star',[2] one of his admirers has called him. Barnes was perhaps a bit more tricky, given as he was both to conceit and, irritatingly, to adolescent practical jokes which never quite seemed to come off. Of the newer players, only Keith Miller was inclined to treat Bradman with anything other than the greatest respect – even awe. But their respect was tinged with affection; he was, after all, their senior by many years, and seemed to command a fatherly loyalty which he had been unable to achieve in the pre-War period of his captaincy. This in turn made Bradman himself more relaxed, and more ready to join in the fun – and even, it was said, on occasions to buy the others a drink.

Altogether it was a happy group which assembled in Melbourne on 4 March 1948 to fly to Tasmania for the first two matches of the tour. Admittedly, Bradman was one of the least euphoric among them; partly because, from his 1938 experience, he knew what was in store for a touring captain of Australia; partly because the rib cartilage which he had torn in the last Test against India had not properly healed; and partly – a continuing theme – 'because of resultant airsickness'.[3] The airsickness was reasonably predictable given his record of seasickness (although the critics were not slow to ask why he had applied initially for the Air Force in 1940), but it was 'disturbing', in his own words, that the torn cartilage in his side continued to trouble him. So painful was it, indeed, that he threw his wicket away in Hobart and rested for the match at Launceston.

It took time and care for the injury finally to mend, and indeed it was still giving residual trouble when the tourists arrived in England. During the journey itself, Bradman had taken a great deal of care with his team – and also with his own plans for the tour. After the experience of 1938 he was determined to be throughly prepared. By the time the *Strathaird* – now owned by the Peninsular and Orient line, but just as plush as in the old Orient days – left Fremantle, he had already given one talk to his team-mates. That had been just before they left Melbourne, but there were to be others during the long voyage to England. Although the Board of Control had relented in their opposition to wives accompanying their husbands, only Barnes had taken advantage of the new ruling, and then only because his wife had relatives in Scotland. The general view had been that Britain in 1948 was not quite the place for a relaxed holiday. The men had to make their own company; this made plenty of time for their captain's lectures.

There were two major events on the way to England. The first was the customary stop at Colombo. In truth, the town had not changed much since Bradman's first visit in 1930, and the bustle and noise of the place were just as confusing; the only change was that the newer cars made an even louder din with their horns. As always, boats rowed out to meet the incoming liner as she slowly and hesitantly manoeuvred her way into Colombo harbour. There was the usual clamour for the visiting Australians; but in reality, there was only one person they wanted to see. Bradman duly appeared to screams of delight, waved his hat in the air and smiled at the crowd. He even went so far as to play in the cricket game arranged for the tourists, and batted – perhaps somewhat eccentrically – in a topee. Strangely, the bowling seemed to come faster than the Australians expected; it was only when they went out to bowl that the pitch was measured and found to be no more than twenty yards long. Even Bradman had not noticed the missing two yards. But that, as they all said, was the way it was in Colombo.

The second event was unusual. The P & O liners, unlike the old Orient liners, stopped on their way to England at Bombay. For the Australians, it might have been a welcome port of call. The Indians had toured Australia not long before, and had made many friends. Furthermore, the country was overflowing with cricket enthusiasm, and Bombay had a new stadium, the Brabourne stadium, which the local authorities wanted desperately to show off to the tourists. As it turned out, however, it was an unsatisfactory visit. At Colombo the Australians had heard rumours of smallpox and even bubonic plague in India, and were reluctant to disembark. To the great disappointment of the Indians, only the manager, Keith Johnson, and one or two players were prepared to leave their ship when the *Strathaird* tied up at Ballard Pier. Bradman, for instance, was nowhere to be seen. The chanting of the crowd, however, became so raucous that he was forced to appear at the deck rail and wave wildly back at them; but there was no question of his disembarking. Moreover, unsurprisingly to those who knew India but grievously disappointing to the hosts, there was a formal embargo on eating the food which was liberally offered by the Indians.

The *Strathaird* eventually docked at Tilbury on the morning of 16 April 1948. It was the first time an Australian touring team had sailed into the Thames estuary rather than arriving at Southampton and travelling onwards by rail into London. The welcoming party was thus all the more frenetic. Apart from the press, the modern cameras and microphones, there was the Australian Deputy High Commissioner Norman Mitchell, the President of the MCC – no less than the seemingly omnipresent Earl of Gowrie – the Secretary of the MCC, Colonel Rait-Kerr, Bill Bowes, Alec Bedser, Maurice Tate and, on the eve of his 76th birthday, C.B. Fry. The English welcome can only be described as little short of ecstatic.

Bradman stood on deck as the liner docked and, it was reported, 'rips off his hat and enthusiastically returns the wild welcome of Tilbury crowds.'[4]

'Bradman is here again,' wrote Robertson-Glasgow, 'captain of Australia for the third time. His old admirers will be glad. After ten years' absence he will also have a new public – those who, in 1938, were still at school or even in perambulator cases. We want him to do well. We feel we have a share in him. He is more than Australian. He is a world batsman.'[5] It was, whatever the hyperbole, a fair reflection of Bradman's new status. He had by now somehow transcended in the mind of the English public the constraints of nationality, and, by a curious combination of nostalgia between the two countries, had become a symbol for the post-War resurgence of the British Empire.

The explanation for this apparently strange phenomenon lies in the circumstances of the day. The Britain which the Australians found in 1948 was quite different to the Britain they had known in 1938. The War had taken its grievous toll, and the euphoria of victory had passed away. Wartime austerity was still in place. The process of orderly demobilisation of the armed forces – the Labour government of the day had been determined not to repeat the mistakes of 1918 – together with the conversion of a wartime economy to peace, and a new order of things to satisfy those who had voted Labour in the General Election of 1945, meant that the fruits of victory had had to be delayed. Not only that, but the winter of 1947 had been exceptionally harsh. In short, Britain looked, and felt, exhausted, shoddy and depressed.

The Australians had been warned what to expect, but even so it came as something of a shock. They had been instructed that they would be living on British rations for the duration of the tour, so as not to offend their hosts; indeed, it was one of the reasons that wives had preferred not to accompany their husbands. Australian diplomats had gone out of their way to impress on the cricket authorities that the tourists should avoid giving the impression of overfed colonials who had escaped the full rigours of the War of which they had been one of the main beneficiaries. In fact, they went so far to counter this impression as to bring with them some thousands of food parcels, which were to be delivered by Bradman and the team manager, Keith Johnson, to John Strachey, the British Minister of Food (who had, as far as is known, no interest in cricket whatsoever), to be distributed to the British people in the manner thought appropriate. The British press, it is reported, thought highly of this gesture, although there were those, perhaps not unreasonably, who thought the whole thing a touch patronising.

There is little doubt that many English people, of all stations in life – to use an expression common at the time – saw the arrival of the Australian cricketers as something of a symbol of the revival of Empire. This may not have been so true of the Scots or the Welsh, but that is a different matter. Just as Australia had turned its back on the Pacific to return to its British roots, so the English, in the midst of their post-War travails, were again turning their back on the reconstruction of the devastated Europe to re-create – even in their imagination – the days of old. God, it was widely assumed, was still in His Heaven and the Empire could still prevail.

The Australian tour of 1948 was an overt and visible manifestation of this mood. Cricket was, after all, an English game which had spread throughout the British Empire. Nobody could possibly imagine the Americans, or the French, or – perish the thought – the Russians engaging in this extraordinary pursuit. Even Mr Attlee, the Labour Prime Minister, only opened his newspaper, it was said, to read the cricket scores. Cricket was part of the life-blood of the Empire, and the English, from the Royal Family downwards, wished it to remain so; and if cricket was part of the life-blood of the Empire, Don Bradman, the greatest cricketer of his day, was part of the life-blood of cricket.

It is hardly surprising that Bradman himself described the next few days 'as a nightmare'.[6] He had known before he left Australia that the reception would be overwhelming, but even he was taken aback by the programme which he had in front of him: '. . . rub shoulders with leaders of the Empire . . . the principal guest and speaker when all around him are the most brilliant orators in the land . . . a frightening prospect'. The day after their arrival, for instance, the tourists were received formally at Australia House by the High Commissioner. Bradman had to stand to shake the hand of some two hundred guests, an experience during which he 'suddenly acquired a new-found respect for the duties of Royalty . . .'; Bradman, of course, would not have been Bradman if he had not added '. . . together with a fear that my right hand would not recover prior to the first match at Worcester'.[7]

In fact Bradman turned out not only to be capable of handling the publicity and the social round but of seeming to enjoy it all. During the ten days in London before the first match at Worcester, there were all kinds of what many might now regard as tedious functions: lunches given by the British Sportsman's Club, the Royal Empire Society, the Institute of Journalists and a dinner given by the Cricket Writers' Club; visits to the theatre (*Annie Get Your Gun*, for instance, at the Coliseum) and, by no means least, attendance – in the unexpected company of Mr and Mrs John Strachey – at St Paul's Cathedral for the Silver Jubilee service for the King and Queen. Almost to everybody's surprise,

Bradman carried off all these events with dignity and great skill. His speech at the Cricket Writers' Club dinner, for instance, was not only broadcast live by the BBC but proved to be so witty that the night editor decided to postpone the nine o'clock news until Bradman had sat down.

On top of all this the post every morning brought large bags of mail. There were thousands of requests for Australian autographs. Bradman had tried to anticipate this problem by getting all his colleagues to sign 5,000 autographs, each on blank sheets of paper, during the sea voyage to England. But 'they lasted just about a week',[8] Bradman recorded, and when the tourists finally took the train to Worcester for their first match, Bradman was carrying with him a large suitcase full of so many letters that it took him the whole three-hour journey, and a further three hours in his hotel in the evening, simply to open them and stack them up ready for answering. Invitations, of course, came top of the pile. Many were perhaps far-fetched, but they had to be answered, and Bradman insisted that they 'demanded an early reply'.[9] Courtesy required no less.

On arrival at Worcester, the Australians were welcomed almost as visitors from another world. They were met at the station by the Mayor and other local dignitaries, and conveyed to their hotel in the greatest style that the city could afford. On their way, Bradman's car was stopped while a girl from a florist's shop pushed a cricket bat made of flowers – marigolds and green leaves to represent the Australian colours – through the car window. When he looked at it closely, Bradman saw the word 'Don' woven as a pattern on the blade. It could hardly have been more touching. But it was not to be unique. The gesture, and the obvious effort that had gone into it, was to be repeated on many occasions in the reception which Bradman was to receive wherever he went during the next few months.

But cricket was another matter. Bradman had determined, as he told his players even before they left Australia, that their aim would be to complete an England tour without losing a match. No previous touring side had ever managed it, but such was the balance of ability between Australia and England that the ambition was not unreasonable. The first gauntlet was thrown down at Worcester.

Bradman put out his strongest side against what was then a weak county. The weather was cold and unpleasant – at one point play was held up for twenty-five minutes because of a hailstorm – but Worcester still treated the match as a holiday. Flags were flying everywhere, many shops closed, schoolchildren were given time off and, on the morning of 28 April, a queue formed outside the ground several hours before the gates were opened.

In spite of the weather, the Australians struck immediate form. Lindwall and Miller opened the attack – announcing in the clearest terms the threat they were going to pose to England in the Test matches – and Toshack, McCool and Johnson followed up. By the time Bradman went in to bat, Worcestershire had been bowled out for 233, and the only question was whether he, coming in first wicket down, or the young opener Arthur Morris would be the first to reach a century. Morris just made it, taking three hours and forty-five minutes against Bradman's two hours and five minutes. The next question was whether Bradman would go on to make his customary double century. He had, after all, done so in 1930, 1934 and 1938, and there seemed to be no reason why he should not do so again. The pre-War Bradman would certainly have persevered; but the post-War Bradman was more cautious. He was still worried about his torn cartilage, and much more worried about a possible recurrence of his frozen shoulder. He gave his wicket away soon after reaching his first century.

This set the pattern for the summer. As he said himself, 'I never went for the second hundred'[10]; and, indeed, that is the story of Bradman's batting on the 1948 tour. There were going to be no risks taken with his physique – in other words, no thumping double centuries just for the sake of it. At Leicester, in the Australians' next match, he was content with 81; at the Oval, against Surrey, it was 146; at Southend, against Essex, it was 187 – in two hours and five minutes, in a match in which the Australians scored 721 in a single day.

It was perhaps in the Essex match at Southend that Bradman individually, and the Australians collectively, announced their true intentions. Opponents were there to be defeated; and were, whenever possible, not just to be defeated, but to be annihilated. It was not simply for the fun of it; there was a serious purpose.

The purpose was to establish a psychological ascendancy over any and every opposition which would carry through to the Test matches. England were to know, even before an England XI took the field, that the combination of bowling, fielding and batting against which they would have to compete was invincible.

The massacre of lowly Essex, thanks to the press team which by now followed the Australians' every step, was reported almost as though it were a Test match. Conclusions were immediately drawn. On the Monday following Saturday's bloodshed, the *News Chronicle* was clear on the matter. 'Bradman,' it reported, 'has not changed one whit . . . he remains the coolest and most ruthless strategist in cricket . . . that mammoth 721 total against Essex on Saturday . . . was all part of his deliberate, merciless, efficient plan, brilliant in its execution, to build up the biggest possible psychological advantage for the Australians over the English bowlers as a whole.'[11] Even O'Reilly, travelling with Fingleton – they were almost inseparable – as a press commentator, was moved to write: 'Never have I seen Bradman annihilate an attack in such convincing manner in such a short space of time.'[12] The same medicine, in fact, was applied at Lord's in the match against the MCC which started on 22 May. Bradman himself scored 98 – nobody could remember him ever getting out before in the 90s – and the Australians won by an innings and 158 runs.

By this time the English press were becoming irritated at what appeared to be an unstoppable Australian steam-roller. Some niggling criticism started to appear. Barnes, it was said, was fielding too close to the batsman. (The same reporters neglected to point out that the batsman had a simple and effective riposte – hitting the ball straight at the fielder's midriff.) Lord Tennyson, a former captain of England and the son of a former Governor-General of Australia, was reported as having been refused entry to the Australian dressing room at Lord's to ask Bradman 'to dine with him at White's'.[13] (Nobody bothered to report that his Lordship was quite clearly drunk, and that Bradman – reasonably enough – did not want him to be a figure of fun to the tourists in their dressing room.) There was also an attempt to cast doubt on the Australians' true ability. For instance, in the next game, against Lancashire at Old Trafford, the young left-arm bowler Hilton took Bradman's wicket twice – and was immediately promoted by the English press into the England Test side. (It did not happen, and, indeed, Hilton was dropped later in the season from the Lancashire first team.)

None of this, of course, was of any significance – it was merely the measure of the Australians' psychological advantage. Furthermore, Bradman was by now used to this sort of treatment, and could shrug it off. Indeed, on the very day that Tennyson had been refused his erratic entry into the Australian dressing room at Lord's, the *Star* carried a leader which approved of Bradman 'not only as the world's greatest batsman . . . As the years have added to his skill, he has become the perfect cricket ambassador.'[14]

Ambassador he was certainly trying to be, and, on all the evidence, was succeeding in being. The effort and application, as in all things that he did, were intense. But there was, perhaps, an extra dimension. There was still in the 'boy from Bowral' a great – some would say exaggerated – respect for the English establishment. In the presence of a member of the Royal Family, or of a senior politician or high-born aristocrat, Bradman felt something akin to reverence. For example, the Sunday of the Nottinghamshire match was marked by a visit to Welbeck Abbey, where 'we were entertained by the Duke and Duchess of Portland'. The Duke's parents had put up Don and Jessie after his operation in 1934, and Bradman was respectfully delighted to find the old Duchess 'still a beautiful woman, and her intellect razor-keen'. Recalling the visit, Bradman later wrote revealingly: 'I must admit this visual evidence of a change in the social structure brought about by modern economic conditions caused me to think deeply. If the people as a whole are benefiting one cannot complain, though I could not escape the feeling that I had witnessed the passing of a traditional element of English life . . . It left,' he went on, 'a deep pang of remorse.'[15]

But cricket was cricket; and when it came to cricket, particularly against England, Bradman was not given to pangs of remorse. The first Test match, at Nottingham, began on Thursday 10 June. The weather, as so often in that summer, was grey, cold and depressing; and it had rained overnight. The two captains, Bradman and Yardley, both in overcoats and scarves, came out at around 11:30, took one look at the pitch and retreated to the pavilion. It was midday before they came out again, this time in flannels and ready to toss. Bradman lost the toss again, and play started soon after. Immediately Bradman set a most aggressive field for his two opening bowlers, Lindwall and Miller, and, in between bouts of rain, the English batting slowly folded. By the end of the day England were all out for 165. Australia made a good start, and by the time Bradman went in to bat, just before lunch on the second day, Barnes and Morris had put on 73 for the first wicket. The weather was still miserable, and the English tactics were very defensive. Yardley's main aim was to prevent Bradman from cutting the English bowling to pieces. In that sense the English tactic was successful: Bradman took an hour and forty minutes to score 50, and by tea was only 78 – after spending a quarter of an hour without scoring. On one occasion he even had to watch a whole over from Yardley meander down the leg side without needing to play a stroke. By the end of the day, he was 130 not out; his eighteenth century in Tests against England, and one of the slowest. The cricket, frankly, was rather tedious.

But it was on that evening that the so-called 'Hutton/Bedser' trap was thought up. O'Reilly (who else?) happened to be having a drink with Bedser and, as bowlers do the world over, they discussed technique, field placing and, above all, wickets. O'Reilly thought that Bedser had bowled well on the day but that his field placing was not right. Pencil and paper were then produced, and a leg-side field planned for Bedser's in-swinger, with a backward short leg, rather wider than leg slip and about twelve yards from the bat, waiting for the leg glance. That, O'Reilly said, is how he would set a field if he were, as he put it, 'having a pop at Don'.[16]

On the following morning Bedser set his field accordingly and, almost to script, soon had Bradman caught by Hutton in precisely the position O'Reilly had described. Not only that, but there was an exact repeat in the second innings, with the difference that Bradman, instead of making a century, had failed to score. By now, of course, the English thought that they had the answer to Bradman. Although Australia had won the game comfortably, it was believed – with a certain amount of truth – that if Bedser could achieve psychological advantage over Bradman the future

Tests were already half won for England. The pendulum seemed, for once, to be swinging England's way.

There was excitement in England, and even some consternation in Australia. By 1948, of course, the radio broadcasts were live – and the effect immediate. The listening public, too, was much larger than in the 1930s. That public, naturally, included the Bradman family, which had been following Don's progress with the attention which was only to be expected. They were perhaps just starting to get worried by the turn of events. 'Mummy is going to let me listen in on Friday night,' John wrote to his father; and indeed there were photographs in the Adelaide *Advertiser* of Jessie and her two children – Jessie with her knitting and the children in their dressing gowns – clustered round their radio set. The Hutton/Bedser trap, and its consequences for Don's future performance, was widely discussed. John at least, however, was able to keep the whole thing in perspective. 'I am very glad you made a century in the Test match,' he wrote later. 'Daddy I know I want everything but please can I have a pellet gun for my birthday they arent wery dangerous because they cant even kill a chook.'[17] It was obviously much more important than the thought that there might be a chink in his father's hitherto impregnable armour.

But it happened again in the Lord's Test match. On another damp and grey morning Bradman was always in difficulty against Bedser's swing and was caught again by Hutton – for 38 – in exactly the same position as at Nottingham. By now it was beginning to look as though the technique was not quite so sharp and confident as it had been. The 'run-machine' was showing signs of missing a gear. Certainly, Bradman himself accepted that he was not the player he had been in the 1930s and that he was limiting the range of his strokes. On the other hand, he claimed that he would not have been caught at backward short leg 'if I had not been trying to score runs off the ball'. Indeed, he demonstrated this in his second innings by eliminating the stroke altogether and allowing Bedser's in-swinger to hit his pads. Admittedly, Bedser did have him caught in the slips when he was 89 – and left him duly disappointed not to have scored a century in his last Test innings at Lord's – but the leg side was now sealed off. The Hutton/Bedser trap was no longer effective. It had worked three times, but that was more than enough for Bradman.

He had decided that he would never again get out playing a leg glance. Nor did he.

Australia won the Lord's Test quite easily – by 409 runs, after declaring their second innings closed with three wickets still standing. The next Test, at Manchester, began in the following week (Bradman in the intervening period having time to score 128 against Surrey). Old Trafford had never been a lucky ground for Bradman, and so it proved once again. In the first innings, yet again in what seemed to many like semi-darkness, he came in at 3 for 1 on the second afternoon, facing an England total of 363. Nine minutes later he was out for 7. By the end of the third day, it looked as though England were set to win the match, but the Manchester rain was true to its reputation, and there was no play until after lunch on the fifth and last day. The wicket was soft, and unresponsive either to pace or spin. Australia lost the first wicket at 10, but Bradman and Morris held on, helped by interruptions due to rain, until the close of play. It was perhaps one the most important and least typical of all Bradman's Test innings. He was playing as captain of Australia rather than as Bradman. In his last forty-two minutes he scored only two runs – almost unheard of in his whole career. But only one ball – from Bedser – got past his bat. It was a model of defensive batting on a wet wicket. He had saved the game.

The Manchester Test drawn, the Ashes were now safely with Australia, and the Australians could afford to relax. But with Bradman as captain there was no question of allowing slackness to set in, or even any sort of anti-climax to the tour as a whole. In fact, the next Test match, at Leeds, was a tense and high-scoring game, and ended in what Bradman himself considered to be the finest win by Australia of a Test match in England.

Quite apart from all else, Headingley at Leeds had always been for Bradman the reverse of Old Trafford at Manchester: a ground where he almost always did well. He was also a great favourite with the Yorkshire crowd. This was evident, for instance, in what both he and the crowd knew would be his last Leeds Test. When he went out to bat on the second day of the Test he was, according to one commentator, 'greeted like an emperor by the crowd'.[18] The ground was full, as it was every day. Indeed, the reserved accommodation had been oversubscribed in the first post on the first day of applications. There was little doubt who it was that they had come to see. As he walked out through the long narrow opening from the dressing room on to the field Bradman was surrounded by a crowd which had poured towards him over the low barriers. It took three policemen to see him safely through the crush, and when he emerged, the applause, in his own words, 'rose in a crescendo to a deafening roar, which caused me to make a special acknowledgement and certainly raised a lump in my throat'.[19]

This Test, starting on 22 July, was to prove a triumphant last chapter in the story of Bradman's success at Headingley. Although England made 496 in the first innings, thanks to centuries from Washbrook and Edrich, and although Bradman was out for 33, Australia, by reaching 458 after a century from Harvey in his first Test against England, were nearly on level terms by the end of the third day. England batted well on the fourth day and by the evening held a large lead. The outlook for Australia was gloomy. 'We are set 400 to win,' wrote Bradman in his diary, 'and I fear we may be defeated.'[20]

On the following morning Yardley decided to bat on for a further few minutes before declaring. Nobody could quite understand why. Some supposed that the use of the heavy roller, to which Yardley would not have been entitled had he declared overnight, would help break up the wicket, others assumed that Yardley wanted to make the target for Australia that much harder so that, if the worst did really come to the worst, England would escape with a draw. Whatever the motive, the result was that Australia were set 404 runs in 345 minutes – a 'colossal task', as Bradman wrote, '. . . on the last day of a Test match'.[21]

Bradman went in for his last Test innings at Headingley at 1 P.M. with the Australian score at 57 for 1. Again he had to find his way through a line of spectators who wanted to slap him on the back as he made his way to the wicket. As he finally came out the whole crowd rose and applauded him all the rest of the way. It was more than respect, more even than enthusiasm. The 'little feller' had somehow found his way into Yorkshire hearts. Bradman was deeply touched. 'I have learned to appreciate both the players and the public of Yorkshire,' he was to say later when presented with life membership of Yorkshire Cricket Club at Leeds in September, 'and I know that I shall never cherish any memory more than the reception at Leeds at the Test here. Not only was it the greatest I have ever received in this country, but the greatest I have ever received from any public in the world.'[22]

Bradman rewarded Yorkshire by playing one of the greatest innings of his life. At first, as he wrote later, 'my thoughts weren't altogether clear. We wanted to win. We didn't want to lose. What should I do?'[23] The answer, oddly enough, was provided by Yardley, who, failing a proper wrist-spinner, brought on Hutton, who was at best only a part-time bowler for Yorkshire. In the half-hour before lunch Bradman and his partner Morris put on 62 runs.

This sudden spurt set the stage for the events of the afternoon. The wicket was dry and dusty, the day hot and sunny. At that time the Headingley ground had no sight-screens. The conditions were thus perfect for a wrist-spinner, but the English had only Compton with his – frequently somewhat picturesque – left arm off-breaks and googlies. Of course, both Bradman and Morris had their share of luck. Bradman might have been caught twice in the slips, once at deep point, and there was a possible stumping as well – all difficult chances, but chances nonetheless. Morris, too, might have been stumped – but, again, it was a difficult chance; an easier catch, after he had reached his century, was badly missed. Almost worse than any of these moments of fortune, Bradman's muscles started to give him trouble half-way through the afternoon, going periodically into spasm; he had to nurse himself carefully. Morris was asked, politely, to take his full share, and more than his full share, of the bowling.

In the event, Bradman and Morris shared in a partnership of 301 runs at 83 an hour. Morris was out for 183, and Bradman himself ended not out with 173, made in four and a quarter hours. As the match was drawing to a close, Bradman, generously and – on this tour – characteristically, allowed the youngest member of the side, Harvey, to hit the winning run. Australia had made 404 for 3, to win by seven wickets with fifteen minutes to spare. It had indeed been a great victory. 'This was the finest Test match,' wrote one commentator, 'that it has ever been my privilege to watch.'[24] Yet it was Bradman himself who said that if England had had in their side a proper leg-spinner, say a Wright or a Hollies, Australia would not have made 250.

As is the case in many walks of life, so in cricket. The glorious and uplifting moment was followed by a return to the prosaic necessities. Within three-quarters of an hour of the triumphal end to the Test, the Australians were on a train to Derby for their next match. In Bradman's case the feeling of descent to earth was more than usually acute. He had, after all, just led his side to victory, and the cheers and the shouts of 'Well done, Don' and 'Good on you, Braddles' – the nickname of the 1930s had been restored for the 1948 tour – were ringing in his ears; the adrenalin had flowed copiously for four and a half hours; and, of course, the crowd did not want to let him go. Furthermore, the muscles around his ribs were still painful. Nevertheless, duty had to be done, and within the allotted time Bradman had showered, changed, packed his bags and, together with his team-mates, caught the train from Leeds to Derby, where they were due to start their match against Derbyshire the following morning.

It was not much fun. The train was stiflingly hot, and dirty; the windows could not be opened because of the smuts drifting in from the pre-War steam engine; there was only a small packed meal on offer and nothing to drink; the train, for no apparent reason, stopped frequently on its journey, and finally arrived late at Derby. The Australians were getting a true taste of post-War Britain. Spirits lightened a bit with a celebration dinner on the second evening – the Ashes, after all, had been retained, and 'you couldn't have seen a happier band of chaps'[25] – but sank again as they boarded the train which was to take them overnight from Derby to Swansea.

By this time Bradman had had enough. Although he had played against Derbyshire – a 'reflex innings', he called it – he was tired and needed a rest. Leaving Hassett to shepherd the players on the long night journey into Welsh territory, Bradman took the train down to London for a bit of peace. On the Sunday he went to the Albert Hall to listen to a recital by Eileen Joyce, herself an Australian. She had had a riding accident only a few days before, and no sooner had she completed the Beethoven 'Emperor' concerto than she collapsed on stage and had to be carried to her dressing room. The incident made Bradman reflect: 'Perhaps I understood better than most people in the audience the mental strain she had endured to get through. The human nervous system is so marvellous in its ability to produce untold reserves of energy . . .'[26] He certainly knew better than most how the mind can overcome the deficiences of the body; but it is a rare – and revealing – piece of self-analysis.

There was to be a good deal of strain, both mental and physical, before the tour came to its conclusion. Bradman rejoined his team for the match against Warwickshire at Edgbaston (where, ominously in the light of subsequent events, he was bowled by Hollies, the Warwickshire leg-spinner, with a top-spinner which he seemed not to pick), and then it was on to Old Trafford for the Washbrook benefit game against Lancashire. Again, Bradman was far from his best in the first innings, taking forty minutes for his first 4 runs. The wicket had been covered, and seemed to have sweated under the covers. Bradman gave two stumping chances, both against the left-arm spinner Roberts – in each case jumping down the pitch and missing a ball turning away from him – and was caught at the wicket for an unhappy 28. When Lancashire batted, Lindwall and Miller both made the ball rear off a good length, and the innings collapsed; in fact, Washbrook himself was hit so many times that he was unable to play again for the rest of the season. Bradman could have enforced the follow-on, but that would almost certainly have finished the match in two days – and lost a day's money for Washbrook. The Australians batted again. Not only that, but Bradman put on a sparkling performance, making 108 runs before lunch. It was his last innings at Old Trafford. He had done his best for Washbrook; and he had finally beaten the Manchester jinx.

The fifth Test match started at the Oval in London on 14 August. It was always bound to be an emotional occasion. The great cricketer was saying goodbye to Test cricket in England, and, perhaps, to Test cricket for all time. In Wagnerian terms – and the occasion was one which Wagner, in his own way, would have fully understood – the young Siegfried of 1930 had become the Wotan of 1948, giving way to a new generation of heroes. But it was not just a matter of farewells. Bradman needed only four runs to achieve a total of 7,000 runs in Test cricket. Furthermore, his Test average, when the last Test started, was 101.39. He needed only to score those four runs to keep that average above 100, a record never achieved before or since.

Farewells there were in plenty. As the Australians followed Bradman on to the field on the first day – Bradman had lost the toss yet again – the commentators intoned 'a great leader emerges with his men for the last time'.[27] What they had not perhaps appreciated was that the 'great leader' was still quite as determined as he ever was on the cricket field. He was going not just to win the series convincingly but to take Australia through the whole tour without losing a match.

The English batting was swept away. It was not a difficult wicket – 'wet but easy', it was said – but the English were unable to cope with the now fearsome Australian out-cricket. Bradman had aimed for psychological advantage since the beginning of the tour. He now had it, and once he had it, it was a matter of exploiting it. It was, as Learie Constantine had said, without pity. England were all out for 52, only Hutton showing resistance – with 30 out of the 46 English runs scored off the bat. Lindwall had removed the English tail as though it had never existed, ending with 6 for 20; Miller and Johnston had taken the early wickets of Dewes and Edrich, and finished with 2 for 5 and 2 for 20 respectively. By the end of their innings, England had achieved a new record: they had sunk lower than their previous lowest score in England–Australia Test matches at home: 53, at Leeds in 1888.

It took the Australian opening pair, Barnes and Morris, less than an hour to pass the England total. The partnership reached 117 before Barnes was caught at the wicket, sparring at a leg-break from Hollies. 'I dearly wanted to do well,' Bradman recalled, '. . . as I walked out to another wonderful ovation . . .'[28] Collar turned up, baggy Australian cap squarely on his head, the small figure walked at his usual slow pace to the wicket. The crowd stood to him all the way. When he arrived at the crease, Yardley called the English fielders round and called for three cheers. Bradman stood, his cap in his hand and, some said, even with a tear in his eye. 'That reception,' he later wrote, 'stirred me deeply.' It had also, he goes on, '. . . made me anxious – a dangerous state of mind for any batsman to be in. I played the first ball from Hollies' (bowling, curiously enough in those days, round the wicket) 'though not sure I really saw it. The second was a perfect-length googly which deceived me. I just touched it with the inside edge of the bat and the off bail was dislodged.'[29] Bradman, in his last Test innings, had been bowled out without scoring.

For a moment, the whole Oval crowd – and the whole cricketing world listening in – held its breath. Then the crowd, realising what had happened, and realising the disappointment of the man, stood to cheer him all the way back to the pavilion. It had been, and still is today, a solemn moment.

But there was one sad and sour postscript. Fingleton and O'Reilly, the main thorns in Bradman's side over the years, were in the press box. When Bradman was out, said a fellow commentator who was with them at the time, 'I thought they were going to have a stroke – they were laughing so much.'[30] The brutal side of Australian cricket had never been so openly on view. Bradman's riposte came much, much later: 'O'Reilly nakedly exposes the disloyalty I had to endure during my early years as Australian captain, a disloyalty based purely on jealousy and religion. Fingleton was the ring-leader. He conducted a vendetta against me all his life and it was most distasteful because he was a prolific writer of books and articles. Conversely, with these fellows out of the way the loyalty of my 1948 side was a big joy and made a big contribution to the outstanding success of that tour.'[31]

There was little more to be said.

The 'Ikin incident': the First Test, Brisbane, November 1946.

With admirers before the Second Test, Sydney, December 1946

Leading the team out with Stan McCabe at the start of the
First Test, Trent Bridge, June 1938.

A brief meeting with
Winston Churchill at
Victoria Station, 1938.

Lieutenant Bradman, 1940.

England-bound again: on board the *Orontes* at the beginning of the 1938 tour.

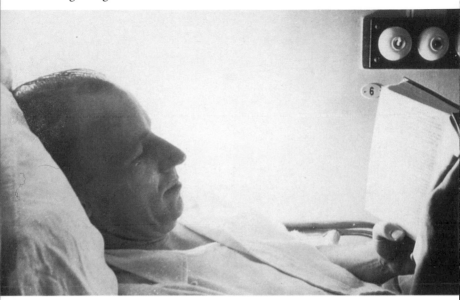

Chatting to G.O. 'Gubby' Allen upon arrival at Waterloo, April 1938.

The Bradman stance.

With his children John
and Shirley before
leaving Adelaide for
the 1948 tour.

Worcester, 29 April
1948: Bradman
had to forego his
customary double
century and make do
with 107.

Walking out for the toss with England captain Norman
Yardley, Trent Bridge, June 1948.

Cutting past the outstretched hand of Edrich at the Second Test, Lord's, June 1948.

The Oval, 14 August 1948: Yardley (centre right), leads his team in three cheers for Bradman, playing his final Test innings.

At his farewell lunch at the Savoy, September 1948, MCC President Lord Gowrie presents Bradman with a silver replica of the Warwick Vase.

Walking off the Sydney Cricket Ground after his last innings there, February 1949.

13

'A COLLECTION OF PRIMA DONNAS'

'THEIR MAJESTIES THE KING AND QUEEN will entertain the Australian Test team at tea at Balmoral Castle today.' So read the official press release of 19 September 1948. It was, of course, no ordinary tea party. It was to be, so the public was informed, 'one of the biggest parties ever held at Balmoral', and would include 'over 50 guests when the Queen presides at tea in the drawing room'. Not only that, but other members of the Royal Family were to be in attendance. Princess Elizabeth, Princess Margaret, the Duke of Edinburgh, as well as the Duchess of Kent, 'will help to entertain the Australians'. On a somewhat lower note, it was also announced that 'the party will be informal'.[1]

As it turned out, the party was not without its own particular form of hilarity. The King had given his 'gracious' permission to the press for photographs to be taken, but it was discreetly mentioned that Princess Elizabeth was in an advanced stage of pregnancy. It would perhaps be better if she were left out of any press shots. It would not be, it was said, 'appropriate'. Furthermore, the King himself, for no immediately obvious reason, had decided to wear a kilt of Balmoral tartan. The tartan, as far as anybody knew, had no particular Australian connection. Indeed it was designed, it was said, by the King's great-grandfather Prince Albert (of Saxe-Coburg-Gotha, as is known, but anxious to please his formidable wife, of almost equally German ancestry, Queen Victoria). The King's decision, whatever the reason, led to unfortunate embarrassments. The fact was that the kilt had no pockets into which the King could put his hands in this atmosphere of supposed 'informality', whereas the Australians, wearing ordinary trousers, quite naturally walked with hands in pockets. This in turn aroused the indignation of the British press, which considered such behaviour in the royal presence to be a form of *lèse-majesté*. Finally, the day, like Balmoral itself, was gloomy and sunless and, by Australian standards, bitterly cold. Skirts and kilts were blown about, and royal hats tended to lose their – admittedly precarious – balance.

Nevertheless, the party was presented as a social, and consequentially a Commonwealth, success. The Royals shook hands with the whole party, and 'chatted with each player'. The visit, it was reported, closed with 'members of the Royal Family seeing visitors off from the front hall of the castle in a hum of lively chat and laughing exchanges'. It is not easy, over a span of nearly fifty years and in view of the characters of the time, to imagine precisely what that meant, but the Australians were suitably bemused. Keith Johnson, the Australian manager, announced that 'the Royal Family are marvellous. They made a deep impression on all of us.'[2] Bradman himself was also much impressed, particularly with the Queen. Much later in life, when she was Queen Mother, he repeated his view that she was 'a wonderful woman'.[3]

As a farewell to Bradman and recognition of his sporting achievement, it could hardly have been better stage-managed. Admittedly, an irreverent English newspaper cut one corner out of one photograph to show Bradman, apparently accompanied only by the King, with his hands in his pockets, but that did no more than show a side of journalism that seemed, at least to those who moved in royal circles, and at that date, to be distinctly lacking in taste. As a matter of fact, the paper might just as easily have shown the Queen walking with Keith Johnson – also with his hands in his pockets; but that, of course, was not nearly as newsworthy as Bradman walking with the King in an attitude of such 'patent disrespect'. It was all very silly and, to his credit, the King thought so too.

But there was more to the occasion than mere social frippery. It was further disclosed that the King and Queen wanted to talk to Bradman about their proposed visit to Australia in the following year. It was a surprising and revealing indication of the stature which Bradman had now attained. He was not just any cricketer; he was now an ambassador to be consulted on royal visits. Furthermore, it was whispered, there was 'something in the wind'. A high honour for Bradman, rumour had it, was being considered.

In retrospect, it is possible to see in this event not only one of the pinnacles of Bradman's own life – the boy from Bowral being entertained by the head of the old Empire – but as an undoubted high point in post-War relations between Australia and Britain. After the wartime strains, the family was pulling together once again. Of course, it was said, there were family spats; there always are. But these could be settled without any suggestion of fundamental rupture. Apart from all else, cricket held the family together.

This theme was taken up the very next day at a lunch given by the *People* newspaper, at which a presentation was made to Bradman of a replica of the 'Warwick Vase', made with the proceeds of a 'shilling fund' run by the newspaper. It was a fine occasion. Quite why the Warwick Vase was chosen as a suitable object for replication and subsequent presentation to the captain of the Australian cricket team was, and still is, something of a mystery. The original itself, after all, appears to be a Roman copy of an artifact of the Greek colonists of southern Italy, which had been discovered by the peppery British Ambassador at the court of Naples, Sir William Hamilton. At the time of discovery, one head was found to be missing from the side of the vase. The Ambassador had the idea of filling in the space with a model of the head of his even more peppery wife who, as is now common knowledge, was the mistress of the Admiral, Lord Nelson. It was a dreadful mistake. The artist who was commissioned gave her Ladyship not her own ears but the ears of a satyr. The result was satisfactory neither to the Ambassador nor to Lady Hamilton, and was promptly given by the Ambassador to his sister's son, the Earl of Warwick.

It was a replica of this somewhat bizarre piece which was presented to Bradman at the very grand lunch at the Savoy Hotel – the balance of the 'shilling fund' after the replica of the vase had been paid for, going, at Bradman's request, to the much more useful purpose of providing cricket pitches for 'budding cricketers' in England. In celebration of the renewed ties between

England and Australia which the 1948 tour had brought, speaker after speaker at the lunch emphasised the importance of cricket in binding the two countries. The matter was even confirmed subsequently in a letter to Bradman from the Minister at the Commonwealth Relations Office, Philip Noel-Baker.

Those at the lunch recalled, too, the blaze of glory in which Bradman had taken leave of English cricket after the Oval Test: 150 in two and a half hours in his last innings at Lord's, against the Gentlemen of England, two days before his fortieth birthday; 143 against the South of England; and a final 153 in the Scarborough festival before leaving England to wind up with 123 in an hour and a half against a Scottish side at Aberdeen. There were even those who remembered, painful as it was, that he had led, for the first time ever, an Australian tour of England without suffering a defeat. Perhaps even more remarkable for those who professed to know their man, it was noted that Bradman had presented each member of his team with a silver ashtray inscribed with the words 'From your admiring skipper'. Autumn had certainly been working its subtle magic.

'The final act of renunciation of an active playing career is never easy, and the irrevocable decision to retire is so often delayed in the search for some final gesture of pleasurable farewell.'[4] Thus Bradman in the Foreword to his book *The Art of Cricket*. For Bradman himself there was to be one 'final pleasurable farewell'; and two less pleasurable. He received a rapturous welcome – from over 3,000 people, it was said – when the old *Orontes*, encrusted with its memories of earlier and more youthful days, berthed at Adelaide. The welcome was the more rapturous in that it was known that the returning champion had made up his mind that he would not play in another first-class match.

There was one temptation, however, that was too much. He was offered a final Testimonial match at Melbourne. The negotiations had taken place during the return journey, and by the time he had arrived back home the pact had been sealed. As it turned out, he was right to surrender to the temptation. The match, in which Bradman, the outgoing captain of Australia, captained one team and Hassett, his obvious successor (remarkable in that he would be the first Catholic captain of the Australian national side since McDonnell in 1888) captained the other, could hardly have been more successful. Nearly 53,000 spectators turned out to see the game. Bradman made a century (dropped, quite obviously intentionally, by McCool at 97) and the game ended in a tie. Bradman gave all the participants a set of gold cuff-links, of a cricket bat and a cricket ball joined by a chain. He himself took away a cheque for £9,000. It seemed a large amount at the time, but in truth it was hardly an over-generous reward for a career played entirely as an amateur.

The other two 'farewells' were very much less satisfactory. Having played in his own Testimonial, Bradman felt that he ought not to refuse to play both in the joint Testimonial for Kippax and Oldfield – they had both, after all, played in his first Sheffield Shield match in 1927 and in his first Test in 1928; and also in the Testimonial for A.J. Richardson, who had toured England himself in 1926 and had watched Bradman's triple century at Leeds in 1930. The first game, Bradman's last at the Sydney Cricket Ground, went reasonably well: he scored 53 and walked off the field, slowly as usual, to the roars of appreciation from over 40,000 Sydneyites who had come to say goodbye to their old hero. The second was sad. Bradman never timed the ball properly, was out for 30, and, while fielding, trod on the ball, which had lodged in a sunken water tap, sprained his ankle and had to be helped off the field. The gods, who had given him so much genius, had had their last, sardonic laugh.

But there was one consolation at least. The whispers at the royal tea party at Balmoral turned out to have truth. In the New Year's honours list of 1949, Bradman's name appeared in the Australian list of Knights Bachelor; it was, the citation said, in recognition of his services to cricket and the Commonwealth. It was the first time that a sportsman had been knighted before retirement, and such was Bradman's reputation and, by now, popularity that, in the words of one English correspondent, 'I think I can say, without attempting to flatter you in any way, that this is one of the most popular of the New Year honours among all the people in this country, and I am sure the same applies in Australia also.'[5] The ceremony itself was not long delayed. Bradman's accolade finally came from the Governor-General, W.J. McKell, in Queen's Hall, Melbourne, on 15 March.

For her part, Jessie was glad Don's career had come to an end. The 'limelight days' had passed, and she for one was mightily relieved. 'I was never keen,' she said during the Testimonial match at Melbourne, after Don had touchingly pinned a gardenia on to the lapel of her coat, 'on having the international news spotlight focused on my home and family. Don's long absences left me with the reponsibility of home and children, and it was something of a strain. The children, John and Shirley, were too young to miss him on his earlier tours, and as long as I was there they were happy.'[6] Nevertheless, she went on, she could not bear to think that Don would shed entirely his cricket connections, and was glad that he would remain an Australian selector.

So that was that. The career which had started some thirty years earlier had now finally come to its conclusion. But retirement for Bradman was not to be easy. His post was full of letters from all over the world asking for his autograph or his opinion on this, that or the other matter, and suggestions that he might follow his cricket career with a further career in politics or diplomacy. It was even suggested that he should become Australian High Commissioner in London – but only suggested, since the professional diplomats in Canberra quickly squashed the idea. In any event, the suggestion did not seem to spark any great enthusiasm in Kensington Park.

The result was that Bradman started to settle down, with his wife and children, to what the world would regard as a normal family life. He rose early, went to his office, saw his clients, met acquaintances at lunch, went back to the office, and left in good time to get home for supper with his family in the evening. It was no more than anybody would expect of millions of business people throughout the developed world. And, indeed, like many of those millions, he took seriously to golf. Yet it was not some idle whim. Bradman had been a good golfer all his cricketing life. But 'serious' to him meant an application which was beyond the range of most weekend business golfers. He announced to his family that he was going to get his handicap down to scratch. There was to be no argument. Nor was there; Jessie knew her husband too well for that. The result was that for two years, until he had achieved his aim, family meal times were altered and the basis of all conversations changed. Within the time allotted, Bradman duly became a scratch golfer.

None of this was palatable to his critics. There were those who said that he had become a 'recluse', unwilling to live up to the reputation which his knighthood and his cricketing history required. There were also those who lamented his withdrawal from Australian cricket – and at the same time criticised his performance as a selector. Certainly it was recognised that he had continued to write about cricket, and that he had produced, in June 1950, his own account of his cricket life under the title of *Farewell to Cricket*. But the book got no better than a mixed reception. It was of interest as a book of record, and, indeed, for Bradman's considered views on the controversies of his day and the colleagues with whom he played. Furthermore, in the book he is surprisingly generous to other cricketers and modest about his own record. But the language is terse, at times to the point of being abrupt, and it was felt not to be particularly well presented. Nevertheless, Bradman being Bradman, the book was an instant bestseller.

But writing about cricket, or playing golf, was on the periphery of Bradman's new life. The fact was that it was difficult, and perhaps more than difficult, for him to become what he always at heart wanted to be, a private person living an ordinary life, in financial security, with a wife and family, in the company of friends and in an environment which reflected the certainties of his youth. It was not only difficult as far as the outside world was concerned. His long absences from his family had made it difficult for him to get to know his children in the way of any average father.

The situation was made very much worse by the epidemic of poliomyelitis, or 'infantile paralysis' as it used to be known, which struck South Australia in the summer of 1951–52. The strain was particularly virulent, and attacked the twelve-year-old John. It was, for Don and Jessie, a desperate moment. Their first child had died in infancy and their third child was badly spastic. To lose their only fully healthy child at the age of twelve would have been tragedy almost beyond belief. Indeed, the situation was so serious, and the worry so great, that Bradman gave up his duties as a selector to help look after his son. The help was much needed, since John was forced to spend most of one year in a steel frame and there were moments when recovery was far from certain.

Crises such as this usually have a lasting effect on both parents, and the Bradman home was no different to others. The two parents, Don and Jessie, were brought even closer together, but Don particularly seemed to wish to retire into what some have called 'his shell'. In the end, John recovered – and, indeed, more than recovered, since he became a fine athlete, setting, later on, a new South Australian record for the 120 yards hurdles. The crisis had passed.

With John's recovery, Bradman seemed somehow to feel released. He felt able to wander abroad again. He resumed his positions as an Australian and South Australian selector, travelling widely to see and assess the new players in Australian cricket. He further agreed to write articles for the London *Daily Mail* on the Test matches during the 1953 Australian tour of England; and in June 1953 the Bradmans took their two children with them to England for the purpose. It was, however, by all accounts a dull visit. Apart from seeing a few old friends – and sitting next to Jardine in the press box at the Headingley Test match – there was little to stir the Bradman adrenalin. Writing was all very well, but it was not a substitute for batting. Besides, there were no royal visits or celebratory dinners. A retired sporting hero is just another individual. The appearance tells the story: the trilby hat was again set square on his head, and the face, as he watched the cricket, even looked slightly bored. The analysis of what was happening at the wicket was as acute as ever, and there were one or two appearances in public. But it was soon quite obviously time to go home.

'Home', of course, was no longer what it used to be. In the post-War period, Australia entered a phase of change which even today has not come to its conclusion. For a start, immigration policy shifted. Instead of being restrictive, the new policy was to raise the growth rate of the Australian population – 'populate or perish', as the new policy was known. But that could not be enough. Although the idea was to increase immigration from Britain, the fact was that Britain was also short of labour. Not only that, but there were few British ships to transport the supposed new Australians. 'Bring out a Briton'[7] had been a popular slogan when it was produced, but the results were meagre. Between 1947 and 1951, nearly 500,000 migrants entered Australia; but of these, only 40% were British. This, to the regret of many conservatives, was quite at variance with the 'White Australia' policy which had hitherto governed immigration.

Furthermore, by the time Menzies became Prime Minister in 1949, the new policy was well under way, and could not be put into reverse. Not only that, but Menzies himself, while professing that he was 'British to the boot-straps', was in reality encouraging non-British immigration. He was particularly enthusiastic about immigration from Eastern Europe, believing – rightly, as it turned out – that anyone who had fled a Communist régime would not be likely to vote for even the watered-down version of socialism offered by the Australian Labor Party.

There was a further change, this time in foreign policy. Although Menzies proclaimed himself a proud supporter of the British Commonwealth, in practice he continued the policy of his Labor predecessor in turning towards the United States. The upshot was not just a formal defence pact but a wave of increasingly populist Americanism in the major cities. To some extent, Adelaide was less affected than the cities of the east coast, but even in Adelaide the younger generation were asserting independence from their parents' culture in a way which would have been unthinkable before the War.

These shifts in policy and fashion had their effect on Australian sport. Immigrants from Eastern Europe had no interest in cricket; the gradual 'Americanisation' of Australia led to emphasis on sports in which Australians could pit their strengths against Americans; and the expansion of university education provided the opportunities for young men and women to train in a carefully prepared environment. The result was the rise of a new generation of sporting heroes whose view of success was quite different to that of the pre-War generation. Frank Sedgman, for instance, took on the Americans at tennis and beat them, not just in the Davis Cups of 1950, 1951 and 1952, but at Wimbledon and at Forest Hills. He was followed by Lew Hoad, Ken Rosewall, Rod Laver and others. Nor were they alone. In athletics, John Landy ran the mile in under four minutes and Herb Elliott followed with Olympic Golds in middle-distance running. The climax of this process of change came in the Olympics of 1956, which were held – at the outset with great diffidence but with gradually increasing confidence – in Melbourne. All in all, the 1950s saw the rise of activity and public interest in sports which had little or no connection with the old Empire; and cricket, which had been one of its greatest symbols, was the loser.

The relative decline in cricket as the Australian national sport was accompanied by lack of success. Hassett lost the Ashes, which Australia had held since 1934, in the last Test match at the Oval in 1953; Johnson failed to recover them in 1954–55 and again in 1956. Bradman, it was said, had made all the difference. Indeed Hutton, the new English captain, said roundly that 'Bradman had been worth three batsmen to Australia'.[8] As might be imagined, there was a good deal of muttering in Australia about the team selections, particularly of the 1954–55 and 1956 sides, in which Bradman had an important say.

Even after John's recovery, it was not easy to combine the roles of selector, businessman and family man. Yet Bradman was far from old; for a man of forty-five it should not have been impossible to carry that triple load. But fortune took another twist. On 28 June 1954 there was an announcement to the effect that Sir Donald Bradman, on the order of his doctor, was retiring from his stockbroking business. Bradman himself amplified the statement by saying that he had received 'a serious warning' from his doctor only a few days before. 'For nearly thirty years,' he went on, 'I have been subjected to stresses and strains of a somewhat abnormal character, which only those closest to me understand.'[9] His statement, of course, left more questions in the air than they resolved. A 'serious warning' is normally a coded expression for a heart problem – perhaps not a heart attack but at least a bad flutter. The major question, of course, was simple: had

Bradman indeed had a heart attack? The answer is: probably not. His supporters say that there was a cardiac event which forced him to give up his stockbroking but allowed him to continue a life which was less immediately stressful. His detractors say that the whole matter was exaggerated by his hypochondria, and that he was getting tired of stockbroking anyway.

Whatever the true nature of the problem, Len Bullock took over the stockbroking business and ran it with only an occasional intervention from its former proprietor. At the age of only forty-five, Bradman's business career seemed to be almost over. In the event, the situation was retrieved by the Adelaide business community, by whom he had been, at long last, substantially accepted. Invitations came in to join the boards of Adelaide companies – many of them anxious to cash in on the Bradman name, but considerable operations none the less. The combined remuneration was enough for him to feel 'comfortable'[10] – his own word.

So it was, in a sense, another new life. In spite of the 'severe warning' Bradman still had plenty of energy and, like any energetic man in what might be described as early middle age, set himself to find an occupation. In reality, however, there was only one choice. Since business was excluded on medical grounds, the only sensible alternative was a career in the administration of the game which he loved and to which he had given most of his active life.

There was, however, writing still to be done, and the Bradmans followed the 1956 Australian tour of England, Don writing his usual crisp analyses of the Tests for the *Daily Mail*. There was, furthermore, another book to be written, and that took time. In his Foreword to what emerged in 1958 as *The Art of Cricket*, Bradman recognises that 'during my playing career I thought I had learnt a great deal about the game, but I humbly admit that I have learnt a great deal more since retiring. And I am still learning.'[11] It was a candid enough admission for somebody who, in the view of one his admirers, 'has the sharpest cricket mind of all the cricketers I have met', and is universally thought to be one of the shrewdest captains cricket has ever seen. But Bradman was never one to boast about his achievements. The book itself is simply written, and does no more than its title suggests: to provide a guide to playing cricket while recognising that the playing methods can never be defined precisely – hence the expression 'Art'.

By the time of the book's publication, Bradman had resumed his place as one of South Australia's members on the Australian Board of Control. He had also been made a life member of the MCC in London. The timing of both events was fortunate, in that it was by then clearly recognised that Australian cricket was still in a slump following his retirement (Barnes had described the Australian side which toured England in 1953 as a 'collection of prima donnas, schoolboys and playboy types'[12]) and badly needed firm direction from a figure of Bradman's stature. Bradman was ready, and now had the time, to give that firm direction. But before he could do so, the world of cricket was shaken by the eruption of yet another volcano – the controversy over 'throwing'.

Throwing, or 'illegal bowling' as the whole controversy should perhaps be called, since it included the problem of fast bowlers' 'drag', became a matter of dispute during the MCC tour of Australia in the 1958–59 season. Neither problem was new. Law 26, which stated that 'for a delivery to be fair the ball must be bowled, not thrown or jerked', had been in place as long as anybody could remember, and the expression 'or jerked' was a relic from the days of underarm bowling. Most umpires, both English and Australian, thought that that was enough, and needed no further interpretation; indeed, the matter had been discussed, to no great effect, prior to the 1958 English season. As for 'drag', it was not uncommon for any fast bowler to land his back foot behind the bowling crease just before delivery, but for his momentum to carry him past it before the ball was actually released.

The two problems were exacerbated in the 1958–59 MCC tour of Australia. As a matter of fact, the whole tour was considered 'very controversial',[13] not least because Richie Benaud, Australia's new captain, introduced tactics which were defensive to the point of boredom and an element of 'gamesmanship' which, to be fair, was quickly adopted by many of the English players. But the most controversial aspect lay in the Australian umpires' relaxed attitude towards the bowling actions of at least two Australian bowlers, Meckiff and Rorke, and of one English bowler, Lock.

The row, of course, was nothing like the row over 'bodyline' a quarter of a century before. It never became an acute diplomatic incident; cricket was simply no longer as important as that. But it was enough to arouse accusations between the two sets of players and their supporters in the press which were tantamount to allegations of cheating. At the very least, it showed a difference between Australian umpires and English umpires on the interpretation of what was or was not a 'fair delivery' as stipulated in Law 26. Indeed, on his return to England, Lock substantially modified his bowling action to eliminate all suspicion (and was a much less effective bowler as a result).

'Drag' was the easier problem to solve since, as with Lindwall in 1948, all that had to be done was to put a line or a marker behind the bowling crease (behind which the bowler's back foot had to fall). But 'throwing' was much more difficult. As it was, only the square-leg umpire could properly see whether or not the bowler's arm was bent at the point just prior to delivery, and since he would normally be standing some thirty yards from the bowler at the time, he could hardly be expected to see – in the twinkling, as it were, of an eye – the exact position of the bowler's elbow.

Nevertheless, it was clear that the matter of throwing needed to be resolved; and the 1959 Imperial Cricket Conference said so without dissent. Furthermore, it was urgent, since the Australians were due to tour England in 1961. It was evident that some of their bowlers would be roughly handled by the English press, and conceivably by the English umpires. It was therefore with this in mind that in early 1959 the South Australian Cricket Association set up a Select Committee on Throwing, of which the Chairman was Sir Donald Bradman.

Bradman settled down to the task with his usual thoroughness. But even after sifting through all the evidence, it was difficult to come to any conclusion other than that the umpire was the only possible arbiter in the matter. True, there was a case for changing the text of Law 26 to leave out the words 'or jerked', mainly on the grounds that nobody knew what they meant. But this was obviously not going to solve the problem by itself. It was, however, because of his great technical understanding of the problem and the importance of the problem itself that Bradman, against all previous precedent, was appointed one of Australia's two delegates – the other being the then Chairman of the Board of Control – to the Imperial Cricket Conference of 1960.

The prelude to the 1960 Conference could hardly have been more startling. The South Africans were touring England that year. They had with them a young bowler by the name of Geoff Griffin, on whom high expectations rested. Griffin had been no-balled for throwing in South African provincial matches, and the English press had already picked his bowling action to pieces by the time he came to play against MCC at Lord's. But worse was to come. At Lord's he was no-balled by both umpires. In the next match, against Nottinghamshire, he was no-balled for throwing no fewer than eleven times. It was then announced by the South African manager that Griffin was to be sent for coaching to the veteran Surrey fast bowler Alf Gover, to see, as it was phrased – with the greatest of delicacy – whether there was anything wrong and whether it could be put right. But it was all to no avail. True, in the first Test match Griffin was not no-balled, but his length was uncertain and his direction little short of random. He then appeared to revert to his previous action – and was promptly no-balled for throwing six times in the match against Hampshire.

The climax came in the second Test match at Lord's. To general astonishment, Griffin took a hat-trick, the first ever in a Lord's Test. He was a hero. But during the England innings Griffin was no-balled eleven times, all by the square-leg umpire, for throwing. That might have been that, but for one further difficulty. The match – 'Griffin's match' it probably would have been called – ended just after lunch on the fourth day; but by coincidence that was the afternoon chosen for the traditional royal visit to meet the two teams. It was obviously absurd for the field to be empty on such an occasion; it simply would not do.

The two captains therefore decided to play an exhibition game. The unfortunate Griffin was put on to bowl. In the event, he only bowled one over in the whole afternoon, but it was an over of eleven balls. Umpire Buller, at square leg, no-balled him four times out of five; after consultation with his captain, Griffin changed to underarm, but was promptly no-balled again, this time by Umpire Lee at the bowler's end, for failing to notify the batsman of his change of action. Thus mortified, the humbled Griffin completed his over with underarm lobs. At that point their Majesties walked on to the field.

These events gave an extra sense of urgency to the problem and to the Conference. Admittedly, Griffin did not bowl again during the South African tour, but the South Africans were so angry that they prevented Buller from umpiring again during the 1960 Test series. This reaction, whatever its merits, destroyed at a stroke the argument that the matter of throwing was up to umpires and nobody else. Bradman's conclusion was to that extent undermined.

The Imperial Cricket Conference thus met in July with the tragi-comedy of Geoff Griffin at Lord's still in its collective mind. Two days were allotted to the Conference instead of the usual single day. At the outset, H.S. Altham, speaking for MCC, gave a 'solemn undertaking'[14] that England would not select bowlers whose action was suspect. But this was no good either. It meant, as the Australians and West Indians pointed out, that selectors could find themselves in the absurd position of declining to select for overseas tours a bowler whose action was accepted as fair by their own country's umpires. Needless to say, Bradman himself was very conscious of this dilemma: the life of an Australian selector was hard enough as it was without being accused by the press of arbitrary and subjective decision about a favourite bowler's action. Bradman argued the point long and hard.

Discussion became difficult, and at times acrimonious. Evidence was taken, films of suspect bowling actions were watched, and the argument was long and, at times, tedious. In the end, a further definition of what constituted 'throwing' was reached. It was not particularly convincing, since it simply re-affirmed what everybody knew, that a throw was, broadly speaking, a throw. This authoritative view was, however, accompanied by an equally majestic assertion that throwing was 'a complicated and difficult problem, especially for the umpires who are solely responsible for interpreting the Laws'. That, it need hardly be said, was a long way from providing a solution to the problem. Indeed, it was difficult to avoid the conclusion that the whole Conference had turned into something of a farce.

On his return from England in August 1960, Bradman was forthright. He said that the forthcoming Australian tour of England in 1961 could lead to 'the greatest catastrophe in cricket history'. 'It is,' he went on, 'the most complex problem I have known in cricket, because it is not a matter of fact but of opinion.'[15] What he did not mention was the clear sub-text: that Australian bowlers had been considered 'fair' not just by Australian umpires but by umpires of other countries as well – South Africa, New Zealand, India and Pakistan. True, there had been in London a definition, agreed unanimously and, in the end, amicably, but the problem of the difference in each country of umpires' interpretation of that definition still remained as acute as it ever had been.

On 13 September 1960, a month or so after his return, the Australian Board of Control unanimously elected Bradman as its Chairman. It was obvious then, if it had not been so before, that Bradman was the only person who could sort out the whole mess. And sort it out he did. Three days later the Board issued a combative statement – Bradman was always one to take the initiative – to the effect that the Board could not guarantee that the bowling action of every bowler who was selected to tour England in 1961 would 'meet with the complete approval of English umpires'. The challenge, however, was accompanied by an announcement that the Board would be sending to the MCC a proposal to ensure that the tour could take place without undue friction.

The proposal, when it came, was one of Byzantine subtlety – so subtle, indeed, that it was agreed almost without discussion by the MCC. English umpires, it said, should not object to any Australian bowler's action before 7 June 1961. Until that time, any umpire who had doubts about the fairness of delivery of an Australian bowler should complete a form – in duplicate – specifying whether in his opinion the bowler had infringed Law 26, 'Basically – that is every ball,' 'Frequently,' 'Occasionally,' or 'Very rarely' ('Please mark category thus [X] and make any comments you may wish and especially any which you think may help the bowler concerned'). The seventh of June 1961 was, by no coincidence, the day before the start of the first Test match.

It was, of course, the greatest nonsense. Literally interpreted, it meant that any Australian could throw as much as he liked up until the first Test match. But, like many pieces of great nonsense, it equally had great political advantages. If Law 26 were enforced as it should be, the tour might lapse into chaos, revenues would be lost, tempers inflamed, relations ruptured, the press in fury, and so on. If, on the other hand, English umpires did not enforce Law 26 as they should have in their own – unfettered – opinion, then the tour would go ahead without trouble; but the umpires would be recognising that their own interpretation of the law was open to question, and that other interpretations were admissible. For the umpires it was indeed Morton's fork.

The English counties would have none of it. Law 26 was the law of cricket, and should be enforced. In the event, the English umpires adopted one practice for county matches and another for matches involving the Australians. Fortunately for all concerned, however, the chief 'suspects', Meckiff and Rorke, had lost form and were not selected for the tour. Furthermore Benaud, the Australian captain, announced on arrival – presumably after heavy hints from Bradman – that his aim was to do away with dull cricket (although there were those who claimed that he was the person most responsible for 'dull cricket' in the previous MCC tour of Australia) and to bowl as many overs as possible (again apparently condemning the time-wasting tactics that he was said to have adopted). Nevertheless, as Fingleton, ever the assiduous journalist, remarked about Benaud in 1961, 'In one respect [he] stood head and shoulders over any international captain I have known . . . His public relations work was simply superb.'[16] It was a combination of Bradman's aggressive tactics and Benaud's public relations skills – and a bit of luck – that put the throwing controversy at least to temporary rest.

Bradman, throughout the whole row, had shown exactly the same characteristics in negotiation as he had in batting: total concentration, mastery of his brief, honesty in accepting another point of view if it was clearly demonstrated, great analytical intelligence, and complete calm in the face of crisis. If he was tough – some said he was too tough – that was because the mature Bradman, like the young Bradman, could not understand why those he was with were not as gifted as he. He was never one to suffer fools gladly, whether they were cricket fools or administrative fools. If fools did not like his treatment of them, that was their problem, not his.

14

SIR DONALD

SIR ROBERT MENZIES KT, PRIME MINISTER of Australia throughout the 1950s and for half the 1960s, was by all accounts something of a political thug. His career up until his assumption of the highest office seems to have been one of tough and unprincipled manoeuvre, and during his years in power he appeared to continue in the same manner, exploiting with pitiless skill the divisions and confusions of his opponents. Although he was consistently popular with his natural power base, the hard-nosed business community and the Returned Services League, and although he was electorally successful, history has not treated him well. Even supporters of his own party are doubtful about his legacy. Indeed, to quote one such source, 'far too much of his rule was a thing of expedients and feints' and 'he did not give enough of the intellectual and moral leadership Australia wanted'.[1] Of course, Menzies was a man of his time, and the 1950s, in Australia as elsewhere in the developed world, have had a particularly bad press. It was the decade of 'indolent consumerism', of 'prosperity without conscience', and of 'unthinking and ill-considered optimism'. In that sense, Menzies, like Eisenhower and Macmillan, was a figurehead for a sleazy decade.

To be fair, Menzies was a much respected figure in the British Commonwealth. It is not entirely clear why, since he was so patently a supporter of white supremacy, and the Commonwealth of the time, if it stood for anything, stood for constructive co-existence of countries of differing races, religions, cultures and colours. Perhaps it was his obvious devotion, which at times sounded almost like the passion of love, to Queen Elizabeth II; perhaps it was his often stated belief in the old-fashioned disciplines of Empire; perhaps it was simply his seniority both in years and in the length of time he had spent in office. But whatever the reason, there is no doubt that his opinion carried weight. His reward from the Queen was the Order of the Thistle in 1963 – in honour, it was said, of his Scottish origins. Given all this, it comes as no surprise to find that he was a fervent enthusiast for the old imperial game of cricket, and that, as such, he was Bradman's friend.

Physically, the two made a curious pair. Menzies was tall, bull-headed, with a 48-inch chest and a 51-inch waist, 'burly', said an opponent, 'with the ingestion of too many carbohydrates'.[2] Bradman, on the other hand, was small, trim and birdlike. Intellectually, by contrast, the two had a great deal in common. Both had a nimbleness of mind and a power of application which were the prerequisites for success in their chosen fields; and both recognised these characteristics in the other. Furthermore, Menzies had great respect not just for Bradman as a cricketer. He also admired Bradman's financial expertise. He said openly to all who wished to hear that Bradman knew more about certain aspects of Australian finance than any man in the country. It is a measure of how much Bradman's mind had developed – untrained, uneducated and ill-focused as it had been in his early years – that a Prime Minister of Australia could give such an accolade to someone who had always seemed in the public mind to be a cricketer, 'the boy from Bowral'. Nobody knew whether to take the accolade seriously or not, since Menzies, like any politician, was skilled in paying compliments to those he wished to please. But the fact that the compliment was paid without it looking ridiculous is significant enough. It is hard to identify any English Test cricketer about whom a British Prime Minister might, even with the greatest goodwill, make a similar comment.

It was during Bradman's first period as Chairman of the Board of Control, from 1960 to 1963, while Menzies was still Prime Minister, that the relationship seems to have been at its closest. Indeed, Bradman's last game of cricket was at Menzies' request. Bradman was invited to captain the Prime Minister's XI against the MCC tourists towards the end of their 1962–63 tour. The game was to be played in Canberra at the Manuka Oval. Possibly as a bait, the new pavilion there was to be opened by Menzies himself and was to be named the 'Bradman Pavilion'. It was an invitation which could not be refused. As it turned out, the occasion was one of mixed fortune. It was all very agreeable, but Bradman, at the age of fifty-four, after coming in to bat to prolonged and reverential applause from both the crowd and the MCC players, could only manage four runs before being bowled. 'I have just played my last game of cricket,' he announced the following day; 'the cricket bat has seen the last of me.'[3] And so it had. But the high points of the occasion were social rather than sporting. On the evening before the game Menzies gave a dinner for most of his team, including Bradman and Richie Benaud, the captain of the Australian national side at the time, and followed that by a further dinner party for Bradman at the Prime Minister's official residence on the next evening.

The presence of Benaud at the two dinners was no accident. During Bradman's period of office as Chairman of the Board of Control the two men had formed a relationship of what would properly be described as mutual respect. It was not, in the true sense, friendship – the difference in age and temperament was too great for that. But Benaud recognised to the full Bradman's knowledge and experience, while Bradman for his part recognised Benaud's willingness, and ability, to engage in a cricket match with the same intensity as had Bradman himself. Furthermore, they had a shared objective: to try to stem the flow of popular opinion which was driving the Australian public into the shallower waters of other summer entertainments. The plain fact was that by the end of the 1950s cricket was in danger of losing its position as Australia's national game. Attendances at Test matches and Sheffield Shield matches had fallen off badly – it was not unusual to see fewer than 10,000 spectators for a Test at Sydney or Melbourne. If the trend continued, both Bradman and Benaud knew that cricket would wither and, at least in its traditional form, die.

The proof of this particular pudding had come during the summer of 1960–61, when the West Indies had toured Australia. If the tide was to be reversed, this was to be the time. The West Indies, after all, were an enterprising set of players, and the series promised well. It was time for cricket to make its come-back as an Australian spectator sport. Both Bradman and Benaud had taken the point. On the eve of the first Test match at Brisbane, Bradman had asked Benaud whether he could speak to the Australian side. His message was simple and cogent: they were there to play attractive cricket which would bring back the lost spectators. In future, they should take note, the selectors would favour those who had followed his advice. It was not a lecture or a sermon; it was a simple statement of fact.

The result of Bradman's homily was little short of spectacular. In the Test which followed, West Indies made 453 in their first innings, Australia replied with 505 and then bowled West Indies out for 284 in their second innings. On the last day Australia needed 233 to win in five and a quarter hours. The odds quite clearly favoured Australia. But by tea, they were 110 for 6, needing 123 to win in the last session of two hours. The game had swung round, it seemed decisively, in West Indies' favour. During the tea interval, Bradman came into the Australian dressing room. He poured himself a cup of tea and sat next to Benaud, who was one of the not-out batsmen.

'What are the tactics?' he asked. 'We're going for a win,' replied Benaud – courageously, under the circumstances. 'Pleased to hear it,' said Bradman in his usual dry voice, and went on his way.[4] The 4,000 or so spectators who had had the faith to turn up then saw one of the most exciting finishes in Test cricket. Benaud was as good as his word, and, together with Davidson, went for the win. The scramble at the end was hectic – and the match ended in a tie. At least for the moment, the excitement had come back into cricket. The next Test at Melbourne showed the effect. On the Saturday, 90,000 spectators were there to watch the game. 'Positive' cricket, as played by both Bradman and Benaud, seemed to be working its old magic.

Bradman finished his term of office in 1963, while remaining a selector, with Australian cricket restored to the position of primacy in the world which it had lost in the 1950s. It would be wrong, however, to suggest that the traditional game of cricket had permanently regained its old appeal, whatever the attendance at the odd Test match. Indeed, it is hard to see how it might have done so. Australia herself, after all, was by now changing rapidly. For instance, the demographic change which was the result of the post-War immigration policy was having its effect. In the 1930s and 1940s (the span, as it happened, of Bradman's Test career), it had been possible for Australians to announce that they were '98 per cent British'. They were merely announcing a fact which was indisputable. By the mid-1960s, however, for Australians even to say that they were '80 per cent British' would have been an overstatement. Furthermore, the effect of that demographic change was, as far as cricket was concerned, even more concentrated. The major immigration from the European continent had been into the cities; the country areas were much slower to change their British – and cricket – allegiance. But it was in the cities that first-class and Test cricket was played.

Demographic change was one thing. The cricket optimists could argue that in the process of 'Australianisation' the new immigrants, from Turkey, Greece, Germany, Poland or Italy or from wherever it was, would learn the national game – complicated as it was. Whether the optimists would have been proved right is neither here nor there. But that, as it turned out, was yesterday's battle. Another battle was under way: the revolt of the young. However confusing it was at the time, with hindsight it is now clear that by the mid-1960s the youth of Australia, like the youth of the world elsewhere, was, in some wholly unco-ordinated and confused way, in the process of mounting a sustained attack on the cultural assumptions with which they had been brought up. The pretext for the revolt varied from country to country. In Australia, it was the Vietnam War.

On 29 April 1965 Menzies announced to a startled House of Representatives that Australia was to send an infantry battalion to South Vietnam to support, if necessary in armed action, the South Vietnamese against the Communist threat from the north. It was, he said, Australia's willing and correct response to a request from the South Vietnamese government and an indication of firm support for the United States. As a matter of possibly irrelevant fact, Menzies, not for the first or the last time, was not telling the truth. The truth was that the South Vietnamese request arrived several hours after his announcement in the House. Why the lie was told is something of a mystery; but it did not matter much, since there is no doubt that once the initial shock had passed, the bulk of Australian opinion, press and public, supported Menzies' decision. Only the *Australian*, recently set up as a national daily by the young Rupert Murdoch, dared to mount a challenge. Intervention in South Vietnam, it contended, would only stir up Asian opinion against Australia without materially helping the United States. It was 'a reckless decision . . . which this nation may live to regret'.[5] As it turned out, the prediction was surprisingly accurate, but as the troops paraded before their departure there were the customary scenes of patriotic fervour and rowdy contempt for the 'pacifists'. To those old enough to remember such things, of course, it was all eerily reminiscent of the departure of the Anzacs on their way to Gallipoli fifty years earlier.

Apart from the *Australian*, such opposition as there was ran along the traditional channels – academics, Anglican bishops, 'open forums' at universities and so on. Equally traditionally, it was all rather woolly, and none of it was very effective. This, after all, was the British method of protest. But gradually, just as the Australian government was following American policy, so, in a curiously exact mirror-image, the protest movement began to follow the American model. Associations started to form, with names like 'Save our Sons', holding long, silent vigils. Protesters, appearing seemingly at random, disrupted Sydney rush-hour traffic by sitting down in Martin Place. Students set light to a cross beside the War Memorial at Perth. Needless to say, the reaction to these events became equally fierce. Robert Askin, the Premier of New South Wales, when confronted with such a demonstration, reportedly instructed his driver to 'drive over the bastards'. The New South Wales president of the RSL was even more forthright. 'A baton behind the bloody ear,' he insisted firmly. 'There's nothing will calm the bloody ardour quicker than that.'[6] He could have spared his breath; the effect was to give further encouragement to the protesters.

There was, in fact, much to protest about. There was the question – up to now unanswered – of Australia's defence policy. It was all very well to regard the United States as the ultimate protector, but this surely did not mean that Australia would have to do whatever the United States asked. The subsidiary question, of course, was whether the communist 'threat from the north' was any more than a drive by the states of South-East Asia to independence, in which case it should be encouraged rather than suppressed. But these were complex questions, and not of the kind to engage popular emotions. There was, however, one which hit home: conscription. This was offensive on two counts: first, that the method of selection was nothing if not bizarre; and, second, that conscription for service, and possible death, outside the home territory had been rejected in both World Wars. As such, it could not be, and was not now, acceptable.

The protesters certainly had a point. On the first count, recruitment, odd as it seems, was by ballot among young Australians, all of whom were required to register when they reached the age of twenty. It was thus a lottery who went to fight and who stayed at home. In this lottery, brother was pitted against brother. Moreover, there was no provision to exempt conscientious objectors. It is difficult to imagine a system better designed to foment social conflict. On the second count, Australia had apparently gone to war in the same way as she had gone to war in 1939 – without any public debate. But Australia in 1965 was not Australia in 1939, and the United States imperium, such as it was, was not the maternal British Empire. There were no old loyalties to call on, and the protest was to that extent the more heartfelt.

In reality, for Australia Vietnam was hardly a major war, and the Australian numbers involved were small. In the whole Vietnam War no more than 475 Australians were killed and 4,307 wounded. But that was not the point, any more than it was the point at Gallipoli. The emotions that both events brought out were nothing to do with statistics. Given that, however, the difficulty for the protesters was to keep to Vietnam issues, and not to be side-tracked into the generalised self-indulgence of student politics. As the years rolled on, and as the Vietnam War became a burden, particularly so since the United States had started to look for a way out, the two got badly muddled up. Encouraged by events in the United States and France, student groups in 1967 and 1968 started to demand an immediate end to capitalism, or a non-nuclear Southern Hemisphere, or whatever happened to be the current adolescent political fad, and to link their demands to the anti-Vietnam movement. In July 1968 the United States consulate in Melbourne was stoned. In April 1969 'Students for a Democratic Society' occupied the Sydney offices of the federal attorney-general – until roughly turfed out by the police. At that moment, the whole Vietnam protest movement seemed to be on the point of turning into a conflict not about the War but between young and old within Australia herself.

In the end matters sorted themselves out. The United States beat an undignified retreat from Vietnam in 1973 and the Australian troops came back, as had their predecessors from Gallipoli – from a battle gallantly lost or a war gallantly lost made little difference – praising their own performance and blaming the foreign generals. By that time, however, Australia herself had undergone the same kind of menopausal shift as she had after Gallipoli. British imperial credibility had been undermined, in the end fatally, on the shores of the sea of Marmara; American credibility as policeman of the Southern Hemisphere had been undermined, just as fatally, in the brothels of Saigon. At the same time, and in curious parallel, the Americanisation of Australian culture, in the widest sense, had accelerated. Whereas before Vietnam the American alliance had been a matter for the politicians and the military – in other words, if such words may be used in an Australian context, for the upper-middle class – the new relationship was with the young. American films, for instance *Easy Rider* and *Zabriskie Point*, were all the fashion. Pop stars were idols. Each new Californian fad became high fashion in Sydney. Australia, it was said gloomily, had finally lost her cultural virginity.

But it was not just Americanisation that was changing Australia. One of Menzies' last and, given his professed loyalties, startling acts before his retirement in 1966 was to relax immigration policy in favour of non-Europeans – carefully selected, of course. In fact, there were two perfectly good reasons for this: first, that Australia's image in Asia and the United States was suffering badly from the 'White Australia' policy; and, second, that it became more and more difficult to accept a Turk, for instance, and deny a Malaysian. Besides, apart from all else, the policy shift gravely embarrassed the Labor opposition, and that was always one of Menzies' favourite sports. The upshot was that non-Europeans, and particularly Asians, of suitable qualifications were allowed to settle in Australia and that those who had lived there for five years could bring in dependents. In practice, it was the end of the 'White Australia' policy.

Through all these sociological upheavals Bradman stuck, as it were, to his last. A royal visit came and went, teams were selected for South Australia and Australia, his companies were visited and the occasional formal dinner addressed. Golf took up a good deal of his time, and he even managed a game of real tennis with Colin Cowdrey during the England tour of 1965–66. Even at this complex game, needless to say, Bradman was not satisfied until he had mastered the rules ('he became quite impatient at my apparent inability to explain all the implications of a certain rule in a single sentence . . .'). By the time the game began Bradman 'understood every tactical situation' and began to concentrate. 'He was conscious,' Cowdrey goes on, 'of no mortal thing outside those walls. His concentration and determination were absolute.' Furthermore, he surprised Cowdrey by 'racing from one corner to another to retrieve a ball which a man half his age would have ignored'.[7] Having mastered the game, Bradman then delivered himself of the opinion that he could not see much point in it.

In truth, Bradman's lifestyle was all part of what was coming to be seen as an old world. Furthermore, if an old world was what was wanted, the suburbs of Adelaide were the place to live. Television interviews could be, and were, refused. Offers to write more books could be, and were, turned down. Letters, of course, would be replied to unless they were from obvious cranks. The day was full, and absences on selection duty frequent, but it is difficult to avoid the impression that Bradman was wishing gradually to withdraw, perhaps even to start to take stock of his life. It could even be, perhaps, that Australia was moving beyond him.

In fact, there was to be one last throw. In 1969, Bradman was again elected Chairman of the Board of Control. His acceptance of the post, perhaps, was rather more reluctant than before. He was, after all, over sixty, and he had always felt, after the dramas of the 1930s, that his health was fragile. But duty was duty, and the influence of the senior and most knowledgeable of Australian cricketers was, for the next three years, to be exercised, it was said in London, at least from the regional office at Melbourne rather than from the branch office of Adelaide. As it turned out, Bradman's presence was much needed at what was to prove a difficult time in international relations, let alone international cricket.

The issue of the day was South Africa. In 1961, on the back of a programme of outright racial segregation inspired by the strictest Dutch Calvinism, South Africa had declared herself a republic. Not only that, but she had removed herself from the British Commonwealth before, it should be clear, she was pushed out. Since then, political links were almost non-existent – Menzies was one of the few Commonwealth Prime Ministers who failed to join the line-up of those who condemned from a convenient distance – but sporting links continued in a somewhat desultory manner. The Australian Board of Control, however, under Bradman's chairmanship, stuck to the normal calendar of events and invited the South Africans, since it was their turn, to tour Australia in the summer of 1971–72.

It was not a wise move. Not only did it pass over the fact that the British government had intervened to prevent a South African tour of England in 1970, but it also failed to recognise the changes which had occurred in Australia herself following the Vietnam War. It was not just that the techniques of protest were that much more sophisticated; the race issue itself had risen, if not to the top, at least to the upper half of the Australian political agenda. The majority of Australians, if the polls were any indication – 70% if the poll in the *Australian* was to be believed – may have been in favour of the South African tour, as indeed was Bradman himself, but the heavyweights of the Australian establishment, the bishops and the universities, were decidedly against. The whole matter became almost overnight a matter of the most acute political controversy.

Nothing could have been more distasteful. Bradman hoped

that 'politics' could be kept out of 'sport'. It was, then as now, far from clear how this could be achieved. He therefore found himself in the unpleasant position of being landed with a political problem but with little political experience in how to deal with it. He had always professed to a dislike of 'politics', in the same way that he had disliked 'publicity'. What he had not realised was that he himself had been part of the whole general process of 'politics' since the 1930s. Like so many other sportsmen, before and since, he seemed to have confused the generality of politics with the narrower activity of party politics.

Bradman set about the unwelcome task with little enthusiasm but with his usual thoroughness. He watched one of the rugby Tests between the then visiting Springboks and Australia, and saw for himself the barricades and the barbed wire needed to protect the visitors, the heavy police presence and the disruption of the game by invasions of the pitch, and the continual stream of bad-tempered abuse levelled at both the visitors and the authorities. 'The police were ready for things such as smoke bombs and flares,' he later said, 'but the barricades didn't stop the protesters; they invaded the arena.'[8] That night, Bradman had dinner with the South Africans, and noted the police guard around their hotel. From there, he and his colleagues went out to canvass the views of State governments, police authorities, groundsmen and cricket administrators. The conclusions were obvious. Indeed, they had been obvious even before the consultation exercise started. It was only Bradman and his colleagues on the Board, all of whom wanted the tour to go ahead, who had been trying to find a way round the political realities in the first place. The tour could not possibly go ahead without a security risk, to the tourists and to the Australian authorities, of a level which could not be accepted.

On 9 September 1971, the Board met to consider what was by then a foregone conclusion: the cancellation of the tour. There was a long press statement, meandering through the arguments, the reluctance of the Board, and so on. But the conclusion was clear: the Board had accepted the politics of the situation. The Adelaide *News* commented that 'the board's decision must go down as one of the utmost wisdom and sagacity – and a great personal victory for Sir Donald'. Rupert Murdoch's *Australian* was more terse: 'An example,' it said, 'of dignified common sense in trying circumstances.' Only the Sydney *Bulletin* struck a more sarcastic note: 'Sir Donald,' it recommended, should be installed 'at once' as Prime Minister with a cabinet of other sportsmen since 'Australia is a sportocracy and the people we love best are our sportsmen.'[9]

The cancellation of the South African tour left something of a blank in the 1971–72 Australian cricketing summer. Bradman and his Board colleagues decided that there was only one way to fill it: another tour would have to be organised in its place. It needed all Bradman's organising ability, his contacts and his reputation to pull it off; for what was proposed was a tour by a scratch team of international players of the highest standard. There was no point in anything less. The tour was duly organised and, in the event, was a resounding success, the climax being the 254 made by Gary Sobers in the third Test match at Melbourne. Bradman himself thought it was the greatest innings ever played in Australia. (Even given Bradman's usual modesty about his own achievements, it was the most generous of compliments.) At the conclusion of the tour, the Rest of the World team gave a farewell dinner in Adelaide for Bradman; no other guests were invited. It was, Don told them when thanking them, an emotional occasion, because it demonstrated at an important moment the way in which sport, and particularly cricket, could cut across barriers of race or colour. That was the true and effective answer to the South African government.

It was on this high note that Bradman's career as a cricket administrator ended. Now in his early sixties, he felt that he had given of his best to the game, as indeed he had. Others should now shoulder the burden. As it happened, his final retirement was marked soon afterwards by a family event which both Don and Jessie would have preferred to avoid. For some time they had been aware of the problems confronting their son John as a result of his bearing the Bradman name. The phenomenon is not without precedent. The child of a famous father, particularly when the name is uncommon, is often asked, when introducing himself or being introduced, whether he is the son of that father.

In that sense, however proud he may be of his father and mother, the child is bound to feel difficulty in establishing his own identity. It has happened before and will no doubt happen again.

Bradman vividly recalled the day in 1972 when he, Jessie and John were sitting at home at a table in the back yard alongside the swimming pool. John quietly informed his parents of his decision to change his name. There was no argument or recrimination. However disappointed Don and Jessie were at John's decision, there was no question of the family bond being broken. There was, of course, discussion. If John wanted to change his name, Bradman said, why did he not change it to something as far removed from 'Bradman' as possible, say 'Smith' or 'Jones' rather than 'Bradsen', which was John's choice? It was a fair point, at least in logic. What it may have missed, however, is the underlying psychology of John's decision; he might only have wanted to put a small distance between him and his father's name, and he certainly never intended a break from his father, which a more radical change might have implied.

In fact, the family bond remained as it always was, strong and affectionate. John made his own career, to his parents' great satisfaction, as a lecturer in constitutional and environmental law, and when he married and children came the grandchildren were almost every day to be seen with their proud and no doubt indulgent grandparents. The bond was equally strong with Shirley. Whatever the difficulties, she had fallen in love, and her love was returned. She married, and for five years the love was sustained, but in the end the marriage came to grief.

To cap it all both parents had difficulties with their health. Jessie developed a heart problem, and in 1978, had to undergo an open-heart bypass operation. Not only that, but Don himself, after a visit to London in the spring of 1974, developed his own heart problems, and, on his return to Adelaide, was advised by his doctors to slow up. None of this, however, prevented the occasional sortie during the 1970s. In January 1974 the big 'Bradman Stand' at the Sydney Cricket Ground was formally opened. Bradman appeared, to adulatory roars from the crowd, during the lunch interval of an Australia–New Zealand Test match. 'They usually leave this sort of thing,' he was heard to remark, 'until you're dead.'[10] In the English spring of that year, Don and Jessie made a trip to London for a dinner of the Lord's Taverners, at which Bradman was presented with – yet another – cut-glass decanter. Then, in September 1976, in spite of another 'serious warning' about his health, Don and Jessie went back to Bowral for the opening of their new cricket ground, named, as might be expected, the 'Bradman Oval'. The following March there was the Centenary Test between England and Australia at Melbourne, and a dinner at which Bradman made a forty-minute speech. Finally, there was a reunion dinner for the 1948 Australian tourists in Sydney – thirty years on, as it were. It was another nostalgic occasion, and difficult to refuse.

There was one temptation which Bradman was able to resist. Even at the time of the Centenary Test, Australian cricket was poised for one of the great rows of its history. A successful entrepreneur, Kerry Packer, had spotted an opening. The one-day limited overs game was attracting support in England, and there seemed no reason why it should not attract similar support in Australia. Besides, Australian cricketers could only look with envy at the money earned by players in other sports; they were only amateurs. Packer, together with a few powerful financial backers and – it should be said – greedy cricketers, launched what he described as 'World Series Cricket'. Packer had contracted enough players to stage one-day games (played in what seemed like particularly colourful pyjamas) but he had so irritated the Australian Board that the Board refused him permission to use the grounds, or even practice wickets, of those clubs which accepted the Board's jurisdiction. There was some talk of compromise, but nothing came of it. Australian cricket was broken in half.

Bradman's view on the matter was quite clear. He accepted that cricket in Australia had to become professional. He also realised that the days when spectators would sit enthusiastically through three-, four- or five-day games belonged to the past – indeed to the days of Empire, when he had been supreme. Nevertheless, what was intolerable was the intrusion from outside the game and the purchase of cricketers as though they were sides of beef. That lowered the dignity of the greatest of all games. In the end, of course, there was an uneasy compromise. What was clear, however, was that Bradman had refused to intervene publicly. Many had expected him to do so, but he knew, as did everybody else, that, if he did, he would be thrown again immediately into the spotlight – and another few gruelling months, if not years, of publicity.

Retirement at that point meant what it said. True, Bradman was awarded the Companionship of the Order of Australia, but beyond that both Bradmans were content to let the world go by as it wished. Don played golf and watched cricket; Jessie got on with her knitting and her grandchildren. There were to be no radio or television interviews, no articles written, no views or comments expressed in public. Over the years, there were one or two exceptions to the rule – a letter to the *Advertiser* about bodyline, a series of prepared interviews with the Australian Broadcasting Corporation for radio, and a television video, all, as it happened, in 1983, around his 75th birthday. After that, there was silence.

If silence is needed, there are few better places than Adelaide in which to keep it. In the relatively small community, 'Sir Donald' came to occupy a position almost like that of royalty. The visitor who wished to see him had to go through an elaborate ritual. The proper way was to establish *bona fides*, probably through the good offices of the South Australian Cricket Association. Once agreed, a meeting would be arranged, possibly at the Adelaide Oval to coincide with a Sheffield Shield or Test match which Bradman wanted to watch. The visitor would be instructed by the Secretary of the Association in the procedure he was to follow. At a particular time – given precisely – he should go to a particular gate, where he would find a ticket waiting for him. He should then walk round to the Committee Room and introduce himself to the Secretary, who would guide him solicitously to a seat and inform him at what precise time 'Sir Donald' would arrive and which steps he would walk up. The Secretary would go on to explain that 'Sir Donald' would talk with the visitor for a specified period of time and then, if there had been prior agreement, invite the visitor into the Committee room for lunch. After lunch, there would be further discussion, until 'Sir Donald' decided that it was time for him to go home.

It would all have happened according to the script. But

instead of a 'Sir Donald', the visitor would have been received by a much more friendly 'Don', with the greatest courtesy, humour and charm. Discussion would have been wide-ranging and lively – about the state of the world, the British Royal Family, one-day cricket, Bradman's career, mutual acquaintances – in short, anything which caught the imagination. The Bradman mind would be as sharp as ever. The visitor would have had to be very careful to avoid a slipshod comment or unsupported assertion; it would have been picked up immediately. One visitor, himself a lawyer of the greatest distinction, remarked after one such discussion: 'The way he answered questions, his summary of events, made me feel that (although it would have been a waste of his wonderful talents) he would have made a very good judge.'[11]

In all this, the visitor would have noticed some very marked characteristics: quietness, a firmness of view without assertiveness, great modesty – not false modesty (Bradman knew perfectly well how great a player he had been) – and considerable respect both for his fellow players and for the devilish nature of the game of cricket. If there was a tendency not to commit himself, to stand back and observe, to play the role of an interested bystander, that was a reflection of the way he wanted his life to be. Party politics was not for him, nor the High Commission in London, nor the Governor-General's palace. 'Altogether,' the same legal visitor remarked, 'an example of someone who has attained the heights in his own area and carries genuine but quiet greatness in his personality.'[12]

As the 'little feller' said his goodbyes, said that he thought perhaps he ought to be getting back to Jessie, and walked slowly down the steps until he was out of sight, the visitor, any visitor, would have been hard put not to endorse that view.

EPILOGUE

'YOU CAN'T TELL YOUNGSTERS TODAY OF the attraction of the fellow. I mean, business used to stop in the town when Bradman was playing and likely to go in – all the offices closed, the shops closed; everybody went up to see him play.'[1] Thus Bill Bowes, speaking on the fiftieth anniversary of the 'bodyline' tour, in 1983. That, of course, was in England. In Australia, his home territory, the attraction was even more compelling, to the point where not only would businesses shut down but the crowds of urban unemployed – who could not even afford the entrance fee into the great cricket grounds and many of whom never saw him bat – would stand in the streets to cheer him on as the numbers clanked up on outdoor mechanical scoreboards. During the Ashes Test series of 1932–33 and 1936–37, city centres would come to a standstill.

But it is not enough simply to state the facts, impressive though they are, since the facts themselves provoke questions. First, and possibly foremost, how good a player – in the whole pantheon of cricketers past and present – was this man who inspired what almost amounted to worship? Second, what sort of Australia was it which was prepared to lay herself at his feet? Third – and for the understanding of the man, most important – what was the effect of all this on his life and character?

As a cricketer, Bradman, in many people's eyes, wears the supreme crown as the best that ever lived. Even his old antagonist O'Reilly had to admit it. 'Don Bradman,' he said towards the end of his life, 'was the greatest cricketer ever to put boots on and to walk on to a cricket field.'[2] In spite of his personal dislike, O'Reilly was forced to recognise Bradman's playing genius. His verdict is echoed by countless others. Of course, and as is natural, there have been those who have been less convinced. R.E.S. Wyatt, for instance, thought that Hobbs was a better player, albeit not such a consistent run-getter; there has been a long-running debate in Australia whether Bradman ever reached the grandeur of Victor Trumper; and there are those in England who argue the case for W.G. Grace. But the weight of opinion clearly follows O'Reilly.

There is little point in pursuing the argument, as it will never end. Indeed, the appearance of Brian Lara on the scene has given it new, although perhaps ephemeral, life. Certainly Trumper and Hobbs were more stylish than Bradman, and the wickets on which Grace had to play were inferior to those of Bradman's Australia. But Bradman's statistical record has outshone all others, as the Appendix bears out. He simply made more runs per innings, at every level of cricket, than anybody before or since. Not only that, but he made his runs at a pace which has never been equalled. Furthermore, his record in Test match cricket, in spite of the 'missing years' of 1939–46, when he could have expected to be in his prime, was far and away superior to any other, and, to cap it all, his runs were mostly made against England – at that time the only other major power in world cricket. O'Reilly's case is certainly formidable.

Style, of course, was another matter, and what is indisputable is that Bradman's batting technique was wholly his own. He was as far removed from the orthodoxy of a Hobbs or a Hutton as it was possible to be. He had, after all, taught himself, with his cricket stump and his golf ball; and such was the speed of his reactions that he never felt the need for coaching into a more traditionally acceptable batting style. 'I've always said,' Bradman claimed in later life, 'that the two main ways to learn cricket are, one, experience for yourself of actually playing and, two, watching somebody else.'[3] Fortunately enough for him, in the Australia of his day, both were amply available.

No more than five feet eight inches tall, with small shoulders, but with long, powerful arms and wrists which could clamp on to a bat handle like a vice, he had a method of batting which it was almost impossible for others to imitate. To begin with, he held his bat in what for anyone else would have been an uncomfortable position. Instead of the bat handle running across the palm of the right hand and resting against the ball of the right thumb, with the left wrist in front of or to the side of the handle, Bradman twisted his right hand round so that the handle pressed directly against the ball of the right thumb, while his left hand was turned round so that the wrist lay almost behind the handle. Furthermore, he rested his bat on the ground, before the bowler's delivery, between his feet rather than behind his right foot, as is usual, and made no movement (except during the 'bodyline' series) until the bowler was committed to a particular length of ball.

From this grip and stance there followed two natural results: first, that his bat was lifted at an angle of almost 45 degrees from the line of trajectory of the ball which was coming at him; and, second, that if the chosen stroke was across the line of the ball rather than directed straight back down the wicket his instinctive movement was to roll his wrists over in making the stroke. It was this second movement that made him such a powerful player on the leg side, particularly in his favourite shots, a push wide of mid-on and – almost his trademark – the pull to mid-wicket from a ball short of a length just on or outside the off stump, and that made him such a master of the late cut through the slips. For anybody else, of course, it would have been impossible with such a grip to hit the ball with any force in the arc between mid-off and cover point. Bradman's off-drive, however, was one of his fiercest shots, achieved as it was by exercising – with exact timing – the full power of his formidable right wrist at the point of impact with the ball. What was impossible for anybody else was a lethal weapon for Bradman.

It was Bradman's footwork that served to counter dangers deriving from his unorthodox grip. And dangers there certainly were. It was, for instance, often said that Bradman was not the player on wet wickets, particularly against the turning ball, that he was on dry wickets, and that his grip of the bat and consequent back-lift were part of his difficulty. There is no final proof either way, since, although his record on wet wickets was far from his normal high level of consistency, Bradman's supporters could well argue, and did argue, that he could easily have adapted his footwork to cope with wet wickets (particularly English wet wickets) had he wanted to, but that wet wickets which allowed sharp turn, as opposed to being merely soggy and therefore easy enough, were sufficiently rare not to warrant any fundamental technical re-appraisal.

There certainly was danger at the beginning of an innings – if Bradman had a weakness it was at that point (as, incidentally, does every other batsman) – but, when he was set, his sharp – and often balletic – footwork enabled him to get his head over the line of the oncoming ball, allowing him in turn to bring his bat into a straight position for defensive play. In the case of the quicker bowlers he gave himself time for this manoeuvre by taking his first step backwards. This left him in position to play defensively or offensively off the back foot, or to move forward to drive. As for the slow bowlers, he was always ready to dance down the wicket to take the ball on the full or on the half-volley.

Technical unorthodoxy, speed of decision allied to a natural sense of timing, dancing footwork, the ability to bring all the movements of his body into synchronised force at the moment he struck the ball: these qualities combined to make Bradman such a difficult batsman to bowl to, and thus allowed him to score runs so quickly. The style was not, it must be admitted, particularly elegant, but it was supremely effective in the destruction of a bowling attack. As though that were not enough, even at a young age he had three characteristics which were unnerving to any bowler whom he was facing: the first was the grin, which made the bowler feel that there was nothing that could possibly come as a surprise to this confident young man; the second was the fact that he stood absolutely still, not tapping the ground with his bat as the bowler ran in, thus giving the appearance of total nervelessness; and third, he never sweated, remaining apparently as cool after three hundred runs as he had been after one. 'As I ran up to bowl,' an English bowler remarked, 'Bradman seemed to know where the ball was going to pitch, what stroke he was going to play and how many runs he was going to score. That was exactly the uncanny impression he gave.'[4]

Although batting was his main preoccupation and his supreme achievement, Bradman was also one of the best out-fielders the game has seen. The practice against the paling fence had not been in vain. His throwing, even from the longest boundary, was flat, accurate and straight to the top of the stumps; from closer in he seemed to be able hit the stumps directly almost at will. He was not a great catcher of the ball – surprising in view of his speed of vision – and rarely fielded in the slips. But it would have been a waste; as an out-fielder he saved so many runs for his side that the balance was always with him even before he went out to bat.

Both in batting and in fielding, his two additional weapons were his power of concentration and his willingness always to learn about the game. Of his concentration there are examples enough. His willingness to learn is perhaps less well understood. But right from the day when his father first took him to Sydney Cricket Ground and he saw both Woolley and Macartney bat, he was learning from others; and the fact that he went out of his way to acquire a qualification in umpiring showed how highly he valued a profound knowledge of the game. Indeed, it was that which made him one of Australia's greatest tactical captains.

Just as it is difficult to explain to 'youngsters today', to use Bowes' expression, Bradman's attraction as a cricketer, so is it equally difficult to explain to the same audience his iconic role at an important point in Australian history. Indeed, a casual conversation in today's Sydney with one of the 'youngsters' is apt to elicit the comment: 'Bradman? He's way back in history.'[5]

Quite so. It may be that young Australians hold his name in less reverence than did the previous generation. The Americanisation of Australia may have seen to that. But the Australia of Bradman's heyday was quite different from the Australia of today. Indeed, the years of Depression were years which the modern Australian can only wonder at, such has been the change; but in those years Bradman was without a doubt the brightest star – almost the only bright star – in what was a particularly gloomy firmament. In the period when day after day went by without hope for a large section of Australia's manhood and in unremitting drudgery for Australian women, Bradman was the one hero with whom it was possible to identify and who stood firm for the pride of a young nation. 'Susso' might be degrading, but as long as 'Our Don' was savaging the English bowling attack, whether in Melbourne or Leeds, there was at least something to cheer. Those who lived through the period say, with the ring of absolute truth, that they will never forget the sense of hope and confidence that Bradman symbolised.

It might, and probably would, all have been different had the colonisation of the Australian continent come from Asia to the north rather than from Britain on the other side of the globe. Instead of staying near the sea and founding a country based on the largest safe anchorages, the Asian colonists would perhaps have penetrated more quickly into the vast areas of desert or near-desert which make up the bulk of the continent. The development of the Chinese hinterland might reasonably be taken as a plausible model. Under those circumstances, the further evolution of Australia would not have been confined to a seemingly inexorable spread of suburbia out from the harbour cities but would have taken on a more balanced – if perhaps less prosperous – shape. From this a culture would have emerged which was not forever looking towards the sea but, like China, would have been more isolated and less derivative. There would have been no British convicts – and certainly no cricket.

Seen in the light of an Australia perched, sometimes uncomfortably, on the edge of the Pacific and Indian Oceans, the Bradman phenomenon can more easily be understood. Culturally, the population was British, even if geographically its home country belonged to Asia. Bradman represented the best possible source of compromise: maintaining the cultural Britishness while asserting an Asian independence against British authority, in particular the assumed authority of the English upper class. It is in this sense that no history of the sociology of Australia is worth writing unless it encompasses Bradman and what he represented. It is, of course, equally not worth writing unless it traces the way Australia, like a great liner, slipped gradually away from her mooring in the British harbour to chart a cultural course into and across the Pacific.

Bradman himself was part of this troubled sociology, even if he was also, for a time, its undoubted icon. For the boy from a lonely childhood in the New South Wales bush it was almost too much to take. In fact, it is perhaps not too much to say that, had he not found a wife who supported him unfailingly through the bad periods, Bradman might have found it altogether too much, and have given up cricket for good in the 1930s. He certainly hinted at the possibility. Furthermore, he said in later life about his knighthood: 'I would have preferred to remain just Mister.'[6] He had accepted the honour, he went on, partly because the official at Government House who told him about it looked so shocked when asked whether there was an option to refuse, and partly because he interpreted the gesture as an honour to Australian cricket rather than to himself. True, self-deprecating comments about honours should normally be taken with a large measure of salt. But Bradman's remark has the ring of sincerity; and it reveals much about what many have hitherto thought to be his 'enigmatic' character.

In his playing days he was a curious mixture of modesty and confident self-assertion. The modesty was genuine. Of course, he knew that he was good, and, like many young men before and since, he was apt to be cocky; but unlike many other players of all sports – and indeed those in other professions – he was generous in his recognition of the achievements and qualities of his competitors. On the other hand, he was at times puritanical, quick to resent criticism, particularly of his conduct outside cricket, and was rarely prepared to accept that he was wrong. To that extent, the legacy of childhood had been one of defence.

Coupled with this defensiveness was intense dislike of the burden placed on him as a national hero, particularly in the 1930s and late 1940s when 'Bradmania', as it was known, was at its height. Nothing in his upbringing had remotely prepared him for the pressure of constant public visibility. He had been used to making his way back from school, in the small town of Bowral, unrecognised except as the boy who was always throwing a golf ball against a paling fence, to a home where the evening's entertainment consisted of a few songs around a piano. It was a far cry from the raucous cheers of 80,000 spectators at Melbourne or the handshake of King George V. As a result, and understandably, his character seemed to develop what some have called an uncertain volatility; in turn, and often unpredictably, he could be brusque or courteous with the press, disciplinarian or considerate to his own players, mutinous or respectfully obedient to the authorities. Age and a happy marriage smoothed over the rougher edges and allowed the old-fashioned rural courtesy of his background to break through the shell of acquired suspicion, but, even then, it would be a mistake to engage in argument with him without a sure knowledge of the facts at issue.

On his retirement, given his self-trained but sharp analytical intelligence and his determinedly accumulated wisdom, he could have followed almost any second career he chose. What in the event he did choose was the relatively modest course of a provincial businessman. The contrast between the glory of his playing days and the relative obscurity of his later life could hardly be more marked. But that, without a doubt, was what he wanted. He had had enough of glory. Besides, there was a consistent theme in his life, dating from the poverty of his childhood. He was determined not to have to rely on cricket for his living, and determined to reach financial security for himself and his wife. As with his cricket, so with his life: when Don Bradman was determined on an objective it was almost invariably achieved.

In a life as long as Bradman's – indeed in any life – there will always be moments where good fortune and bad fortune interrupt the steady course of events. Bradman's bad fortune was partly in his health but more in the timing of the Second World War; his good fortune was to find a wife as the other half of what he himself called 'the greatest partnership of my life'.[7] In the sunset of old age, contentment settled on them both. He had achieved, as the poet Pindar wrote of Xenophon of Corinth two and a half thousand years ago, 'things that no mortal man had achieved before'.[8] It is only right that fortune allowed them time to enjoy, in tranquillity and reflection, the respect and admiration of their country and the cricketing world.

ACKNOWLEDGEMENTS

M Y FIRST THANKS MUST GO TO Don himself – more formally, to Sir Donald Bradman. Apart from showing me the greatest courtesy when I saw him in Adelaide, he gave seemingly endless attention to the smallest question I asked in our subsequent correspondence. Not only that, he set aside two whole days to read the draft I had prepared and commented on it in great, and frequently trenchant, detail. We did not always agree in our opinions, but disagreement, when it came, was always friendly and adult. My second thanks go to Jessie – again more formally, to Lady Bradman. She followed the whole enterprise from a distance but with sympathy, and kindly allowed me to dedicate this book to her.

Many people helped in the course of my journey. Pride of place goes to Brian Matthews, professor at the Sir Robert Menzies Centre for Australian Studies in London, who has firmly guided my steps in the unfamiliar territory of Australian social history and saved me from many traps. Furthermore, he was extremely generous in the time he gave to reading through my drafts and making valuable suggestions. I cannot thank him enough. Colin Cowdrey and Doug Insole (both former captains under whom I served on the cricket field) were authoritative and informed on Don's career, and Jim Swanton – whose generous gift to an impoverished undergraduate of a pair of batting gloves in the Parks in 1954 will always be remembered – dug deep into his copious memory as well as his wide knowledge. All of them accepted without hesitation the penance of reading through the bulk of the final draft and made life-saving corrections. The final product, imperfect as it is, is very much better for their attentions.

Many others, too numerous to mention, contributed to my

283

understanding of Bradman and of Australian sociology. Almost everybody I talked to had an anecdote or a reminiscence – all of which, whether true or not, helped my perception. For practical help, my thanks go to Graham Halbish of the Australian Cricket Board; to Dean Hazel of the Official Receiver's Office, Adelaide; to Stephen Young and Hugh Piper of Arthur Andersen in Adelaide; to Sir Victor Garland; to Sir Richard Kingsland for guidance through the intricacies of Canberra; to Michael Whelan of the British Broadcasting Corporation; to the Australian Broadcasting Corporation; to Col Egar and his colleagues in the South Australian Cricket Association; to Elizabeth Warburton and Hilary Browne-Wilkinson; to the House of Lords Library; to Stephen Green of the MCC Library at Lord's; to the State Library of South Australia; to the Bradman Museum in Bowral; to the Public Records Office in Kew and to Dr Angus Blair, for his expert advice on health matters. I should also mention, in case it goes unnoticed, that the titles of Chapters 5 and 6 are from the words to 'Waltzing Maltilda' by A.J. ('Banjo') Paterson.

I am immensely grateful to the master statistician, Bill Frindall, for compiling the statistical appendix, and to Alan Samson and Andrew Gordon at Little, Brown for their patience and hard work – and inspiration – in the editing and production of the book; but finally, my debt, as always, is to my wife, who has had to put up, while the book was in my mind, with what I can now perceive to be a succession of random bouncers, half-volleys and long hops. She has dealt with all of them in the most patient and loving manner. She is by far my best and most truthful critic. All that I can give in return is my own love, which, as she knows, I do unstintingly.

APPENDIX
Bradman's Career Statistics
Compiled by Bill Frindall

HIS FIRST-CLASS CAREER

Match-by-Match Summary

(* not out; + captain; Brisbane[1] = Exhibition Ground; Brisbane[2] = Woolloongabba; Test matches in **bold**)

Season	Match	Venue	1st Innings No	Runs	HO	2nd Innings No	Runs	HO
1927–28	1 NSW v S Aus	Adelaide	7	118	c	6	33	b
	2 NSW v Vic	Melbourne	6	31	lbw	6	5	b
	3 NSW v Qld	Sydney	8	0	b	8	13	c wk
	4 NSW v S Aus	Sydney	6	2	c & b	6	73	st
	5 NSW v Vic	Sydney	6	7	st	6	134	*

1 Batted 188 minutes (8 fours) despite an injured finger to record a chanceless hundred in his initial first-class innings. Reached his 50 in 67 minutes and his 100 in 161 minutes.

Season	Match	Venue	1st Innings No	Runs	HO	2nd Innings No	Runs	HO
1928–29	6 Rest v Aus XI	Melbourne	6	14	c wk	6	5	b
	7 NSW v Qld	Brisbane[1]	3	131	c wk	3	133	*
	8 NSW v MCC	Sydney	5	87	b	5	132	*
	9 Aus XI v MCC	Sydney	5	58	*	5	18	lbw
	10 **AUS v ENG**	**Brisbane[1]**	7	18	lbw	6	1	c

Season	Match	Venue	1st Innings No	Runs	HO	2nd Innings No	Runs	HO
1928–29	11 NSW v Vic	Melbourne	5	1	b	3	71	★
	12 **AUS v ENG**	**Melbourne**	6	79	b	6	112	**c wk**
	13 NSW v S Aus	Adelaide	2	5	c	1	2	b
	14 NSW v Vic	Sydney	3	340	★			
	15 **AUS v ENG**	**Adelaide**	6	40	c	6	58	ro
	16 NSW v MCC	Sydney	5	15	c			
	17 NSW v S Aus	Sydney	3	35	c wk	3	175	c wk
	18 **AUS v ENG**	**Melbourne**	5	123	c	7	37	★

7 His first instance of scoring a hundred in each innings: 131 in 212 minutes with 14 fours and 133★ in 264 minutes with 11 fours.

8 Innings of 87 (131 minutes, 8 fours) and 132★ (207 minutes, 14 fours; sharing an unbroken match-saving partnership of 249 with A.F. Kippax) secured his selection for the First Test.

14 His chanceless 340★ (488 minutes, 38 fours) was a record for the Sydney ground. Completing his hundred in 189 minutes, he progressed from 196 to 301 in the post-lunch session on the second day.

18 His tally of 1,690 runs (average 93.88) created the record (still current) for any batsman in an Australian first-class season.

Season	Match	Venue	1st Innings No	Runs	HO	2nd Innings No	Runs	HO
1929–30	19 NSW v Qld	Brisbane[1]	3	48	ro	4	66	c wk
	20 NSW v MCC	Sydney	3	157	b			
	21 Woodfull's XI v Ryder's XI	Sydney	4	124	c	2	225	lbw
	22 NSW v S Aus	Adelaide	3	2	ro	2	84	b
	23 NSW v Vic	Melbourne	3	89	b	4	26	★
	24 NSW v Qld	Sydney	1	3	c wk	3	452	★
	25 NSW v S Aus	Sydney	3	47	c			
	26 NSW v Vic	Sydney	3	77	c			
	27 Aus XI v Tas	Launceston	5	20	lbw			
	28 Aus XI v Tas	Hobart	3	139	c			
	29 Aus XI v WA	Perth	3	27	c			

20 He batted 175 minutes and hit 16 fours (50 in 45 minutes, 100 in 103 minutes).

21 His second instance of a hundred in each innings involved an aggregate of 275 runs in 325 minutes on the third day. His 225 (252 minutes, 28 fours) included 120 in the post-tea session.

24 His score of 452★ (in 415 minutes) remains the highest in Australian first-class

cricket and was the world record for 29 years until Hanif Mohammad (499) surpassed it in January 1959. It occupied 415 minutes and eclipsed the previous world record of 437 by W.H. Ponsford. He reached 100 in 104 minutes, 200 in 185, 300 in 288 and 400 in 377. Commencing his innings shortly after lunch on the second day (4 January), he reached 85 at tea and was 205 at stumps. Following the rest day, he added 105 before lunch and had scored a further 142 when A.F. Kippax declared at tea. As New South Wales won by 685 runs (still the world record victory margin of runs) with almost two days to spare, Bradman could easily have been allowed to reach his 500 and extend the record even beyond B.C. Lara's eventual reach.

29 His aggregate of 1,586 (average 113.28) was the second-highest by an Australian in a home first-class season until R.N. Harvey scored 1,659 in 1952–53.

| Season | Match | Venue | 1st Innings | | | 2nd Innings | | |
			No	Runs	HO	No	Runs	HO
1930	30 Aus v Worcs	Worcester	3	236	c			
	31 Aus v Leics	Leicester	3	185	*			
	32 Aus v Yorks	Sheffield	3	78	c & b			
	33 Aus v Lancs	Liverpool	3	9	b	3	48	*
	34 Aus v MCC	Lord's	3	66	b	3	4	lbw
	35 Aus v Derbys	Chesterfield	3	44	c wk			
	36 Aus v Surrey	The Oval	3	252	*			
	37 Aus v OU	Oxford	3	32	b			
	38 Aus v Hants	Southampton	1	191	c			
	39 Aus v Middx	Lord's	3	35	b	3	18	b
	40 Aus v CU	Cambridge	3	32	c			
	41 **AUS v ENG**	**Nottingham**	**4**	**8**	**b**	**3**	**131**	**b**
	42 Aus v Surrey	The Oval	3	5	c			
	43 Aus v Lancs	Manchester	3	38	c wk	3	23	*
	44 **AUS v ENG**	**Lord's**	**3**	**254**	**c**	**3**	**1**	**c**
	45 Aus v Yorks	Bradford	3	1	lbw			
	46 **AUS v ENG**	**Leeds**	**3**	**334**	**c wk**			
	47 Aus v Scotland	Edinburgh		–				
	48 **AUS v ENG**	**Manchester**	**3**	**14**	**c**			
	49 Aus v Somerset	Taunton	3	117	c & b			
	50 Aus v Glam	Swansea	3	58	b	3	19	*
	51 Aus v Northants	Northampton	3	22	b	3	35	c
	52 **AUS v ENG**	**The Oval**	**3**	**232**	**c wk**			
	53 Aus v Glos	Bristol	3	42	c	3	14	b
	54 Aus v Kent	Canterbury	3	18	lbw	3	205	*
	55 Aus v Eng XI	Folkestone	3	63	lbw			
	56 Aus v Leveson-Gower's XI	Scarborough	3	96	b			

30 He scored 236 out of 423 in just over 4½ hours with 28 fours in his initial first-class innings in Britain.

36 Batting 335 minutes and hitting 21 fours, he progressed from 100 to 200 in 80 minutes.

38 He took his tour aggregate to 1,001 runs before rain ended play on 31 May and remains the only Australian to reach this landmark before June. He added 109 before lunch on the second day.

Season	Match	Venue	1st Innings			2nd Innings		
			No	Runs	HO	No	Runs	HO
1930–31	57 NSW v S Aus	Sydney	3	61	c	3	121	c
	58 Aus XI v Rest	Sydney	3	73	b	1	29	c & b
	59 NSW v WI	Sydney	3	73	c wk	3	22	c
	60 **AUS v WI**	**Adelaide**	**3**	**4**	**c**			
	61 NSW v S Aus	Adelaide	3	258	b			
	62 NSW v Vic	Melbourne	3	2	c			
	63 **AUS v WI**	**Sydney**	**3**	**25**	**c wk**			
	64 **AUS v WI**	**Brisbane**[1]	**3**	**223**	**c**			
	65 NSW v Vic	Sydney	3	33	c wk	2	220	c
	66 **AUS v WI**	**Melbourne**	**3**	**152**	**c**			
	67 NSW v WI	Sydney	3	10	b	3	73	lbw
	68 **AUS v WI**	**Sydney**	**3**	**43**	**c**	**3**	**0**	**b**

61 His innings, completed on the first day with 116 in the post-tea session, lasted 282 minutes and included 37 fours. He added 334 in 223 minutes for the second wicket with A.A. Jackson.

Season	Match	Venue	1st Innings			2nd Innings		
			No	Runs	HO	No	Runs	HO
1931–32	69 NSW v Qld	Brisbane[2]	3	0	c wk			
	70 NSW v SA	Sydney	3	30	c & b	3	135	c
	71 **AUS v SA**	**Brisbane**[2]	**3**	**226**	**lbw**			
	72 NSW v SA	Sydney	3	219	c			
	73 **AUS v SA**	**Sydney**	**4**	**112**	**c**			
	74 **AUS v SA**	**Melbourne**	**3**	**2**	**c wk**	**3**	**167**	**lbw**
	75 NSW v Vic	Sydney	3	23	c	3	167	b
	76 **AUS v SA**	**Adelaide**	**3**	**299**	**★**			
	77 **AUS v SA**	**Melbourne**		**–**	**abs ht**			
	78 NSW v S Aus	Sydney	5	23	b	3	0	b

76 His sixth hundred against the South Africans, a tally which included four in successive innings, took his aggregate to 1,190 (average 170.00). He was the first

to score 1,000 runs against a team visiting Australia and it remains the highest such aggregate.

Season	Match	Venue	1st Innings No	Runs	HO	2nd Innings No	Runs	HO
1932–33	79 Aus XI v MCC	Perth	3	3	c	3	10	c
	80 NSW v Vic	Sydney	3	238	c	3	52	★
	81 Aus XI v MCC	Melbourne	3	36	lbw	3	13	b
	82 NSW v MCC	Sydney	3	18	lbw	6	23	b
	83 NSW v Vic	Melbourne	3	157	c			
	84 **AUS v ENG**	**Melbourne**	**4**	**0**	**b**	**4**	**103**	**★**
	85 **AUS v ENG**	**Adelaide**	**3**	**8**	**c**	**4**	**66**	**c & b**
	86 NSW v MCC	Sydney	3	1	b	3	71	c
	87 NSW v S Aus	Sydney	3	56	c	1	97	lbw
	88 **AUS v ENG**	**Brisbane**[2]	**3**	**76**	**b**	**3**	**24**	**c**
	89 **AUS v ENG**	**Sydney**	**3**	**48**	**b**	**3**	**71**	**b**

80 During this chanceless 238 out of 339 (200 minutes, 32 fours) he reached 50 in 30 minutes, 100 in 73, 150 in 129 and 200 in 172 – still the fastest double hundred in Sheffield Shield cricket. He scored 126 in the post-lunch session on the second day.

Season	Match	Venue	1st Innings No	Runs	HO	2nd Innings No	Runs	HO
1933–34	90 NSW v Qld	Brisbane[2]	3	200	c			
	91 Richardson's XI v Woodfull's XI	Melbourne	3	55	c	3	101	c
	92 NSW v Rest	Sydney	3	22	c wk	3	92	b
	93 NSW v S Aus	Adelaide	3	1	b	3	76	c
	94 NSW v Vic	Melbourne	3	187	★	1	77	★
	95 NSW v Qld	Sydney	3	253	b			
	96 NSW v Vic	Sydney	3	128	c			

90 Batting 184 minutes (26 fours) he reached 50 in 34 minutes and 100 in 92, scoring 120 runs in a post-lunch session. He added 294 in 171 minutes for the second wicket with W.A. Brown.

95 During this 253 (204 minutes, 4 sixes, 29 fours) he completed 1,000 first-class runs for the sixth successive season. He added 131 before lunch on the third day.

96 His final innings for NSW lasted 96 minutes and included 17 fours and 4 sixes, including three off one over from L.O. Fleetwood-Smith. His hundred took 87 minutes.

Season	Match	Venue	1st Innings			2nd Innings		
			No	Runs	HO	No	Runs	HO
1934	97 Aus v Worcs	Worcester	3	206	b			
	98 Aus v Leics	Leicester	3	65	b			
	99 Aus v CU	Cambridge	3	0	b			
	100 Aus v MCC	Lord's	3	5	c & b			
	101 Aus v OU	Oxford	3	37	lbw			
	102 Aus v Hants	Southampton	3	0	c			
	103 Aus v Middx	Lord's	3	160	c			
	104 Aus v Surrey	The Oval	3	77	c			
	105 **AUS v ENG**	**Nottingham**	4	**29**	c	4	**25**	**c wk**
	106 Aus v Northants	Northampton	6	65	c	6	25	b
	107 **AUS v ENG**	**Lord's**	3	**36**	**c & b**	4	**13**	**c wk**
	108 Aus v Somerset	Taunton	3	17	c wk			
	109 Aus v Surrey	The Oval	4	27	c wk	4	61	★
	110 **AUS v ENG**	**Manchester**	6	**30**	**c wk**			
	111 Aus v Derbys	Chesterfield	3	71	c wk	3	6	★
	112 Aus v Yorks	Sheffield	3	140	b			
	113 **AUS v ENG**	**Leeds**	5	**304**	**b**			
	114 **AUS v ENG**	**The Oval**	3	**244**	**c wk**	3	**77**	**b**
	115 Aus v Sussex	Hove	7	19	b			
	116 Aus v Kent	Canterbury		–				
	117 Aus v Eng XI	Folkestone	5	149	★			
	118 Aus v Leveson-Gower's XI	Scarborough	3	132	st			

97 His second double hundred at Worcester took under 3½ hours and included 27 fours.

103 He scored a chanceless 160 out of 225 in just over 2 hours.

117 He batted approximately 105 minutes, hitting four sixes and 17 fours and reached his hundred in 90 minutes. He scored 30 (466464) off an over from A.P. Freeman.

118 Hitting a six and 24 fours, he batted 90 minutes and completed his entire innings before lunch on the first day. Serious illness postponed his next first-class innings until November 1935.

Season	Match	Venue	1st Innings			2nd Innings		
			No	Runs	HO	No	Runs	HO
1935–36	119 +S Aus v MCC	Adelaide	3	15	lbw	3	50	lbw
	120 +S Aus v NSW	Adelaide	3	117	c & b			
	121 +S Aus v Qld	Adelaide	3	233	c			
	122 +S Aus v Vic	Melbourne	3	357	c wk			

Season	Match	Venue	1st Innings			2nd Innings		
			No	Runs	HO	No	Runs	HO
1935–36	123 +S Aus v Qld	Brisbane[2]	4	31	c			
	124 +S Aus v NSW	Sydney	3	0	c			
	125 +S Aus v Vic	Adelaide	3	1	c			
	126 +S Aus v Tas	Adelaide	3	369	c & b			

120 He celebrated his first Shield match for South Australia with a chanceless 117 in 158 minutes (7 fours).

121 Batting 191 minutes (a six and 28 fours), he completed his third double hundred against Queensland in successive innings in 168 minutes. He progressed from 43 to 200 in a two-hour post-lunch session on the first day, moving from 150 to 200 in 14 minutes.

122 His 357 (62.7% of the total) occupied 421 minutes and included 40 fours. He reached 50 in 70 minutes, 100 in 152, 150 in 222, 200 in 267, 250 in 328, 300 in 399 and 350 in 413. He scored 229 on the first day and added 109 in 105 minutes before lunch on the second.

126 His 369 (253 minutes) remains the highest score for South Australia and a record for the Adelaide Oval. The last of his six triple hundreds, it included 4 sixes and 46 fours, the record tally of boundaries in a first-class innings in Australia until 1989–90. He scored 127 in 95 minutes after tea on the first day, followed by 135 in 105 minutes before lunch and a further 107 before tea on the second.

Season	Match	Venue	1st Innings			2nd Innings		
			No	Runs	HO	No	Runs	HO
1936–37	127 +Bradman's XI v Richardson's XI	Sydney	6	212	c	3	13	c
	128 +S Aus v Vic	Melbourne	4	192	c			
	129 +Aus XI v MCC	Sydney	3	63	b			
	130 **+AUS v ENG**	**Brisbane[2]**	3	38	c	5	0	c
	131 **+AUS v ENG**	**Sydney**	3	0	c	3	82	b
	132 **+AUS v ENG**	**Melbourne**	3	13	c	7	270	c
	133 +S Aus v MCC	Adelaide	4	38	c wk			
	134 +AUS v ENG	**Adelaide**	4	26	b	3	212	c & b
	135 +S Aus v Qld	Brisbane[2]	5	123	st			
	136 +S Aus v NSW	Sydney	4	24	lbw	4	38	★
	137 **+AUS v ENG**	**Melbourne**	3	169	b			
	138 +S Aus v Vic	Adelaide	4	31	c	4	8	c

127 By scoring 212 in 202 minutes (2 sixes, 26 fours) he compiled successive double

hundreds for the fourth and last time, all four occurring in Australia. It remains the record number of instances of this feat (one more than W.R. Hammond and E. de C. Weekes achieved).

Season	Match	Venue	1st Innings No	Runs	HO	2nd Innings No	Runs	HO
1937–38	139 +S Aus v NZ XI	Adelaide	4	11	c wk			
	140 +Bradman's XI v							
	Richardson's XI	Adelaide	3	17	b			
	141 +S Aus v WA	Adelaide	6	101	c			
	142 +S Aus v NSW	Adelaide	3	91	c	5	62	c
	143 +S Aus v Qld	Adelaide	3	246	c	3	39	★
	144 +S Aus v Vic	Melbourne	3	54	c	3	35	c
	145 +S Aus v Qld	Brisbane[2]	3	107	c wk	3	113	c
	146 +S Aus v NSW	Sydney	3	44	c	4	104	★
	147 +S Aus v Vic	Adelaide	3	3	b	3	85	c
	148 +Aus XI v Tas XI	Launceston	4	79	c			
	149 +Aus XI v Tas	Hobart	4	144	b			
	150 +Aus XI v WA	Perth	3	102	st			

145 He scored a hundred in each innings for the third time (107 in 164 minutes, 9 fours, and 113 in 143 minutes, 10 fours) and became the first to achieve this feat twice in the Sheffield Shield.
149 His 144 in 98 minutes included sixes off three consecutive balls from S.W.L. Putman and 6 fours off an over from G.T.H. James.

Season	Match	Venue	1st Innings No	Runs	HO	2nd Innings No	Runs	HO
1938	151 +Aus v Worcs	Worcester	3	258	c			
	152 +Aus v OU	Oxford	3	58	lbw			
	153 +Aus v CU	Cambridge	3	137	c			
	154 +Aus v MCC	Lord's	3	278	c			
	155 +Aus v Northants	Northampton	3	2	c wk			
	156 +Aus v Surrey	The Oval	3	143	c wk			
	157 +Aus v Hants	Southampton	3	145	★			
	158 +Aus v Middx	Lord's	3	5	c	3	30	★
	159 **+AUS v ENG**	**Nottingham**	3	**51**	c wk	3	**144**	★
	160 +Aus v Gentlemen	Lord's	6	104	c			
	161 +Aus v Lancs	Manchester	3	12	c	3	101	★
	162 **+AUS v ENG**	**Lord's**	3	**18**	b	3	**102**	★
	163 +Aus v Yorks	Sheffield	3	59	st	3	42	c

Season	Match	Venue	1st Innings			2nd Innings		
			No	Runs	HO	No	Runs	HO
1938	164 +Aus v Warks	Birmingham	3	135	c			
	165 +Aus v Notts	Nottingham	3	56	lbw	3	144	c
	166 +AUS v ENG	**Leeds**	**4**	**103**	**b**	**3**	**16**	**c**
	167 +Aus v Somerset	Taunton	3	202	b			
	168 +Aus v Glam	Swansea	3	17	st			
	169 +Aus v Kent	Canterbury	3	67	c			
	170 +AUS v ENG	**The Oval**		**–**	**abs ht**			

151 His third successive double hundred at Worcester occupied 290 minutes and included 33 fours.

154 His 278 (in 6 hours with a six and 35 fours) was then the equal fourth-highest first-class score at Lord's. It remains the second-highest by an Australian (W.H. Ponsford 281* in 1934).

157 He completed 1,000 runs before June (1,056 average 150.85) for the second time and remains alone in achieving this feat more than once. Both instances were completed at Southampton.

161 His 100 took 73 minutes and was the fastest of the season at that point.

167 His tally of 13 hundreds in a season remains the record by a visiting batsman.

Season	Match	Venue	1st Innings			2nd Innings		
			No	Runs	HO	No	Runs	HO
1938–39	171 +Bradman's XI v							
	Rigg's XI	Melbourne	3	118	b			
	172 +S Aus v NSW	Adelaide	3	143	b			
	173 +S Aus v Qld	Adelaide	3	225	c			
	174 +S Aus v Vic	Melbourne	3	107	c			
	175 +S Aus v Qld	Brisbane[2]	3	186	c			
	176 +S Aus v NSW	Sydney	3	135	*			
	177 +S Aus v Vic	Adelaide	3	5	c			

175 His chanceless 186 in 287 minutes (19 fours) was his fifth hundred in successive first-class innings and established an Australian record.

176 His sixth consecutive hundred (a chanceless 135* in 201 minutes with 7 fours) equalled the world record set by C.B. Fry in 1901 and extended his sequence of first-class hundreds in Australia to eight.

177 A crowd of 17,777, Adelaide's record for a Sheffield Shield match, saw their hero fall 95 short of eclipsing Fry's record.

Season	Match	Venue	1st Innings			2nd Innings		
			No	Runs	HO	No	Runs	HO
1939–40	178 +S Aus v Vic	Adelaide	3	76	ro	4	64	lbw
	179 +S Aus v NSW	Adelaide	3	251	*	3	90	*
	180 +S Aus v Qld	Adelaide	3	138	c			
	181 +S Aus v Vic	Melbourne	3	267	c			
	182 +S Aus v Qld	Brisbane[2]	3	0	c	4	97	c wk
	183 +S Aus v NSW	Sydney	4	39	lbw	4	40	c
	184 +S Aus v WA	Perth	4	42	c wk	3	209	*
	185 +S Aus v WA	Perth	3	135	c			
	186 +Rest v NSW	Sydney	3	25	c	3	2	c

180 His 10th hundred in a sequence of 12 innings against Queensland and his fifth in succession.

Season	Match	Venue	1st Innings			2nd Innings		
			No	Runs	HO	No	Runs	HO
1940–41	187 +S Aus v Vic	Adelaide	3	0	c	3	6	b
	188 +Bradman's XI							
	v McCabe's XI	Melbourne	3	0	c	3	12	b

Season	Match	Venue	1st Innings			2nd Innings		
			No	Runs	HO	No	Runs	HO
1945–46	189 +S Aus v Qld	Adelaide	4	68	c wk	3	52	*
	190 +S Aus v Services	Adelaide	4	112	c			

Season	Match	Venue	1st Innings			2nd Innings		
			No	Runs	HO	No	Runs	HO
1946–47	191 +S Aus v MCC	Adelaide	4	76	c & b	4	3	c
	192 +Aus XI v MCC	Melbourne	3	106	c			
	193 +S Aus v Vic	Adelaide	5	43	st	5	119	st
	194 **+AUS v ENG**	**Brisbane[2]**	**3**	**187**	**b**			
	195 **+AUS v ENG**	**Sydney**	**6**	**234**	**lbw**			
	196 **+AUS v ENG**	**Melbourne**	**3**	**79**	**b**	**3**	**49**	**c & b**
	197 +S Aus v MCC	Adelaide	3	5	c			
	198 **+AUS v ENG**	**Adelaide**	**3**	**0**	**b**	**3**	**56**	*****
	199 **+AUS v ENG**	**Sydney**	**3**	**12**	**b**	**3**	**63**	**c**

Season	Match	Venue	1st Innings			2nd Innings		
			No	Runs	HO	No	Runs	HO
1947–48	200 +S Aus v Ind	Adelaide	3	156	c	3	12	st
	201 +S Aus v Vic	Adelaide	3	100	lbw			
	202 +Aus XI v Ind	Sydney	3	172	c	3	26	c
	203 **+AUS v IND**	**Brisbane**[2]	3	185	**hw**			
	204 **+AUS v IND**	**Sydney**	3	13	**b**			
	205 **+AUS v IND**	**Melbourne**	3	132	**lbw**	6	127	⋆
	206 **+AUS v IND**	**Adelaide**	3	201	**b**			
	207 **+AUS v IND**	**Melbourne**	3	57	⋆ (rh)			
	208 +Aus XI v WA	Perth	3	115	c			

201 His 36th and final Sheffield Shield hundred.

202 'Bradman gave a glorious display in completing his hundredth hundred in first-class cricket . . .' (*Wisden*). He was the eleventh to achieve this feat and remains the only Australian. He reached the landmark in 295 innings, still 257 fewer than any other batsman.

207 He took his aggregate against the Indian touring team to 1,081 (average 135.12).

Season	Match	Venue	1st Innings			2nd Innings		
			No	Runs	HO	No	Runs	HO
1948	209 +Aus v Worcs	Worcester	3	107	b			
	210 +Aus v Leics	Leicester	4	81	c wk			
	211 +Aus v Surrey	The Oval	3	146	b			
	212 +Aus v Essex	Southend	3	187	b			
	213 +Aus v MCC	Lord's	3	98	c			
	214 +Aus v Lancs	Manchester	3	11	b	3	43	st
	215 +Aus v Notts	Nottingham	3	86	b			
	216 +Aus v Sussex	Hove	3	109	b			
	217 **+AUS v ENG**	**Nottingham**	3	138	**c**	3	0	**c**
	218 +Aus v Yorks	Sheffield	3	54	c	3	86	c
	219 **+AUS v ENG**	**Lord's**	3	38	**c**	3	89	**c**
	220 +Aus v Surrey	The Oval	3	128	c			
	221 **+AUS v ENG**	**Manchester**	3	7	**lbw**	3	30	⋆
	222 +Aus v Middx	Lord's	3	6	c			
	223 **+AUS v ENG**	**Leeds**	3	33	**b**	3	173	⋆
	224 +Aus v Derbys	Derby	3	62	b			
	225 +Aus v Warks	Birmingham	3	31	b	3	13	⋆
	226 +Aus v Lancs	Manchester	3	28	c wk	3	133	⋆

Season	Match	Venue	1st Innings No Runs HO			2nd Innings No Runs HO		
1948	227 **+AUS v ENG**	**The Oval**	**3**	**0**	**b**			
	228 +Aus v Kent	Canterbury	3	65	c			
	229 +Aus v Gentlemen	Lord's	3	150	c			
	230 +Aus v South	Hastings	3	143	c			
	231 +Aus v Leveson–							
	Gower's XI	Scarborough	3	153	c			

209 His fourth successive hundred against Worcestershire.

212 His 187 in 125 minutes (32 fours), his only innings against Essex, enabled the Australians to amass 721, still the world record total of runs by any team or teams in a day (6 hours).

231 He celebrated his final appearance in England by completing his tenth sequence of three or more hundreds in consecutive innings. He batted 190 minutes, hitting two sixes and 19 fours. He bowled the final over of the match.

Season	Match	Venue	1st Innings No Runs HO			2nd Innings No Runs HO		
1948–49	232 +Bradman's XI							
	v Hassett's XI	Melbourne	4	123	c	3	10	c
	233 Morris's XI							
	v Hassett's XI	Sydney	3	53	c			
	234 S Aus v Vic	Adelaide	4	30	b	–	abs ht	

232 Spurred on by a crowd approaching 53,000, he commemorated his testimonial match with the last of his 117 first-class hundreds, completing a sequence of four in succession for the third time.

233 Recently knighted and welcomed to his former home ground by a crowd of 41,575, he batted 65 minutes in a testimonial match for two of his former State captains, A.F. Kippax and W.A. Oldfield.

234 In his final first-class appearance (in a testimonial match for A.J. Richardson) he batted 82 minutes for his team's top score of 30. He sprained his ankle on a sunken water tap while fielding and was unable to bat in the second innings.

APPENDIX

Season-by-Season Summary

Season	M	I	NO	HS	Runs	Avge	100	50
1927–28	5	10	1	134	416	46.22	2	1
1928–29	13	24	6	340★	1,690	93.88	7	5
1929–30	11	16	2	452★	1,586	113.28	5	4
1930	27	36	6	334	2,960	98.66	10	5
1930–31	12	18	–	258	1,422	79.00	5	4
1931–32	10	13	1	299★	1,403	116.91	7	–
1932–33	11	21	2	238	1,171	61.63	3	7
1933–34	7	11	2	253	1,192	132.44	5	4
1934	22	27	3	304	2,020	84.16	7	6
1935–36	8	9	–	369	1,173	130.33	4	1
1936–37	12	19	1	270	1,552	86.22	6	2
1937–38	12	18	2	246	1,437	89.81	7	5
1938	20	26	5	278	2,429	115.66	13	5
1938–39	7	7	1	225	919	153.16	6	–
1939–40	9	15	3	267	1,475	122.91	5	4
1940–41	2	4	–	12	18	4.50	–	–
1945–46	2	3	1	112	232	116.00	1	2
1946–47	9	14	1	234	1,032	79.38	4	4
1947–48	9	12	2	201	1,296	129.60	8	1
1948	23	31	4	187	2,428	89.92	11	8
1948–49	3	4	–	123	216	54.00	1	1
Totals	**234**	**338**	**43**	**452★**	**28,067**	**95.14**	**117**	**69**

Summary by Venue

Venue	M	I	NO	HS	Runs	Avge	100	50
Adelaide	40	60	6	369	4,840	89.62	18	15
Brisbane[1]	4	7	1	223	620	103.33	3	1
Brisbane[2]	12	16	–	226	1,593	99.56	8	2
Hobart	2	2	–	144	283	141.50	2	–
Launceston	2	2	–	79	99	49.50	2	–
Melbourne	29	45	8	357	3,922	106.00	19	8
Perth	6	8	1	209★	643	91.85	4	–
Sydney	47	78	9	452★	6,230	90.28	22	18
In Australia	**142**	**218**	**25**	**452★**	**18,230**	**94.45**	**76**	**45**

Summary by Venue

Venue	M	I	NO	HS	Runs	Avge	100	50
Birmingham	2	3	1	135	179	89.50	1	–
Bradford	1	1	–	1	1	1.00	–	–
Bristol	1	2	–	42	56	28.00	–	–
Cambridge	3	3	–	137	169	56.33	1	–
Canterbury	4	4	1	205★	355	118.33	1	2
Chesterfield	2	3	1	71	121	60.50	–	1
Derby	1	1	–	62	62	62.00	–	1
Edinburgh	1	–						
Folkestone	2	2	1	149★	212	212.00	1	1
Hastings	1	1	–	143	143	143.00	1	–
Hove	2	2	–	109	128	64.00	1	–
Leeds	4	6	1	334	963	192.60	4	–
Leicester	3	3	1	185★	331	165.50	1	2
Liverpool	1	2	1	48★	57	57.00	–	–
Lord's	14	21	2	278	1,510	79.47	6	3
Manchester	7	12	4	133★	470	58.75	2	–
Northampton	3	5	–	65	149	29.80	–	1
Nottingham	6	11	1	144★	812	81.20	4	3
Oxford	3	3	–	58	127	42.33	–	1
Scarborough	3	3	–	153	381	127.00	2	1
Sheffield	4	6	–	140	459	76.50	1	4
Southampton	3	3	1	191	336	168.00	2	–
Southend	1	1	–	187	187	187.00	1	–
Swansea	2	3	1	58	94	47.00	–	1
Taunton	3	3	–	202	336	112.00	2	–
The Oval	11	12	2	252	1,392	139.20	6	3
Worcester	4	4	–	258	807	201.75	4	–
In England	**92**	**120**	**18**	**334**	**9,837**	**96.44**	**41**	**24**
Totals	**234**	**338**	**43**	**452★**	**28,067**	**95.14**	**117**	**69**

HIS PLACE IN FIRST-CLASS RECORDS
(Updated to the end of the 1995 English season)

Highest Individual Innings

501*	B.C. Lara	Warwickshire v Durham	Birmingham	1994
499	Hanif Mohammad	Karachi v Bahawalpur	Karachi	1958–59
452*	**D.G. Bradman**	**New South Wales v Queensland**	**Sydney**	**1929–30**
443*	B.B. Nimbalkar	Maharashtra v Kathiawar	Poona	1948–49
437	W.H. Ponsford	Victoria v Queensland	Melbourne	1927–28
429	W.H. Ponsford	Victoria v Tasmania	Melbourne	1922–23
428	Aftab Baloch	Sind v Baluchistan	Karachi	1973–74
424	A.C. MacLaren	Lancashire v Somerset	Taunton	1895
405*	G.A. Hick	Worcestershire v Somerset	Taunton	1988
385	B. Sutcliffe	Otago v Canterbury	Christchurch	1952–53
383	C.W. Gregory	New South Wales v Queensland	Brisbane	1906–07
377	S.V. Manjrekar	Bombay v Hyderabad	Bombay	1990–91
375	B.C. Lara	West Indies v England	St John's	1993–94
369	**D.G. Bradman**	**South Australia v Tasmania**	**Adelaide**	**1935–36**
366	N.H. Fairbrother	Lancashire v Surrey	The Oval	1990
366	M.V. Sridhar	Hyderabad v Andhra	Secunderabad	1993–94
365*	C. Hill	South Australia v NSW	Adelaide	1900–01
365*	G. St A. Sobers	West Indies v Pakistan	Kingston	1957–58
364	L. Hutton	England v Australia	The Oval	1938
359*	V.M. Merchant	Bombay v Maharashtra	Bombay	1943–44
359	R.B. Simpson	New South Wales v Queensland	Brisbane	1963–64
357*	R. Abel	Surrey v Somerset	The Oval	1899
357	**D.G. Bradman**	**South Australia v Victoria**	**Melbourne**	**1935–36**
356	B.A. Richards	South Australia v W Australia	Perth	1970–71
355*	G.R. Marsh	W Australia v S Australia	Perth	1989–90
355	B. Sutcliffe	Otago v Auckland	Dunedin	1949–50
352	W.H. Ponsford	Victoria v New South Wales	Melbourne	1926–27
350	Rashid Israr	Habib Bank v National Bank	Lahore	1976–77

Most Quadruple Hundreds

2 W.H. Ponsford

Most Triple Hundreds

6 D.G. Bradman
4 W.R. Hammond

Most Double Hundreds

37 D.G. Bradman
36 W.R. Hammond
22 E.H. Hendren

Most Hundreds in Successive Innings

6	C.B. Fry	Sussex and Rest of England	1901
6	**D.G. Bradman**	**South Australia and D.G. Bradman's XI**	**1938–39**
6	M.J. Procter	Rhodesia	1970–71

Most Hundreds in a Career

		Total		100th Hundred	
	Hundreds	Inns	Inns/100	Season	Inns
J.B. Hobbs	197	1,315	6.67	1923	821
E.H. Hendren	170	1,300	7.64	1928–29	740
W.R. Hammond	167	1,005	6.01	1935	679
C.P. Mead	153	1,340	8.75	1927	892
G. Boycott	151	1,014	6.71	1977	645
H. Sutcliffe	149	1,088	7.30	1932	700
F.E. Woolley	145	1,532	10.56	1929	1,031
L. Hutton	129	814	6.31	1951	619
W.G. Grace	126	1,493	11.84	1895	1,113
D.C.S. Compton	123	839	6.82	1952	552
T.W. Graveney	122	1,223	10.02	1964	940
G.A. Gooch	120	941	7.84	1992–93	820
D.G. Bradman	**117**	**338**	**2.88**	**1947–48**	**295**
I.V.A. Richards	114	796	6.98	1988–89	658
Zaheer Abbas	108	768	7.11	1982–83	658
A. Sandham	107	1,000	9.34	1935	871
M.C. Cowdrey	107	1,130	10.56	1973	1,035
T.W. Hayward	104	1,138	10.94	1913	1,076
J.H. Edrich	103	979	9.50	1977	945
G.M. Turner	103	792	7.68	1982	779
G.E. Tyldesley	102	961	9.42	1934	919
L.E.G. Ames	102	951	9.32	1950	915
D.L. Amiss	102	1,139	11.16	1986	1,081

Highest Career Average
(Qualifications: 10,000 runs; avge 55.00)

Dates in italic denote the first half of an overseas season, i.e. *1927–48* denotes 1927–28 to 1948–49.

Avge		Career	I	NO	HS	Runs	100
95.14	**D.G. Bradman**	*1927–48*	**338**	43	452★	**28,067**	117
71.22	V.M. Merchant	*1929–51*	229	43	359★	13,248	44
65.18	W.H. Ponsford	*1920–34*	235	23	437	13,819	47
64.99	W.M. Woodfull	*1921–34*	245	39	284	13,388	49
58.24	A.L. Hassett	*1932–53*	322	32	232	16,890	59
58.19	V.S. Hazare	*1934–66*	365	45	316★	18,621	60
57.22	A.F. Kippax	*1918–35*	256	33	315★	12,762	43
57.00	G.A. Hick	*1983–95*	492	50	405★	25,194	84
56.83	G. Boycott	1962–86	1,104	162	261★	48,426	151
56.55	C.L. Walcott	*1941–63*	238	29	314★	11,820	40
56.37	K.S. Ranjitsinhji	1893–1920	500	62	285★	24,692	72
56.22	R.B. Simpson	*1952–77*	436	62	359	21,029	60
56.10	W.R. Hammond	1920–51	1,005	104	336★	50,551	167
56.03	M.D. Crowe	*1979–94*	406	61	299	19,333	69
55.67	M.E. Waugh	*1985–95*	356	46	229★	17,260	57
55.51	L. Hutton	1934–60	814	91	364	40,140	129
55.34	E. de C. Weekes	*1944–64*	241	24	304★	12,010	36

Highest Batting Average in an English Season
(Qualification: 12 innings)

Avge			I	NO	HS	Runs	100	Season
115.66	**D.G. Bradman**	**Australians**	26	5	278	2,429	13	1938
102.53	G. Boycott	Yorkshire	20	5	175★	1,538	6	1979
102.00	W.A. Johnston	Australians	17	16	28★	102	–	1953
101.70	G.A. Gooch	Essex	30	3	333	2,746	12	1990
100.12	G. Boycott	Yorkshire	30	5	233	2,503	13	1971

HIS TEST MATCH CAREER

Match-by-Match Summary

(* not out; + captain; Brisbane¹ = Exhibition Ground; Brisbane² = Woolloongabba)

Season	Match	Venue	1st Innings			2nd Innings		
			No	Runs	HO	No	Runs	HO
1928–29	1 ENGLAND 1	Brisbane¹	7	18	lbw	6	1	c
	2 ENGLAND 3	Melbourne	6	79	b	6	112	c wk
	3 ENGLAND 4	Adelaide	6	40	c	6	58	ro
	4 ENGLAND 5	Melbourne	5	123	c	7	37	*
1930	5 ENGLAND 1	Nottingham	4	8	b	3	131	b
	6 ENGLAND 2	Lord's	3	254	c	3	1	c
	7 ENGLAND 3	Leeds	3	334	c wk			
	8 ENGLAND 4	Manchester	3	14	c			
	9 ENGLAND 5	The Oval	3	232	c wk			
1930–31	10 WEST INDIES 1	Adelaide	3	4	c			
	11 WEST INDIES 2	Sydney	3	25	c wk			
	12 WEST INDIES 3	Brisbane¹	3	223	c			
	13 WEST INDIES 4	Melbourne	3	152	c			
	14 WEST INDIES 5	Sydney	3	43	c	3	0	b
1931–32	15 SOUTH AFRICA 1	Brisbane²	3	226	lbw			
	16 SOUTH AFRICA 2	Sydney	4	112	c			
	17 SOUTH AFRICA 3	Melbourne	3	2	c wk	3	167	lbw
	18 SOUTH AFRICA 4	Adelaide	3	299	*			
	19 SOUTH AFRICA 5	Melbourne	–		abs ht			
1932–33	20 ENGLAND 2	Melbourne	4	0	b	4	103	*
	21 ENGLAND 3	Adelaide	3	8	c	4	66	c & b
	22 ENGLAND 4	Brisbane²	3	76	b	3	24	c
	23 ENGLAND 5	Sydney	3	48	b	3	71	b
1934	24 ENGLAND 1	Nottingham	4	29	c	4	25	c wk
	25 ENGLAND 2	Lord's	3	36	c & b	4	13	c wk
	26 ENGLAND 3	Manchester	6	30	c wk			
	27 ENGLAND 4	Leeds	5	304	b			
	28 ENGLAND 5	The Oval	3	244	c wk	3	77	b
1936–37	29 +ENGLAND 1	Brisbane²	3	38	c	5	0	c
	30 +ENGLAND 2	Sydney	3	0	c	3	82	b
	31 +ENGLAND 3	Melbourne	3	13	c	7	270	c
	32 +ENGLAND 4	Adelaide	4	26	b	3	212	c & b
	33 +ENGLAND 5	Melbourne	3	169	b			

Season	Match	Venue	1st Innings			2nd Innings		
			No	Runs	HO	No	Runs	HO
1938	34 +ENGLAND 1	Nottingham	3	51	c wk	3	144	*
	35 +ENGLAND 2	Lord's	3	18	b	3	102	*
	36 +ENGLAND 4	Leeds	4	103	b	3	16	c
	37 +ENGLAND 5	The Oval	–		abs ht			
1946–47	38 +ENGLAND 1	Brisbane[2]	3	187	b			
	39 +ENGLAND 2	Sydney	6	234	lbw			
	40 +ENGLAND 3	Melbourne	3	79	b	3	49	c & b
	41 +ENGLAND 4	Adelaide	3	0	b	3	56	*
	42 +ENGLAND 5	Sydney	3	12	b	3	63	c
1947–48	43 +INDIA 1	Brisbane[2]	3	185	hw			
	44 +INDIA 2	Sydney	3	13	b			
	45 +INDIA 3	Melbourne	3	132	lbw	6	127	*
	46 +INDIA 4	Adelaide	3	201	b			
	47 +INDIA 5	Melbourne	3	57	* (rh)			
1948	48 +ENGLAND 1	Nottingham	3	138	c	3	0	c
	49 +ENGLAND 2	Lord's	3	38	c	3	89	c
	50 +ENGLAND 3	Manchester	3	7	lbw	3	30	*
	51 +ENGLAND 4	Leeds	3	33	b	3	173	*
	52 +ENGLAND 5	The Oval	3	0	b			

Highlights of his Test Career

2 He scored his first Test hundred when aged 20 years 129 days.

5 He celebrated his first Test in England by registering Australia's first hundred in five Tests at Trent Bridge.

6 He batted 339 minutes and hit 25 fours in the highest Test innings at Lord's until 1990. He reached 50 in 46 minutes, 100 in 106 and 200 in 234.

7 At 21 years 318 days he was then the youngest to score 300 in a Test innings. With his score 138, he completed 1,000 runs in only seven Test matches (13 innings). He reached 50 in 49 minutes, 100 in 99 and 200 in 214 – still the fastest double hundred in Test cricket – and 300 in 336. His tally of 309 runs on the first day remains the record for Test cricket; he made 105 before lunch (the third instance on the first day), 115 between lunch and tea, and 89 in the final session. His 334 (383 minutes, 46 fours) was the highest Test innings until W.R. Hammond surpassed it in April 1933.

9 His feats of scoring three double hundreds and achieving an aggregate of 974, average 139.14, remain unequalled in any Test series.

15 This innings of 226 in 277 minutes (22 fours) surpassed his own home record.

16 His hundred was his fourth in successive first-class innings – a record for Australia.

18 This innings of 299* (396 minutes, 23 fours) remains the highest in Adelaide Tests, was the record for Australia in a home Test until 1965–66 and took his tally of runs in the series to 806 (average 201.50). He reached 100 in 133 minutes and 200 in 284.

20 Dismissed first ball in the first innings (Bowes' only Test wicket in Australia), he batted 185 minutes (146 balls, 7 fours) for his only hundred of the 'bodyline' series.

27 His second triple hundred in successive Tests at Headingley occupied 430 minutes and included 2 sixes and 43 fours. His fourth-wicket partnership of 388 in 341 minutes with W.H. Ponsford was then the highest for any wicket by either side in Ashes Tests.

28 Batting 316 minutes (a six and 32 fours), he shared a partnership of 451 with W.H. Ponsford which was the world Test record for any wicket until 1990–91 and which retains that status for the second wicket.

31 Countering a 'gluepot' pitch by opening with his tailenders and batting at the fall of the fifth wicket, he amassed the (then) highest home score for Australia against England (270 in 458 minutes off 375 balls with 22 fours and 110 singles) and shared with J.H.W. Fingleton what remains the world Test record sixth-wicket partnership of 346. His innings remains the highest second innings score in Ashes Tests and the record for a number 7 batsman in all Test cricket.

32 During this innings (212 in 437 minutes, 14 fours), he exceeded C. Hill's record aggregate of first-class runs scored in Australia (11,137) and became the first to score 17 Test match hundreds.

33 His aggregate of 810, average 90.00, remains the highest by a captain in any Test series.

34 His 13th hundred against England set a record for either side in Ashes Tests.

35 This hundred was the 200th of this series and took him beyond the record aggregate of 3,636 by J.B. Hobbs for these Tests.

38 His partnership of 276 in 278 minutes with A.L. Hassett remains the third wicket record for this series.

39 With S.G. Barnes (also 234) he added 405 in 393 minutes to establish the present world Test record partnership for the fifth wicket. His chanceless innings took 393 minutes and included 24 fours.

45 His only instance in Test cricket (fourth in all first-class matches) of scoring a hundred in each innings. He was the first to achieve this feat against India.

46 He recorded the last of his record Test match tally of 12 double hundreds. His closest challenger, W.R. Hammond, registered seven and played 60 more innings. For the first time he completed a sequence of three hundreds in successive Test innings.

51 His match-winning innings took 255 minutes and contained 29 fours. The last of his 29 hundreds in Test cricket, it was his 14th as captain, his 19th against England and his fourth in six innings at Headingley. Australia's total of 404 for 3 remained the highest in a fourth innings to win a Test match until 1975–76.

Series-by-Series Summary

Series	v	M	I	NO	HS	Runs	Avge	100	50
1928–29	E	4	8	1	123	468	66.85	2	2
1930	E	5	7	–	334	974	139.14	4	–
1930–31	WI	5	6	–	223	447	74.50	2	–
1931–32	SA	5	5	1	299★	806	201.50	4	–
1932–33	E	4	8	1	103★	396	56.57	1	3
1934	E	5	8	–	304	758	94.75	2	1
1936–37	E	5	9	–	270	810	90.00	3	1
1938	E	4	6	2	144	434	108.50	3	1
1946–47	E	5	8	1	234	680	97.14	2	3
1947–48	I	5	6	2	201	715	178.75	4	1
1948	E	5	9	2	173★	508	72.57	2	1
Totals		**52**	**80**	**10**	**334**	**6,996**	**99.94**	**29**	**13**

Summary by Venue

Venue	M	I	NO	HS	Runs	Avge	100	50
Adelaide	7	11	2	299	970	107.77	3	3
Brisbane[1]	2	3	–	223	242	80.66	1	–
Brisbane[2]	5	7	–	226	736	105.14	3	1
Melbourne	11	17	4	270	1,671	128.53	9	3
Sydney	8	12	–	234	703	58.58	2	3
In Australia	**33**	**50**	**6**	**299★**	**4,322**	**98.22**	**18**	**10**
Leeds	4	6	1	334	963	192.60	4	–
Lord's	4	8	1	254	551	78.71	2	1
Manchester	3	4	1	30★	81	27.00	–	–
Nottingham	4	8	1	144★	526	75.14	3	1
The Oval	4	4	–	244	553	138.25	2	1
In England	**19**	**30**	**4**	**334**	**2,674**	**102.84**	**11**	**3**
Totals	**52**	**80**	**10**	**334**	**6,996**	**99.94**	**29**	**13**

305

Summary by Opponents

Opponents	M	I	NO	HS	Runs	Avge	100	50
England	37	63	7	334	5,028	89.78	19	12
South Africa	5	5	1	299★	806	201.50	4	–
West Indies	5	6	–	223	447	74.50	2	–
India	5	6	2	201	715	178.75	4	1
Totals	**52**	**80**	**10**	**334**	**6,996**	**99.94**	**29**	**13**

HIS PLACE IN TEST MATCH RECORDS
(Updated to 1st April 1996)

Leading Test Match Averages
(Qualifications: 25 innings; avge 55.00)

Avge			M	I	NO	HS	Runs	100
99.94	**D.G. Bradman**	**A**	**52**	**80**	**10**	**334**	**6,996**	**29**
62.15	J.C. Adams	WI	22	34	8	174★	1,616	4
60.97	R.G. Pollock	SA	23	41	4	274	2,256	7
60.96	B.C. Lara	WI	31	52	2	375	3,048	7
60.83	G.A. Headley	WI	22	40	4	270★	2,190	10
60.73	H. Sutcliffe	E	54	84	9	194	4,555	16
59.23	E. Paynter	E	20	31	5	243	1,540	4
58.67	K.F. Barrington	E	82	131	15	256	6,806	20
58.61	E. de C. Weekes	WI	48	81	5	207	4,455	15
58.45	W.R. Hammond	E	85	140	16	336★	7,249	22
57.78	G. St A. Sobers	WI	93	160	21	365★	8,032	26
56.94	J.B. Hobbs	E	61	102	7	211	5,410	15
56.68	C.L. Walcott	WI	44	74	7	220	3,798	15
56.67	L. Hutton	E	79	138	15	364	6,971	19

Most Hundreds

100			200	I	E	A	Opponents SA	WI	NZ	I	P	SL	Z
34	S.M. Gavaskar	I	4	214	4	8	–	13	2	–	5	2	–
29	**D.G. Bradman**	A	12	80	19	–	4	2	–	4	–	–	–
27	A.R. Border	A	2	265	8	–	–	3	5	4	6	1	–
26	G. St A. Sobers	WI	2	160	10	4	–	–	1	8	3	–	–
24	G.S. Chappell	A	4	151	9	–	–	5	3	1	6	–	–
24	I.V.A. Richards	WI	3	182	8	5	–	–	1	8	2	–	–
23	Javed Miandad	P	6	189	2	6	–	2	7	5	–	1	–

Most Runs in a Series

Runs		Series	Season	M	I	NO	HS	Avge	100	50
974	**D.G. Bradman**	**A v E**	**1930**	**5**	**7**	**–**	**334**	**139.14**	**4**	**–**
905	W.R. Hammond	E v A	1928–29	5	9	1	251	113.12	4	–
839	M.A. Taylor	A v E	1989	6	11	1	219	83.90	2	5
834	R.N. Harvey	A v SA	1952–53	5	9	–	205	92.66	4	3
829	I.V.A. Richards	WI v E	1976	4	7	–	291	118.42	3	2
827	C.L. Walcott	WI v A	1954–55	5	10	–	155	82.70	5	2
824	G. St A. Sobers	WI v P	1957–58	5	8	2	365★	137.33	3	3
810	**D.G. Bradman**	**A v E**	**1936–37**	**5**	**9**	**–**	**270**	**90.00**	**3**	**1**
806	**D.G. Bradman**	**A v SA**	**1931–32**	**5**	**5**	**1**	**299★**	**201.50**	**4**	**–**

Highest Partnership for each Wicket

1st	413	V. Mankad/Pankaj Roy	I v NZ	Madras	1955–56
2nd	**451**	**W.H. Ponsford/D.G. Bradman**	**A v E**	**The Oval**	**1934**
3rd	467	A.H. Jones/M.D. Crowe	NZ v SL	Wellington	1990–91
4th	411	P.B.H. May/M.C. Cowdrey	E v WI	Birmingham	1957
5th	**405**	**S.G. Barnes/D.G. Bradman**	**A v E**	**Sydney**	**1946–47**
6th	**346**	**J.H.W. Fingleton/D.G. Bradman**	**A v E**	**Melbourne**	**1936–37**
7th	347	D. St E. Atkinson/C.C. Depeiaza	WI v A	Bridgetown	1954–55
8th	246	L.E.G. Ames/G.O.B. Allen	E v NZ	Lord's	1931
9th	190	Asif Iqbal/Intikhab Alam	P v E	The Oval	1967
10th	151	B.F. Hastings/R.O. Collinge	NZ v P	Auckland	1972–73

Highest Individual Innings

375	B.C. Lara	WI v E	St John's	1993–94
365*	G. St A. Sobers	WI v P	Kingston	1957–58
364	L. Hutton	E v A	The Oval	1938
337	Hanif Mohammad	P v WI	Bridgetown	1957–58
336*	W.R. Hammond	E v NZ	Auckland	1932–33
334	**D.G. Bradman**	**A v E**	**Leeds**	**1930**
333	G.A. Gooch	E v I	Lord's	1990
325	A. Sandham	E v WI	Kingston	1929–30
311	R.B. Simpson	A v E	Manchester	1964
310*	J.H. Edrich	E v NZ	Leeds	1965
307	R.M. Cowper	A v E	Melbourne	1965–66
304	**D.G. Bradman**	**A v E**	**Leeds**	**1934**
302	L.G. Rowe	WI v E	Bridgetown	1973–74
299*	**D.G. Bradman**	**A v SA**	**Adelaide**	**1931–32**
299	M.D. Crowe	NZ v SL	Wellington	1990–91
291	I.V.A. Richards	WI v E	The Oval	1976
287	R.E. Foster	E v A	Sydney	1903–04
285*	P.B.H. May	E v WI	Birmingham	1957
280*	Javed Miandad	P v I	Hyderabad	1982–83
278	D.C.S. Compton	E v P	Nottingham	1954
277	B.C. Lara	WI v A	Sydney	1992–93
274	R.G. Pollock	SA v A	Durban	1969–70
274	Zaheer Abbas	P v E	Birmingham	1971
271	Javed Miandad	P v NZ	Auckland	1988–89
270*	G.A. Headley	WI v E	Kingston	1934–35
270	**D.G. Bradman**	**A v E**	**Melbourne**	**1936–37**
268	G.N. Yallop	A v P	Melbourne	1983–84
267	P.A. de Silva	SL v NZ	Wellington	1990–91
266	W.H. Ponsford	A v E	The Oval	1934
266	D.L. Houghton	Z v SL	Bulawayo	1994–95
262*	D.L. Amiss	E v WI	Kingston	1973–74
261	F.M.M. Worrell	WI v E	Nottingham	1950
260	C.C. Hunte	WI v P	Kingston	1957–58
260	Javed Miandad	P v E	The Oval	1987
259	G.M. Turner	NZ v WI	Georgetown	1971–72
258	T.W. Graveney	E v WI	Nottingham	1957
258	S.M. Nurse	WI v NZ	Christchurch	1968–69
256	R.B. Kanhai	WI v I	Calcutta	1958–59
256	K.F. Barrington	E v A	Manchester	1964
255*	D.J. McGlew	SA v NZ	Wellington	1952–53
254	**D.G. Bradman**	**A v E**	**Lord's**	**1930**

NOTES

Further publication and source details are provided in the Select Bibliography.

PROLOGUE (pages 1 to 8)

1 Vamplew & Stoddart (eds), *Sport in Australia: A Social History*, p.1.
2 Blainey, *A Shorter History of Australia*, p.114.
3 In a letter dated 19 November 1849.

1: FROM SUFFOLK TO SYDNEY (pages 9 to 25)

1 Letter to author from Elizabeth Warburton, dated 8 September 1994.
2 DGB in radio interview, ABC, 1988.
3 Ibid.
4 Ibid.
5 Quoted in *The Oxford History of Australia*, vol. 4, p.147.
6 Ibid.
7 Op. cit., p.159.
8 Op. cit., p.160.
9 DGB in radio interview, ABC, 1988.
10 Quoted in Page, *Bradman: The Illustrated Biography*, p.7.
11 DGB's school report, Public High School, Bowral, 1922.
12 O'Reilly, *'Tiger'*; quoted in Derriman, *Our Don Bradman*, p.5.
13 Letter to DGB from the Secretary of the New South Wales Cricket Association, dated 5 October 1926.
14 Quoted in Page, op. cit., p.15.
15 Op. cit., p.27.
16 Press report reproduced in *The Bradman Albums*, p.27.

2: 'A POOR WANDERING DREAMER' (pages 26 to 44)

1 Clark, *A History of Australia*, p.496.
2 Ibid.
3 Op. cit., p.497.
4 Kirkpatrick, *The Sea Coast of Bohemia*, p.179.
5 Quoted in Page, *Bradman: The Illustrated Biography*, p.28.

[6] Author interview with Sir Colin Cowdrey, 24 October 1994.
[7] Clark, *A History of Australia*, pp. 173–4.
[8] Reproduced in *The Bradman Albums*, p.24.
[9] Op. cit., p.25.
[10] A doctor's wife quoted in *The Oxford History of Australia*, vol. 4, p.251.
[11] H. Fisher, quoted in Rosenwater, *Sir Donald Bradman*, p.53.
[12] Press report reproduced in *The Bradman Albums*, p.39.
[13] DGB in radio interview, ABC, 1988.
[14] Ibid.
[15] Ibid.
[16] Match commentator Lionel Watt, 3 January 1929; recording played during ABC radio interview.
[17] Quoted in Page, op. cit., p.42.
[18] DGB in radio interview, ABC, 1988.
[19] Author interview with Sir Colin Cowdrey, 24 October 1994.
[20] Quoted in Page, op. cit., p.45.
[21] Op. cit., p.47.
[22] Bradman, *Don Bradman's Book*; quoted in *The Bradman Albums*, p.205.
[23] Quoted in Page, op. cit., p.48.
[24] Quoted in *The Oxford History of Australia*, vol. 4, p.257.
[25] Quoted in Page, op. cit., p.56.
[26] Op. cit., p.60.

3: BOWRAL VS. ENGLAND (pages 45 to 63)

[1] Press report reproduced in *The Bradman Albums*, p.82.
[2] Op. cit., p.83.
[3] Quoted in Page, *Bradman: The Illustrated Biography*, p.71.
[4] DGB's diary, quoted in *The Bradman Albums*, p.85.
[5] Op. cit., p.86.
[6] Op. cit., p.87.
[7] Press photograph and caption reproduced in *The Bradman Albums*, p.88.
[8] Quoted in Page, op. cit., p.79.
[9] DGB's diary, quoted in *The Bradman Albums*, p.107.
[10] Author interview with E.W. Swanton, 8 July 1994.
[11] DGB's diary, quoted in the *Bradman Albums*, pp. 121, 122.
[12] Quoted in Page, op. cit., pp.91–2.
[13] Op. cit., p.93.
[14] *Manchester Guardian*, 14 July 1930.
[15] Quoted in Page, op. cit., pp.95, 97.
[16] Telegram from A.E. Whitelaw to William Kelly, 12 July 1930.
[17] DGB's diary, quoted in *The Bradman Albums*, p.147.
[18] Quoted in Page, op. cit., p.102.
[19] Press report quoted in *The Bradman Albums*, p.153.
[20] Author interview with Sir Colin Cowdrey, 24 October 1994.

21   Quoted in Page, op. cit., p.103.
22   Op. cit., p.104.
23   Quoted in *The Bradman Albums*, p.170.
24   R.E.S. Wyatt in *Forty Minutes: Bodyline*, BBC TV, 1983.
25   DGB's diary, quoted in *The Bradman Albums*, p.181.
26   Quoted in Rosenwater, *Sir Donald Bradman*, p.130.

4: FOR BETTER OR FOR WORSE (pages 64 to 82)

1   Quoted in *The Bradman Albums*, p.195.
2   Quoted in *The Oxford History of Australia*, vol. 4, p.279.
3   Bradman, *Farewell to Cricket*, p.259.
4   Quoted in Page, *Bradman: The Illustrated Biography*, p.109.
5   Op. cit., p.111.
6   Op. cit., p.112.
7   Ibid.
8   Op. cit., p.113.
9   Op. cit., p.114.
10   Op. cit., p.115.
11   Ibid.
12   DGB's diary, quoted in *The Bradman Albums*, p.193.
13   Quoted in Page, op. cit., p.117.
14   DGB's diary, quoted in *The Bradman Albums*, p.193.
15   Ibid.
16   Quoted in Rosenwater, *Sir Donald Bradman*, p.138.
17   Op. cit., p.139.
18   Op. cit., p.140.
19   Ibid.
20   Op. cit., p.145.
21   Quoted in Page, op. cit., p.119.
22   Adelaide *Chronicle* of 27 November 1930, quoted in *The Bradman Albums*, p.220.
23   Statement by DGB in the *Referee*, quoted in *The Bradman Albums*, p.221.
24   Quoted in Rosenwater, op. cit., p.144.
25   Ibid.
26   Author interview with DGB, 2 January 1995.
27   Quoted in Page, op. cit., p.140.
28   Op. cit., p.142.
29   Op. cit., p.143.
30   Rosenwater, op. cit., pp.162–3.
31   DGB in *The Bradman Albums*, p.255.
32   A.J. Bell, quoted in *The Bradman Albums*, p.278.
33   Bradman, op. cit., p.259.
34   Quoted in Page, op. cit., p.147.
35   Bradman, op. cit., p.60.

5: Up Came the Troopers (pages 83 to 101)

1   Amos, *The New Guard Movement 1931–35*, p.82.
2   Op. cit., p.83.
3   Author interview with E.W. Swanton, 8 July 1994. (Rockley Wilson was Jardine's master at Winchester.)
4   Lord Wyatt of Weeford, quoted in Pawle, *R.E.S. Wyatt: Fighting Cricketer*, p.1.
5   R.E.S. Wyatt, interviewed by Ned Sherrin on BBC Radio 4, 1992.
6   Author interview with E.W. Swanton, 8 July 1994.
7   Quoted in Le Quesne, *The Bodyline Controversy*, p.128.
8   DGB in radio interview, ABC, 1988.
9   Quoted in *The Bradman Albums*, p.317.
10   Fingleton, *Cricket Crisis*, p.48.
11   Op. cit., p.52.
12   Quoted in *The Bradman Albums*, p.319.
13   DGB in radio interview, ABC, 1988.
14   Quoted in Fingleton, op. cit., p.59.
15   Quoted in Page, *Bradman: The Illustrated Biography*, p.176.
16   DGB in radio interview, ABC, 1988.
17   Quoted in *The Bradman Albums*, p.323.
18   L.P. O'Brien in DGB's radio interview, ABC, 1988.
19   DGB in radio interview, ABC, 1988.
20   W.E. Bowes in *Forty Minutes: Bodyline*, BBC TV, 1983.
21   Fingleton, op. cit., p.63.
22   W.E. Bowes in *Forty Minutes: Bodyline*, BBC TV, 1983.
23   L.P. O'Brien in DGB's radio interview, ABC, 1988.
24   Fingleton, op. cit., p.63.
25   Quoted during DGB's radio interview, ABC, 1988.
26   DGB in radio interview, ABC, 1988.
27   Arthur Mailey's press report, quoted in Rosenwater, *Sir Donald Bradman*, p.190.
28   Quoted in Page, op. cit., p.182.

6: One – Two – Three (pages 102 to 120)

1   DGB in radio interview, ABC, 1988.
2   Le Quesne, *The Bodyline Controversy*, p.28.
3   Ibid.
4   Ibid.
5   Quoted in Derriman, *Our Don Bradman*, p.5.
6   L.P. O'Brien in DGB's radio interview, ABC, 1988.
7   Ibid.
8   DGB in radio interview, ABC, 1988.
9   Fingleton, *Cricket Crisis*, p.91.

10 Op. cit., p.103.
11 DGB in radio interview, ABC, 1988.
12 Shown during *Forty Minutes: Bodyline*, BBC TV, 1983.
13 DGB in radio interview, ABC, 1988.
14 Quoted in Le Quesne, op. cit., p.38.
15 Op. cit., p.55.
16 MCC to Australian Board of Control, 23 January 1933.
17 H. Larwood, interviewed by F.S. Trueman for *Forty Minutes: Bodyline*, BBC TV, 1983.
18 Australian Board of Control to MCC, 30 January 1933.
19 MCC to Australian Board of Control, 2 February 1933.
20 Australian Board of Control to MCC, 8 February 1933.
21 Quoted in *The Bradman Albums*, p.337.
22 Quoted in Rosenwater, *Sir Donald Bradman*, p.197.
23 Quoted in Le Quesne, op. cit., p.83.
24 H. Larwood on an excerpt from Movietone News, shown during *Forty Minutes: Bodyline*, BBC TV, 1983.
25 Quoted in Le Quesne, op. cit., p.167.
26 W.J. O'Reilly in DGB's radio interview, ABC, 1988.
27 Quoted in Derriman, op. cit., p.5.
28 Quoted in Page, *Bradman: The Illustrated Biography*, p.191.
29 Quoted in Rosenwater, op. cit., p.205.
30 Quoted in Le Quesne, op. cit., p.193.
31 MCC to Australian Board of Control, 9 October 1933.
32 H. Larwood, interviewed by F.S. Trueman for *Forty Minutes: Bodyline*, BBC TV, 1983.
33 Author interview with Lord Hailsham of St Marylebone, 10 May 1995.
34 A.G. Moyes, quoted in *The Bradman Albums*, p.358.
35 Author interview with DGB, 2 January 1995.
36 Letter to DGB from the New South Wales Cricket Association, dated 20 February 1934.

7: In Health and in Sickness (pages 121 to 139)

1 W.A. Brown in DGB's radio interview, ABC, 1988.
2 DGB in radio interview, ABC, 1988.
3 Quoted in Page, *Bradman: The Illustrated Biography*, p.115.
4 DGB in radio interview, ABC, 1988.
5 Letter from J.H. Fingleton to W.M. Woodfull, February 1934, housed in the Mitchell Library, NSW.
6 DGB in radio interview, ABC, 1988.
7 Trevor Wignall, quoted in Rosenwater, *Sir Donald Bradman*, p.219.
8 Ibid.
9 Press report quoted in *The Bradman Albums*, p.365.
10 Ibid.

11 DGB in radio interview, ABC, 1988.
12 Author interview with Lord Hailsham of St Marylebone, 10 May 1995.
13 W.M. Woodfull, quoted by DGB in radio interview, ABC, 1988.
14 Quoted in Page, op. cit., p.197.
15 DGB in radio interview, ABC, 1988.
16 Ibid.
17 Quoted in Derriman, *Our Don Bradman*, p.103.
18 Quoted in *The Bradman Albums*, p.377.
19 DGB in radio interview, ABC, 1988.
20 Ibid.
21 W.A. Brown in DGB's radio interview, ABC, 1988.
22 Quoted in *The Bradman Albums*, p.385.
23 Quoted in Page, op. cit., p.200.
24 W.A. Brown in DGB's radio interview, ABC, 1988.
25 Commentator quoted during DGB's radio interview, ABC, 1988.
26 DGB in radio interview, ABC, 1988.
27 Quoted in *The Bradman Albums*, p.394.
28 Ibid.
29 Op. cit., p.395.
30 Quoted in Rosenwater, op. cit., p.228.
31 Quoted in DGB's radio interview, ABC, 1988.
32 Quoted in *The Bradman Albums*, p.397.
33 Op. cit., p.398.
34 Quoted in Rosenwater, op. cit., p.229.
35 Ibid.
36 Quoted in Page, op. cit., pp.205, 206.
37 DGB in radio interview, ABC, 1988.
38 Quoted in Rosenwater, op. cit., p.230.
39 Bradman, *Farewell to Cricket*, p.88.
40 DGB in radio interview, ABC, 1988.
41 Bradman, op. cit., p.90.
42 Op. cit., p.91.
43 Quoted in Rosenwater, op. cit., p.240.
44 Op. cit., p.239.
45 Op. cit., p.240.
46 Bradman, op. cit., p.92.
47 Ibid.

8: 'FINGLETON WAS THE RING–LEADER' (pages 140 to 160)

1   R.S. Whitington, *Cricket Caravan*, quoted in Derriman, *Our Don Bradman*, p.123.
2   Press report quoted in *The Bradman Albums*, p.438.
3   Clem Hill, quoted in op. cit., p.440.
4   Clem Hill, quoted in Page, *Bradman: The Illustrated Biography*, p.217.

5   Quoted in Rosenwater, *Sir Donald Bradman*, p.251.

6   Op. cit., p.250.

7   Op. cit., p.251.

8   DGB in radio interview, ABC, 1988.

9   Author interview with DGB, 2 January 1995.

10   Quoted in Rosenwater, op. cit., p.251.

11   Hartley Gratton, quoted in *The Oxford History of Australia*, vol. 4, p.322.

12   DGB in radio interview, ABC, 1988.

13   Neville Cardus, quoted in Rosenwater, op. cit., p.252.

14   Op. cit., p.253.

15   Ibid.

16   Press report quoted in *The Bradman Albums*, p.467.

17   Ibid.

18   Sydney *Daily Telegraph*, 23 December 1936.

19   Letter from J.H. Fingleton to Ian Wooldridge, 28 September 1980, housed in the Mitchell Library, NSW.

20   W.J. O'Reilly in the Australian Oral History Archives, quoted by Gideon Haigh in *Wisden Cricket Monthly*, February 1995.

21   Quoted in *The Bradman Albums*, p.471.

22   DGB in radio interview, ABC, 1988.

23   Ibid.

24   Ibid.

25   W.J. O'Reilly in the Australian Oral History Archives.

26   DGB in radio interview, ABC, 1988.

27   W.J. O'Reilly in the Australian Oral History Archives.

28   Alan Fairfax, quoted in Rosenwater, op. cit., p.254.

29   Op. cit., p.253.

30   DGB in radio interview, ABC, 1988.

31   Ibid.

32   Ibid.

33   Quoted in *The Bradman Albums*, p.499.

34   Op. cit., p.505.

35   Op. cit., p.508.

36   Op. cit., p.509.

37   Quoted in Rosenwater, op. cit., p.260.

38   Op. cit., p.257.

39   W.J. O'Reilly in the Australian Oral History Archives.

9: THIRD TIME ROUND (pages 161 to 180)

1   William Pollock, quoted in Rosenwater, *Sir Donald Bradman*, p.260.

2   Quoted in *The Oxford History of Australia*, vol.4, p.313.

3   Quoted in Rosenwater, op. cit., p.247.

4   Author interview with Sir Colin Cowdrey, 24 October 1994.

5   Ibid.

6   Moyes, *Bradman*, p.93.
7   Bradman, *Farewell to Cricket*, p.107.
8   Quoted in *The Bradman Albums*, p.519.
9   Quoted, ibid.
10 Bradman, op. cit., p.107.
11 Press report quoted in *The Bradman Albums*, p.523.
12 DGB's diary, ibid.
13 Quoted in Page, *Bradman: The Illustrated Biography*, p.241.
14 Press report quoted in *The Bradman Albums*, p.523.
15 DGB's diary, quoted in op. cit., p.524.
16 Op. cit., p.430.
17 Quoted in op. cit., p.529.
18 DGB's diary, quoted in op. cit., p.530.
19 A.G. Gardiner, quoted in Rosenwater, op. cit., p.267.
20 Quoted in op. cit., p.269.
21 Excerpt from the Australian touring contract, 1938, quoted in Page, op. cit., p.242.
22 Quoted in *The Bradman Albums*, p.544.
23 Op. cit., p.540.
24 Quoted in Page, op. cit., p.246.
25 Moyes, op. cit., p.103.
26 Bradman, op. cit., p.114.
27 DGB's diary, quoted in *The Bradman Albums*, p.556.
28 Press report, ibid.
29 DGB's diary, ibid.
30 Quoted in Page, op. cit., p.248.
31 Op. cit., p.249.
32 Ibid.
33 Quoted in Rosenwater, op. cit., p.274.
34 Quoted in *The Bradman Albums*, p.563.
35 Op. cit., p.562.
36 W.J. O'Reilly in the Australian Oral History Archives.
37 Quoted in Page, op. cit., p.256.
38 W.J. O'Reilly in the Australian Oral History Archives.
39 Ibid.
40 Bradman, op. cit., p.118.

10: THE BUSINESS OF WAR (pages 181 to 202)

1   Quoted in Rosenwater, *Sir Donald Bradman*, p.282.
2   Op. cit., p.284.
3   Bradman, *Farewell to Cricket*, p.119.
4   Op. cit., p.120.
5   Quoted in *The Oxford History of Australia*, vol. 4, p.325.
6   Ibid.

[7] Op. cit., p.328.

[8] W.J. O'Reilly in the Australian Oral History Archives.

[9] Quoted in *The Oxford History of Australia*, vol. 4, p.329.

[10] Bradman, op. cit., p.122.

[11] Quoted in *The Bradman Albums*, p.598.

[12] Ibid.

[13] Press report quoted in Page, *Bradman: The Illustrated Biography*, p.264.

[14] Bradman, op. cit., p.122.

[15] Quoted in Moyes, *Bradman*, p.125.

[16] Quoted in *The Oxford History of Australia*, vol. 4, p.335.

[17] Gibbs, *Bulls, Bears and Wildcats*, pp.297–8.

[18] Adelaide *Advertiser*, 5 June 1945.

[19] Gibbs, op. cit., p.304.

[20] Bradman, op. cit., p.122.

[21] Sydney Deamer in the Sydney *Daily Telegraph*, October 1946.

[22] Ibid.

[23] Adelaide *Advertiser*, 1 January 1946.

[24] Sydney Deamer in the Sydney *Daily Telegraph*, October 1946.

11: WILL HE OR WON'T HE? (pages 203 to 220)

[1] Grant, *The Australian Dilemma*, p.7.

[2] Quoted in *The Oxford History of Australia*, vol. 5, p.7.

[3] W.J. O'Reilly in the Australian Oral History Archives.

[4] DGB in radio interview, ABC, 1988.

[5] DGB in *The Bradman Albums*, p.605.

[6] Adelaide *Advertiser*, 24 October 1946.

[7] D.C.S. Compton, quoted in Rosenwater, *Sir Donald Bradman*, p.303.

[8] Adelaide *Advertiser*, 24 October 1946.

[9] DGB in *The Bradman Albums*, p.605.

[10] E.M. Wellings, quoted in Rosenwater, op. cit., p.304.

[11] J.M. Kilburn, quoted in Rosenwater, op. cit., p.307.

[12] Bradman, *Farewell to Cricket*, p.128.

[13] W.R. Hammond, quoted in Rosenwater, op. cit., p.308.

[14] Bradman, op. cit., p.128.

[15] W.J. O'Reilly, quoted in Rosenwater, op. cit., p.310.

[16] Quoted in Rosenwater, ibid., although the expletive has been restored. Rosenwater, rather coyly, preferred an ellipsis.

[17] Bradman, op. cit., p.129.

[18] N.W.D. Yardley, *Cricket Campaigns*, quoted in Rosenwater, op. cit., p.310.

[19] Quoted in Rosenwater, op. cit., p.313.

[20] Ibid.

[21] Ibid.

[22] Bradman, op. cit., p.131.

[23] R.S. Whitington, quoted in Page, *Bradman: The Illustrated Biography*, p.282.

[24] Quoted in Rosenwater, op. cit., p.314.
[25] E.M. Wellings, quoted in *The Bradman Albums*, p.640.
[26] L.N. Bailey, ibid.
[27] Quoted in op. cit., p.641.
[28] DGB in op. cit., p.645.
[29] Quoted in Rosenwater, op. cit., p.316.
[30] Quoted in *The Bradman Albums*, p.645.
[31] Quoted in op. cit., p.656.
[32] Quoted in op. cit., p.659.
[33] Ibid.
[34] Rosenwater, op. cit., p.317.
[35] Quoted in *The Bradman Albums*, p.663.
[36] Ibid.
[37] Letter from H. Blinman, President of SACA, quoted in Bradman, op. cit., p.14.
[38] Letter from DGB to the Adelaide *Advertiser*, quoted in Page, op. cit., p.286.
[39] Bradman, op. cit., p.142.
[40] Op. cit., p.143.
[41] S.P. Foenander, quoted in *The Bradman Albums*, p.693.

12: 1948 (pages 221 to 240)

[1] L. Constantine, *Cricketers' Carnival*, quoted in Rosenwater, *Sir Donald Bradman*, p.336.
[2] Author interview with Sir Colin Cowdrey, 24 October 1994.
[3] Bradman, *Farewell to Cricket*, p.153.
[4] Quoted in *The Bradman Albums*, p.703.
[5] Op. cit., p.704.
[6] Bradman, op. cit., p.157.
[7] Ibid.
[8] Op. cit., p.164.
[9] Ibid.
[10] Author interview with DGB, 2 January 1995.
[11] Quoted in Rosenwater, op. cit., p.336.
[12] Op. cit., p.335.
[13] D. McNicoll in the Sydney *Daily Telegraph*, quoted in op. cit., p.338.
[14] Quoted in op. cit., p.339.
[15] Bradman, op. cit., p.173.
[16] Fingleton, *Brightly Fades the Don*, p.90.
[17] Reproduced in *The Bradman Albums*, pp.718–19.
[18] E.W. Swanton, quoted in Rosenwater, op. cit., p.345.
[19] Bradman, op. cit., p.198.
[20] Op. cit., p.202.
[21] Op. cit., p.203.
[22] Quoted in Rosenwater, op. cit., p.346.

23 Bradman, op. cit., p.203.
24 Charles Bray, quoted in op. cit., p.205.
25 Bradman, op. cit., p.206.
26 Op. cit., p.209.
27 Quoted in *The Bradman Albums*, p.752.
28 Bradman, op. cit., p.211.
29 Ibid.
30 Author interview with E.W. Swanton, 8 July 1994.
31 Letter from DGB to author, dated 27 July 1995.

13: 'A COLLECTION OF PRIMA DONNAS' (pages 241 to 258)

1   Associated Press, 19 September 1948.
2   Ibid.
3   Author interview with DGB, 2 January 1995.
4   Bradman, *The Art of Cricket*, p.5.
5   Quoted in Page, *Bradman: The Illustrated Biography*, p.335.
6   Quoted in *The Bradman Albums*, p.772.
7   Grant, *The Australian Dilemma*, p.241.
8   *Wisden*, 1954.
9   Quoted in Rosenwater, *Sir Donald Bradman*, p.378.
10 Quoted in Perry, *The Don*, p.569.
11 Bradman, op. cit., p.5.
12 Quoted in Page, op. cit., p.343.
13 *Wisden*, 1960.
14 Rait Kerr & Peebles, *Lord's 1946–1970*, p.153.
15 Quoted in Rosenwater, op. cit., p.373.
16 *Wisden*, 1962.

14: SIR DONALD (pages 259 to 274)

1   Sir Ronald Crocker, quoted in *The Oxford History of Australia*, vol. 5, p.161.
2   Quoted in *The Oxford History of Australia*, vol. 5, p.178.
3   Quoted in Rosenwater, *Sir Donald Bradman*, p.380.
4   R. Benaud, in his Foreword to Allen & Kemsley, *Images of Bradman*.
5   *Australian*, 30 April 1965.
6   Quoted in *The Oxford History of Australia*, vol. 5, p.168.
7   M C Cowdrey, *The Autobiography of a Cricketer*, quoted in Derriman, *Our Don Bradman*, p.200.
8   Quoted in Perry, *The Don*, p.575.
9   Quoted in Page, *Bradman: The Illustrated Biography*, p.353–4.
10 Quoted in Page, op. cit., p.356.
11 Letter to author from Lord Alexander of Weedon QC, dated 22 February 1995.
12 Ibid.

EPILOGUE (pages 275 to 282)

1   W.E. Bowes in *Forty Minutes: Bodyline*, BBC TV, 1983.
2   W.J. O'Reilly, ibid.
3   DGB in radio interview, ABC, 1988.
4   J.C. Laker, quoted in Rosenwater, *Sir Donald Bradman*, p.358.
5   Unknown youth in a Sydney pub, in conversation with author on 28 December 1994.
6   DGB in radio interview, ABC, 1988.
7   DGB at the opening of the Bradman Oval in Bowral, 1976.
8   Pindar, Oxford Text (1947) of *Olympia* XIII, lines 41–2; tr. author.

SELECT BIBLIOGRAPHY

BOOKS BY SIR DONALD BRADMAN

The Art of Cricket (London: Hodder & Stoughton, 1958)
Don Bradman's Book (London: Hutchinson, 1930)
Farewell to Cricket (London: Pavilion Books, 1988; first published in Great Britain by Hodder & Stoughton in 1950)
My Cricketing Life (London: Stanley Paul, 1938)

BIOGRAPHIES AND OTHER BOOKS ABOUT SIR DONALD BRADMAN

Allen, P., and Kemsley, J. (eds), *Images of Bradman* (Welby, NSW: Allen & Kemsley, 1994)
The Bradman Albums (2 vols.; Adelaide: Rigby, 1987)
Davis, A., *Sir Donald Bradman* (London: Cassell, 1960)
Derriman, P., *Our Don Bradman* (Melbourne: Macmillan, 1987)
Docker, E.W., *Bradman and the Bodyline Series* (Sydney: Angus & Robertson, 1978)
Fingleton, J.H., *Brightly Fades the Don* (London: Collins, 1949)
Flanagan, A., *On Tour with Bradman* (Sydney: Halstead Press, 1950)
Lindsay, P., *Don Bradman* (London: Phoenix House, 1951)
Morris, B., *Bradman: What They Said About Him* (Sydney: ABC Books, 1994)
Moyes, A.G., *Bradman* (Sydney: Angus & Robertson, 1948)
Page, M., *Bradman: The Illustrated Biography* (Melbourne: Sun Books, 1983)
Perry, R., *The Don* (Sydney: Macmillan, 1995)
Roberts, E.L., *Bradman 1927–1941* (Birmingham: Hudson, 1944)
Rosenwater, I., *Sir Donald Bradman* (London: B.T. Batsford, 1978)
Wakley, B.J., *Bradman the Great* (London: Nicholas Kay, 1959)

SOME RELEVANT BOOKS ABOUT CRICKET

Cardus, N., *Australian Summer* (London: Souvenir Press, 1987)

Derriman, P., *Bodyline* (Melbourne: Fontana, 1984)

Douglas, C., *Douglas Jardine: Spartan Cricketer* (London: Allen & Unwin, 1984)

Fingleton, J.H., *Cricket Crisis* (London: Cassell, 1946)

——, *Four Chukkas to Australia* (London: Heinemann, 1959)

Hill, A., *Hedley Verity* (Tadworth: Kingswood Press, 1986)

Larwood, H., *The Larwood Story* (London: W.H. Allen, 1965)

Le Quesne, L., *The Bodyline Controversy* (London: Secker & Warburg, 1983)

Pawle, G., *R.E.S. Wyatt: Fighting Cricketer* (London: Allen & Unwin, 1985)

Peebles, I., *Straight from the Shoulder* (London: Hutchinson, 1968)

O'Reilly, W.J., *'Tiger'* (Sydney: Collins, 1985)

Rait Kerr, D., and Peebles, I., *Lord's 1946–1970* (London: Harrap, 1971)

Swanton, E.W., *Gubby Allen: Man of Cricket* (London: Hutchinson, 1985)

——, *Sort of Cricket Person* (London: Collins, 1972)

Tebbutt, G., *With the 1930 Australians* (London: Hodder & Stoughton, 1930)

SOME RELEVANT BOOKS ABOUT AUSTRALIA

Amos, K., *The New Guard Movement 1931–35* (Melbourne: MUP, 1976)

Blainey, G., *A Shorter History of Australia* (Melbourne: Heinemann, 1994)

Bolton, G. (ed.), *The Oxford History of Australia* (5 vols.; Oxford: OUP, 1986–90)

Bunting, J., *R.G. Menzies – A Portrait* (London: Allen & Unwin, 1988)

Clark, C.M.H. (abridged by M. Cathcart), *A History of Australia* (Melbourne: MUP, 1993)

Darian-Smith, K., *On the Home Front: Melbourne in Wartime* (Melbourne: OUP, 1990)

Day, D., *The Great Betrayal: Britain, Australia and the Onset of the Pacific War* (Melbourne: OUP, 1988)

Gibbs, R.M., *Bulls, Bears and Wildcats: A Centenary History of the Stock Exchange of Adelaide* (Norwood, SA: Peacock Publications, 1988)

Grant, B., *The Australian Dilemma* (London: Macdonald, 1983)

Kirkpatrick, P.J., *The Sea Coast of Bohemia: Literary Life in Sydney's Roaring Twenties* (St Lucia, Qld.: UQP, 1992)

Martin, A., *Robert Menzies: A Life* (Melbourne: MUP, 1993)

Menzies, R.G., *Afternoon Light* (London: Cassell, 1967)

——, *The Measure of the Years* (London: Cassell, 1970)

Thomson, A., *Anzac Memories* (Melbourne: OUP, 1994)

Vamplew, W., and Stoddart, B. (eds), *Sport in Australia: A Social History* (Melbourne: CUP, 1994)

Ward, R., *A Concise History of Australia* (St Lucia, Qld.: UQP, 1992)

White, R., *Inventing Australia* (London: Allen & Unwin, 1981)

TELEVISION AND RADIO SOURCES

Bradman (dir. Jack Egan; ABC TV, 1991)

Bradman radio interviews with Norman May (series of eight; ABC, 1988)

England vs. Australia: 100 Not Out (BBC TV, first broadcast on 5 March 1977)

Forty Minutes: Bodyline (BBC TV, first broadcast on 6 November 1983)

R.E.S. Wyatt interview with Ned Sherrin (BBC Radio 4, 1991)

INDEX

Accrington CC, 76–7, 78

Adelaide, 30–1, 141, 142, 249, 267, 273; business community, 251; Regent Theatre, 67; Stock Exchange, 141, 193, 194–6, 197, 222; unrest over 'bodyline' tactics, 102–4

Adelaide, Commonwealth Club of, 198

Adelaide Club, 197, 198

Adelaide Electric Supply Company, 199

Advertiser (Adelaide), 110, 197, 201, 233, 273

Age (Melbourne), 214–15

AIF, *see* Australian Imperial Force

Allen, G.O. ('Gubby'), 87–8, 92, 97; background, 86, 146–7; as captain of England, 146–7, 152, 154, 157, 159; disagrees with 'bodyline' tactics, 100, 147

Altham, H.S., 255

amateur cricket: and elitism, 87–8; payments 47–8

Anzac troops, 18, 22, 26, 185

Argus (Melbourne), 73

Armstrong, Warwick, 112

army: physical training schools, 188–9

Art of Cricket, The (Bradman), 244, 251–2

Ashes series, 4, 20, 34, 45, 158; 1928–29, in Australia, 34–40, 86; 1930, in England, 56–63; 1932–33, in Australia ('bodyline'), 83, 85–91, 94–5, 97–117; 1934, in England, 128–34; 1936–37, in Australia, 151–60; 1938, in England, 173–5, 177–9; 1946–47, in Australia, 209–17; 1948, in England, 231–7, 239–41; 1950s, 248, 250

Askin, Robert, 264

Associated Newspapers, 96

athletics, Australian, 250

Attlee, Clement, 227

Australia: early sporting history, 1–8; gold rush, 2, 12–13; 1890–1914, 14; First World War, 5–6, 17–19, 26, 100; 1920s economic and social problems, 21, 26–8, 32–4, 41–2, 47; 1930s depression, 64, 65, 75, 79, 83–5, 102, 116; new optimism from 1935, 138, 150–1; late-thirties, 162–3, 182; Second World War, 185–7, 192–5, 200, 203–5; post-War period, 199, 201, 203, 204–6, 217, 248–50;